Advanced Blockchain Development

Build highly secure, decentralized applications and conduct secure transactions

Imran Bashir
Narayan Prusty

BIRMINGHAM - MUMBAI

Advanced Blockchain Development

First published: May 2019

Production reference: 1200519

Published by Packt Publishing Ltd.
Livery Place
35 Livery Street
Birmingham
B3 2PB, UK.

ISBN 978-1-83882-319-1

www.packtpub.com

`mapt.io`

Mapt is an online digital library that gives you full access to over 5,000 books and videos, as well as industry leading tools to help you plan your personal development and advance your career. For more information, please visit our website.

Why subscribe?

- Spend less time learning and more time coding with practical eBooks and Videos from over 4,000 industry professionals

- Improve your learning with Skill Plans built especially for you

- Get a free eBook or video every month

- Mapt is fully searchable

- Copy and paste, print, and bookmark content

Packt.com

Did you know that Packt offers eBook versions of every book published, with PDF and ePub files available? You can upgrade to the eBook version at `www.packt.com` and as a print book customer, you are entitled to a discount on the eBook copy. Get in touch with us at `customercare@packtpub.com` for more details.

At `www.packt.com`, you can also read a collection of free technical articles, sign up for a range of free newsletters, and receive exclusive discounts and offers on Packt books and eBooks.

Contributors

About the authors

Imran Bashir has a master's degree in information security from Royal Holloway, University of London. He has a background in software development, solution architecture, infrastructure management, and IT service management. He is also a member of the Institute of Electrical and Electronics Engineers (IEEE) and British Computer Society (BCS). Imran has an experience of sixteen years in the public and financial sectors. He worked on large-scale IT projects for public sector before moving to the financial services industry. Since then he has worked in various technical roles for different financial companies in Europe's financial capital, London. Currently, he is working for an investment bank in London.

Narayan Prusty is a full-stack developer. He works as a consultant for various start-ups around the world. He has worked on various technologies and programming languages but is very passionate about JavaScript, WordPress, Ethereum, Solr, React, Cordova, MongoDB, and AWS. Apart from consulting for various start-ups, he also runs a blog titled QNimate (http://qnimate.com) and a video tutorial site titled QScutter (http://qscutter.com), where he shares information about a lot of the technologies he works on.

Packt is searching for authors like you

If you're interested in becoming an author for Packt, please visit authors.packtpub.com and apply today. We have worked with thousands of developers and tech professionals, just like you, to help them share their insight with the global tech community. You can make a general application, apply for a specific hot topic that we are recruiting an author for, or submit your own idea.

Table of Contents

Preface

Blockchain technology is a distributed ledger with applications in industries such as finance, government, and media. This Learning Path is your guide to building blockchain networks using Ethereum, JavaScript, and Solidity. You will get started by understanding the technical foundations of blockchain technology, including distributed systems, cryptography and how this digital ledger keeps data secure. Further into the chapters, you'll gain insights into developing applications using Ethereum and Hyperledger. As you build on your knowledge of Ether security, mining , smart contracts, and Solidity, you'll learn how to create robust and secure applications that run exactly as programmed without being affected by fraud, censorship, or third-party interference. Toward the concluding chapters, you'll explore how blockchain solutions can be implemented in applications such as IoT apps, in addition to its use in currencies. The book will also highlight how you can increase blockchain scalability and even discusses the future scope of this fascinating and powerful technology. By the end of this Learning Path, you'll be equipped with the skills you need to tackle pain points encountered in the blockchain life cycle and confidently design and deploy decentralized applications.

This Learning Path includes content from the following Packt products:

- Mastering Blockchain - Second Edition by Imran Bashir
- Building Blockchain Projects by Narayan Prusty

Who this book is for

This Learning Path is designed for blockchain developers who want to build decentralized applications and smart contracts from scratch using Hyperledger. Basic familiarity with any programming language will be useful to get started with this course

What this book covers

Chapter 1, Blockchain 101, introduces the basic concepts of distributed computing on which blockchain technology is based. It also covers history, definitions, features, types, and benefits of blockchains along with various consensus mechanisms that are at the core of the blockchain technology.

Chapter 2, Decentralization, covers the concept of decentralization and its relationship with blockchain technology. Various methods and platforms that can be used to decentralize a process or a system have also been introduced.

Chapter 3, Understanding How Ethereum Works, explains how Ethereum works.

Chapter 4, Smart Contracts, provides an in-depth discussion on smart contracts. Topics such as history, the definition of smart contracts, Ricardian contracts, Oracles, and the theoretical aspects of smart contracts are presented in this chapter.

Chapter 5, Symmetric Cryptography, introduces the theoretical foundations of symmetric cryptography, which is necessary to understand how various security services such as confidentiality and integrity are provided.

Chapter 6, Public Key Cryptography, introduces concepts such as public and private keys, digital signatures and hash functions with practical examples. Finally, an introduction to financial markets is also included as there are many interesting use cases for blockchain technology in the financial sector.

Chapter 7, Getting Started with web3.js, introduces web3js and how to import and connect to geth. It also explains how to use it in Node.js or client-side JavaScript.

Chapter 8, Introducing Bitcoin, covers Bitcoin, the first and largest blockchain. It introduces technical concepts related to bitcoin cryptocurrency in detail.

Chapter 9, Building a Wallet Service, explains how to build a wallet service that users can use to create and manage Ethereum Wallets easily, even offline. We will specifically use the LightWallet library to achieve this.

Chapter 10, Alternative Coins, introduces alternative cryptocurrencies that were introduced after the invention of Bitcoin. It also presents examples of different altcoins, their properties, and how they have been developed and implemented.

Chapter 11, Development Tools and Frameworks, provides a detailed practical introduction to the Solidity programming language and different relevant tools and frameworks that are used for Ethereum development.

Chapter 12, Building a Betting App, explains how to use Oraclize to make HTTP requests from Ethereum smart contracts to access data from the World Wide Web. We will also learn how to access files stored in IPFS, use the strings library to work with strings, and more.

Chapter 13, Hyperledger, presents a discussion about the Hyperledger project from the Linux Foundation, which includes different blockchain projects introduced by its members.

Chapter 14, Alternative Blockchains, introduces alternative blockchain solutions and platforms. It provides technical details and features of alternative blockchains and relevant platforms.

Chapter 15, Blockchain - Outside of Currencies, provides a practical and detailed introduction to applications of blockchain technology in fields others than cryptocurrencies, including Internet of Things, government, media, and finance.

Chapter 16, Scalability and Other Challenges, is dedicated to a discussion of the challenges faced by blockchain technology and how to address them.

Chapter 17, Building a Consortium Blockchain, will discuss consortium blockchain.

Chapter 18, Current Landscape and What's Next, is aimed at providing information about the current landscape, projects, and research efforts related to blockchain technology. Also, some predictions based on the current state of blockchain technology have been made.

To get the most out of this book

You require Windows 7 SP1+, 8, 10 or Mac OS X 10.8+, examples in this book have been developed on Ubuntu 16.04.1 LTS (Xenial)
and macOS version 10.13.2. As such, it is recommended to use Ubuntu or any other Unix like system. However, any appropriate operating system, either Windows or Linux, can be used, but examples, especially those related to installation, may need to be changed accordingly.

Examples related to cryptography have been developed using the OpenSSL 1.0.2g 1 Mar 2016 command-line tool.

Ethereum Solidity examples have been developed using Remix IDE, available online at https://remix.ethereum.org

Ethereum Byzantine release is used to develop Ethereum-related examples. At the time of writing, this is the latest version available and can be downloaded from https://www.ethereum.org/ .

Examples related to IoT have been developed using a Raspberry Pi kit by Vilros, but any aapropriate latest model or kit can be used. Specifically, Raspberry Pi 3 Model B V 1.2 has been used to build the hardware example of IoT. Node.js V8.9.3 and npm V5.5.1 have been used to download related packages and run Node js server for IoT examples.

The Truffle framework has been used in some examples of smart contract deployment, and is available at http://truffleframework.com/. Any latest version available via npm should be appropriate.

Download the example code files

You can download the example code files for this book from your account at `www.packt.com`. If you purchased this book elsewhere, you can visit `www.packt.com/support` and register to have the files emailed directly to you.

You can download the code files by following these steps:

1. Log in or register at `www.packt.com`.
2. Select the **SUPPORT** tab.
3. Click on **Code Downloads & Errata**.
4. Enter the name of the book in the **Search** box and follow the onscreen instructions.

Once the file is downloaded, please make sure that you unzip or extract the folder using the latest version of:

- WinRAR/7-Zip for Windows
- Zipeg/iZip/UnRarX for Mac
- 7-Zip/PeaZip for Linux

The code bundle for the book is also hosted on GitHub at `https://github.com/TrainingByPackt/Advanced-Blockchain-Development` .In case there's an update to the code, it will be updated on the existing GitHub repository.

We also have other code bundles from our rich catalogue of books and videos available at `https://github.com/PacktPublishing/`. Check them out!

Download the color images of this book

We also provide you with a PDF file that has color images of the screenshots/diagrams used in this book. The color images will help you better understand the changes in the output. You can download this file from `https://www.packtpub.com/sites/default/files/downloads/9781838823191_ColorImages.pdf`

Conventions used

There are a number of text conventions used throughout this book.

`CodeInText`: Indicates code words in text, database table names, folder names, filenames, file extensions, pathnames, dummy URLs, user input, and Twitter handles. Here is an example: "The `input()` method is used to get an input from the user."

A block of code is set as follows:

```
pragma solidity ^0.4.0;
contract TestStruct {
  struct Trade
  {
    uint tradeid;
    uint quantity;
    uint price;
    string trader;
  }
  //This struct can be initialized and used as below
  Trade tStruct = Trade({tradeid:123, quantity:1, price:1,
trader:"equinox"});
}
```

Any command-line input or output is written as follows:

```
$ sudo apt-get install solc
```

Bold: Indicates a new term, an important word, or words that you see onscreen. For example, words in menus or dialog boxes appear in the text like this. Here is an example: "If you need something different, click on the **DOWNLOADS** link in the header for all possible downloads:"

Warnings or important notes appear like this.

Tips and tricks appear like this.

Get in touch

Feedback from our readers is always welcome.

General feedback: If you have questions about any aspect of this book, mention the book title in the subject of your message and email us at customercare@packtpub.com.

Errata: Although we have taken every care to ensure the accuracy of our content, mistakes do happen. If you have found a mistake in this book, we would be grateful if you would report this to us. Please visit www.packt.com/submit-errata, selecting your book, clicking on the Errata Submission Form link, and entering the details.

Piracy: If you come across any illegal copies of our works in any form on the Internet, we would be grateful if you would provide us with the location address or website name. Please contact us at copyright@packt.com with a link to the material.

If you are interested in becoming an author: If there is a topic that you have expertise in and you are interested in either writing or contributing to a book, please visit authors.packtpub.com.

Reviews

Please leave a review. Once you have read and used this book, why not leave a review on the site that you purchased it from? Potential readers can then see and use your unbiased opinion to make purchase decisions, we at Packt can understand what you think about our products, and our authors can see your feedback on their book. Thank you!

For more information about Packt, please visit packt.com.

1
Blockchain 101

If you are reading this book, it is very likely that you already have heard about blockchain and have some fundamental appreciation of its enormous potential. If not, then let me tell you that this is a technology that has promised to positively alter the existing paradigms of nearly all industries including, but not limited to IT, finance, government, media, medical, and law.

This chapter serves an introduction to blockchain technology, its technical foundations, the theory behind it, and various techniques that have been combined together to build what is known today as blockchain.

In this chapter, we first describe the theoretical foundations of distributed systems. Next, we address the precursors of Bitcoin by which blockchain technology was introduced to the world. Finally, we introduce you to blockchain technology. This approach is a logical way to understanding blockchain technology, as the roots of blockchain are in distributed systems. We will cover a lot of ground quickly here, but don't worry—we will go over a great deal of this material in much greater detail as you move through the book.

The growth of blockchain technology

With the invention of Bitcoin in 2008, the world was introduced to a new concept, which is now likely to revolutionize the whole of society. It is something that promises to have an impact on every industry, including but not limited to the financial sector, government, media, law, and arts. Some describe blockchain as a revolution, whereas another school of thought believes that it is going to be more evolutionary, and it will take many years before any practical benefits of blockchain reach fruition. This thinking is correct to some extent, but in my opinion, the revolution has already begun.

Many prominent organizations all around the world are already writing proofs of concept using blockchain technology, as its disruptive potential has now been fully recognized. However, some organizations are still in the preliminary exploration stage, though they are expected to progress more quickly as the technology matures. It is a technology that has an impact on current technologies too and possesses the ability to change them at a fundamental level.

If we look at the last few years, we notice that in 2013 some ideas started to emerge that suggested usage of blockchain in other areas than cryptocurrencies. Around that time the primary usage of blockchain was cryptocurrencies, and many new coins emerged during that time. The following graph shows a broad-spectrum outline of year wise progression and adaption trend of blockchain technology. Years shown on the *x* axis indicate the range of time in which a specific phase of blockchain technology falls. Each phase has a name which represents the action and is shown on the *x* axis starting from the period of **IDEAS & THOUGHTS** to eventually **MATURITY & FURTHER STANDARDIZATION**. The *y* axis shows level of activity, involvement and adoption of blockchain technology. The graph shows that eventually, roughly around **2025** blockchain technology is expected to become mature with a high number of users.

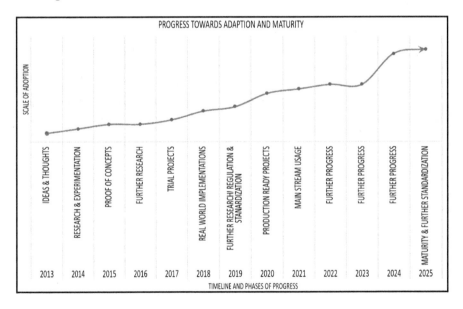

Blockchain technology adoption and maturity

The preceding graph shows that in 2013 **IDEAS & THOUGHTS** emerged related to other usages of blockchain technology apart from cryptocurrencies. Then in 2014 some **RESEARCH & EXPERIMENTATION** started which led to **PROOF OF CONCEPTS**, **FURTHER RESEARCH**, and full-scale **TRIAL PROJECTS** between 2015 and 2017. In 2018 we will see **REAL WORLD IMPLEMENTATIONS**. Already many projects are underway and set to replace existing systems, for example, **Australian Securities Exchange** (**ASX**) is soon to become the first organization to replace its legacy clearing and settlement system with blockchain technology.

More information on this topic can be found at
`https://www.asx.com.au/services/chess-replacement.htm`.

It is expected that during 2019 more research will be carried out along with some interest towards regulation and standardization of blockchain technology. After this, production ready projects and off the shelf products utilizing blockchain technology will be available from 2020 and by 2021 mainstream usage of blockchain technology is expected to start. Progress in blockchain technology almost feels like the internet *dot-com boom* of the late 1990s. More research is expected to continue along with adaption and further maturity of blockchain technology, and finally, in 2025 it is expected that the technology will be mature enough to be used on day to day basis. Please note that the timelines provided in the chart are not strict and can vary as it is quite difficult to predict that when exactly blockchain technology will become mature. This graph is based on the progress made in the recent years and the current climate of research, interest and enthusiasm regarding this technology which suggests that by 2025 blockchain technology is expected to become mature.

Interest in blockchain technology has risen quite significantly over the last few years. Once dismissed as simply geek money from a cryptocurrency point of view, or as something that was just not considered worth pursuing, blockchain is now being researched by the largest companies and organizations around the world. Millions of dollars are being spent to adapt and experiment with this technology. This is evident from recent actions taken by European Union where they have announced plans to increase funding for blockchain research to almost 340 million euros by 2020.

Interested readers can read more about this at
`https://www.irishtimes.com/business/technology/boost-for-blockch`
`ain-research-as-eu-increases-funding-four-fold-1.3383340`.

Another report suggests that global spending on blockchain technology research could reach 9.2 billion dollars by 2021.

More information regarding this can be found at
`https://bitcoinmagazine.com/articles/report-suggests-global-spen`
`ding-blockchain-tech-could-reach-92-billion-2021/`.

There are various consortiums such as **Enterprise Ethereum Alliance (EEA)**, **Hyperledger**, and **R3**, which have been established for research and development of blockchain technology. Moreover, a large number of start-ups are providing blockchain-based solutions already. A simple trend search on Google reveals the immense scale of interest in blockchain technology over the last few years. Especially, since early 2017 the increase in the search term *blockchain* is quite significant, as shown in the following graph:

Google trend graph for blockchain

Various benefits of this technology are envisioned, such as decentralized trust, cost savings, transparency, and efficiency. However, there are multiple challenges too that are an area of active research on blockchain, such as scalability and privacy.

In this book, we are going to see how blockchain technology can help bring about the benefits mentioned earlier. You are going to learn about what exactly is blockchain technology, and how it can reshape businesses, multiple industries, and indeed everyday life by bringing about a plenitude of benefits such as efficiency, cost saving, transparency, and security. We will also explore what is distributed ledger technology, decentralization, and smart contracts and how technology solutions can be developed and implemented using mainstream blockchain platforms such as Ethereum, and Hyperledger. We will also investigate that what challenges need to be addressed before blockchain can become a mainstream technology.

Chapter 16, *Scalability and Other Challenges*, is dedicated to a discussion of the limitations and challenges of blockchain technology.

Distributed systems

Understanding distributed systems is essential to the understanding of blockchain technology, as blockchain is a distributed system at its core. It is a distributed ledger which can be centralized or decentralized. A blockchain is originally intended to be and is usually used as a decentralized platform. It can be thought of as a system that has properties of both decentralized and distributed paradigms. It is a decentralized-distributed system.

Distributed systems are a computing paradigm whereby two or more nodes work with each other in a coordinated fashion to achieve a common outcome. It is modeled in such a way that end users see it as a single logical platform. For example, Google's search engine is based on a large distributed system, but to a user, it looks like a single, coherent platform.

A **node** can be defined as an individual player in a distributed system. All nodes are capable of sending and receiving messages to and from each other. Nodes can be honest, faulty, or malicious, and they have memory and a processor. A node that exhibits irrational behavior is also known as a **Byzantine node** after the Byzantine Generals Problem.

The Byzantine Generals problem

In 1982, a thought experiment was proposed by Lamport and others in their research paper, *The Byzantine Generals Problem* which is available at: `https://www.microsoft.com/en-us/research/publication/byzantine-generals-problem/` whereby a group of army generals who lead different parts of the Byzantine army are planning to attack or retreat from a city. The only way of communicating among them is via a messenger. They need to agree to strike at the same time in order to win. The issue is that one or more generals might be traitors who could send a misleading message. Therefore, there is a need for a viable mechanism that allows for agreement among the generals, even in the presence of the treacherous ones, so that the attack can still take place at the same time. As an analogy to distributed systems, the generals can be considered nodes, the traitors as Byzantine (malicious) nodes, and the messenger can be thought of as a channel of communication among the generals.

This problem was solved in 1999 by Castro and Liskov who presented the **Practical Byzantine Fault Tolerance** (**PBFT**) algorithm, where consensus is reached after a certain number of messages are received containing the same signed content.

This type of inconsistent behavior of Byzantine nodes can be intentionally malicious, which is detrimental to the operation of the network. Any unexpected behavior by a node on the network, whether malicious or not, can be categorized as Byzantine.

A small-scale example of a distributed system is shown in the following diagram. This distributed system has six nodes out of which one (**N4**) is a Byzantine node leading to possible data inconsistency. **L2** is a link that is broken or slow, and this can lead to partition in the network.

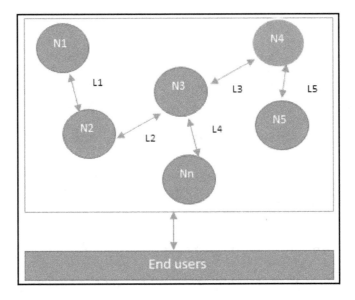

Design of a distributed system: N4 is a Byzantine node, L2 is broken or a slow network link

The primary challenge in distributed system design is coordination between nodes and fault tolerance. Even if some of the nodes become faulty or network links break, the distributed system should be able to tolerate this and continue to work to achieve the desired result. This problem has been an active area of distributed system design research for many years, and several algorithms and mechanisms have been proposed to overcome these issues.

Distributed systems are so challenging to design that a hypothesis known as the **CAP theorem** has been proven, which states that a distributed system cannot have all three of the much-desired properties simultaneously; that is, consistency, availability, and partition tolerance. We will dive into the CAP theorem in more detail later in this chapter.

The history of blockchain and Bitcoin

Blockchain was introduced with the invention of Bitcoin in 2008. Its practical implementation then occurred in 2009. For the purposes of this chapter, it is sufficient to review Bitcoin very briefly, as it will be explored in great depth in Chapter 8, *Introducing Bitcoin*. However, it is essential to refer to Bitcoin because, without it, the history of blockchain is not complete.

Electronic cash

The concept of electronic cash or digital currency is not new. Since the 1980s, e-cash protocols have existed that are based on a model proposed by David Chaum.

Just as understanding the concept of distributed systems is necessary to comprehend blockchain technology, the idea of electronic cash is also essential in order to appreciate the first and astonishingly successful application of blockchain, Bitcoin, or more broadly cryptocurrencies in general.

Two fundamental e-cash system issues need to be addressed: accountability and anonymity.

Accountability is required to ensure that cash is spendable only once (double-spend problem) and that it can only be spent by its rightful owner. Double spend problem arises when same money can be spent twice. As it is quite easy to make copies of digital data, this becomes a big issue in digital currencies as you can make many copies of same digital cash. **Anonymity** is required to protect users' privacy. As with physical cash, it is almost impossible to trace back spending to the individual who actually paid the money.

David Chaum solved both of these problems during his work in 1980s by using two cryptographic operations, namely **blind signatures** and **secret sharing**. These terminologies and related concepts will be discussed in detail in Chapter 5, *Symmetric Cryptography* and Chapter 6, *Public Key Cryptography*. For the moment, it is sufficient to say that *blind signatures* allow for signing a document without actually seeing it, and *secret sharing* is a concept that enables the detection of double spending, that is using the same e-cash token twice (double spending).

In 2009, the first practical implementation of an electronic cash (e-cash) system named Bitcoin appeared. The term cryptocurrency emerged later. For the very first time, it solved the problem of distributed consensus in a trustless network. It used **public key cryptography** with a **Proof of Work (PoW)** mechanism to provide a secure, controlled, and decentralized method of minting digital currency. The key innovation was the idea of an ordered list of blocks composed of transactions and cryptographically secured by the PoW mechanism. This concept will be explained in greater detail in Chapter 8, *Introducing Bitcoin*.

Other technologies used in Bitcoin, but which existed before its invention, include Merkle trees, hash functions, and hash chains. All these concepts are explained in appropriate depth in Chapter 6, *Public Key Cryptography*.

Looking at all the technologies mentioned earlier and their relevant history, it is easy to see how concepts from electronic cash schemes and distributed systems were combined to create Bitcoin and what now is known as blockchain. This concept can also be visualized with the help of the following diagram:

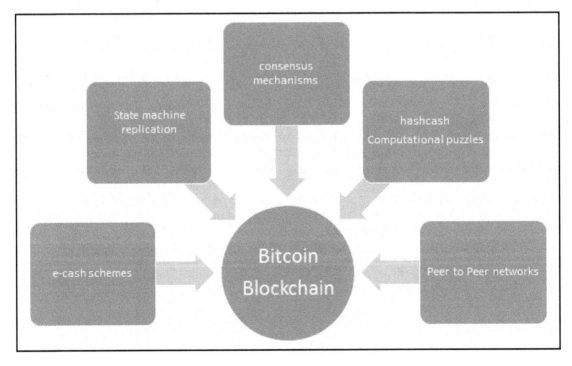

The various ideas that supported the invention of Bitcoin and blockchain

Blockchain

In 2008, a groundbreaking paper entitled *Bitcoin: A Peer-to-Peer Electronic Cash System* was written on the topic of peer-to-peer electronic cash under the pseudonym *Satoshi Nakamoto*. It introduced the term **chain of blocks**. No one knows the actual identity of Satoshi Nakamoto. After introducing Bitcoin in 2009, he remained active in the Bitcoin developer community until 2011. He then handed over Bitcoin development to its core developers and simply disappeared. Since then, there has been no communication from him whatsoever, and his existence and identity are shrouded in mystery. The term *chain of blocks* evolved over the years into the word *blockchain*.

As stated earlier, blockchain technology incorporates a multitude of applications that can be implemented in various economic sectors. Particularly in the finance sector, significant improvement in the performance of financial transactions and settlements is seen as resulting in desirable time and cost reductions. It is sufficient to say that parts of nearly all economic sectors have already realized the potential and promise of blockchain and have embarked, or will do so soon, on the journey to capitalize on the benefits of blockchain technology.

Blockchain defined

Layman's definition: Blockchain is an ever-growing, secure, shared record keeping system in which each user of the data holds a copy of the records, which can only be updated if all parties involved in a transaction agree to update.

Technical definition: Blockchain is a peer-to-peer, distributed ledger that is cryptographically-secure, append-only, immutable (extremely hard to change), and updateable only via consensus or agreement among peers.

Now let's examine the preceding definitions in more detail. We will look at all keywords in the definitions one by one.

Peer-to-peer

The first keyword in the technical definition is *peer-to-peer*. This means that there is no central controller in the network, and all participants talk to each other directly. This property allows for cash transactions to be exchanged directly among the peers without a third-party involvement, such as by a bank.

Distributed ledger

Dissecting the technical definition further reveals that blockchain is a *distributed ledger*, which simply means that a ledger is spread across the network among all peers in the network, and each peer holds a copy of the complete ledger.

Cryptographically-secure

Next, we see that this ledger is *cryptographically-secure*, which means that cryptography has been used to provide security services which make this ledger secure against tampering and misuse. These services include non-repudiation, data integrity, and data origin authentication. You will see how this is achieved later in Chapter 5, *Symmetric Cryptography* which introduces the fascinating world of cryptography.

Append-only

Another property that we encounter is that blockchain is *append-only*, which means that data can only be added to the blockchain in *time-ordered sequential order*. This property implies that once data is added to the blockchain, it is almost impossible to change that data and can be considered practically immutable. Nonetheless, it can be changed in rare scenarios wherein collusion against the blockchain network succeeds in gaining more than 51 percent of the power. There may be some legitimate reasons to change data in the blockchain once it has been added, such as the *right to be forgotten* or *right to erasure* (also defined in **General Data Protection (GDPR)** ruling, https://gdpr-info.eu/art-17-gdpr/).

However, those are individual cases that need to be handled separately and that require an elegant technical solution. For all practical purposes, blockchain is indeed immutable and cannot be changed.

Updateable via consensus

Finally, the most critical attribute of a blockchain is that it is *updateable* only via consensus. This is what gives it the power of decentralization. In this scenario, no central authority is in control of updating the ledger. Instead, any update made to the blockchain is validated against strict criteria defined by the blockchain protocol and added to the blockchain only after a consensus has been reached among all participating peers/nodes on the network. To achieve consensus, there are various consensus facilitation algorithms which ensure that all parties are in agreement about the final state of the data on the blockchain network and resolutely agree upon it to be true. Consensus algorithms are discussed later in this chapter and throughout the book as appropriate.

Blockchain can be thought of as a layer of a distributed peer-to-peer network running on top of the internet, as can be seen in the following diagram. It is analogous to SMTP, HTTP, or FTP running on top of TCP/IP.

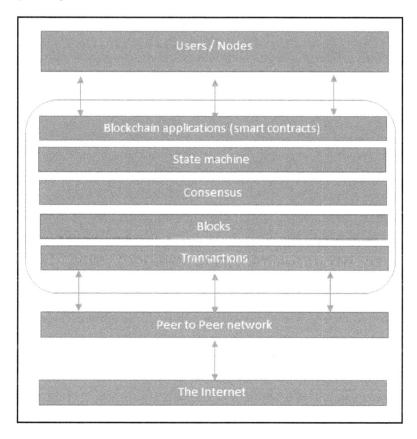

The network view of a blockchain

At the bottom layer in the preceding diagram, there is the internet, which provides a basic communication layer for any network. In this case, a peer-to-peer network runs on top of the internet, which hosts another layer of blockchain. That layer contains transactions, blocks, consensus mechanisms, state machines, and blockchain smart contracts. All of these components are shown as a single logical entity in a box, representing blockchain above the peer-to-peer network. Finally, at the top, there are users or nodes that connect to the blockchain and perform various operations such as consensus, transaction verification, and processing. These concepts will be discussed in detail later in this book.

From a business standpoint, a blockchain can be defined as a platform where peers can exchange value / electronic cash using transactions without the need for a centrally-trusted arbitrator. For example, for cash transfers, banks act as a trusted third party. In financial trading, a central clearing house acts as an arbitrator between two trading parties. This concept is compelling, and once you absorb it, you will realize the enormous potential of blockchain technology. This disintermediation allows blockchain to be a decentralized consensus mechanism where no single authority is in charge of the database. Immediately, you'll see a significant benefit of decentralization here, because if no banks or central clearing houses are required, then it immediately leads to cost savings, faster transaction speeds, and trust.

A **block** is merely a selection of transactions bundled together and organized logically. A **transaction** is a record of an event, for example, the event of transferring cash from a sender's account to a beneficiary's account. A block is made up of transactions, and its size varies depending on the type and design of the blockchain in use.

A reference to a previous block is also included in the block unless it is a genesis block. A **genesis block** is the first block in the blockchain that is hardcoded at the time the blockchain was first started. The structure of a block is also dependent on the type and design of a blockchain. Generally, however, there are just a few attributes that are essential to the functionality of a block: the block header, which is composed of pointer to previous block, the timestamp, nonce, Merkle root, and the block body that contains transactions. There are also other attributes in a block, but generally, the aforementioned components are always available in a block.

A **nonce** is a number that is generated and used only once. A nonce is used extensively in many cryptographic operations to provide replay protection, authentication, and encryption. In blockchain, it's used in PoW consensus algorithms and for transaction replay protection.

Merkle root is a hash of all of the nodes of a Merkle tree. Merkle trees are widely used to validate the large data structures securely and efficiently. In the blockchain world, Merkle trees are commonly used to allow efficient verification of transactions. Merkle root in a blockchain is present in the block header section of a block, which is the hash of all transactions in a block. This means that verifying only the Merkle root is required to verify all transactions present in the Merkle tree instead of verifying all transactions one by one. We will elaborate further on these concepts in Chapter 6, *Public Key Cryptography*.

The generic structure of a block.

This preceding structure is a simple block diagram that depicts a block. Specific block structures relative to their blockchain technologies will be discussed later in the book with greater in-depth technical detail.

Generic elements of a blockchain

Now, let's walk through the generic elements of a blockchain. You can use this as a handy reference section if you ever need a reminder about the different parts of a blockchain. More precise elements will be discussed in the context of their respective blockchains in later chapters, for example, the Ethereum blockchain. The structure of a generic blockchain can be visualized with the help of the following diagram:

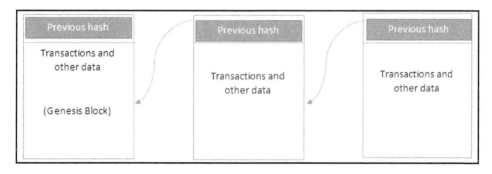

Generic structure of a blockchain

Elements of a generic blockchain are described here one by one. These are the elements that you will come across in relation to blockchain:

- **Address**: Addresses are unique identifiers used in a blockchain transaction to denote senders and recipients. An address is usually a public key or derived from a public key. While addresses can be reused by the same user, addresses themselves are unique. In practice, however, a single user may not use the same address again and generate a new one for each transaction. This newly-created address will be unique. Bitcoin is, in fact, a pseudonymous system. End users are usually not directly identifiable, but some research in removing the anonymity of Bitcoin users has shown that they can be identified successfully. A good practice is for users to generate a new address for each transaction in order to avoid linking transactions to the common owner, thus preventing identification.

- **Transaction**: A transaction is the fundamental unit of a blockchain. A transaction represents a transfer of value from one address to another.

- **Block**: A block is composed of multiple transactions and other elements, such as the previous block hash (hash pointer), timestamp, and nonce.

- **Peer-to-peer network**: As the name implies, a peer-to-peer network is a network topology wherein all peers can communicate with each other and send and receive messages.

- **Scripting or programming language**: Scripts or programs perform various operations on a transaction in order to facilitate various functions. For example, in Bitcoin, transaction scripts are predefined in a language called **Script**, which consist of sets of commands that allow nodes to transfer tokens from one address to another. Script is a limited language, however, in the sense that it only allows essential operations that are necessary for executing transactions, but it does not allow for arbitrary program development. Think of it as a calculator that only supports standard preprogrammed arithmetic operations. As such, Bitcoin script language cannot be called *Turing complete*. In simple words, Turing complete language means that it can perform any computation. It is named after Alan Turing who developed the idea of Turing machine that can run any algorithm however complex. Turing complete languages need loops and branching capability to perform complex computations. Therefore, Bitcoin's scripting language is not Turing complete, whereas Ethereum's Solidity language is.

To facilitate arbitrary program development on a blockchain, Turing complete programming language is needed, and it is now a very desirable feature of blockchains. Think of this as a computer that allows development of any program using programming languages. Nevertheless, the security of such languages is a crucial question and an essential and ongoing research area. We will discuss this in greater detail in Chapter 8, *Introducing Bitcoin*, Chapter 4, *Smart Contracts*, and Chapter 11, *Development Tools and Frameworks*, later in this book.

- **Virtual machine**: This is an extension of the transaction script introduced earlier. A *virtual machine* allows Turing complete code to be run on a blockchain (as smart contracts); whereas a transaction script is limited in its operation. However, virtual machines are not available on all blockchains. Various blockchains use virtual machines to run programs such as **Ethereum Virtual Machine** (**EVM**) and **Chain Virtual Machine** (**CVM**). EVM is used in Ethereum blockchain, while CVM is a virtual machine developed for and used in an enterprise-grade blockchain called **Chain Core**.

- **State machine**: A blockchain can be viewed as a state transition mechanism whereby a state is modified from its initial form to the next one and eventually to a final form by nodes on the blockchain network as a result of a transaction execution, validation, and finalization process.

- **Node**: A node in a blockchain network performs various functions depending on the role that it takes on. A node can propose and validate transactions and perform mining to facilitate consensus and secure the blockchain. This goal is achieved by following a **consensus protocol** (most commonly PoW). Nodes can also perform other functions such as simple payment verification (lightweight nodes), validation, and many other functions depending on the type of the blockchain used and the role assigned to the node. Nodes also perform a transaction signing function. Transactions are first created by nodes and then also digitally signed by nodes using private keys as proof that they are the legitimate owner of the asset that they wish to transfer to someone else on the blockchain network. This asset is usually a token or virtual currency, such as Bitcoin, but it can also be any real-world asset represented on the blockchain by using tokens.

- **Smart contract**: These programs run on top of the blockchain and encapsulate the business logic to be executed when certain conditions are met. These programs are enforceable and automatically executable. The smart contract feature is not available on all blockchain platforms, but it is now becoming a very desirable feature due to the flexibility and power that it provides to the blockchain applications. Smart contracts have many use cases, including but not limited to identity management, capital markets, trade finance, record management, insurance, and e-governance. Smart contracts will be discussed in more detail in `Chapter 4`, *Smart Contracts*.

How blockchain works

We have now defined and described blockchain. Now let's see how a blockchain actually works. Nodes are either *miners* who create new blocks and mint cryptocurrency (coins) or *block signers* who validates and digitally sign the transactions. A critical decision that every blockchain network has to make is to figure out that which node will append the next block to the blockchain. This decision is made using a *consensus mechanism*. The consensus mechanism will be described later in this chapter.

Now we will look at the how a blockchain validates transactions and creates and adds blocks to grow the blockchain.

How blockchain accumulates blocks

Now we will look at a general scheme for creating blocks. This scheme is presented here to give you a general idea of how blocks are generated and what the relationship is between transactions and blocks:

1. A node starts a transaction by first creating and then digitally signing it with its private key. A transaction can represent various actions in a blockchain. Most commonly this is a data structure that represents transfer of value between users on the blockchain network. Transaction data structure usually consists of some logic of transfer of value, relevant rules, source and destination addresses, and other validation information. This will be covered in more detail in specific chapters on Bitcoin and Ethereum later in the book.
2. A transaction is propagated (flooded) by using a flooding protocol, called Gossip protocol, to peers that validate the transaction based on preset criteria. Usually, more than one node are required to verify the transaction.

3. Once the transaction is validated, it is included in a block, which is then propagated onto the network. At this point, the transaction is considered confirmed.

4. The newly-created block now becomes part of the ledger, and the next block links itself cryptographically back to this block. This link is a hash pointer. At this stage, the transaction gets its second confirmation and the block gets its first confirmation.

5. Transactions are then reconfirmed every time a new block is created. Usually, six confirmations in the Bitcoin network are required to consider the transaction final.

It is worth noting that steps 4 and 5 are considered non-compulsory, as the transaction itself is finalized in step 3; however, block confirmation and further transaction reconfirmations, if required, are then carried out in step 4 and step 5.

This completes the basic introduction to blockchain. In the next section, you will learn about the benefits and limitations of this technology.

Benefits and limitations of blockchain

Numerous advantages of blockchain technology have been discussed in many industries and proposed by thought leaders around the world who are participating in the blockchain space. The notable benefits of blockchain technology are as follows:

- **Decentralization**: This is a core concept and benefit of the blockchain. There is no need for a trusted third party or intermediary to validate transactions; instead, a consensus mechanism is used to agree on the validity of transactions.

- **Transparency and trust**: Because blockchains are shared and everyone can see what is on the blockchain, this allows the system to be transparent. As a result, trust is established. This is more relevant in scenarios such as the disbursement of funds or benefits where personal discretion in relation to selecting beneficiaries needs to be restricted.

- **Immutability**: Once the data has been written to the blockchain, it is extremely difficult to change it back. It is not genuinely immutable, but because changing data is so challenging and nearly impossible, this is seen as a benefit to maintaining an immutable ledger of transactions.

- **High availability**: As the system is based on thousands of nodes in a peer-to-peer network, and the data is replicated and updated on every node, the system becomes highly available. Even if some nodes leave the network or become inaccessible, the network as a whole continues to work, thus making it highly available. This redundancy results in high availability.

- **Highly secure**: All transactions on a blockchain are cryptographically secured and thus provide network integrity.

- **Simplification of current paradigms**: The current blockchain model in many industries, such as finance or health, is somewhat disorganized. In this model, multiple entities maintain their own databases and data sharing can become very difficult due to the disparate nature of the systems. However, as a blockchain can serve as a single shared ledger among many interested parties, this can result in simplifying the model by reducing the complexity of managing the separate systems maintained by each entity.

- **Faster dealings**: In the financial industry, especially in post-trade settlement functions, blockchain can play a vital role by enabling the quick settlement of trades. Blockchain does not require a lengthy process of verification, reconciliation, and clearance because a single version of agreed-upon data is already available on a shared ledger between financial organizations.

- **Cost saving**: As no trusted third party or clearing house is required in the blockchain model, this can massively eliminate overhead costs in the form of the fees which are paid to such parties.

As with any technology, some challenges need to be addressed in order to make a system more robust, useful, and accessible. Blockchain technology is no exception. In fact, much effort is being made in both academia and industry to overcome the challenges posed by blockchain technology. The most sensitive blockchain problems are as follows:

- Scalability
- Adaptability
- Regulation
- Relatively immature technology
- Privacy

All of these issues and possible solutions will be discussed in detail in Chapter 16, *Scalability and Other Challenges*.

Tiers of blockchain technology

In this section, various layers of blockchain technology are presented. It is thought that due to the rapid development and progress being made in blockchain technology, many applications will evolve. Some of these advancements have already been realized, while others are anticipated in the near future based on the current rate of advancement in blockchain technology.

The three levels discussed here were initially described in the book *Blockchain: Blueprint for a New Economy* by *Melanie Swan, O'Reilly Media, 2015* as blockchain tiers categorized by applications in each category. This is how blockchain is evolving, and this versioning shows different tiers of evolution and usage of blockchain technology. In fact, all blockchain platforms, with limited exceptions, support these functionalities and applications. This versioning is just a logical segregation of various blockchain categories based on the way that they are currently being used, are evolving, or predicted to evolve.

Also note that this versioning is being presented here for completeness and for historic reasons, as these definitions are somewhat blurred now, and with the exception of Bitcoin (Blockchain 1.0), all newer blockchain platforms that support smart contract development can be programmed to provide the functionalities and applications mentioned in all blockchain tiers: 1.0, 2.0, 3.0, and beyond.

In addition to Tier 1, Tier 2 and Tier 3, or Tier X in the future, the following represents my own vision of what blockchain technology eventually could become as this technology advances:

- **Blockchain 1.0**: This tier was introduced with the invention of Bitcoin, and it is primarily used for cryptocurrencies. Also, as Bitcoin was the first implementation of cryptocurrencies, it makes sense to categorize this first generation of blockchain technology to include only cryptographic currencies. All alternative cryptocurrencies as well as Bitcoin fall into this category. It includes core applications such as payments and applications. This generation started in 2009 when Bitcoin was released and ended in early 2010.

- **Blockchain 2.0**: This second blockchain generation is used by financial services and smart contracts. This tier includes various financial assets, such as derivatives, options, swaps, and bonds. Applications that go beyond currency, finance, and markets are incorporated at this tier. Ethereum, Hyperledger, and other newer blockchain platforms are considered part of Blockchain 2.0. This generation started when ideas related to using blockchain for other purposes started to emerge in 2010.

- **Blockchain 3.0**: This third blockchain generation is used to implement applications beyond the financial services industry and is used in government, health, media, the arts, and justice. Again, as in Blockchain 2.0, Ethereum, Hyperledger, and newer blockchains with the ability to code smart contracts are considered part of this blockchain technology tier. This generation of blockchain emerged around 2012 when multiple applications of blockchain technology in different industries were researched.

- **Blockchain X.0**: This generation represents a vision of blockchain singularity where one day there will be a public blockchain service available that anyone can use just like the Google search engine. It will provide services for all realms of society. It will be a public and open distributed ledger with general-purpose rational agents (*Machina economicus*) running on a blockchain, making decisions, and interacting with other intelligent autonomous agents on behalf of people, and regulated by code instead of law or paper contracts. This does not mean that law and contracts will disappear, instead law and contracts will be implementable in code.

Machina Economicus is a concept which comes from the field of **Artificial Intelligence** (**AI**) and computational economics. It can be defined as a machine that makes logical and perfect decisions. There are various technical challenges that need to be addressed before this dream can be realized.

 Discussion of Machina Economicus is beyond the scope of this book, interested readers can refer to `https://www.infosys.com/insights/purposeful-ai/Documents/machina -economicus.pdf`, for more information.

This concept in the context of blockchain and its convergence with AI will be elaborated on in `Chapter 18`, *Current Landscape and What's Next*.

Features of a blockchain

A blockchain performs various functions which are supported by various features. These functions include but are not limited to transfer of value, managing assets and agreements. All of the blockchain tiers described in the previous section perform these functions with the help of features offered by blockchain, but with some exceptions. For example, smart contracts are not supported by all blockchain platforms, such as Bitcoin. Another example is that not all blockchain platforms produce cryptocurrency or tokens, such as Hyperledger Fabric, and MultiChain.

The features of a blockchain are described here:

- **Distributed consensus**: Distributed consensus is the primary underpinning of a blockchain. This mechanism allows a blockchain to present a single version of the truth, which is agreed upon by all parties without the requirement of a central authority.
- **Transaction verification**: Any transactions posted from the nodes on the blockchain are verified based on a predetermined set of rules. Only valid transactions are selected for inclusion in a block.
- **Platform for smart contracts**: A blockchain is a platform on which programs can run to execute business logic on behalf of the users. Not all blockchains have a mechanism to execute *smart contracts*; however, this is a very desirable feature, and it is available on newer blockchain platforms such as Ethereum and MultiChain.

Smart Contracts

Blockchain technology provides a platform for running smart contracts. These are automated, autonomous programs that reside on the blockchain network and encapsulate the business logic and code needed to execute a required function when certain conditions are met. For example, think about an insurance contract where a claim is paid to the traveler if the flight is canceled. In the real world, this process normally takes a significant amount of time to make the claim, verify it, and pay the insurance amount to the claimant (traveler). What if this whole process were automated with cryptographically-enforced trust, transparency, and execution so that as soon as the smart contract received a feed that the flight in question has been canceled, it automatically triggers the insurance payment to the claimant? If the flight is on time, the smart contract pays itself.

This is indeed a revolutionary feature of blockchain, as it provides flexibility, speed, security, and automation for real-world scenarios that can lead to a completely trustworthy system with significant cost reductions. Smart contracts can be programmed to perform any actions that blockchain users need and according to their specific business requirements.

- **Transferring value between peers**: Blockchain enables the transfer of value between its users via tokens. Tokens can be thought of as a carrier of value.

- **Generation of cryptocurrency**: This feature is optional depending on the type of blockchain in use. A blockchain can create cryptocurrency as an incentive to its miners who validate the transactions and spend resources to secure the blockchain. We will discuss cryptocurrencies in great detail in `Chapter 8, Introducing Bitcoin`.

- **Smart property**: It is now possible to link a digital or physical asset to the blockchain in such a secure and precise manner that it cannot be claimed by anyone else. You are in full control of your asset, and it cannot be double-spent or double-owned. Compare this with a digital music file, for example, which can be copied many times without any controls. While it is true that many **Digital Rights Management** (**DRM**) schemes are being used currently along with copyright laws, but none of them is enforceable in such a way as blockchain based DRM can be. Blockchain can provide DRM functionality in such a way that it can be enforced fully. There are famously broken DRM schemes which looked great in theory but were hacked due to one limitation or another. One example is Oculus hack (`http://www.wired.co.uk/article/oculus-rift-drm-hacked`).

Another example is PS3 hack, also copyrighted digital music, films and e-books are routinely shared on the internet without any limitations. We have copyright protection in place for many years, but digital piracy refutes all attempts to fully enforce the law on a blockchain, however, if you own an asset, no one else can claim it unless you decide to transfer it. This feature has far-reaching implications, especially in DRM and electronic cash systems where double-spend detection is a crucial requirement. The double-spend problem was first solved without the requirement of a trusted third party in Bitcoin.

- **Provider of security**: The blockchain is based on proven cryptographic technology that ensures the integrity and availability of data. Generally, confidentiality is not provided due to the requirements of transparency. This limitation is the leading barrier to its adoption by financial institutions and other industries that require privacy and confidentiality of transactions. As such, the privacy and confidentiality of transactions on the blockchain is being researched very actively, and advancements are already being made. It could be argued that, in many situations, confidentiality is not needed and transparency is preferred. For example, with Bitcoin, confidentiality is not an absolute requirement; however, it is desirable in some scenarios. A more recent example is Zcash, which provides a platform for conducting anonymous transactions. This scheme will be discussed in detail in `Chapter 10`, *Alternative Coins*. Other security services, such as non-repudiation and authentication, are also provided by blockchain, as all actions are secured using private keys and digital signatures.
- **Immutability**: This is another critical feature of blockchain: once records are added to the blockchain, they are immutable. There is the remote possibility of rolling back changes, but this is to be avoided at all costs as doing so would consume an exorbitant amount of computing resources. For example, with Bitcoin if a malicious user wants to alter previous blocks, then it would require computing the PoW once again for all those blocks that have already been added to the blockchain. This difficulty makes the records on a blockchain essentially immutable.
- **Uniqueness**: This blockchain feature ensures that every transaction is unique and has not already been spent (double-spend problem). This feature is especially relevant with cryptocurrencies, where detection and avoidance of double spending are a vital requirement.

Types of blockchain

Based on the way that blockchain has evolved over the last few years, it can be divided into multiple categories with distinct though sometimes partially-overlapping attributes. You *should* note that the tiers described earlier in the chapter are a different concept whereby the logical categorization of blockchain based on its evolution and usage is presented.

In this section, we will examine the different types of blockchains from a technical and business usage perspective. These blockchain types can occur on any blockchain tier, as there is no direct relationship between those tiers and the various types of blockchain.

In this section we'll examine:

- Distributed ledgers
- Distributed Ledger Technology (DLT)
- Blockchains
- Ledgers

Distributed ledgers

First, I need to clarify an ambiguity. It should be noted that a *distributed ledger* is a broad term describing shared databases; hence, all blockchains technically fall under the umbrella of shared databases or distributed ledgers. Although all blockchains are fundamentally distributed ledgers, all distributed ledgers are not necessarily a blockchain.

A critical difference between a distributed ledger and blockchain is that a distributed ledger does not necessarily consist of blocks of transactions to keep the ledger growing. Rather, a blockchain is a special type of shared database that is comprised of blocks of transactions. An example of a distributed ledger that does not use blocks of transactions is R3's Corda. Corda is a distributed ledger which is developed to record and manage agreements and is especially focused on financial services industry. On the other hand, more widely-known blockchains like Bitcoin and Ethereum make use of blocks to update the shared database.

As the name suggests, a distributed ledger is distributed among its participants and spread across multiple sites or organizations. This type of ledger can be either private or public. The fundamental idea here is that, unlike many other blockchains, the records are stored contiguously instead of being sorted into blocks. This concept is used in Ripple which is a blockchain and cryptocurrency based global payment network.

Distributed Ledger Technology

It should be noted that over the last few years, the terms distributed ledger or **Distributed Ledger Technology** (**DLT**) have grown to be commonly used to describe blockchain in finance industry. Sometimes, blockchain and DLT are used interchangeably. Though this is not entirely accurate, it is how the term has evolved recently, especially in the finance sector. In fact, DLT is now a very active and thriving area of research in the financial sector. From a financial sector point of view, DLTs are permissioned blockchains that are shared and used between known participants. DLTs usually serve as a shared database, with all participants known and verified. They do not have a cryptocurrency or do not require mining to secure the ledger.

Public blockchains

As the name suggests, public blockchains are not owned by anyone. They are open to the public, and anyone can participate as a node in the decision-making process. Users may or may not be rewarded for their participation. All users of these *permissionless* or *unpermissioned* ledgers maintain a copy of the ledger on their local nodes and use a distributed consensus mechanism to decide the eventual state of the ledger. Bitcoin and Ethereum are both considered public blockchains.

Private blockchains

As the name implies, private blockchains are just that—private. That is, they are open only to a consortium or group of individuals or organizations who have decided to share the ledger among themselves. There are various blockchains now available in this category, such as HydraChain and Quorum. Optionally, both of these blockchains can also run in public mode if required, but their primary purpose is to provide a private blockchain.

Semiprivate blockchains

With *semiprivate blockchains*, part of the blockchain is private and part of it is public. Note that this is still just a concept today, and no real world POCs have yet been developed. With a semi-private blockchain, the private part is controlled by a group of individuals, while the public part is open for participation by anyone.

This hybrid model can be used in scenarios where the private part of the blockchain remains internal and shared among known participants, while the public part of the blockchain can still be used by anyone, optionally allowing mining to secure the blockchain. This way, the blockchain as a whole can be secured using PoW, thus providing consistency and validity for both the private and public parts. This type of blockchain can also be called a *semi-decentralized* model, where it is controlled by a single entity but still allows for multiple users to join the network by following appropriate procedures.

Sidechains

More precisely known as *pegged sidechains,* this is a concept whereby coins can be moved from one blockchain to another and moved back again. Typical uses include the creation of new *altcoins* (alternative cryptocurrencies) whereby coins are burnt as a proof of an adequate stake. *Burnt* or *burning the coins* in this context means that the coins are sent to an address which is unspendable and this process makes the *burnt* coins irrecoverable. This mechanism is used to bootstrap a new currency or introduce scarcity which results in increased value of the coin.

This mechanism is also called **Proof of Burn** (**PoB**) and is used as an alternative method for distributed consensus to PoW and **Proof of Stake** (**PoS**). The aforementioned example for burning coins applies to a **one-way pegged sidechain**. The second type is called a **two-way pegged sidechain**, which allows the movement of coins from the main chain to the sidechain and back to the main chain when required.

This process enables the building of smart contracts for the Bitcoin network. Rootstock is one of the leading examples of a sidechain, which enables smart contract development for Bitcoin using this paradigm. It works by allowing a two-way peg for the Bitcoin blockchain, and this results in much faster throughput.

Permissioned ledger

A *permissioned ledger* is a blockchain where participants of the network are already known and trusted. Permissioned ledgers do not need to use a distributed consensus mechanism; instead, an agreement protocol is used to maintain a shared version of the truth about the state of the records on the blockchain. In this case, for verification of transactions on the chain, all verifiers are already preselected by a central authority and typically there is no need for a mining mechanism.

By definition, there is also no requirement for a permissioned blockchain to be private, as it can be a public blockchain but with regulated access control. For example, Bitcoin can become a permissioned ledger if an access control layer is introduced on top of it that verifies the identity of a user and then allows access to the blockchain.

Shared ledger

This is a generic term that is used to describe any application or database that is shared by the public or a consortium. Generally, all blockchains, fall into the category of a shared ledger.

Fully private and proprietary blockchains

There is no mainstream application of these types of blockchains, as they deviate from the core concept of decentralization in blockchain technology. Nonetheless, in specific private settings within an organization, there could be a need to share data and provide some level of guarantee of the authenticity of the data.

An example of this type of blockchain might be to allow for collaboration and the sharing data between various government departments. In that case, no complex consensus mechanism is required, apart from simple state machine replication and an agreement protocol with known central validators. Even in private blockchains, tokens are not really required, but they can be used as means of transferring value or representing some real-world asset.

Tokenized blockchains

These blockchains are standard blockchains that generate cryptocurrency as a result of a consensus process via mining or initial distribution. Bitcoin and Ethereum are prime examples of this type of blockchain.

Tokenless blockchains

These blockchains are designed in such a way that they do not have the basic unit for the transfer of value. However, they are still valuable in situations where there is no need to transfer value between nodes and only the sharing of data among various trusted parties is required. This is similar to full private blockchains, the only difference being that use of tokens is not required. This can also be thought of as a shared distributed ledger used for storing data. It does have its benefits when it comes to immutability, security, and consensus driven updates but are not used for common blockchain application of value transfer or cryptocurrency.

This ends our examination of the various type of blockchain, we'll now move in the next section to discuss the concept of census.

Consensus

Consensus is the backbone of a blockchain and, as a result, it provides decentralization of control through an optional process known as **mining**. The choice of the **consensus algorithm** is also governed by the type of blockchain in use; that is, not all consensus mechanisms are suitable for all types of blockchains. For example, in public permissionless blockchains, it would make sense to use PoW instead of a simple agreement mechanism that is perhaps based on proof of authority. Therefore, it is essential to choose an appropriate consensus algorithm for a particular blockchain project.

Consensus is a process of agreement between distrusting nodes on the final state of data. To achieve consensus, different algorithms are used. It is easy to reach an agreement between two nodes (in client-server systems, for example), but when multiple nodes are participating in a distributed system and they need to agree on a single value, it becomes quite a challenge to achieve consensus. This process of attaining agreement common state or value among multiple nodes despite the failure of some nodes is known as **distributed consensus**.

Consensus mechanism

A **consensus mechanism** is a set of steps that are taken by most or all nodes in a blockchain to agree on a proposed state or value. For more than three decades, this concept has been researched by computer scientists in industry and academia. Consensus mechanisms have most recently come into the limelight and gained considerable popularity with the advent of blockchain and Bitcoin.

There are various requirements that must be met to provide the desired results in a consensus mechanism. The following describes these requirements:

- **Agreement**: All honest nodes decide on the same value
- **Termination**: All honest nodes terminate execution of the consensus process and eventually reach a decision
- **Validity**: The value agreed upon by all honest nodes must be the same as the initial value proposed by at least one honest node
- **Fault tolerant**: The consensus algorithm should be able to run in the presence of faulty or malicious nodes (Byzantine nodes)
- **Integrity**: This is a requirement that no node can make the decision more than once in a single consensus cycle

Types of consensus mechanisms

All consensus mechanisms are developed to deal with faults in a distributed system and to allow distributed systems to reach a final state of agreement. There are two general categories of consensus mechanisms. These categories deal with all types of faults (fail stop type or arbitrary). These common types of consensus mechanisms are as follows:

- **Traditional Byzantine Fault Tolerance (BFT)-based**: With no compute-intensive operations, such as partial hash inversion (as in Bitcoin PoW), this method relies on a simple scheme of nodes that are publisher-signed messages. Eventually, when a certain number of messages are received, then an agreement is reached.
- **Leader election-based consensus mechanisms**: This arrangement requires nodes to compete in a leader-election lottery, and the node that wins proposes a final value. For example, the PoW used in Bitcoin falls into this category.

Many practical implementations of consensus protocols have been proposed. **Paxos** is the most famous of these protocols. It was introduced by Leslie Lamport in 1989. With Paxos, nodes are assigned various roles such as Proposer, Acceptor, and Learner. Nodes or processes are named replicas, and consensus is achieved in the presence of faulty nodes by agreement among a majority of nodes.

An alternative to Paxos is RAFT, which works by assigning any of three states; that is, follower, candidate, or leader to the nodes. A leader is elected after a candidate node receives enough votes, and all changes then have to go through the leader. The leader commits the proposed changes once replication on the majority of the follower nodes is completed. More detail on the theory of consensus mechanisms from a distributed system point of view are beyond the scope of this chapter. Later in this chapter, however, a full section is dedicated to the introduction of consensus protocols. Specific algorithms will be discussed in chapters dedicated to Bitcoin and other blockchains later in this book.

Consensus in blockchain

Consensus is a distributed computing concept that has been used in blockchain in order to provide a means of agreeing to a single version of the truth by all peers on the blockchain network. This concept was previously discussed in the distributed systems section of this chapter. In this section, we will address consensus in the context of blockchain technology. Some concepts presented here are still relevant to distributed systems theory, but they are explained from a blockchain perspective.

Roughly, the following describes the two main categories of consensus mechanisms:

- Proof-based, leader-election lottery based, or the Nakamoto consensus whereby a leader is elected at random (using an algorithm) and proposes a final value. This category is also referred to as the *fully decentralized* or *permissionless* type of consensus mechanism. This type is well used in the Bitcoin and Ethereum blockchain in the form of a PoW mechanism.
- BFT-based is a more traditional approach based on rounds of votes. This class of consensus is also known as the *consortium* or *permissioned* type of consensus mechanism.

BFT-based consensus mechanisms perform well when there are a limited number of nodes, but they do not scale well. On the other hand, leader-election lottery based (PoW) type consensus mechanisms scale very well but perform very slowly. As there is significant research being conducted in this area, new types of consensus mechanism are also emerging, such as the semi-decentralized type, which is used in the Ripple network. Ripple network will be discussed in detail in Chapter 14, *Alternative Blockchains*. There are also various other proposals out there, which are trying to find the right balance between scalability and performance. Some notable projects include PBFT, Hybrid BFT, BlockDAG, Tezos, Stellar, and GHOST.

The consensus algorithms available today, or that are being researched in the context of blockchain, are presented here. The following is not an exhaustive list, but it includes all notable algorithms.

- **Proof of Work (PoW)**: This type of consensus mechanism relies on proof that adequate computational resources have been spent before proposing a value for acceptance by the network. This scheme is used in Bitcoin, Litecoin, and other cryptocurrency blockchains. Currently, it is the only algorithm that has proven to be astonishingly successful against any collusion attacks on a blockchain network, such as the Sybil attack. The Sybil attack will be discussed in Chapter 8, *Introducing Bitcoin*.
- **Proof of Stake (PoS)**: This algorithm works on the idea that a node or user has an adequate stake in the system; that is, the user has invested enough in the system so that any malicious attempt by that user would outweigh the benefits of performing such an attack on the network. This idea was first introduced by Peercoin, and it is going to be used in the Ethereum blockchain version called *Serenity*. Another important concept in PoS is **coin age**, which is a criterion derived from the amount of time and number of coins that have not been spent. In this model, the chances of proposing and signing the next block increase with the coin age.

- **Delegated Proof of Stake (DPoS)**: This is an innovation over standard PoS, whereby each node that has a stake in the system can delegate the validation of a transaction to other nodes by voting. It is used in the BitShares blockchain.

- **Proof of Elapsed Time (PoET)**: Introduced by Intel in 2016, PoET uses a **Trusted Execution Environment** (**TEE**) to provide randomness and safety in the leader election process via a guaranteed wait time. It requires the Intel **Software Guard Extensions** (**SGX**) processor to provide the security guarantee for it to be secure. This concept is discussed in more detail in `Chapter 13`, *Hyperledger*, in the context of the Intel's *Sawtooth Lake* blockchain project.

- **Proof of Deposit (PoD)**: In this case, nodes that wish to participate in the network have to make a security deposit before they can mine and propose blocks. This mechanism is used in the Tendermint blockchain.

- **Proof of Importance (PoI)**: This idea is significant and different from PoS. PoI not only relies on how large a stake a user has in the system, but it also monitors the usage and movement of tokens by the user in order to establish a level of trust and importance. It is used in the NEM coin blockchain. More information about this coin is available at NEM's website `https://nem.io`.

- **Federated consensus or federated Byzantine consensus**: This mechanism is used in the stellar consensus protocol. Nodes in this protocol retain a group of publicly-trusted peers and propagate only those transactions that have been validated by the majority of trusted nodes.

- **Reputation-based mechanisms**: As the name suggests, a leader is elected by the reputation it has built over time on the network. It is based on the votes of other members.

- **PBFT**: This mechanism achieves state machine replication, which provides tolerance against Byzantine nodes. Various other protocols including PBFT, PAXOS, RAFT, and **Federated Byzantine Agreement** (**FBA**) are also being used or have been proposed for use in many different implementations of distributed systems and blockchains.

- **Proof of Activity** (**PoA**): This scheme is a combination of PoS and PoW, which ensures that a stakeholder is selected in a pseudorandom but uniform fashion. This is a comparatively more energy-efficient mechanism as compared to PoW. It utilizes a new concept called *Follow the Satoshi*. In this scheme, PoW and PoS are combined together to achieve consensus and good level of security. This scheme is more energy efficient as PoW is used only in the first stage of the mechanism, after the first stage it switches to PoS which consumes negligible energy.

- **Proof of Capacity (PoC)**: This scheme uses hard disk space as a resource to mine the blocks. This is different from PoW, where CPU resources are used. In in PoC, hard disk space is utilized for mining and as such is also known as *hard drive mining*. This concept was first introduced in the Burstcoin cryptocurrency.
- **Proof of Storage (PoS)**: This scheme allows for the outsourcing of storage capacity. This scheme is based on the concept that a particular piece of data is probably stored by a node *which* serves as a means to participate in the consensus mechanism. Several variations of this scheme have been proposed, such as Proof of Replication, Proof of Data Possession, Proof of Space, and Proof of Space-Time.

CAP theorem and blockchain

CAP theorem, also known as Brewer's theorem, was introduced by Eric Brewer in 1998 as conjecture. In 2002, it was proven as a theorem by Seth Gilbert and Nancy Lynch. The theory states that any distributed system cannot have consistency, availability, and partition tolerance simultaneously:

- **Consistency** is a property which ensures that all nodes in a distributed system have a single, current, and identical copy of the data.
- **Availability** means that the nodes in the system are up, accessible for use, and are accepting incoming requests and responding with data without any failures as and when required. In other words, data is available at each node and the nodes are responding to requests.
- **Partition tolerance** ensures that if a group of nodes is unable to communicate with other nodes due to network failures, the distributed system continues to operate correctly. This can occur due to network and node failures.

It has been proven that a distributed system cannot have consistency, availability, and partition tolerance simultaneously. This is explained with the following example. Let's imagine that there is a distributed system with two nodes. Now let us apply the three theorem properties on this smallest of possible distributed systems only with two nodes.

- **Consistency** is achieved if both nodes have the same shared state; that is, they have the same up-to-date copy of the data.
- **Availability** is achieved if both nodes are up and running and responding with the latest copy of data.
- **Partition tolerance** is achieved if communication does not break down between two nodes (either due to network issues, Byzantine faults, and so forth), and they are able to communicate with each other.

Now think of scenario where a partition occurs and nodes can no longer communicate with each other. If no new updated data comes in, it can only be updated on one node only. In that case, if the node accepts the update, then only that one node in the network is updated and therefore consistency is lost. Now, if the update is rejected by the node, that would result in loss of availability. In that case due to partition tolerance, both availability and consistency are unachievable.

This is strange because somehow blockchain manages to achieve all of these properties—or does it? This will be explained shortly. To achieve fault tolerance, replication is used. This is a standard and widely-used method to achieve fault tolerance. Consistency is achieved using consensus algorithms in order to ensure that all nodes have the same copy of the data. This is also called **state machine replication**. The blockchain is a means for achieving state machine replication. In general, there are two types of faults that a node can experience. Both of these types fall under the broader category of faults that can occur in a distributed system:

- **Fail-stop fault**: This type of fault occurs when a node merely has crashed. Fail-stop faults are the easier ones to deal with of the two fault types. Paxos protocol, introduced earlier in this chapter, is normally used to deal with this type of fault. These faults are simple to deal with

- **Byzantine faults**: The second type of fault is one where the faulty node exhibits malicious or inconsistent behavior arbitrarily. This type is difficult to handle since it can create confusion due to misleading information. This can be a result of an attack by adversaries, a software bug, or data corruption. State machine replication protocols such as PBFT was developed to address this second type of faults.

Strangely, it seems that the CAP theorem is violated in the blockchain, especially in its most successful implementation, Bitcoin. However, this is not the case. In blockchains, consistency is sacrificed in favor of availability and partition tolerance. In this scenario, **Consistency (C)** on the blockchain is not achieved simultaneously with **Partition tolerance (P)** and **Availability (A)**, but it is achieved over time. This is called eventual consistency, where consistency is achieved as a result of validation from multiple nodes over time. The concept of mining was introduced in Bitcoin for this purpose. **Mining** is a process that facilitates the achievement of consensus by using the PoW consensus algorithm. At a higher level, mining can be defined as a process that is used to add more blocks to the blockchain. More on this later in Chapter 8, *Introducing Bitcoin*.

Summary

In this chapter, we introduced you to the blockchain technology at an advanced level. First, we discussed some basic concepts of distributed systems, and then we reviewed the history of blockchain. We also discussed concepts such as electronic cash.

Furthermore, we presented various definitions of blockchain from different point of views. We also introduced you to few applications of blockchain technology. Next, we explored different types of blockchain. Finally, we examined the benefits and limitations of this new technology. Few topics such as blockchain scalability and adaptability issues were intentionally introduced only briefly, as these will be discussed in depth, in later chapters.

In the next chapter, we will introduce you to the concept of decentralization, which is central to the idea behind blockchains and their vast number of applications.

2
Decentralization

Decentralization is not a new concept. It has been used in strategy, management, and the government, for a long time. The basic idea of decentralization is to distribute control and authority to the peripheries of an organization instead of one central body being in full control of the organization. This configuration produces several benefits for organizations, such as increased efficiency, expedited decision making, better motivation, and a reduced burden on top management.

In this chapter, we will discuss the concept of decentralization in the context of blockchain. The fundamental basis of blockchain is that no single central authority is in control, and, in this chapter, we will present examples of various methods of decentralization and routes to achieve this. Furthermore, we will discuss the decentralization of the blockchain ecosystem, decentralized applications, and platforms for achieving decentralization, in detail. Also, we will introduce you to numerous exciting applications and ideas that emerge out of the decentralized blockchain technology.

Decentralization using blockchain

Decentralization is a core benefit and service provided by blockchain technology. By design, blockchain is a perfect vehicle for providing a platform that does not need any intermediaries and that can function with many different leaders chosen via consensus mechanisms. This model allows anyone to compete to become the decision-making authority. This competition is governed by a consensus mechanism, and the most commonly used method is known as **Proof of Work** (**PoW**).

Decentralization is applied in varying degrees from a semi-decentralized model to a fully decentralized one depending on the requirements and circumstances. Decentralization can be viewed from a blockchain perspective as a mechanism that provides a way to remodel existing applications and paradigms, or to build new applications, in order to give full control to users.

Information and Communication Technology (ICT) has conventionally been based on a centralized paradigm whereby database or application servers are under the control of a central authority, such as a system administrator. With Bitcoin and the advent of blockchain technology, this model has changed and now the technology exists, which allows anyone to start a decentralized system and operate it with no single point of failure or single trusted authority. It can either be run autonomously or by requiring some human intervention, depending on the type and model of governance used in the decentralized application running on blockchain.

The following diagram shows the different types of systems that currently exist: central, decentralized, and distributed. This concept was first published by Paul Baran in *On Distributed Communications: I. Introduction to Distributed Communications Networks* (Rand Corporation, 1964):

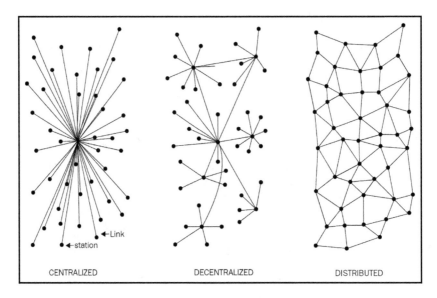

Different types of networks/systems

Centralized systems are conventional (client-server) IT systems in which there is a single authority that controls the system, and who is solely in charge of all operations on the system. All users of a centralized system are dependent on a single source of service. The majority of online service providers including Google, Amazon, eBay, Apple's App Store, and others use this conventional model for delivering services.

A **distributed system**, data and computation are spread across multiple nodes in the network. Sometimes, this term is confused with *parallel computing*. While there is some overlap in the definition, the main difference between these systems is that in a parallel computing system, computation is performed by all nodes simultaneously in order to achieve the result; for example, parallel computing platforms are used in weather research and forecasting, simulation and financial modeling. On the other hand, in a distributed system, computation may not happen in parallel and data is replicated across multiple nodes that users view as a single, coherent system. Variations of both of these models are used with to achieve fault tolerance and speed. In the parallel system model, there is still a central authority that has control over all nodes, which governs processing. This means that the system is still centralized in nature.

The critical difference between a decentralized system and distributed system is that in a distributed system, there still exists a central authority that governs the entire system; whereas, in a decentralized system, no such authority exists.

A **decentralized system** is a type of network where nodes are not dependent on a single master node; instead, control is distributed among many nodes. This is analogous to a model where each department in an organization is in charge of its own database server, thus taking away the power from the central server and distributing it to the subdepartments who manage their own databases.

A significant innovation in the decentralized paradigm that has given rise to this new era of decentralization of applications is **decentralized consensus**. This mechanism came into play with Bitcoin, and it enables a user to agree on something via a consensus algorithm without the need for a central, trusted third party, intermediary, or service provider.

Methods of decentralization

Two methods can be used to achieve decentralization: disintermediation and competition (Contest-driven decentralization). These methods will be discussed in detail in the sections that follow.

Disintermediation

The concept of **disintermediation** can be explained with the aid of an example. Imagine that you want to send money to a friend in another country. You go to a bank who, for a fee, will transfer your money to the bank in that country. In this case, the bank maintains a central database that is updated, confirming that you have sent the money. With blockchain technology, it is possible to send this money directly to your friend without the need for a bank. All you need is the address of your friend on the blockchain. This way, the intermediary; that is, the bank, is no longer required, and decentralization is achieved by *disintermediation*. It is debatable, however, how practical decentralization through disintermediation is in the financial sector due to massive regulatory and compliance requirements. Nevertheless, this model can be used not only in finance but in many different industries as well.

Contest-driven decentralization

In the method involving **competition**, different service providers compete with each other in order to be selected for the provision of services by the system. This paradigm does not achieve complete decentralization. However, to a certain degree, it ensures that an intermediary or service provider is not monopolizing the service. In the context of blockchain technology, a system can be envisioned in which smart contracts can choose an external data provider from a large number of providers based on their reputation, previous score, reviews, and quality of service.

This method will not result in full decentralization, but it allows smart contracts to make a free choice based on the criteria just mentioned. This way, an environment of competition is cultivated among service providers where they compete with each other to become the data provider of choice.

In the following diagram, varying levels of decentralization are shown. On the left-hand side, the conventional approach is shown where a central system is in control; on the right-hand side, complete disintermediation is achieved as intermediaries are entirely removed. Competing intermediaries or service providers are shown in the center. At that level, intermediaries or service providers are selected based on reputation or voting, thus achieving partial decentralization.

Scale of decentralization

While there are many benefits of decentralization, including transparency, efficiency, cost saving, development of trusted ecosystems, and in some cases privacy and anonymity, some challenges, such as security requirements, software bugs, and human errors need to be examined thoroughly.

For example, in a decentralized system such as Bitcoin or Ethereum where security is normally provided by private keys, how can one ensure that a smart property associated with these private keys cannot be rendered useless if the private keys are lost or, due to a bug in the smart contract code or the decentralized application becomes vulnerable to attack? Before embarking on a journey to decentralize everything using blockchain and decentralized applications, it is essential that you understand that not everything can or needs to be decentralized.

This view raises few fundamental questions. Is a blockchain really needed? When is a blockchain required? In what circumstances is blockchain preferred over traditional databases? To answer these questions, go through the simple set of questions presented here:

1. Is high data throughput required? If the answer to this question is yes, then use a traditional database.
2. Are updates centrally controlled? If yes, then use a conventional database.
3. Do users trust each other? If yes, then use a traditional database.
4. Are users anonymous? If yes, then use a public blockchain; if not, then use a private blockchain.
5. If consensus is required to be maintained within a consortium then use a private blockchain, otherwise use a public blockchain.

Answering all of these questions can provide an understanding of whether or not a blockchain is required. Beyond the questions posed in this model there are many other issues to consider, such as latency, choice of consensus mechanisms, whether consensus is required or not, and where consensus is going to be achieved. If consensus is maintained internally by a consortium, then a private blockchain should be used; otherwise, if consensus is required publicly among multiple entities, then a public blockchain solution should be considered. Other aspects like immutably should also be considered while making a decision about whether to use a blockchain or a traditional database. If strict data immutability is required, then a public blockchain should be used; otherwise, a central database may be an option.

As blockchain technology matures, there will be more questions raised regarding this model. For now, however, this set of questions is sufficient to decide whether a blockchain-based solution is required or not.

Routes to decentralization

Even though there were systems that pre-existed blockchain and Bitcoin, including BitTorrent and the Gnutella file sharing system, which to a certain degree could be classified as decentralized. However, with the advent of blockchain technology, many initiatives are now being taken to leverage this new technology for achieving decentralization. The Bitcoin blockchain is typically the first choice for many, as it has proven to be the most resilient and secure blockchain and has a market cap of nearly $145 billion at the time of this writing. Alternatively, other blockchains, such as Ethereum, serve as the tool of choice for many developers for building decentralized applications. As compared to Bitcoin, Ethereum has become a more prominent choice because of the flexibility it allows for programming any business logic into the blockchain by using *smart contracts*.

How to decentralize

Arvind Narayanan and others have proposed a framework in their book, *Bitcoin and Cryptocurrency Technologies, Princeton University Press*, that can be used to evaluate the decentralization requirements of a variety of issues in the context of blockchain technology. The framework raises four questions whose answers provide a clear understanding as to how a system can be decentralized:

1. What is being decentralized?
2. What level of decentralization is required?
3. What blockchain is used?
4. What security mechanism is used?

The first question simply asks you to identify what system is being decentralized. This can be any system, such as an identity system or a trading system.

The second question asks you to specify the level of decentralization required by examining the scale of decentralization as discussed earlier. It can be full disintermediation or partial disintermediation.

The third question asks developers to determine which blockchain is suitable for a particular application. It can be Bitcoin blockchain, Ethereum blockchain, or any other blockchain that is deemed fit for the specific application.

Finally, a fundamental question that needs to be addressed is how the security of a decentralized system will be guaranteed. For example, the security mechanism can be atomicity-based, where either the transaction executes in full or does not execute at all. This deterministic approach ensures the integrity of the system. Other mechanisms may include one based on reputation, which allows for varying degrees of trust in a system.

The decentralization framework example

Let's evaluate a money transfer system as an example of an application selected to be decentralized. The four questions discussed previously are used to evaluate the decentralization requirements of this application. The answers to these questions are as follows:

1. Money transfer system
2. Disintermediation
3. Bitcoin
4. Atomicity

The responses indicate that the money transfer system can be decentralized by removing the intermediary, implemented on the Bitcoin blockchain, and that a security guarantee will be provided via atomicity. Atomicity will ensure that transactions execute successfully in full or not execute at all. We have chosen Bitcoin blockchain because it is the longest established blockchain which has stood the test of time.

Similarly, this framework can be used for any other system that needs to be evaluated in terms of decentralization. The answers to these four simple questions help clarify what approach to take to decentralize the system.

Blockchain and full ecosystem decentralization

To achieve complete decentralization, it is necessary that the environment around the blockchain also be decentralized. The blockchain is a distributed ledger that runs on top of conventional systems. These elements include storage, communication, and computation. There are other factors, such as identity and wealth, which are traditionally based on centralized paradigms, and there's a need to decentralize these aspects as well in order to achieve a sufficiently decentralized ecosystem.

Storage

Data can be stored directly in a blockchain, and with this fact it achieves decentralization. However, a significant disadvantage of this approach is that a blockchain is not suitable for storing large amounts of data by design. It can store simple transactions and some arbitrary data, but it is certainly not suitable for storing images or large blobs of data, as is the case with traditional database systems.

A better alternative for storing data is to use **Distributed Hash Tables** (**DHTs**). DHTs were used initially in peer-to-peer file sharing software, such as BitTorrent, Napster, Kazaa, and Gnutella. DHT research was made popular by the CAN, Chord, Pastry, and Tapestry projects. BitTorrent is the most scalable and fastest network, but the issue with BitTorrent and the others is that there is no incentive for users to keep the files indefinitely. Users generally don't keep files permanently, and if nodes that have data still required by someone leave the network, there is no way to retrieve it except by having the required nodes rejoin the network so that the files once again become available.

Two primary requirements here are high availability and link stability, which means that data should be available when required and network links also should always be accessible. **InterPlanetary File System** (**IPFS**) by Juan Benet possesses both of these properties, and its vision is to provide a decentralized World Wide Web by replacing the HTTP protocol. IPFS uses Kademlia DHT and Merkle **Directed Acyclic Graph** (**DAG**) to provide storage and searching functionality, respectively. The concept of DHTs and DAGs will be introduced in detail in `Chapter 6`, *Public Key Cryptography*.

The incentive mechanism for storing data is based on a protocol known as Filecoin, which pays incentives to nodes that store data using the Bitswap mechanism. The Bitswap mechanism lets nodes keep a simple ledger of bytes sent or bytes received in a one-to-one relationship. Also, a Git-based version control mechanism is used in IPFS to provide structure and control over the versioning of data.

There are other alternatives for data storage, such as Ethereum Swarm, Storj, and MaidSafe. Ethereum has its own decentralized and distributed ecosystem that uses Swarm for storage and the Whisper protocol for communication. MaidSafe aims to provide a decentralized World Wide Web. All of these projects are discussed later in this book in greater detail.

BigchainDB is another storage layer decentralization project aimed at providing a scalable, fast, and linearly-scalable decentralized database as opposed to a traditional filesystem. BigchainDB complements decentralized processing platforms and file systems such as Ethereum and IPFS.

Communication

The internet (the communication layer in blockchain) is considered to be decentralized. This belief is correct to some extent, as the original vision of the internet was to develop a decentralized communications system. Services such as email and online storage are now all based on a paradigm where the service provider is in control, and users trust such providers to grant them access to the service as requested. This model is based on unconditional trust of a central authority (the service provider) where users are not in control of their data. Even user passwords are stored on trusted third-party systems.

Thus, there is a need to provide control to individual users in such a way that access to their data is guaranteed and is not dependent on a single third party. Access to the internet (the communication layer) is based on **Internet Service Providers** (**ISPs**) who act as a central hub for internet users. If the ISP is shut down for any reason, then no communication is possible with this model.

An alternative is to use **mesh networks**. Even though they are limited in functionality when compared to the internet, they still provide a decentralized alternative where nodes can talk directly to each other without a central hub such as an ISP.

 An example of a Meshnet is FireChat (`http://www.opengarden.com/firechat.html`), which allows iPhone users to communicate with each other directly in a peer-to-peer fashion without an internet connection.

Now imagine a network that allows users to be in control of their communication; no one can shut it down for any reason. This could be the next step toward decentralizing communication networks in the blockchain ecosystem. It must be noted that this model may only be vital in a jurisdiction where the internet is censored and controlled by the government.

As mentioned earlier, the original vision of the internet was to build a decentralized network; however, over the years, with the advent of large-scale service providers such as Google, Amazon, and eBay, control is shifting towards these big players. For example, email is a decentralized system at its core; that is, anyone can run an email server with minimal effort and can start sending and receiving emails. There are better alternatives available, for example, Gmail and Outlook.com, which already provide managed services for end users, so there is a natural inclination toward selecting from these large centralized services as they are more convenient and free. This is one example that shows how the internet has moved toward centralization.

Free services, however, are offered at the cost of exposing valuable personal data, and many users are unaware of this fact. Blockchain has once again given this vision of decentralization to the world, and now concerted efforts are being made to harness this technology and take advantage of the benefits that it can provide.

Computing power and decentralization

Decentralization of computing or processing power is achieved by a blockchain technology such as Ethereum, where smart contracts with embedded business logic can run on the blockchain network. Other blockchain technologies also provide similar processing-layer platforms, where business logic can run over the network in a decentralized manner.

The following diagram shows a decentralized ecosystem overview. At the bottom layer, the internet or Meshnets provide a decentralized communication layer. On the next layer up, a storage layer uses technologies such as IPFS and BigchainDB to enable decentralization. Finally, at the next level up, you can see that blockchain serves as a decentralized processing (computation) layer. Blockchain can, in a limited way, provide a storage layer too, but that severely hampers the speed and capacity of the system. Therefore, other solutions such as IPFS and BigchainDB are more suitable to store large amounts of data in a decentralized way. The Identity, Wealth layers are shown at the top level. Identity on the internet is a vast topic, and systems such as BitAuth and OpenID provide authentication and identification services with varying degrees of decentralization and security assumptions:

Decentralized ecosystem

The blockchain is capable of providing solutions to various issues relating to decentralization. A concept relevant to identity known as **Zooko's Triangle** requires that the naming system in a network protocol be secure, decentralized, and is able to provide human-meaningful and memorable names to the users. Conjecture has it that a system can have only two of these properties simultaneously. Nevertheless, with the advent of blockchain in the form of Namecoin, this problem was resolved. It is now possible to achieve security, decentralization, and human-meaningful names with the Namecoin blockchain. However, this is not a panacea, and it comes with many challenges, such as reliance on users to store and maintain private keys securely. This opens up other general questions about the suitability of decentralization to a particular problem.

Decentralization may not be appropriate for every scenario. Centralized systems with well-established reputations tend to work better in many cases. For example, email platforms from well reputed companies such as Google or Microsoft would provide a better service as compared to a scenario where individual email servers are hosted by users on the internet.

There are many projects underway that are developing solutions for a more comprehensive distributed blockchain system. For example, Swarm and Whisper are developed to provide decentralized storage and communication for Ethereum blockchain.

With the emergence of the decentralization paradigm, different terminologies and buzzwords are now appearing in the media and academic literature. With the advent of blockchain technology, it is now possible to build software versions of traditional physical organizations in the form of **Decentralized Organizations** (**DOs**) and other similar constructs, which we will examine in detail shortly.

The following concepts are worth discussion in the context of decentralization.

Smart contracts

A **smart contract** is a decentralized program. Smart contracts do not necessarily need a blockchain to run; however, due to the security benefits that blockchain technology provides, blockchain has become a standard decentralized execution platform for smart contracts.

A smart contract usually contains some business logic and a limited amount of data. The business logic is executed if specific criteria are met. Actors or participants in the blockchain use these smart contracts, or they run autonomously on behalf of the network participants.

More information on smart contracts will be provided in Chapter 4, *Smart Contracts*.

Decentralized Organizations

DOs are software programs that run on a blockchain and are based on the idea of actual organizations with people and protocols. Once a DO is added to the blockchain in the form of a smart contract or a set of smart contracts, it becomes decentralized and parties interact with each other based on the code defined within the DO software.

Decentralized Autonomous Organizations

Just like DOs, a **Decentralized Autonomous Organization** (DAO) is also a computer program that runs atop a blockchain and embedded within it are governance and business logic rules. DAO and DO are fundamentally the same thing. The main difference, however, is that DAOs are autonomous, which means that they are fully automated and contain artificially-intelligent logic. DOs, on the other hand, lack this feature and rely on human input to execute business logic.

The Ethereum blockchain led the way with the initial introduction of DAOs. In a DAO, the code is considered the governing entity rather than people or paper contracts. However, a human curator maintains this code and acts as a proposal evaluator for the community. DAOs are capable of hiring external contractors if enough input is received from the token holders (participants).

The most famous DAO project is The DAO, which raised $168 million in its crowdfunding phase. The DAO project was designed to be a venture capital fund aimed at providing a decentralized business model with no single entity as owner. Unfortunately, this project was hacked due to a bug in the DAO code, and millions of dollars' worth in **Ether currency (ETH)** was siphoned out of the project and into a child DAO created by hackers. A hard fork was required on the Ethereum blockchain to reverse the impact of the hack and initiate the recovery of the funds. This incident opened up the debate on the security, quality, and need for thorough testing of the code in smart contracts in order to ensure their integrity and adequate control. There are other projects underway, especially in academia, which are seeking to formalize smart contract coding and testing.

Currently, DAOs do not have any legal status, even though they may contain some intelligent code that enforces certain protocols and conditions. However, these rules have no value in the real-world legal system at present. One day, perhaps an **Autonomous Agent (AA)**; that is, a piece of code that runs without human intervention, commissioned by a law enforcement agency or regulator will contain rules and regulations that could be embedded in a DAO for the purpose of ensuring its integrity from a legalistic and compliance perspective. The fact that DAOs are purely-decentralized entities enables them to run in any jurisdiction. Thus, they raise a large question as to how the current legal system could be applied to such a varied mix of jurisdictions and geographies.

Decentralized Autonomous Corporations

Decentralized Autonomous Corporations (DACs) are similar to DAOs in concept, though considered to be a smaller subset of them. The definitions of DACs and DAOs may sometimes overlap, but the general distinction is that DAOs are usually considered to be nonprofit; whereas DACs can earn a profit via shares offered to the participants and to whom they can pay dividends. DACs can run a business automatically without human intervention based on the logic programmed into them.

Decentralized Autonomous Societies

Decentralized Autonomous Societies (DASs) are a concept whereby an entire society can function on a blockchain with the help of multiple, complex smart contracts and a combination of DAOs and **Decentralized Applications (DApps)** running autonomously. This model does not necessarily translate to a free-for-all approach, nor is it based on an entirely libertarian ideology; instead, many services that a government commonly offers can be delivered via blockchains, such as government identity card systems, passports, and records of deeds, marriages, and births. Another theory is that, if a government is corrupt and central systems do not provide the satisfactory levels of trust that a society needs, then that society can start its own virtual one on a blockchain that is driven by decentralized consensus and transparency. This concept might look like a libertarian's or cypherpunk's dream, but it is entirely possible on a blockchain.

Decentralized Applications (DApps)

All ideas mentioned up to this point come under the broader umbrella of DApps. DAOs, DACs, and DOs are DApps that run on top of a blockchain in a peer-to-peer network. They represent the latest advancement in decentralization technology. DApps, on the other hand, are software programs that can run on their respective blockchains, use an existing established blockchain, or use only the protocols of an existing blockchain. These are called Type I, Type II, and Type III DApps.

Requirements of a Decentralized Application

For an application to be considered decentralized, it must meet the following criteria. This definition was provided in the whitepaper by Johnston and others, *The General Theory of Decentralized Applications, Dapps*:

- The DApp should be fully open source and autonomous, and no single entity should be in control of a majority of its tokens. All changes to the application must be consensus-driven based on the feedback given by the community.
- Data and records of operations of the application must be cryptographically secured and stored on a public, decentralized blockchain to avoid any central points of failure.
- A cryptographic token must be used by the application to provide access and rewards to those who contribute value to the applications, for example, miners in Bitcoin.
- The tokens must be generated by the DApp according to a standard cryptographic algorithm. This generation of tokens acts as a proof of the value to contributors (for example, miners).

Operations of a DApp

Establishment of consensus by a DApp can be achieved using consensus algorithms such as PoW and PoS. So far, only PoW has been found to be incredibly resistant to 51% attacks, as is evident from Bitcoin. Furthermore, a DApp can distribute tokens (coins) via mining, fundraising, and development.

DApp examples

Examples of some decentralized applications are provided here.

KYC-Chain

This application provides the facility to manage **Know Your Customer** (**KYC**) data securely and conveniently based on smart contracts.

OpenBazaar

This is a decentralized peer-to-peer network that enables commercial activities directly between sellers and buyers instead of relying on a central party, such as eBay and Amazon. It should be noted that this system is not built on top of a blockchain; instead, DHTs are used in a peer-to-peer network to enable direct communication and data sharing among peers. It makes use of Bitcoin and various other cryptocurrencies as a payment method.

Lazooz

This is the decentralized equivalent of Uber. It allows peer-to-peer ride sharing and users to be incentivized by proof of movement, and they can earn Zooz coins.

 Many other DApps have been built on the Ethereum blockchain and are showcased at http://dapps.ethercasts.com/.

Platforms for decentralization

Today, there are many platforms available for decentralization. In fact, the fundamental feature of blockchain networks is to provide decentralization. Therefore, any blockchain network such as Bitcoin, Ethereum, Hyperledger Fabric, or Quorum can be used to provide decentralization service. Many organizations around the world have introduced platforms that promise to make distributed application development easy, accessible, and secure. Some of these platforms are described next.

Ethereum

Ethereum tops the list as being the first blockchain to introduce a Turing-complete language and the concept of a virtual machine. This is in stark contrast to the limited scripting language in Bitcoin and many other cryptocurrencies. With the availability of its Turing-complete language called Solidity, endless possibilities have opened for the development of decentralized applications. This blockchain was first proposed in 2013 by Vitalik Buterin, and it provides a public blockchain to develop smart contracts and decentralized applications. Currency tokens on Ethereum are called **Ethers**.

MaidSafe

MaidSafe provides a **Secure Access For Everyone** (**SAFE**) network that is made up of unused computing resources, such as storage, processing power, and the data connections of its users. The files on the network are divided into small chunks of data, which are encrypted and distributed randomly throughout the network. This data can only be retrieved by its respective owner. One key innovation of MaidSafe is that duplicate files are automatically rejected on the network, which helps reduce the need for additional computing resources needed to manage the load. It uses Safecoin as a token to incentivize its contributors.

Lisk

Lisk is a blockchain application development and cryptocurrency platform. It allows developers to use JavaScript to build decentralized applications and host them in their respective sidechains. Lisk uses the **Delegated Proof of Stake** (**DPOS**) mechanism for consensus whereby 101 nodes can be elected to secure the network and propose blocks. It uses the Node.js and JavaScript backend, while the frontend allows the use of standard technologies, such as CSS3, HTML5, and JavaScript.

Lisk uses **LSK** coin as a currency on the blockchain. Another derivative of Lisk is Rise, which is a Lisk-based decentralized application and digital currency platform. It offers a greater focus on the security of the system.

A more practical introduction to these platforms and others will be supplied in later chapters.

Summary

In this chapter, we introduced the concept of decentralization, which is the core service offered by blockchain technology. Although the concept of decentralization is not new, it has gained renewed significance in the world of the blockchain. Consequently, various applications based on a decentralized architecture have recently been introduced.

We began the chapter with an introduction to the concept of decentralization. Next, we discussed decentralization from the blockchain perspective. Moreover, we introduced you to ideas relating to the different layers of decentralization in the blockchain ecosystem and to the several new concepts and terms that have emerged with the advent of blockchain technology and decentralization from the blockchain perspective, including DAOs, DACs, and DApps. Finally, we looked at few examples of decentralized applications.

In the next chapter, we will see how Ethereum works and what we can develop using Ethereum. We will also see the important Ethereum clients and node implementations.

Understanding How Ethereum Works

3

In this chapter, we will learn in depth about how Ethereum works and what we can develop using Ethereum. We will also see the important Ethereum clients and node implementations.

In this chapter, we will cover the following topics:

- Ethereum user accounts
- What are smart contracts and how do they work?
- Ethereum virtual machine
- How does mining work in the proof-of-work consensus protocol?
- Learning how to use the geth command
- Setting up the Ethereum Wallet and Mist
- Overview of Whisper and Swarm
- The future of Ethereum

Overview of Ethereum

Ethereum is a decentralized platform, which allows us to deploy DApps on top of it. Smart contracts are written using the solidity programming language. DApps are created using one or more smart contracts. Smart contracts are programs that run exactly as programmed without any possibility of downtime, censorship, fraud, or third party interface. In Ethereum, smart contracts can be written in several programming languages, including Solidity, LLL, and Serpent. Solidity is the most popular of those languages.

Ethereum has an internal currency called ether. To deploy smart contracts or to call their methods, we need ether. There can be multiple instances of a smart contract just like any other DApp, and each instance is identified by its unique address. Both user accounts and smart contracts can hold ether.

Ethereum uses blockchain data structure and proof-of-work consensus protocol. A method of a smart contract can be invoked via a transaction or via another method. There are two kinds of nodes in the network: regular nodes and miners. Regular nodes are the ones that just have a copy of the blockchain, whereas miners build the blockchain by mining blocks.

Ethereum accounts

To create an Ethereum account, we just need an asymmetric key pair. There are various algorithms, such as RSA, ECC, and so on, for generating asymmetric encryption keys. Ethereum uses **elliptic curve cryptography** (**ECC**). ECC has various parameters. These parameters are used to adjust speed and security. Ethereum uses the `secp256k1` parameter. To go in depth about ECC and its parameters will require mathematical knowledge, and it's not necessary to understand it in depth for building DApps using Ethereum.

Ethereum uses 256-bit encryption. An Ethereum private/public key is a 256-bit number. As processors cannot represent such big numbers, it's encoded as a hexadecimal string of length 64.

Every account is represented by an address. Once we have the keys we need to generate the address, here is the procedure to generate the address from the public key:

1. First, generate the `keccak-256` hash of the public key. It will give you a 256-bit number.
2. Drop the first 96 bits, that is, 12 bytes. You should now have 160 bits of binary data, that is, 20 bytes.
3. Now encode the address as a hexadecimal string. So finally, you will have a bytestring of 40 characters, which is your account address.

Now anyone can send ether to this address.

Transactions

A **transaction** is a signed data package to transfer ether from an account to another account or to a contract, invoke methods of a contract, or deploy a new contract. A transaction is signed using **ECDSA (Elliptic Curve Digital Signature Algorithm)**, which is a digital signature algorithm based on ECC. A transaction contains the recipient of the message, a signature identifying the sender and proving their intention, the amount of ether to transfer, the maximum number of computational steps the transaction execution is allowed to take (called the gas limit), and the cost the sender of the transaction is willing to pay for each computational step (called the gas price). If the transaction's intention is to invoke a method of a contract, it also contains input data, or if its intention is to deploy a contract, then it can contain the initialization code. The product of gas used and gas price is called transaction fees. To send ether or to execute a contract method, you need to broadcast a transaction to the network. The sender needs to sign the transaction with its private key.

A transaction is said to be confirmed if we are sure that it will always appear in the blockchain. It is recommended to wait for 15 confirmations before assuming a transaction to be confirmed.

Consensus

Every node in the Ethereum network holds a copy of the blockchain. We need to make sure that nodes cannot tamper with the blockchain, and we also need a mechanism to check whether a block is valid or not. And also, if we encounter two different valid blockchains, we need to have a way to find out which one to choose.

Ethereum uses the proof-of-work consensus protocol to keep the blockchain tamper-proof. A proof-of-work system involves solving a complex puzzle to create a new block. Solving the puzzle should require a significant amount of computational power thereby making it difficult to create blocks. The process of creating blocks in the proof-of-work system is called mining. Miners are the nodes in the network that mine blocks. All the DApps that use proof-of-work do not implement exactly the same set of algorithms. They may differ in terms of what the puzzle miners need to solve, how difficult the puzzle is, how much time it takes to solve it, and so on. We will learn about proof-of-work with respect to Ethereum.

Anyone can become a miner in the network. Every miner solves the puzzle individually; the first miner to solve the puzzle is the winner and is rewarded with five ether and transaction fees of all the transactions in that block. If you have a more powerful processor than any other node in the network, that doesn't mean that you will always succeed because the parameters for the puzzle are not exactly same for all the miners. But instead, if you have a more powerful processor than any other node in the network, it gives you a higher chance at succeeding. Proof-of-work behaves like a lottery system, and processing power can be thought as the number of lottery tickets a person has. Networks security is not measured by total number of miners; instead, it's measured by the total processing power of the network.

There is no limit to the number of blocks the blockchain can have, and there is no limit to the total ether that can be produced. Once a miner successfully mines a block, it broadcasts the block to all other nodes in the network. A block has a header and a set of transactions. Every block holds hash of the previous block, thereby creating a connected chain.

Let's see what the puzzle the miners need to solve is and how it's solved at a high level. To mine a block, first of all, a miner collects the new un-mined transactions broadcasted to it, and then it filters out the not-valid transactions. A transaction to be valid must be properly signed using the private key, the account must have enough balance to make the transaction, and so on. Now the miner creates a block, which has a header and content. Content is the list of transactions that the block contains. The header contains things such as the hash of the previous block, block number, nonce, target, timestamp, difficulty, address of the miner, and so on. The timestamp represents the time at the block's inception. Then nonce is a meaningless value, which is adjusted in order to find the solution to the puzzle. The puzzle is basically to find such nonce values with which when the block is hashed, the hash is less than or equal to the target. Ethereum uses ethash hashing algorithm. The only way to find the nonce is to enumerate all possibilities. The target is a 256-bit number, which is calculated based on various factors. The difficulty value in the header is a different representation of the target to make it easier to deal with. The lower the target, the more time it takes to find the nonce, and the higher the target, the less time it takes to find the nonce. Here is the formula to calculate the difficulty of the puzzle:

```
current_block_difficulty = previous_block_difficulty +
previous_block_difficulty // 2048 * max(1 - (current_block_timestamp -
previous_blocktimestamp) // 10, -99) + int(2 ** ((current_block_number //
100000) - 2))
```

Now any node in the network can check whether the blockchain they have is valid or not by first checking whether the transactions in the blockchain are valid, the timestamp validation, then whether the target and nonce of all the blocks are valid, a miner has assigned a valid reward itself, and so on.

If a node in the network receives two different valid blockchains, then the blockchain whose combined difficulty of all blocks is higher is considered to be the valid blockchain.

Now, for example, if a node in the network alters some transactions in a block, then the node needs to calculate the nonce of all the succeeding blocks. By the time it re-finds the nonce of the succeeding blocks, the network would have mined many more blocks and therefore reject this blockchain as its combined difficulty would be lower.

Timestamp

The formula to calculate the target of a block requires the current timestamp, and also every block has the current timestamp attached to its header. Nothing can stop a miner from using some other timestamp instead of the current timestamp while mining a new block, but they don't usually because timestamp validation would fail and other nodes won't accept the block, and it would be a waste of resources of the miner. When a miner broadcasts a newly mined block, its timestamp is validated by checking whether the timestamp is greater than the timestamp of the previous block. If a miner uses a timestamp greater than the current timestamp, the difficulty will be low as difficulty is inversely proportional to the current timestamp; therefore, the miner whose block timestamp is the current timestamp would be accepted by the network as it would have a higher difficulty. If a miner uses a timestamp greater than the previous block timestamp and less than the current timestamp, the difficulty would be higher, and therefore, it would take more time to mine the block; by the time the block is mined, the network would have produced more blocks, therefore, this block will get rejected as the blockchain of the malicious miner will have a lower difficulty than the blockchain the network has. Due to these reasons, miners always use accurate timestamps, otherwise they gain nothing.

Nonce

The nonce is a 64-bit unsigned integer. The nonce is the solution to the puzzle. A miner keeps incrementing the nonce until it finds the solution. Now you must be wondering if there is a miner who has hash power more than any other miner in the network, would the miner always find nonce first? Well, it wouldn't.

The hash of the block that the miners are mining is different for every miner because the hash depends on things such as the timestamp, miner address, and so on, and it's unlikely that it will be the same for all miners. Therefore, it's not a race to solve the puzzle; rather, it's a lottery system. But of course, a miner is likely to get lucky depending on its hash power, but that doesn't mean the miner will always find the next block.

Block time

The block difficulty formula we saw earlier uses a 10-second threshold to make sure that the difference between the time a parent and child block mines is in is between 10-20 seconds. But why is it 10-20 seconds and not some other value? And why there such a constant time difference restriction instead of a constant difficulty?

Imagine that we have a constant difficulty, and miners just need to find a nonce to get the hash of the block less and equal to the difficulty. Suppose the difficulty is high; then in this case, users will have no way to find out how long it will take to send ether to another user. It may take a very long time if the computational power of the network is not enough to find the nonce to satisfy the difficulty quickly. Sometimes the network may get lucky and find the nonce quickly. But this kind of system will find it difficult to gain attraction from users as users will always want to know how much time it should take for a transaction to be completed, just like when we transfer money from one bank account to another bank account, we are given a time period within which it should get completed. If the constant difficulty is low, it will harm the security of the blockchain because large miners can mine blocks much faster than small miners, and the largest miner in the network will have the ability to control the DApp. It is not possible to find a constant difficulty value that can make the network stable because the network's computational power is not constant.

Now we know why we should always have an average time for how long it should take for the network to mine a block. Now the question is what the most suitable average time is as it can be anything from 1 second to infinite seconds. A smaller average time can be achieved by lowering the difficulty, and higher average time can be achieved by increasing the difficulty. But what are the merits and demerits of a lower and higher average time? Before we discuss this, we need to first know what stale blocks are.

What happens if two miners mine the next block at nearly the same time? Both the blocks will be valid for sure, but the blockchain cannot hold two blocks with the same block number, and also, both the miners cannot be awarded. Although this is a common issue, the solution is simple. In the end, the blockchain with the higher difficulty will be the one accepted by the network. So the valid blocks that are finally left out are called stale blocks.

The total number of stale blocks produced in the network is inversely proportional to the average time it takes to generate a new block. Shorter block generation time means there would be less time for the newly mined block to propagate throughout the network and a bigger chance of more than one miner finding a solution to the puzzle, so by the time the block is propagated through the network, some other miner would have also solved the puzzle and broadcasted it, thereby creating stales. But if the average block generation time is bigger, there is less chance that multiple miners will be able to solve the puzzle, and even if they solve it, there is likely to be time gap between when they solved it, during which the first solved block can be propagated and the other miners can stop mining that block and proceed towards mining the next block. If stale blocks occur frequently in the network, they cause major issues, but if they occur rarely, they do no harm.

But what's the problem with stale blocks? Well, they delay the confirmation of a transaction. When two miners mine a block at nearly the same time, they may not have the same set of transactions, so if our transactions appears in one of them, we cannot say that it's confirmed as the block in which the transaction appeared may be stale. And we should wait for a few more blocks to be mined. Due to stale blocks, the average confirmation time is not equal to average block generation time.

Do stale blocks impact blockchain security? Yes, they do. We know that the network's security is measured by the total computation power of the miners in the network. When computation power increases, the difficulty is increased to make sure that blocks aren't generated earlier than the average block time. So more difficulty means a more secure blockchain, as for a node to tamper, the blockchain will need much more hash power now, which makes it more difficult to tamper with the blockchain; therefore, the blockchain is said to be more secure. When two blocks are mined at nearly the same time, we will have the network parted in two, working on two different blockchains, but one is going to be the final blockchain. So the part of the network working on the stale block mines the next block on top of the stale block, which ends up in loss of hash power of the network as hash power is being used for something unnecessary. The two parts of the network are likely to take longer than the average block time to mine the next block as they have lost hash power; therefore, after mining the next block, there will be decrease in difficulty as it took more time than the average block time to mine the block. The decrease in difficulty impacts the overall blockchain security. If the stale rate is too high, it will affect the blockchain security by a huge margin.

Ethereum tackles the security issue caused by stale blocks using something known as ghost protocol. Ethereum uses a modified version of the actual ghost protocol. The ghost protocol covers up the security issue by simply adding the stale blocks into the main blockchain, thereby increasing the overall difficulty of the blockchain, as overall difficulty of the blockchain also includes the sum of difficulties of the stale blocks. But how are stale blocks inserted into the main blockchain without transactions conflicting? Well, any block can specify 0 or more stales. To incentivize miners to include stale blocks, the miners are rewarded for including stale blocks. And also, the miners of the stale blocks are rewarded. The transactions in the stale blocks are not used for calculating confirmations, and also, the stale block miners don't receive the transaction fees of the transactions included in the stale blocks. Note that Ethereum calls stale blocks uncle blocks.

Here is the formula to calculate how much reward a miner of a stale block receives. The rest of the reward goes to the nephew block, that is, the block that includes the orphan block:

```
(uncle_block_number + 8 - block_number) * 5 / 8
```

As not rewarding the miners of stale blocks doesn't harm any security, you must be wondering why miners of stale blocks get rewarded? Well, there is another issue caused when stale blocks occur frequently in the network, which is solved by rewarding the miners of stale blocks. A miner should earn a percentage of reward similar to the percentage of hash power it contributes to the network. When a block is mined at nearly the same time by two different miners, then the block mined by the miner with more hash power is more likely to get added to the final blockchain because of the miner's efficiency to mine the next block; therefore, the small miner will lose reward. If the stale rate is low, it's not a big issue because the big miner will get a little increase in reward; but if the stale rate is high, it causes a big issue, that is, the big miner in the network will end up taking much more rewards than it should receive. The ghost protocol balances this by rewarding the miners of stale blocks. As the big miner doesn't take all the rewards but much more than it should get, we don't award stale block miners the same as the nephew block; instead, we award a lesser amount to balance it. The preceding formula balances it pretty well.

Ghost limits the total number of stale blocks a nephew can reference so that miners don't simply mine stale blocks and stall the blockchain.

So wherever a stale block appears in the network, it somewhat affects the network. The more the frequency of stale blocks, the more the network is affected by it.

Forking

A fork is said to have happened when there is a conflict among the nodes regarding the validity of a blockchain, that is, more than one blockchain happens to be in the network, and every blockchain is validated for some miners. There are three kinds of forks: regular forks, soft fork, and hard fork.

A regular fork is a temporary conflict occurring due to two or more miners finding a block at nearly the same time. It's resolved when one of them has more difficulty than the other.

A change to the source code could cause conflicts. Depending on the type of conflict, it may require miners with more than 50% of hash power to upgrade or all miners to upgrade to resolve the conflict. When it requires miners with more than 50% of hash power to upgrade to resolve the conflict, its called a soft fork, whereas when it requires all the miners to upgrade to resolve the conflict, its called a hard fork. An example of a soft fork would be if update to the source code invalidates subset of old blocks/transactions, then it can be resolved when miners more than 50% of hash power have upgraded so that the new blockchain will have more difficulty and finally get accepted by the whole network. An example of a hard fork would be an if update in the source code was to change the rewards for miners, then all the miners needs to upgrade to resolve the conflict.

Ethereum has gone through various hard and soft forks since its release.

Genesis block

A genesis block is the first block of the blockchain. It's assigned to block number 0. It's the only block in the blockchain that doesn't reference to a previous block because there isn't any. It doesn't hold any transactions because there isn't any ether produced yet.

Two nodes in a network will only pair with each other if they both have the same genesis block, that is, blocks synchronization will only happen if both peers have the same genesis block, otherwise they both will reject each other. A different genesis block of high difficulty cannot replace a lower difficult one. Every node generates its own genesis block. For various networks, the genesis block is hardcoded into the client.

Ether denominations

Ether has various denominations just like any other currency. Here are the denominations:

- 1 Ether = 1000000000000000000 Wei
- 1 Ether = 1000000000000000 Kwei
- 1 Ether = 1000000000000 Mwei
- 1 Ether = 1000000000 Gwei
- 1 Ether = 1000000 Szabo
- 1 Ether = 1000 Finney
- 1 Ether = 0.001 Kether
- 1 Ether = 0.000001 Mether
- 1 Ether = 0.000000001 Gether
- 1 Ether = 0.000000000001 Tether

Ethereum virtual machine

EVM (or Ethereum virtual machine) is the Ethereum smart contracts byte-code execution environment. Every node in the network runs EVM. All the nodes execute all the transactions that point to smart contracts using EVM, so every node does the same calculations and stores the same values. Transactions that only transfer ether also require some calculation, that is, to find out whether the address has a balance or not and deduct the balance accordingly.

Every node executes the transactions and stores the final state due to various reasons. For example, if there is a smart contract that stores the names and details of everyone attending a party, whenever a new person is added, a new transaction is broadcasted to the network. For any node in the network to display details of everyone attending the party, they simply need to read the final state of the contract.

Every transaction requires some computation and storage in the network. Therefore, there needs to be a transaction cost, otherwise the whole network will be flooded with spam transactions, and also without a transaction cost, miners will have no reason to include transactions in blocks, and they will start mining empty blocks. Every transaction requires different amount of computation and storage; therefore, every transaction has different transaction costs.

There are two implementations of EVM, that is, byte-code VM and JIT-VM. At the time of writing this book, JIT-VM is available for use, but its development is still not completed. In either case, the Solidity code is compiled to byte code. In the case of JIT-VM, the byte code is further compiled. JIT-VM is more efficient than it's counterpart.

Gas

Gas is a unit of measurement for computational steps. Every transaction is required to include a gas limit and a fee that it is willing to pay per gas (that is, pay per computation); miners have the choice of including the transaction and collecting the fee. If the gas used by the transaction is less than or equal to the gas limit, the transaction processes. If the total gas exceeds the gas limit, then all changes are reverted, except that the transaction is still valid and the fee (that is, the product of the maximum gas that can be used and gas price) can still be collected by the miner.

The miners decide the gas price (that is, price per computation). If a transaction has a lower gas price than the gas price decided by a miner, the miner will refuse to mine the transaction. The gas price is an amount in a wei unit. So, a miner can refuse to include a transaction in a block if the gas price is lower than what it needs.

Each operation in EVM is assigned a number of how much gas it consumes.

Transaction costs affect the maximum ether an account can transfer to another account. For example, if an account has an ether balance of five, it cannot transfer all five ethers to another account because if all ethers are transferred, there would be no balance in the account to deduct transaction fees from.

If a transaction invokes a contract method and the method sends some ether or invokes some other contract method, the transaction fee is deducted from the account that invoked the contract method.

Peer discovery

For a node to be part of the network, it needs to connect to some other nodes in the network so that it can broadcast transactions/blocks and listen to new transactions/blocks. A node doesn't need to connect to every node in the network; instead, a node connects to a few other nodes. And these nodes connect to a few other nodes. In this way, the whole network is connected to each other.

But how does a node find some other nodes in the network as there is no central server that everyone can connect to so as to exchange their information? Ethereum has its own node discovery protocol to solve this problem, which is based on the Kadelima protocol. In the node discovery protocol, we have special kind of nodes called Bootstrap nodes. Bootstrap nodes maintain a list of all nodes that are connected to them over a period of time. They don't hold the blockchain itself. When peers connect to the Ethereum network, they first connect to the Bootstrap nodes ,which share the lists of peers that have connected to them in the last predefined time period. The connecting peers then connect and synchronize with the peers.

There can be various Ethereum instances, that is, various networks, each having its own network ID. The two major Ethereum networks are mainnet and testnet. The mainnet one is the one whose ether is traded on exchanges, whereas testnet is used by developers to test. Until now, we have learned everything with regards to the mainnet blockchain.

> Bootnode is the most popular implementation of an Ethereum Bootstrap node. If you want to host your own Bootstrap node, you can use bootnode.

Whisper and Swarm

Whisper and Swarm are a decentralized communication protocol and a decentralized storage platform respectively, being developed by Ethereum developers. Whisper is a decentralized communication protocol, whereas Swarm is a decentralized filesystem.

Whisper lets nodes in the network communicate with each other. It supports broadcasting, user-to-user, encrypted messages, and so on. It's not designed to transfer bulk data. You can learn more about Whisper at https://github.com/ethereum/wiki/wiki/Whisper, and you can see a code example overview at https://github.com/ethereum/wiki/wiki/Whisper-Overview.

Swarm is similar to Filecoin, that is, it differs mostly in terms of technicalities and incentives. Filecoin doesn't penalize stores, whereas Swarm penalizes stores; therefore, this increases the file availability further. You must be wondering how incentive works in swarm. Does it have an internal currency? Actually, Swarm doesn't have an internal currency, rather it uses ether for incentives. There is a smart contract in Ethereum, which keeps track of incentives. Obviously, the smart contract cannot communicate with Swarm; instead, swarm communicates with the smart contract. So basically, you pay the stores via the smart contract, and the payment is released to the stores after the expiry date. You can also report file missing to the smart contract, in which case it can penalize the respective stores. You can learn more about the difference between Swarm and IPFS/Filecoin at `https://github.com/ethersphere/go-ethereum/wiki/IPFS--SWARM` and see the smart contract code at `https://github.com/ethersphere/go-ethereum/blob/bzz-config/bzz/bzzcontract/swarm.sol`.

At the time of writing this book, Whisper and Swarm are still under development; so, many things are still not clear.

Geth

Geth (or called as go-ethereum) is an implementation of Ethereum, Whisper, and Swarm nodes. Geth can be used to be part of all of these or only selected ones. The reason for combining them is to make them look like a single DApp and also so that via one node, a client can access all three DApps.

Geth is a CLI application. It's written in the go programming language. It's available for all the major operating systems. The current version of geth doesn't yet support Swarm and supports whisper a some of the features of Whisper. At the time of writing this book, the latest version of geth was 1.3.5.

Installing geth

Geth is available for OS X, Linux, and Windows. It supports two types of installation: binary and scripted installation. At the time of writing this book, the latest stable version of geth is 1.4.13. Let's see how to install it in various operating systems using the binary installation method. Scripted installation is used when you have to modify something in the geth source code and install it. We don't want to make any changes to the source code, therefore, we will go with binary installation.

OS X

The recommended way of installing geth in OS X is using brew. Run these two commands in the terminal to install geth:

```
brew tap ethereum/ethereum
brew install ethereum
```

Ubuntu

The recommended way to install geth in Ubuntu is to use `apt-get`. Run these commands in Ubuntu terminal to install geth:

```
sudo apt-get install software-properties-common
sudo add-apt-repository -y ppa:ethereum/ethereum
sudo apt-get update
sudo apt-get install ethereum
```

Windows

Geth comes as an executable file for Windows. Download the zip file from `https://github.com/ethereum/go-ethereum/wiki/Installation-instructions-for-Windows`, and extract it. Inside it, you will find the `geth.exe` file.

 To find more about installing geth on various operating systems, visit `https://github.com/ethereum/go-ethereum/wiki/Building-Ethereum`.

JSON-RPC and JavaScript console

Geth provides JSON-RPC APIs for other applications to communicate with it. Geth serves JSON-RPC APIs using HTTP, WebSocket, and other protocols. The APIs provided by JSON-RPC are divided into these categories: admin, debug, eth, miner, net, personal, shh, txpool, and web3. You can find more information about it these `https://github.com/ethereum/go-ethereum/wiki/JavaScript-Console`.

Geth also provides an interactive JavaScript console to interact with it programmatically using JavaScript APIs. This interactive console uses JSON-RPC over IPC to communicate with geth. We will learn more about the JSON-RPC and the JavaScript APIs in later chapters.

Sub-commands and options

Let's learn some of the important sub-commands and options of the geth command using examples. You can find the list of all sub-commands and options by using the help sub-command. We will see a lot more about geth and its commands throughout the following chapters.

Connecting to the mainnet network

Nodes in the Ethereum network, by default, communicate using `30303` port. But nodes are also free to listen on some other port numbers.

To connect to the mainnet network, you just need to run the `geth` command. Here is an example of how to specify the network ID explicitly and specify a custom directory where geth will store the downloaded blockchain:

```
geth --datadir "/users/packt/ethereum" --networkid 1
```

The `--datadir` option is used to specify where to store the blockchain. If it's not provided, the default path is `$HOME/.ethereum`.

`--networkid` is used to specify the network ID. 1 is the ID of the mainnet network. If it's not provided, the default value is 1. The network ID of testnet is 2.

Creating a private network

To create a private network, you just need to give a random network ID. Private networks are usually created for development purposes. Geth also provide various flags related to logging and debugging, which are useful during development. So, instead of giving a random network ID and putting the various logging and debugging flags, we can simply use the `--dev` flag, which runs a private network with various debugging and logging flags enabled.

Creating accounts

Geth also lets us create accounts, that is, generate keys and addresses associated with them. To create an account, use the following command:

```
geth account new
```

When you run this command, you will be asked to enter a password to encrypt your account. If you forget your password, there is no way to access your account.

To get a list of all accounts in your local Wallet, use the following command:

```
geth account list
```

The preceding command will print a list of all the addresses of the accounts. Keys are, by default, stored in the `--datadir` path, but you can use the `--keystore` option to specify a different directory.

Mining

By default, geth doesn't start mining. To instruct geth to start mining, you just need to provide the `--mine` option. There are a few other options related to mining:

```
geth --mine --minerthreads 16 --minergpus '0,1,2' --etherbase
'489b4e22aab35053ecd393b9f9c35f4f1de7b194' --unlock
'489b4e22aab35053ecd393b9f9c35f4f1de7b194'
```

Here, along with the `--mine` option, we have provided various other options. The `--minerthreads` option specifies the total number of threads to use while hashing. By default, eight threads are used. Etherbase is the address to which the reward earned by mining is deposited. By default, accounts are encrypted. So to access the ether in the account, we need to unlock it, that is, decrypt the account. Decryption is used to decrypt the private key associated with the account. To start mining, we don't need to unlock it because only the address is required to deposit the mining rewards. One or more accounts can be unlocked using the -unlock option. Multiple addresses can be provided by separating the addresses using comma.

`--minergpus` is used to specify the GPUs to use for mining. To get the list of GPUs, use the `geth gpuinfo` command. For each GPU, you need to have 1-2 GB of RAM. By default, it doesn't use GPUs, instead only CPU.

Fast synchronization

At the time of writing this book, the blockchain size is around 30 GB. Downloading it may take several hours or days if you have a slow Internet connection. Ethereum implements a fast synchronization algorithm, which can download the blockchain faster.

Fast synchronization doesn't download the entire blocks; instead, it only downloads the block headers, transactions receipts, and the recent state database. So, we don't have to download and replay all transactions. To check blockchain integrity, the algorithm downloads a full block after every defined number of blocks. To learn more about fast synchronization algorithm, visit `https://github.com/ethereum/go-ethereum/pull/1889`.

To use fast sync while downloading the blockchain, you need to use the `--fast` flag while running geth.

Due to security reasons, fast sync will only run during an initial sync (that is, when the node's own blockchain is empty). After a node manages to successfully sync with the network, fast sync is forever disabled. As an additional safety feature, if a fast sync fails close to or after the random pivot point, it is disabled as a safety precaution, and the node reverts to full, block-processing-based synchronization.

Ethereum Wallet

Ethereum Wallet is an Ethereum UI client that lets you create account, send ether, deploy contracts, invoke methods of contracts, and much more.

Ethereum Wallet comes with geth bundled. When you run Ethereum, it tries to find a local geth instance and connects to it, and if it cannot find geth running, it launches its own geth node. Ethereum Wallet communicates with geth using IPC. Geth supports file-based IPC.

If you change the data directory while running geth, you are also changing the IPC file path. So for Ethereum Wallet to find and connect to your geth instance, you need to use the `--ipcpath` option to specify the IPC file location to its default location so that Ethereum Wallet can find it; otherwise Ethereum Wallet won't be able to find it and will start its own geth instance. To find the default IPC file path, run geth help, and it will show the default path next to the `--ipcpath` option.

Visit `https://github.com/ethereum/mist/releases` to download Ethereum Wallet. It's available for Linux, OS X, and Windows. Just like geth, it has two installation modes: binary and scripted installation.

Here is an image that shows what Ethereum Wallet looks like:

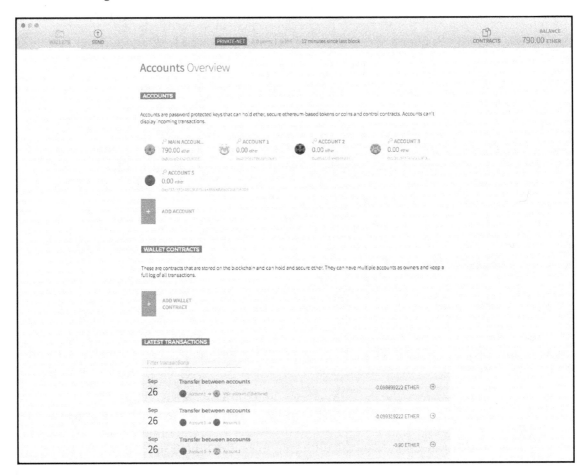

Mist

Mist is a client for Ethereum, Whisper, and Swarm. It lets us send transactions, send Whisper messages, inspect blockchains, and so on.

The relation between Mist and geth is similar to the relation between Ethereum Wallet and geth.

The most popular feature of Mist is that it comes with a browser. Currently, the frontend JavaScript running in the browser can access the web3 APIs of the geth node using the `web3.js` library (a library that provides Ethereum console's JavaScript APIs for other applications to communicate with geth).

The basic idea of Mist is to build the third generation web (Web 3.0), which would wipe out the need to have servers by using Ethereum, Whisper, and Swarm as replacements for centralized servers.

Here is an image, showing what Mist looks like:

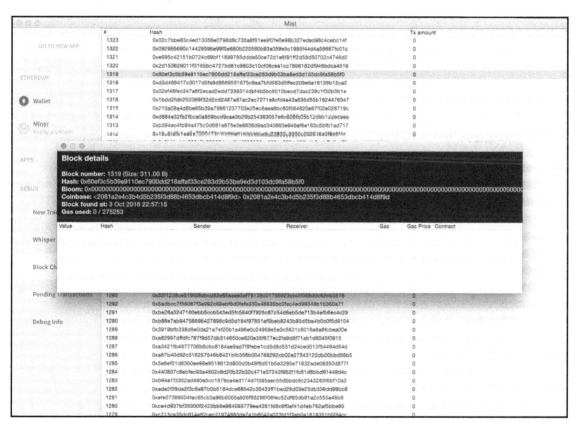

Weaknesses

Every system has some weaknesses. Similarly, Ethereum also has some weaknesses. Obviously, just like any other application, Ethereum source code can have bugs. And also just like any other network-based application, Ethereum is also exposed to DoS attacks. But let's see the unique and most important weaknesses of Ethereum.

Sybil attack

An attacker can attempt to fill the network with regular nodes controlled by him; you would then be very likely to connect only to the attacker nodes. Once you have connected to the attacker nodes, the attacker can refuse to relay blocks and transactions from everyone, thereby disconnecting you from the network. The attacker can relay only blocks that he creates, thereby putting you on a separate network, and so on.

51% attack

If the attacker controls more than half of the network hashrate, the attacker can generate blocks faster than the rest of the network. The attacker can simply preserve his private fork until it becomes longer than the branch built by the honest network and then broadcast it.

With more than 50% of hash power, the miner can reverse transactions, prevent all/some transactions from getting mined, and prevent other miners' mined blocks from getting inserted to the blockchain.

Serenity

Serenity is the name of the next major update for Ethereum. At the time of writing this book, serenity is still under development. This update will require a hard fork. Serenity will change the consensus protocol to casper, and will integrate state channels and sharding. Complete details of how these will work is still unclear at this point of time. Let's see a high level overview of what these are.

Payment and state channels

Before getting into state channels, we need to know what payment channels are. A payment channel is a feature that allows us to combine more than two transactions of sending ether to another account into two transactions. Here is how it works. Suppose X is the owner of a video streaming website, and Y is a user. X charges one ether for every minute. Now X wants Y to pay after every minute while watching the video. Of course, Y can broadcast a transaction every minute, but there are few issues here, such as X has to wait for confirmation, so the video will be paused for sometime, and so on. This is the problem payment channels solve. Using payment channels, Y can lock some ether (maybe 100 ether) for a period of time (maybe 24 hours) for X by broadcasting a lock transaction. Now after watching a 1 minute video, Y will send a signed record indicating that the lock can be unlocked and one ether will go to X's account and the rest to Y's account. After another minute, Y will send a signed record indicating that the lock can be unlocked, and two ether will go to X's account, and the rest will go to Y's account. This process will keep going as Y watches the video on X's website. Now once Y has watched 100 hours of video or 24 hours of time is about to be reached, X will broadcast the final signed record to the network to withdraw funds to his account. If X fails to withdraw in 24 hours, the complete refund is made to Y. So in the blockchain, we will see only two transactions: lock and unlock.

Payment channel is for transactions related to sending ether. Similarly, a state channel allows us to combine transactions related to smart contracts.

Proof-of-stake and casper

Before we get into what the casper consensus protocol is, we need to understand how the proof-of-stake consensus protocol works.

Proof-of-stake is the most common alternative to proof-of-work. Proof-of-work wastes too many computational resources. The difference between POW and POS is that in POS, a miner doesn't need to solve the puzzle; instead the miner needs to prove ownership of the stake to mine the block. In the POS system, ether in accounts is treated as a stake, and the probability of a miner mining the block is directly proportional to the stake the miner holds. So if the miner holds 10% of the stake in the network, it will mine 10% of the blocks.

But the question is how will we know who will mine the next block? We cannot simply let the miner with the highest stake always mine the next block because this will create centralization. There are various algorithms for next block selection, such as randomized block selection, and coin-age-based selection.

Casper is a modified version of POS that tackles various problems of POS.

Sharding

At present, every node needs to download all transactions, which is huge. At the rate at which blockchain size is increasing, in the next few years, it will be very difficult to download the whole blockchain and keep it in sync.

If you are familiar with distributed database architecture, you must be familiar with sharding. If not, then sharding is a method of distributing data across multiple computers. Ethereum will implement sharding to partition and distribute the blockchain across nodes.

You can learn more about sharding a blockchain at `https://github.com/ethereum/wiki/wiki/Sharding-FAQ`.

Summary

In this chapter, we learned in detail about how Ethereum works. We learned how block time affects security and about the weaknesses of Ethereum. We also saw what Mist and Ethereum Wallet are and how to install them. We also saw some of the important commands of geth. Finally, we learned what is going to be new in Serenity updates for Ethereum.

4
Smart Contracts

This chapter provides an introduction to smart contracts. This concept is not new, but, with the advent of the blockchain, interest in this idea was revived, and this is now an active area of research in the blockchain space. Due to the cost-saving benefits that smart contracts can bring to the financial services industry by reducing the cost of transactions and simplifying complex contracts, rigorous research is being carried out by various commercial and academic institutions to formalize and make the implementation of smart contracts easy and practical, as soon as possible.

History

Smart contracts were first theorized by Nick Szabo in the late 1990s in an article named *Formalizing and Securing Relationships on Public Networks,* but it was almost 20 years before the real potential and benefits of them were indeed appreciated with the invention of Bitcoin and subsequent development in blockchain technology. Smart contracts are described by Szabo as follows:

> *"A smart contract is an electronic transaction protocol that executes the terms of a contract. The general objectives are to satisfy common contractual conditions (such as payment terms, liens, confidentiality, and even enforcement), minimize exceptions both malicious and accidental, and minimize the need for trusted intermediaries. Related economic goals include lowering fraud loss, arbitrations and enforcement costs, and other transaction costs."*

 The original article written by Szabo is available at http://firstmonday. org/ojs/index.php/fm/article/view/548.

This idea of smart contracts was implemented in a limited fashion in Bitcoin in 2009, where Bitcoin transactions using a limited scripting language can be used to transfer value between users, over a peer-to-peer network where users do not necessarily trust each other, and there is no need for a trusted intermediary.

Definition

There is no consensus on a standard definition of smart contracts. It is essential to define what a smart contract is, and the following is my attempt to provide a generalized definition of a smart contract:

A smart contract is a secure and unstoppable computer program representing an agreement that is automatically executable and enforceable.

Dissecting this definition further reveals that a smart contract is, in fact, a computer program that is written in a language that a computer or target machine can understand. Also, it encompasses agreements between parties in the form of business logic. Another fundamental idea is that smart contracts are automatically executed when certain conditions are met. They are enforceable, which means that all contractual terms are executed as defined and expected, even in the presence of adversaries.

Enforcement is a broader term that encompasses traditional enforcement in the form of law, along with the implementation of specific measures and controls that make it possible to execute contract terms without requiring any mediation. It should be noted that true smart contracts should not rely on traditional methods of enforcement. Instead, they should work on the principle that code is law, meaning that there is no need for an arbitrator or a third party to control or influence the execution of the smart contract. Smart contracts are self-enforcing as opposed to legally enforceable. This idea might be regarded as a libertarian's dream, but it is entirely possible and is in line with the true spirit of smart contracts.

Moreover, they are secure and unstoppable, which means that these computer programs are required to be designed in such a fashion that they are fault-tolerant and executable in a reasonable amount of time. These programs should be able to execute and maintain a healthy internal state, even if external factors are unfavorable. For example, imagine a typical computer program that is encoded with some logic and executes according to the instruction coded within it. However, if the environment it is running in or external factors it relies on deviate from the normal or expected state, the program may react arbitrarily or simply abort. It is essential that smart contracts be immune to this type of issue.

Secure and unstoppable may well be considered requirements or desirable features but it will provide more significant benefits in the long run if security and unstoppable properties are included in the smart contract definition from the beginning. This will allow researchers to focus on these aspects from the start and will help to build strong foundations on which further research can then be based. There is also a suggestion by some researchers that smart contracts need not be automatically executable; instead, they can be what's called automatable, due to manual human input required in some scenarios. For example, a manual verification of a medical record might be required by a qualified medical professional. In such cases fully automated approaches may not work best. While it is true that in some cases human input and control is desirable, it is not necessary; and, for a contract to be truly smart, in the author's opinion, it has to be fully automated. Some inputs that need to be provided by people can and should also be automated via the use of Oracles. Oracles will be discussed later in this chapter in greater detail.

Smart contracts usually operate by managing their internal state using a state machine model. This allows development of an effective framework for programming smart contracts, where the state of a contract is advanced further based on some predefined criteria and conditions.

There is also on-going debate on the question of whether the code is acceptable as a contract in a court of law. A smart contract is different in presentation from traditional legal prose, albeit they do represent and enforce all contractual clauses but a court of law does not understand the code. This dilemma raises several questions about how a smart contract can be legally binding: can it be developed in such a way that it is readily acceptable and understandable in a court of law? How can dispute resolution be implemented within the code, and is it possible? Moreover, regulatory and compliance requirements is another topic that needs to be addressed before smart contracts can be used as efficiently as traditional legal documents.

Even though smart contracts are named smart, they in fact only do what they have been programmed to do, and that is fine because this very property of smart contracts ensures that smart contracts produce same output every time they are executed. This deterministic nature of smart contracts is highly desirable in blockchain platforms due to consistent consensus requirements. This means that smart contracts are not really smart, they are simply doing what they are programmed to do.

Now this gives rise to a problem whereby a large gap between real world and blockchain world emerges. In this situation, natural language is not understandable by the smart contract, and similarly, the code is not comprehensible to the natural world. So, a few questions arise, how real-life contracts can be deployed on a blockchain? How can this bridge between the real world and smart contract world be built?

The preceding questions open up various possibilities, such as making a smart contract code readable not only by machines but also by people. If humans and machines can both understand the code written in a smart contract it might be more acceptable in legal situations, as opposed to just a piece of code that no-one understands except for programmers. This desirable property is an area ripe for research, and a large research effort has been expended in this area to answer questions around semantics, meaning, and interpretation of a contract.

Some work has already been done to describe natural language contracts formally by combining both smart contract code and natural language contract through linking contract terms with machine understandable elements. This is achieved using a markup language. An example of this type of markup language is called **Legal Knowledge Interchange Format** (**LKIF**), which is an XML schema for representing theories and proofs. It was developed under the ESTRELLA Project in 2008.

 More information is available in a research paper available at `https://doi.org/10.1007/978-3-642-15402-7_30`.

Smart contracts are inherently required to be deterministic. This property will allow a smart contract to be run by any node on a network and achieve the same result. If the result differs even slightly between nodes, then consensus cannot be achieved, and a whole paradigm of distributed consensus on blockchain can fail. Moreover, it is also desirable that the contract language itself is deterministic, thus ensuring integrity and stability of the smart contracts. Deterministic in the sense that there are no non-deterministic functions used in the language, which can produce different results on various nodes.

Let's take, for example, various floating-point operations calculated by various functions in a variety of programming languages can produce different results in different runtime environments. Another example is some math functions in JavaScript, which can produce different results for the same input on different browsers, and which can, in turn, lead to various bugs. This is highly undesirable in smart contracts because if results are inconsistent between nodes, then consensus will never be achieved.

A deterministic feature ensures that smart contracts always produce the same output for a specific input. In other words, programs, when executed, produce a reliable and accurate business logic that is entirely in line with the requirements programmed in the high-level code.

In summary, a smart contract has the following four properties:

- Automatically executable
- Enforceable
- Semantically sound
- Secure and unstoppable

The first two properties are required as a minimum, whereas the latter two may not be required or implementable in some scenarios and can be relaxed. For example, a financial derivatives contract does not perhaps need to be semantically sound and unstoppable but should at least be automatically executable and enforceable at a fundamental level. On the other hand, a title deed needs to be semantically sound and complete, therefore, for it to be implemented as a smart contract, the language must be understood by both computers and people. Ian Grigg addressed this issue of interpretation with his invention of Ricardian contracts, which we will look at in more detail in the next section.

Ricardian contracts

Ricardian contracts were initially proposed in the paper, *Financial Cryptography in 7 Layers*, by *Ian Grigg* in late 1990s. These contracts were used initially in a bond trading and payment system called **Ricardo**. The fundamental idea is to write a document that is understandable and acceptable by both a court of law and computer software. Ricardian contracts address the challenge of issuance of value over the internet. It identifies the issuer and captures all the terms and clauses of the contract in a document to make it acceptable as a legally binding contract.

A Ricardian contract is a document that has several of the following properties:

- A contract offered by an issuer to holders
- A valuable right held by holders and managed by the issuer
- Easily readable by people (like a contract on paper)
- Readable by programs (parsable, like a database)
- Digitally signed
- Carries the keys and server information
- Allied with a unique and secure identifier

The preceding information is based on the original definition by Ian Grigg at `http://iang.org/papers/ricardian_contract.html`.

In practice, the contracts are implemented by producing a single document that contains the terms of the contract in legal prose and the required machine-readable tags. This document is digitally signed by the issuer using their private key. This document is then hashed using a message digest function to produce a hash by which the document can be identified. This hash is then further used and signed by parties during the performance of the contract to link each transaction, with the identifier hash thus serving as an evidence of intent. This is depicted in the next diagram, usually called a bowtie model.

The diagram shows number of elements:

- The **World of Law** on the left-hand side from where the document originates. This document is a written contract in legal prose with some machine-readable tags.
- This document is then hashed.
- The resultant message digest is used as an identifier throughout the **World of Accountancy**, shown on the right-hand side of the diagram.

The **World of Accountancy** element represents any accounting, trading, and information systems that are being used in the business to perform various business operations. The idea behind this flow is that the message digest generated by hashing the document is first used in a so-called **genesis transaction**, or first transaction, and then used in every transaction as an identifier throughout the operational execution of the contract.

This way, a secure link is created between the original written contract and every transaction in the **World of Accounting**:

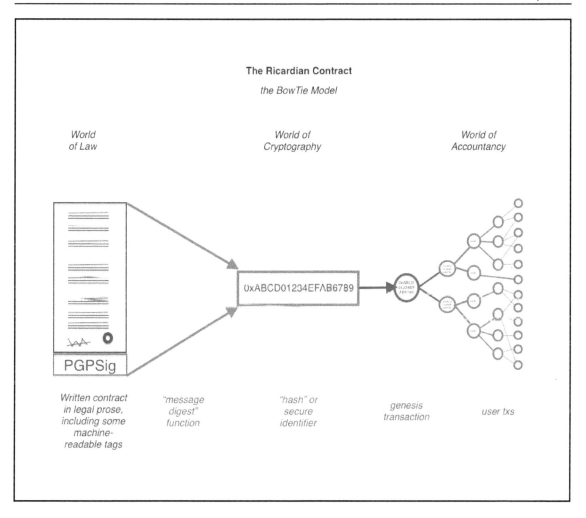

Ricardian contracts, bowtie diagram

A Ricardian contract is different from a smart contract in the sense that a smart contract does not include any contractual document and is focused purely on the execution of the contract. A Ricardian contract, on the other hand, is more concerned with the semantic richness and production of a document that contains contractual legal prose. The semantics of a contract can be divided into two types: operational semantics and denotational semantics.

The first type defines the actual execution, correctness, and safety of the contract, and the latter is concerned with the real-world meaning of the full contract. Some researchers have differentiated between smart contract code and smart legal contracts where a smart contract is only concerned with the execution of the contract. The second type encompasses both the denotational and operational semantics of a legal agreement. It perhaps makes sense to categorize smart contracts based on the difference between semantics, but it is better to consider smart contracts as a standalone entity that is capable of encoding legal prose and code (business logic) in it.

In Bitcoin, a straightforward implementation of basic smart contracts (conditional logic) can be observed, which is entirely oriented towards the execution and performance of the contract, whereas a Ricardian contract is more geared towards producing a document that is understandable by humans with some parts that a computer program can understand. This can be viewed as legal semantics versus operational performance (semantics versus performance) as shown in the following diagram. The diagram shows that Ricardian contracts are more semantically-rich, whereas smart contracts are more performance-rich. This concept was initially proposed by *Ian Grigg* in his paper, *On the intersection of Ricardian and smart contracts*.

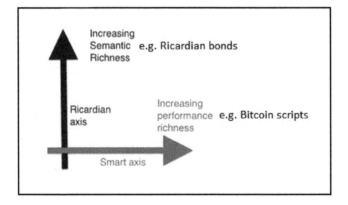

Diagram explaining performance versus semantics are orthogonal issues as described by Ian Grigg; slightly modified to show examples of different types of contracts on both axis

A smart contract is made up to have both of these elements (performance and semantics) embedded together, which completes an ideal model of a smart contract.

A Ricardian contract can be represented as a tuple of three objects, namely *Prose, parameters,* and *code*. Prose represents the legal contract in natural language; code represents the program that is a computer-understandable representation of legal prose; and parameters join the appropriate parts of the legal contract to the equivalent code.

Ricardian contracts have been implemented in many systems, such as CommonAccord, OpenBazaar, OpenAssets, and Askemos.

Smart contract templates

Smart contracts can be implemented for any industry where required, but most current use cases are related to the financial industry. This is due to the fact that blockchain found many use cases in the Finance industry first and sparked great research interest in the financial industry long before other industries. Recent work in smart contract space specific to the financial industry has proposed the idea of smart contract templates. The idea is to build standard templates that provide a framework to support legal agreements for financial instruments.

This idea was proposed by *Clack et al.* in their paper published in 2016, named *Smart Contract Templates: Foundations, design landscape and research directions*. The paper also proposed that domain-specific languages should be built to support design and implementation of smart contract templates. A language named CLACK, a common language for augmented contract knowledge has been proposed, and research has begun to develop the language. This language is intended to be very rich and provide a large variety of functions ranging from supporting legal prose to the ability to be executed on multiple platforms and cryptographic functions.

Recent work to develop smart contract templates that support legally enforceable smart contracts have been carried out by Clack et al. This proposal has been discussed in their research paper *Smart Contract Templates: essential requirements and design options*. The main aim of this paper is to investigate how legal prose can be linked with code using a markup language. It also covers that how smart legal agreements can be created, formatted, executed, and serialized for storage and transmission. This is an ongoing work and an open area for further research and development.

Contracts in the finance industry is not a new concept, and various domain-specific language DSLs are already in use in the financial industry to provide specific language for a specific domain. For example, there are DSLs available that support development of insurance products, represent energy derivatives, or are being used to build trading strategies.

 A comprehensive list of financial domain-specific languages can be found at http://www.dslfin.org/resources.html.

It is also important to understand the concept of domain-specific languages as this type of languages can be developed to program smart contracts. These languages are developed with limited expressiveness for a particular application or area of interest. **Domain-specific languages (DSLs)** are different from **general-purpose programming languages (GPLs)**. DSLs have a small set of features that are sufficient and optimized for the domain they are intended to be used in and, unlike GPLs, are usually not used to build general purpose large application programs.

Based on the design philosophy of DSLs it can be envisaged that such languages will be developed specifically to write smart contracts. Some work has already been done, and Solidity is one such language that has been introduced with Ethereum blockchain to write smart contracts. Vyper is another language that has been recently introduced for Ethereum smart contact development.

This idea of domain-specific languages for smart contract programming can be further extended to a *graphical domain-specific language*, a smart contract modeling platform where a domain expert (not a programmer, for example, a front desk dealer) can use a graphical user interface and a canvas to define and draw the semantics and performance of a financial contract. Once the flow has been drawn and completed, it can be emulated first to test and then be deployed from the same system to the target platform, which can be a blockchain. This is also not a new concept, and a similar approach is used in the Tibco StreamBase product, which is a Java-based system used for building event-driven, high-frequency trading systems.

It is proposed that research should also be conducted in the area of developing high-level DSLs that can be used to program a smart contract in a user-friendly graphical user interface, thus allowing a non-programmer domain expert (for example, a lawyer) to design smart contracts.

Oracles

Oracles are an important component of the smart contract ecosystem. The limitation with smart contracts is that they cannot access external data, which might be required to control the execution of the business logic; for example, the stock price of a security product that is required by the contract to release the dividend payments. Oracles can be used to provide external data to smart contracts. An Oracle is an interface that delivers data from an external source to smart contracts.

Depending on the industry and requirements, Oracles can deliver different types of data ranging from weather reports, real-world news, and corporate actions to data coming from **Internet of Things (IoT)** devices. Oracles are trusted entities that use a secure channel to transfer data to a smart contract.

Oracles are also capable of digitally signing the data proving that the source of the data is authentic. Smart contracts can then subscribe to the Oracles, and the smart contracts can either pull the data or Oracles can push the data to the smart contracts. It is also necessary that Oracles should not be able to manipulate the data they provide and must be able to provide authentic data. Even though Oracles are trusted, it may still be possible in some cases that the data is incorrect due to manipulation. Therefore, it is necessary that Oracles are unable to change the data. This validation can be provided by using various notary schemes, discussed later in the chapter.

In this approach, an issue can already be seen which perhaps is not desirable in some cases, and that is the issue of trust. How do you trust a third party about the quality and authenticity of data they provide? This is especially true in the financial world, where market data must be accurate and reliable. It might be acceptable for a smart contract designer to accept data for an Oracle that is provided by a large, reputable, trusted third party, but the issue of centralization remains. These types of Oracles can be called standard or simple Oracles. For example, the source of the data can be from a reputable weather reporting agency or airport information system relaying the flight delays.

Another concept that can be used to ensure the credibility of data provided by third-party sources for Oracles is that data is sourced from multiple sources; even users or members of the public that have access and knowledge about some data can provide the required data. This data can then be aggregated and if a high number of same information is fed from multiple sources, then there is a high chance that the data is correct and can be trusted.

Another type of Oracle, which essentially emerged due to the decentralization requirements, is called **decentralized** Oracles. These types of Oracles can be built based on some distributed mechanism. It can also be envisaged that the Oracles can find themselves source data from another blockchain, which is driven by distributed consensus, thus ensuring the authenticity of data. For example, one institution running their private blockchain can publish their data feed via an Oracle that can then be consumed by other blockchains.

Another concept of hardware Oracles is also introduced by researchers where real-world data from physical devices is required. For example, this can be used in telemetry and IoT. However, this approach requires a mechanism in which hardware devices are tamperproof. This can be achieved by providing cryptographic evidence (non-repudiation and integrity) of IoT device's data and anti-tampering mechanism on the IoT device, which renders the device useless in case of tampering attempts.

The following diagram shows a generic model of an Oracle and smart contract ecosystem:

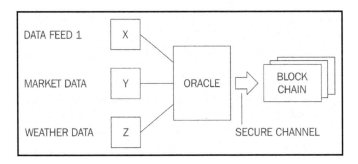

A generic model of an Oracle and smart contract ecosystem

There are platforms available now to enable a smart contract to get external data using an Oracle. There are different methods used by an Oracle to write data into the blockchain depending on the type of blockchain used. For example, in Bitcoin blockchain, an Oracle can write data to a specific transaction and a smart contract can monitor that transaction in the blockchain and read the data.

Various online services such as `http://www.oraclize.it/` and `https://www.realitykeys.com/` are available that provide Oracle services. Another service at `https://smartcontract.com/` is also available, which provides external data and the ability to make payments using smart contracts.

All these services aim to enable the smart contract to get the data it needs to execute and make decisions. To prove the authenticity of the data retrieved by the Oracles from external sources, mechanisms like TLSnotary can be used which produce proof of communication between the data source and the Oracle. This ensures that the data fed back to the smart contract is retrieved from the source.

More details about TLSnotary can be found here: `https://tlsnotary.org/`.

Smart Oracles

An idea of Smart Oracle has also been proposed by *Ripple labs (codius)*. Its original whitepaper is available at `https://github.com/codius/codius/wiki/Smart-Oracles:-A-Simple,-Powerful-Approach-to-Smart-Contracts`. Smart Oracles are entities just like Oracles, but with the added capability of contract code execution. Smart Oracles proposed by Codius run using Google Native Client, which is a sandboxed environment for running untrusted x86 native code.

Deploying smart contracts on a blockchain

Smart contracts may or may not be deployed on a blockchain, but it makes sense to deploy them on a blockchain due to the distributed and decentralized consensus mechanism provided by blockchain. Ethereum is an example of a blockchain platform that natively supports the development and deployment of smart contracts. Smart contracts on Ethereum blockchain are usually part of a broader application such as **Decentralized Autonomous organization** (**DAOs**).

As a comparison, in Bitcoin blockchain, the transaction timelocks such as the `nLocktime` field and CHECKLOCKTIMEVERIFY (CLTV), CHECKSEQUENCEVERIFY script operator in the Bitcoin transaction can be seen as an enabler of a simple version of a smart contract. These timelocks enable a transaction to be locked until a specified time or until a number of blocks, thus enforcing a basic contract that a certain transaction can only be unlocked if certain conditions (elapsed time or number of blocks) are met. For example, you can implement conditions such as "Pay party X, N amount of bitcoins after 3 months". However, this is very limited and should be only viewed as an example of a basic smart contract. In addition to the example mentioned above, Bitcoin scripting language, though limited, can be used to construct basic smart contracts. One example, of a basic smart contract, is to fund a Bitcoin address that can be spent by anyone who demonstrates a "hash collision attack". This was a contest that was announced on the Bitcointalk forum where bitcoins were set as a reward for whoever manages to find hash collisions (we discussed this concept in `Chapter 6`, *Public Key Cryptography*) for hash functions. This conditional unlocking of Bitcoin only on the demonstration of a successful attack is a basic type of smart contract.

 This idea was presented on the Bitcointalk forum, and more information can be found at `https://bitcointalk.org/index.php?topic=293382.0`. This can also be considered a basic form of smart contract.

Various other blockchain platforms support smart contracts such as Monax, Lisk, Counterparty, Stellar, Hyperledger fabric, corda, and Axoni core. Smart contracts can be developed in various languages. The critical requirement, however, is determinism, which is very important because it is vital that regardless of where the smart contract code executes, it produces the same result every time and everywhere. This requirement of deterministic nature of smart contracts also implies that smart contract code is absolutely bug-free. Validation and verification of smart contracts is an active area of research and detailed discussion of this topic will be presented in `Chapter 16`, *Scalability and Other Challenges*. Various languages have been developed to build smart contracts such as Solidity, which runs on **Ethereum Virtual Machine (EVM)**. It's worth noting that there are platforms which already support mainstream languages for smart contract development, such as Lisk which supports JavaScript. However, another prominent example is Hyperledger fabric which supports Golang, Java, and JavaScript for smart contract development.

The DAO

The DAO is one of the highest crowdfunded projects, and it started in April 2016. This was a set of smart contracts written to provide a platform for investment. Due to a bug in the code, this was hacked in June 2016, and an equivalent of 50 million dollars was siphoned out of the DAO into another account.

Even though the term hacked is used above, it was not really hacked, the smart contract simply did what it was asked to do. It was just an unintentional behavior that programmers of the DAO did not foresee. This incident resulted in a hard fork on Ethereum to recover from the attack. It should be noted that the notion of *code is the law* or unstoppable smart contracts should be viewed with some skepticism as the implementation of these concepts is not mature enough to merit full and unquestionable trust. This is evident from the recent events where the Ethereum foundation was able to stop and change the execution of *The DAO* by introducing a hard fork. Though this hard fork was introduced for genuine reasons, it goes against the true spirit of decentralization, and the notion of *code is law*. On the other hand, resistance against this hard fork and some miners who decided to keep mining on the original chain resulted in the creation of Ethereum Classic. This chain is the original, non-forked Ethereum blockchain where *the code is still the law*.

This attack highlights the dangers of not formally and thoroughly testing smart contracts. It also highlights the absolute need to develop a formal language for development and verification of smart contracts. The attack also highlighted the importance of thorough testing to avoid the issues that the DAO experienced. There have been various vulnerabilities discovered in Ethereum recently around the smart contract development language. Therefore, it is of utmost importance that a standard framework is developed to address all these issues. Some work has already begun, for example, an online service at `https://securify.ch`, which provides tools to formally verify smart contract. However, this area is ripe for more research to address limitations in smart contract languages.

Summary

This chapter started by introducing a history of smart contracts and was followed by a detailed discussion on the definition of a smart contract. As there is no agreement on the standard definition of a smart contract, we attempted to introduce a definition that encompasses the crux of smart contracts.

An introduction to Ricardian contracts was also provided, and the difference between Ricardian contracts and smart contracts was explained, highlighting the fact that Ricardian contracts are concerned with the definition of the contract whereas smart contracts are geared towards the actual execution of the contract.

The concept of smart contract templates was discussed, on the subject of which high-quality active research is currently being conducted in academia and industry. Some ideas about the possibility of creating high-level domain-specific languages were also discussed to create smart contracts or smart contract templates. In the later sections of the chapter, the concepts of Oracles were introduced followed by a brief discussion on the DAO, and security issues in DAO and smart contracts.

Discussion regarding formal verification and security of smart contracts will be presented later in this book in `Chapter 16`, *Scalability and Other Challenges.*

In the next chapter, you will be introduced to the concepts, theory, and practical aspects of *symmetric cryptography*

5
Symmetric Cryptography

In this chapter, you will be introduced to the concepts, theory, and practical aspects of *symmetric cryptography*. We will focus more on the elements that are specifically relevant in the context of blockchain technology. We will provide you with concepts that are required to understand the material covered in later chapters.

You will also be introduced to applications of cryptographic algorithms so that you can gain hands-on experience in the practical implementation of cryptographic functions. For this, we'll use the OpenSSL command-line tool. Before starting with the theoretical foundations, we'll look at the installation of OpenSSL in the following section, so that you can do some practical work as you read through the conceptual material.

Working with the OpenSSL command line

On the Ubuntu Linux distribution, OpenSSL is usually already available. However, it can be installed using the following command:

```
$ sudo apt-get install openssl
```

Examples in this chapter have been developed using OpenSSL version 1.0.2g.

 It is available at `https://packages.ubuntu.com/xenial/openssl`.

You are encouraged to use this specific version, as all examples in the chapter have been developed and tested with it. The OpenSSL version can be checked using the following command:

```
$ openssl version
```

You will see the following output:

```
OpenSSL 1.0.2g  1 Mar 2016
```

Now, you are all set to run the examples provided in this chapter. If you are running a version other than 1.0.2g, the examples may still work but that is not guaranteed, as older versions lack the features used in the examples and newer versions may not be backward compatible with version 1.0.2g.

In the sections that follow, the theoretical foundations of cryptography are first discussed and then a series of relevant practical experiments will be presented.

Introduction

Cryptography is the science of making information secure in the presence of adversaries. It does so under the assumption that limitless resources are available to adversaries. **Ciphers** are algorithms used to encrypt or decrypt data, so that if intercepted by an adversary, the data is meaningless to them without **decryption**, which requires a secret key.

Cryptography is primarily used to provide a confidentiality service. On its own, it cannot be considered a complete solution, rather it serves as a crucial building block within a more extensive security system to address a security problem. For example, securing a blockchain ecosystem requires many different cryptographic primitives, such as hash functions, symmetric key cryptography, digital signatures, and public key cryptography.

In addition to a confidentiality service, cryptography also provides other security services such as integrity, authentication (entity authentication and data origin authentication), and non-repudiation. Additionally, accountability is also provided, which is a requirement in many security systems.

Before discussing cryptography further, some mathematical terms and concepts need to be explained in order to build a foundation for fully understanding the material provided later in this chapter.

The next section serves as a basic introduction to these concepts. An explanation with proofs and relevant background for all of these terms would require somewhat involved mathematics, which is beyond the scope of this book. More details on these topics can be found in any standard number theory, algebra, or cryptography-specific book. For example, *A Course in Number Theory and Cryptography* by *Neal Koblitz* provides an excellent presentation of all relevant mathematical concepts.

Mathematics

As the subject of cryptography is based on mathematics, this section will introduce some basic concepts that will help you understand the concepts presented later in the chapter.

Set

A **set** is a collection of distinct objects, for example, $X = \{1, 2, 3, 4, 5\}$.

Group

A **group** is a commutative set with one operation that combines two elements of the set. The group operation is closed and associated with a defined identity element. Additionally, each element in the set has an inverse. **Closure** (closed) means that if, for example, elements A and B are in the set, then the resultant element after performing an operation on the elements is also in the set. **Associative** means that the grouping of elements does not affect the result of the operation.

Field

A **field** is a set that contains both additive and multiplicative groups. More precisely, all elements in the set form an additive and multiplicative group. It satisfies specific axioms for addition and multiplication. For all group operations, the **distributive law** is also applied. The law dictates that the same sum or product will be produced even if any of the terms or factors are reordered.

A finite field

A **finite field** is one with a finite set of elements. Also known as *Galois fields*, these structures are of particular importance in cryptography as they can be used to produce accurate and error-free results of arithmetic operations. For example, prime finite fields are used in **Elliptic Curve Cryptography** (**ECC**) to construct discrete logarithm problems.

Order

The **order** is the number of elements in a field. It is also known as the *cardinality* of the field.

An abelian group

An **abelian group** is formed when the operation on the elements of a set is commutative. The commutative law means that changing the order of the elements does not affect the result of the operation, for example, $A \times B = B \times A$.

Prime fields

A **prime field** is a finite one with a prime number of elements. It has specific rules for addition and multiplication, and each nonzero element in the field has an inverse. Addition and multiplication operations are performed modulo p, that is, prime.

Ring

If more than one operation can be defined over an abelian group, that group becomes a **ring**. There are also specific properties that need to be satisfied. A ring must have closure and associative and distributive properties.

A cyclic group

A **cyclic group** is a type of group that can be generated by a single element called the *group generator*.

Modular arithmetic

Also known as clock arithmetic, numbers in modular arithmetic wrap around when they reach a certain fixed number. This fixed number is a positive number called **modulus**, and all operations are performed concerning this fixed number. Analogous to a clock, there are numbers from 1 to 12. When it reaches 12, the number 1 starts again. In other words, this type of arithmetic deals with the remainders after the division operation. For example, 50 mod 11 is 6 because 50 / 11 leaves a remainder of 6.

This completes a basic introduction to some mathematical concepts involved in cryptography. In the next section, you will be introduced to cryptography concepts.

Cryptography

A generic cryptography model is shown in the following diagram:

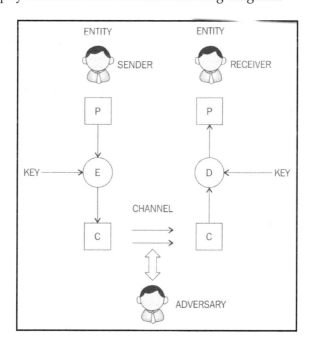

A model of the generic encryption and decryption model

In the preceding diagram, **P**, **E**, **C**, and **D** represent plaintext, encryption, ciphertext, and decryption, respectively. Also based on this model, explanations of concepts such as entity, sender, receiver, adversary, key, and channel follow:

- **Entity**: Either a person or system that sends, receives, or performs operations on data
- **Sender**: This is an entity that transmits the data
- **Receiver**: This is an entity that takes delivery of the data
- **Adversary**: This is an entity that tries to circumvent the security service
- **Key**: A key is data that is used to encrypt or decrypt other data
- **Channel**: Channel provides a medium of communication between entities

Next, we will describe the cryptography services mentioned earlier in the chapter in greater detail.

Confidentiality

Confidentiality is the assurance that information is only available to authorized entities.

Integrity

Integrity is the assurance that information is modifiable only by authorized entities.

Authentication

Authentication provides assurance about the identity of an entity or the validity of a message.

There are two types of authentication mechanisms, namely entity authentication and data origin authentication, which are discussed in the following section.

Entity authentication

Entity authentication is the assurance that an entity is currently involved and active in a communication session. Traditionally, users are issued a username and password that is used to gain access to the various platforms with which they are working. This practice is known as **single-factor authentication**, as there is only one factor involved, namely, *something you know*, that is, the password and username. This type of authentication is not very secure for a variety of reasons, for example, password leakage; therefore, additional factors are now commonly used to provide better security. The use of additional techniques for user identification is known as **multifactor authentication** (or two-factor authentication if only two methods are used).

Various authentication factors are described here:

- The first factor is *something you have*, such as a hardware token or a smart card. In this case, a user can use a hardware token in addition to login credentials to gain access to a system. This mechanism protects the user by requiring two factors of authentication. A user who has access to the hardware token and knows the login credentials will be able to access the system. Both factors should be available to gain access to the system, thus making this method a two-factor authentication mechanism. In case if the hardware token is lost, on its own it won't be of any use unless, *something you know*, the login password is also used in conjunction with the hardware token.

- The second factor is *something you are*, which uses biometric features to identify the user. With this method, a user's fingerprint, retina, iris, or hand geometry is used to provide an additional factor for authentication. This way, it can be ensured that the user was indeed present during the authentication process, as biometric features are unique to every individual. However, careful implementation is required to guarantee a high level of security, as some research has suggested that biometric systems can be circumvented under specific conditions.

Data origin authentication

Also known as *message authentication*, **data origin authentication** is an assurance that the source of the information is indeed verified. Data origin authentication guarantees data integrity because if a source is corroborated, then the data must not have been altered. Various methods, such as **Message Authentication Codes** (**MACs**) and digital signatures are most commonly used. These terms will be explained in detail later in the chapter.

Non-repudiation

Non-repudiation is the assurance that an entity cannot deny a previous commitment or action by providing incontrovertible evidence. It is a security service that offers definitive proof that a particular activity has occurred. This property is essential in debatable situations whereby an entity has denied the actions performed, for example, placement of an order on an e-commerce system. This service produces cryptographic evidence in electronic transactions so that in case of disputes, it can be used as a confirmation of an action.

Non-repudiation has been an active research area for many years. Disputes in electronic transactions are a common issue, and there is a need to address them to increase the confidence level of consumers in such services.

The non-repudiation protocol usually runs in a communication network, and it is used to provide evidence that an action has been taken by an entity (originator or recipient) on the network. In this context, there are two communications models that can be used to transfer messages from originator A to recipient B:

- A message is sent directly from originator A to recipient B.
- A message is sent to a delivery agent from originator A, which then delivers the message to recipient B.

The primary requirements of a non-repudiation protocol are fairness, effectiveness, and timeliness. In many scenarios, there are multiple participants involved in a transaction, as opposed to only two parties. For example, in electronic trading systems, there can be many entities, such as clearing agents, brokers, and traders that can be involved in a single transaction. In this case, two-party non-repudiation protocols are not appropriate. To address this problem, **Multi-Party Non-Repudiation** (**MPNR**) protocols have been developed.

Accountability

Accountability is the assurance which states that actions affecting security can be traced back to the responsible party. This is usually provided by logging and audit mechanisms in systems where a detailed audit is required due to the nature of the business, for example, in electronic trading systems. Detailed logs are vital to trace an entity's actions, such as when a trade is placed in an audit record with the date and timestamp and the entity's identity is generated and saved in the log file. This log file can optionally be encrypted and be part of the database or a standalone ASCII text log file on a system.

In order to provide all of the services discussed earlier, different cryptographic primitives are used that are presented in the next section.

Cryptographic primitives

Cryptographic primitives are the basic building blocks of a security protocol or system. In the following section, you are introduced to cryptographic algorithms that are essential for building secure protocols and systems. A **security protocol** is a set of steps taken to achieve the required security goals by utilizing appropriate security mechanisms. Various types of security protocols are in use, such as authentication protocols, non-repudiation protocols, and key management protocols.

The taxonomy of cryptographic primitives can be visualized as shown here:

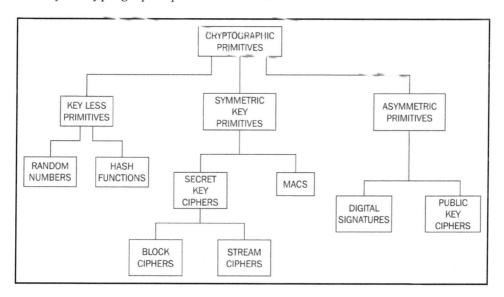

Cryptographic primitives

As shown in the cryptographic primitives taxonomy diagram, cryptography is mainly divided into two categories: *symmetric cryptography* and *asymmetric cryptography*.

These primitives are discussed further in the next section.

Symmetric cryptography

Symmetric cryptography refers to a type of cryptography where the key that is used to encrypt the data is the same one that is used for decrypting the data. Thus, it is also known as **shared key cryptography**. The key must be established or agreed upon before the data exchange occurs between the communicating parties. This is the reason it is also called **secret key cryptography**.

There are two types of symmetric ciphers: *stream ciphers* and *block ciphers*. **Data Encryption Standard (DES)** and **Advanced Encryption Standard (AES)** are typical examples of block ciphers, whereas RC4 and A5 are commonly used stream ciphers.

Stream ciphers

Stream ciphers are encryption algorithms that apply encryption algorithms on a bit-by-bit basis (one bit at a time) to plaintext using a keystream. There are two types of stream ciphers: *synchronous stream ciphers* and *asynchronous stream ciphers*:

- **Synchronous stream ciphers** are those where the keystream is dependent only on the key
- **Asynchronous stream ciphers** have a keystream that is also dependent on the encrypted data

In stream ciphers, encryption and decryption are the same function because they are simple modulo-2 additions or XOR operations. The fundamental requirement in stream ciphers is the security and randomness of keystreams. Various techniques ranging from pseudorandom number generators to true random number generators implemented in hardware have been developed to generate random numbers, and it is vital that all key generators be cryptographically secure:

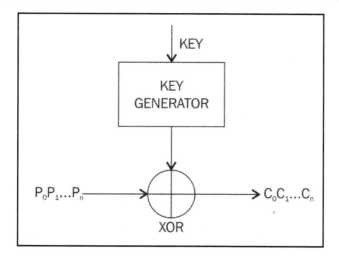

Operation of a stream cipher

Block ciphers

Block ciphers are encryption algorithms that break up the text to be encrypted (plaintext) into blocks of a fixed length and apply the encryption block-by-block. Block ciphers are generally built using a design strategy known as a **Feistel cipher**. Recent block ciphers, such as AES (Rijndael) have been built using a combination of substitution and permutation called a **Substitution-Permutation Network (SPN)**.

Feistel ciphers are based on the Feistel network, which is a structure developed by Horst Feistel. This structure is based on the idea of combining multiple rounds of repeated operations to achieve desirable cryptographic properties known as *confusion* and *diffusion*. Feistel networks operate by dividing data into two blocks (left and right) and processing these blocks via keyed *round functions* in iterations to provide sufficient pseudorandom permutation.

Confusion makes the relationship between the encrypted text and plaintext complex. This is achieved by substitution. In practice, A in plaintext is replaced by X in encrypted text. In modern cryptographic algorithms, substitution is performed using lookup tables called *S-boxes*. The diffusion property spreads the plaintext statistically over the encrypted data. This ensures that even if a single bit is changed in the input text, it results in changing at least half (on average) of the bits in the ciphertext. Confusion is required to make finding the encryption key very difficult, even if many encrypted and decrypted data pairs are created using the same key. In practice, this is achieved by transposition or permutation.

A key advantage of using a Feistel cipher is that encryption and decryption operations are almost identical and only require a reversal of the encryption process to achieve decryption. DES is a prime example of Feistel-based ciphers:

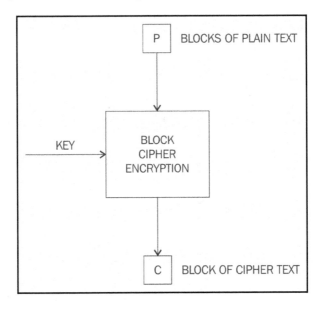

Simplified operation of a block cipher

Various modes of operation for block ciphers are **Electronic Code Book (ECB)**, **Cipher Block Chaining (CBC)**, **Output Feedback (OFB)** mode, and **Counter (CTR)** mode. These modes are used to specify the way in which an encryption function is applied to the plaintext. Some of these modes of block cipher encryption are introduced here.

Block encryption mode

In **block encryption mode**, the plaintext is divided into blocks of fixed length depending on the type of cipher used. Then the encryption function is applied to each block.

The most common block encryption modes are briefly discussed in the following subsections.

Electronic Code Book

Electronic Code Book (**ECB**) is a basic mode of operation in which the encrypted data is produced as a result of applying the encryption algorithm one-by-one to each block of plaintext. This is the most straightforward mode, but it should not be used in practice as it is insecure and can reveal information:

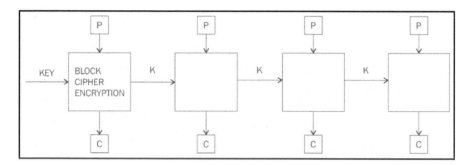

Electronic Code Book mode for block ciphers

The preceding diagram shows that we have plaintext **P** provided as an input to the block cipher encryption function, along with a key **KEY** and ciphertext **C** is produced as output.

Cipher Block Chaining

In **Cipher Block Chaining** (**CBC**) mode, each block of plaintext is XOR'd with the previously-encrypted block. CBC mode uses the **Initialization Vector** (**IV**) to encrypt the first block. It is recommended that the IV be randomly chosen:

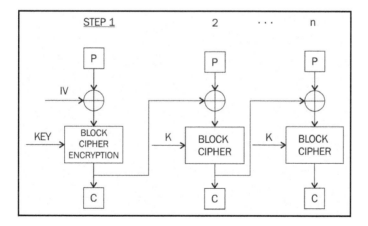

Cipher block chaining mode

Counter mode

The **Counter (CTR)** mode effectively uses a block cipher as a stream cipher. In this case, a unique nonce is supplied that is concatenated with the counter value to produce a **keystream**:

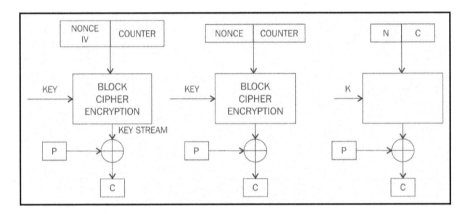

Counter mode

There are other modes, such as **Cipher Feedback (CFB)** mode, **Galois Counter (GCM)** mode, and **Output Feedback (OFB)** mode, which are also used in various scenarios.

Keystream generation mode

In **keystream generation mode**, the encryption function generates a keystream that is then XOR'd with the plaintext stream to achieve encryption.

Message authentication mode

In **message authentication mode**, a **Message Authentication Code (MAC)** results from an encryption function. The MAC is a cryptographic checksum that provides an integrity service. The most common method to generate a MAC using block ciphers is CBC-MAC, where a part of the last block of the chain is used as a MAC. For example, a MAC can be used to ensure that if a message is modified by an unauthorized entity. This can be achieved by encrypting the message with a key using the MAC function. The resultant message and MAC of the message once received by the receiver can be checked by encrypting the message received again by the key and comparing it with the MAC received from the sender. If they both match, then the message has not modified by unauthorized user thus integrity service is provided. If they both don't match, then it means that message is modified by unauthorized entity during the transmission.

Cryptographic hash mode

Hash functions are primarily used to compress a message to a fixed-length digest. In **cryptographic hash mode**, block ciphers are used as a compression function to produce a hash of plaintext.

With this, we have now concluded the introduction to block ciphers. In the following section, you will be introduced to the design and mechanism of a currently market-dominant block cipher known as AES.

Before discussing AES, however, some history is presented about the **Data Encryption Standard** (**DES**) that led to the development of the new AES standard.

Data Encryption Standard

The **Data Encryption Standard** (**DES**) was introduced by the U.S. **National Institute of Standards and Technology** (**NIST**) as a standard algorithm for encryption, and it was in widespread use during the 1980s and 1990s. However, it did not prove to be very resistant to brute force attacks, due to advances in technology and cryptography research. In July 1998, for example, the **Electronic Frontier Foundation** (**EFF**) broke DES using a special-purpose machine called EFF DES cracker (or *Deep Crack*).

DES uses a key of only 56 bits, which raised some concerns. This problem was addressed with the introduction of **Triple DES** (**3DES**), which proposed the use of a 168-bit key by means of three 56-bit keys and the same number of executions of the DES algorithm, thus making brute force attacks almost impossible. However, other limitations, such as slow performance and 64-bit block size, were not desirable.

Advanced Encryption Standard

In 2001, after an open competition, an encryption algorithm named Rijndael invented by cryptographers Joan Daemen and Vincent Rijmen was standardized as **Advanced Encryption Standard** (**AES**) with minor modifications by NIST. So far, no attack has been found against AES that is more effective than the brute-force method. The original version of Rijndael permits different key and block sizes of 128-bit, 192-bit, and 256-bits. In the AES standard, however, only a 128-bit block size is allowed. However, key sizes of 128-bit, 192-bit, and 256-bit are permissible.

How AES works

During AES algorithm processing, a 4 x 4 array of bytes known as the **state** is modified using multiple rounds. Full encryption requires 10 to 14 rounds, depending on the size of the key. The following table shows the key sizes and the required number of rounds:

Key size	Number of rounds required
128-bit	10 rounds
192-bit	12 rounds
256-bit	14 rounds

Once the state is initialized with the input to the cipher, four operations are performed in four stages to encrypt the input. These stages are: AddRoundKey, SubBytes, ShiftRows, and MixColumns:

1. In the AddRoundKey step, the state array is XOR'd with a subkey, which is derived from the master key
2. SubBytes is the substitution step where a lookup table (S-box) is used to replace all bytes of the state array
3. The ShiftRows step is used to shift each row to the left, except for the first one, in the state array to the left in a cyclic and incremental manner
4. Finally, all bytes are mixed in the MixColumns step in a linear fashion, column-wise

The preceding steps describe one round of AES.

In the final round (either 10, 12, or 14, depending on the key size), stage 4 is replaced with AddRoundKey to ensure that the first three steps cannot be simply reversed:

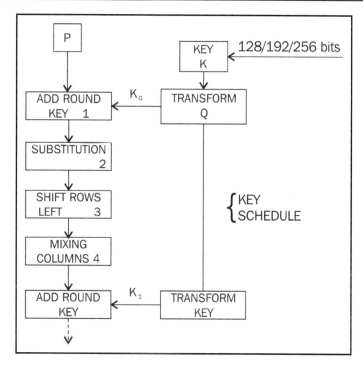

AES block diagram, showing the first round of AES encryption. In the last round, the mixing step is not performed

Various cryptocurrency wallets use AES encryption to encrypt locally-stored data. Especially in Bitcoin wallet, AES-256 in the CBC mode is used.

Here's an OpenSSL example of how to encrypt and decrypt using AES:

```
$ openssl enc -aes-256-cbc -in message.txt -out message.bin
enter aes-256-cbc encryption password:
Verifying - enter aes-256-cbc encryption password:
$ ls -ltr
-rw-rw-r-- 1 drequinox drequinox 14 Sep 21 05:54 message.txt
-rw-rw-r-- 1 drequinox drequinox 32 Sep 21 05:57 message.bin
$ cat message.bin
```

The following are the contents of the message.bin file:

```
Salted__w▒▒▒s_ÿ▒h~▒▒▒▒▒▒▒▒▒▒▒:~/Crypt$
:~/Crypt$
```

Note that `message.bin` is a binary file. Sometimes, it is desirable to encode this binary file in a text format for compatibility/interoperability reasons. The following command can be used to do just that:

```
$ openssl enc -base64 -in message.bin -out message.b64
$ ls -ltr
-rw-rw-r-- 1 drequinox drequinox 14 Sep 21 05:54 message.txt
-rw-rw-r-- 1 drequinox drequinox 32 Sep 21 05:57 message.bin
-rw-rw-r-- 1 drequinox drequinox 45 Sep 21 06:00 message.b64
$ cat message.b64
U2FsdGVkX193uByIcwZf0Z7J1at+4L+Fj8/uzeDAtJE=
```

In order to decrypt an AES-encrypted file, the following commands can be used. An example of `message.bin` from a previous example is used:

```
$ openssl enc -d -aes-256-cbc -in message.bin -out message.dec
enter aes-256-cbc decryption password:
$ ls -ltr
-rw-rw-r-- 1 drequinox drequinox 14 Sep 21 05:54 message.txt
-rw-rw-r-- 1 drequinox drequinox 32 Sep 21 05:57 message.bin
-rw-rw-r-- 1 drequinox drequinox 45 Sep 21 06:00 message.b64
-rw-rw-r-- 1 drequinox drequinox 14 Sep 21 06:06 message.dec
$ cat message.dec
Datatoencrypt
```

Astute readers will have noticed that no IV has been provided, even though it's required in all block encryption modes of operation except ECB. The reason for this is that OpenSSL automatically derives the IV from the given password. Users can specify the IV using the following switch:

```
-K/-iv       , (Initialization Vector) should be provided in Hex.
```

In order to decode from base64, the following commands are used. Follow the `message.b64` file from the previous example:

```
$ openssl enc -d -base64 -in message.b64 -out message.ptx
$ ls -ltr
-rw-rw-r-- 1 drequinox drequinox 14 Sep 21 05:54 message.txt
-rw-rw-r-- 1 drequinox drequinox 32 Sep 21 05:57 message.bin
-rw-rw-r-- 1 drequinox drequinox 45 Sep 21 06:00 message.b64
-rw-rw-r-- 1 drequinox drequinox 14 Sep 21 06:06 message.dec
-rw-rw-r-- 1 drequinox drequinox 32 Sep 21 06:16 message.ptx
$ cat message.ptx
```

The following are the contents of the `message.ptx` file:

```
:~/Crypt$ cat message.ptx
Salted__w    s_ÿ  h~?                    :~/Crypt$
```

There are many types of ciphers that are supported in OpenSSL. You can explore these options based on the preceding examples. A list of supported cipher types is shown in the following screenshot:

```
Cipher Types
-aes-128-cbc          -aes-128-ccm          -aes-128-cfb
-aes-128-cfb1         -aes-128-cfb8         -aes-128-ctr
-aes-128-ecb          -aes-128-ofb          -aes-192-cbc
-aes-192-ccm          -aes-192-cfb          -aes-192-cfb1
-aes-192-cfb8         -aes-192-ctr          -aes-192-ecb
-aes-192-ofb          -aes-256-cbc          -aes-256-ccm
-aes-256-cfb          -aes-256-cfb1         -aes-256-cfb8
-aes-256-ctr          -aes-256-ecb          -aes-256-ofb
-aes128               -aes192               -aes256
-bf                   -bf-cbc               -bf-cfb
-bf-ecb               -bf-ofb               -blowfish
-camellia-128-cbc     -camellia-128-cfb     camellia-128-cfb1
 camellia-128-cfb8    -camellia-128-ecb     -camellia-128-ofb
-camellia-192-cbc     -camellia-192-cfb     -camellia-192-cfb1
-camellia-192-cfb8    -camellia-192-ecb     -camellia-192-ofb
-camellia-256-cbc     -camellia-256-cfb     -camellia-256-cfb1
-camellia-256-cfb8    -camellia-256-ecb     -camellia-256-ofb
-camellia128          -camellia192          -camellia256
-cast                 -cast-cbc             -cast5-cbc
-cast5-cfb            -cast5-ecb            -cast5-ofb
-des                  -des-cbc              -des-cfb
-des-cfb1             -des-cfb8             -des-ecb
-des-ede              -des-ede-cbc          -des-ede-cfb
-des-ede-ofb          -des-ede3             -des-ede3-cbc
-des-ede3-cfb         -des-ede3-cfb1        -des-ede3-cfb8
-des-ede3-ofb         -des-ofb              -des3
-desx                 -desx-cbc             -id-aes128-CCM
-id-aes128-wrap       -id-aes192-CCM        -id-aes192-wrap
-id-aes256-CCM        -id-aes256-wrap       -id-smime-alg-CMS3DESwrap
-idea                 -idea-cbc             -idea-cfb
-idea-ecb             -idea-ofb             -rc2
-rc2-40-cbc           -rc2-64-cbc           -rc2-cbc
-rc2-cfb              -rc2-ecb              -rc2-ofb
-rc4                  -rc4-40               -seed
-seed-cbc             -seed-cfb             -seed-ecb
-seed-ofb
```

Screenshot displaying rich library options available in OpenSSL

OpenSSL tool can be used to experiment with all the ciphers shown in the screenshot.

Summary

In this chapter, we introduced you to symmetric key cryptography. We started with basic mathematical definitions and cryptographic primitives. After this, we introduced you to the concepts of stream and block ciphers along with working modes of block ciphers. Moreover, we introduced you to the practical exercises using OpenSSL to complement the theoretical concepts.

In the next chapter, we will present public key cryptography, which is used extensively in blockchain technology and has very interesting properties.

6
Public Key Cryptography

In this chapter, you will be introduced to the concepts and practical aspects of public key cryptography, also called asymmetric cryptography or asymmetric key cryptography. We will continue to use OpenSSL, as we did in the previous chapter, to experiment with some applications of cryptographic algorithms so that you can gain hands-on experience. We will start with the theoretical foundations of public key cryptography and will gradually build on the concepts with relevant practical exercises. In addition, we will also examine hash functions, which are another cryptographic primitive used extensively in blockchains. After this, we will introduce some new and advanced cryptography constructs.

Asymmetric cryptography

Asymmetric cryptography refers to a type of cryptography where the key that is used to encrypt the data is different from the key that is used to decrypt the data. This is also known as **public key cryptography**. It uses both public and private keys to encrypt and decrypt data, respectively. Various asymmetric cryptography schemes are in use, including RSA, DSA, and ElGammal.

An overview of public key cryptography is shown in the following diagram:

Encryption/decryption using public/private keys

The preceding diagram illustrates how a sender encrypts data **P** using the recipient's public key and encryption function **E** and producing an output encrypted data **C** which is then transmitted over the network to the receiver. Once it reaches the receiver, it can be decrypted using the receiver's private key by feeding the **C** encrypted data into function **D**, which will output plaintext **P**. This way, the private key remains on the receiver's side, and there is no need to share keys in order to perform encryption and decryption, which is the case with symmetric encryption.

The following diagram shows how the receiver uses public key cryptography to verify the integrity of the received message. In this model, the sender signs the data using their private key and transmits the message across to the receiver. Once the message is received, it is verified for integrity by the sender's public key.

It's worth noting that there is no encryption being performed in this model. It is simply presented here to help you understand thoroughly the sections covering message authentication and validation later in this chapter:

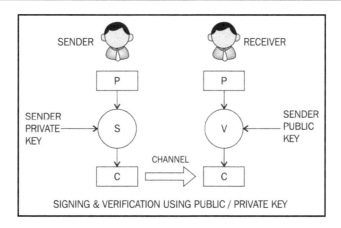

Model of a public-key cryptography signature scheme

The preceding diagram shows that sender digitally signs the plaintext **P** with his private key using signing function **S** and produces data **C** which is sent to the receiver who verifies **C** using sender public key and function **V** to ensure the message has indeed come from the sender.

Security mechanisms offered by public key cryptosystems include key establishment, digital signatures, identification, encryption, and decryption.

Key establishment mechanisms are concerned with the design of protocols that allow the setting up of keys over an insecure channel. Non-repudiation services, a very desirable property in many scenarios, can be provided using **digital signatures**. Sometimes, it is important not only to authenticate a user but also to identify the entity involved in a transaction. This can also be achieved by a combination of digital signatures and **challenge-response protocols**. Finally, the encryption mechanism to provide confidentiality can also be obtained using public key cryptosystems, such as RSA, ECC, and ElGammal.

Public key algorithms are slower in terms of computation than symmetric key algorithms. Therefore, they are not commonly used in the encryption of large files or the actual data that requires encryption. They are usually used to exchange keys for symmetric algorithm. Once the keys are established securely, symmetric key algorithms can be used to encrypt the data.

Public key cryptography algorithms are based on various underlying mathematical functions. The three main categories of asymmetric algorithms are described here.

Integer factorization

Integer factorization schemes are based on the fact that large integers are very hard to factor. RSA is the prime example of this type of algorithm.

Discrete logarithm

A **discrete logarithm scheme** is based on a problem in modular arithmetic. It is easy to calculate the result of modulo function, but it is computationally impractical to find the exponent of the generator. In other words, it is extremely difficult to find the input from the result. This is a one-way function.

For example, consider the following equation:

$$3^2 \; mod \; 10 = 9$$

Now, given 9, the result of the preceding equation finding 2 which is the exponent of the generator 3 in the preceding question, is extremely hard to determine. This difficult problem is commonly used in the Diffie-Hellman key exchange and digital signature algorithms.

Elliptic curves

The **elliptic curves algorithm** is based on the discrete logarithm problem discussed earlier but in the context of elliptic curves. An **elliptic curve** is an algebraic cubic curve over a field, which can be defined by the following equation. The curve is non-singular, which means that it has no cusps or self-intersections. It has two variables a and b, as well as a point of infinity.

$$y^2 = x^3 + ax + b$$

Here, a and b are integers whose values are elements of the field on which the elliptic curve is defined. Elliptic curves can be defined over real numbers, rational numbers, complex numbers, or finite fields. For cryptographic purposes, an elliptic curve over prime finite fields is used instead of real numbers. Additionally, the prime should be greater than 3. Different curves can be generated by varying the value of a and/or b.

The most prominently used cryptosystems based on elliptic curves are the **Elliptic Curve Digital Signature Algorithm** (**ECDSA**) and the **Elliptic Curve Diffie-Hellman** (**ECDH**) key exchange.

To understand public key cryptography, the key concept that needs to be explored is the concept of public and private keys.

Public and private keys

A **private key**, as the name suggests, is a randomly generated number that is kept secret and held privately by its users. Private keys need to be protected and no unauthorized access should be granted to that key; otherwise, the whole scheme of public key cryptography is jeopardized, as this is the key that is used to decrypt messages. Private keys can be of various lengths depending on the type and class of algorithms used. For example, in RSA, typically a key of 1024-bits or 2048-bits is used. The 1024-bit key size is no longer considered secure, and at least a 2048-bit key size is recommended.

A **public key** is freely available and published by the private key owner. Anyone who would then like to send the publisher of the public key an encrypted message can do so by encrypting the message using the published public key and sending it to the holder of the private key. No one else is able to decrypt the message because the corresponding private key is held securely by the intended recipient. Once the public key encrypted message is received, the recipient can decrypt the message using the private key. There are a few concerns, however, regarding public keys. These include authenticity and identification of the publisher of the public keys.

In the following section, we will introduce two examples of asymmetric key cryptography: RSA and ECC. RSA is the first implementation of public key cryptography whereas ECC is used extensively in blockchain technology.

RSA

RSA was invented in 1977 by Ron Rivest, Adi Shamir, and Leonard Adelman, hence the name **Rivest–Shamir–Adleman** (**RSA**). This type of public key cryptography is based on the integer factorization problem, where the multiplication of two large prime numbers is easy, but it is difficult to factor it (the result of multiplication, product) back to the two original numbers.

The crux of the work involved with the RSA algorithm is during the key generation process. An RSA key pair is generated by performing the following steps:

1. **Modulus generation**:

   - Select p and q, which are very large prime numbers
   - Multiply p and q, $n=p.q$ to generate modulus n

2. **Generate co-prime**:

   - Assume a number called e.
   - e should satisfy a certain condition; that is, it should be greater than *1* and less than *(p-1) (q-1)*. In other words, e must be a number such that no number other than *1* can divide e and *(p-1) (q-1)*. This is called **co-prime**, that is, e is the co-prime of *(p-1) (q-1)*.

3. **Generate the public key**:

   The modulus generated in step 1 and co-prime e generated in step 2 is a pair together that is a public key. This part is the public part that can be shared with anyone; however, p and q need to be kept secret.

4. **Generate the private key**:

   The private key, called d here, is calculated from p, q, and e. The private key is basically the inverse of *e modulo (p-1) (q-1)*. In the equation form, it is this as follows:

   $$ed = 1 \bmod (p\text{-}1)\,(q\text{-}1)$$

Usually, the extended Euclidean algorithm is used to calculate d. This algorithm takes p, q, and e and calculates d. The key idea in this scheme is that anyone who knows p and q can easily calculate private key d by applying the extended Euclidean algorithm. However, someone who does not know the value of p and q cannot generate d. This also implies that p and q should be large enough for the modulus n to become extremely difficult (computationally impractical) to factor.

Encryption and decryption using RSA

RSA uses the following equation to produce ciphertext:

$$C = P^e \bmod n$$

This means that plaintext P is raised to e number of times and then reduced to modulo n. Decryption in RSA is provided in the following equation:

$$P = C^d \bmod n$$

This means that the receiver who has a public key pair (n, e) can decipher the data by raising C to the value of the private key d and reducing to modulo n.

Elliptic Curve Cryptography

Elliptic Curve Cryptography (ECC) is based on the discrete logarithm problem founded upon elliptic curves over finite fields (Galois fields). The main benefit of ECC over other types of public key algorithms is that it requires a smaller key size while providing the same level of security as, for example, RSA. Two notable schemes that originate from ECC are ECDH for key exchange and ECDSA for digital signatures.

ECC can also be used for encryption, but it is not usually used for this purpose in practice. Instead, it is used for key exchange and digital signatures commonly. As ECC needs less space to operate, it is becoming very popular on embedded platforms and in systems where storage resources are limited. By comparison, the same level of security can be achieved with ECC only using 256-bit operands as compared to 3072-bits in RSA.

Mathematics behind ECC

To understand ECC, a basic introduction to the underlying mathematics is necessary. An elliptic curve is basically a type of polynomial equation known as the **Weierstrass equation**, which generates a curve over a finite field. The most commonly-used field is where all the arithmetic operations are performed modulo a prime p. Elliptic curve groups consist of points on the curve over a finite field.

An elliptic curve is defined in the following equation:

$$y^2 = x^3 + Ax + B \bmod P$$

Here, A and B belong to a finite field Zp or Fp (prime finite field) along with a special value called the **point of infinity**. The point of infinity (∞) is used to provide identity operations for points on the curve.

Furthermore, a condition also needs to be met that ensures that the equation mentioned earlier has no repeated roots. This means that the curve is non-singular.

The condition is described in the following equation, which is a standard requirement that needs to be met. More precisely, this ensures that the curve is non-singular:

$$4a^3 + 27b^2 \neq 0 \bmod p$$

To construct the discrete logarithm problem based on elliptic curves, a large enough cyclic group is required. First, the group elements are identified as a set of points that satisfy the previous equation. After this, group operations need to be defined on these points.

Group operations on elliptic curves are point addition and point doubling. **Point addition** is a process where two different points are added, and **point doubling** means that the same point is added to itself.

Point addition

Point addition is shown in the following diagram. This is a geometric representation of point addition on elliptic curves. In this method, a diagonal line is drawn through the curve that intersects the curve at two points **P** and **Q**, as shown in the diagram, which yields a third point between the curve and the line. This point is mirrored as **P+Q**, which represents the result of the addition as **R**.

This is shown as **P+Q** in the following diagram:

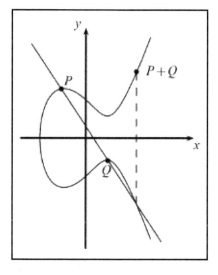

Point addition over R

The group operation denoted by the + sign for addition yields the following equation:

$$P + Q = R$$

In this case, two points are added to compute the coordinates of the third point on the curve:

$$P + Q = R$$

More precisely, this means that coordinates are added, as shown in the following equation:

$$(x_1, y_1) + (x_2, y_2) = (x_3, y_3)$$

The equation of point addition is as follows:

$$X_3 = s^2 - x_1 - x_2 \bmod p$$

$$y_3 = s\ (x_1 - x_3) - y_1 \bmod p$$

Here, we see the result of the preceding equation:

$$S = \frac{(y_2 - y_1)}{(x_2 - x_1)} \bmod p$$

S in the preceding equation depicts the line going through P and Q.

An example of point addition is shown in the following diagram. It was produced using Certicom's online calculator. This example shows the addition and solutions for the equation over finite field $\mathbf{F}_{23}$. This is in contrast to the example shown earlier, which is over real numbers and only shows the curve but provides no solutions to the equation:

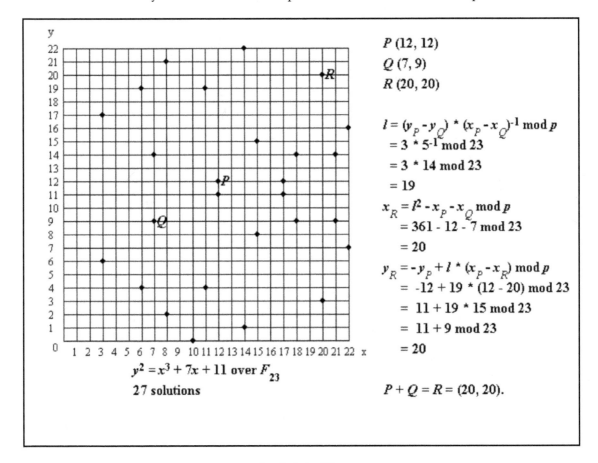

Example of point addition

In the preceding example, the graph on the left side shows the points that satisfy this equation:

$$y^2 = x^3 + 7x + 11$$

There are 27 solutions to the equation shown earlier over finite field F_{23}. P and Q are chosen to be added to produce point R. Calculations are shown on the right side, which calculates the third point R. Note that here, l is used to depict the line going through P and Q.

As an example, to show how the equation is satisfied by the points shown in the graph, a point (x, y) is picked up where $x = 3$ and $y = 6$.

Using these values shows that the equation is indeed satisfied:

$$y^2 \bmod 23 = x^3 + 7x + 11 \bmod 23$$

$$6^2 \bmod 23 = 3^3 + 7(3) + 11 \bmod 23$$

$$36 \bmod 23 = 59 \bmod 23$$

$$13 = 13$$

The next subsection introduces the concept of point doubling, which is another operation that can be performed on elliptic curves.

Point doubling

The other group operation on elliptic curves is called **point doubling**. This is a process where **P** is added to itself. In this method, a tangent line is drawn through the curve, as shown in the following graph. The second point is obtained, which is at the intersection of the tangent line drawn and the curve.

This point is then mirrored to yield the result, which is shown as $2P = P + P$:

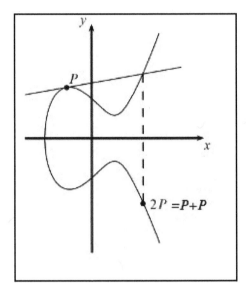

Graph representing point doubling over real numbers

In the case of point doubling, the equation becomes:

$$x_3 = s^2 - x_1 - x_2 \; mod \; p$$

$$y_3 = s(x_1 - x_3) - y_1 \; mod \; p$$

$$S = \frac{3x_1^2 + a}{2y_1}$$

Here, S is the slope of tangent (tangent line) going through P. It is the line shown on top in the preceding diagram. In the preceding example, the curve is plotted over real numbers as a simple example, and no solution to the equation is shown.

The following example shows the solutions and point doubling of elliptic curves over finite field $\mathbf{F}_{23}$. The graph on the left side shows the points that satisfy the equation:

$$y^2 = x^3 + 7x + 11$$

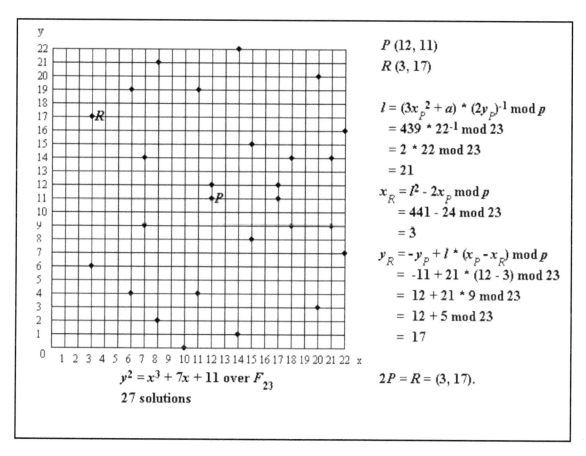

$P\,(12, 11)$

$R\,(3, 17)$

$l = (3x_p^2 + a) * (2y_p)^{-1} \bmod p$

$\quad = 439 * 22^{-1} \bmod 23$

$\quad = 2 * 22 \bmod 23$

$\quad = 21$

$x_R = l^2 - 2x_p \bmod p$

$\quad = 441 - 24 \bmod 23$

$\quad = 3$

$y_R = -y_p + l * (x_p - x_R) \bmod p$

$\quad = -11 + 21 * (12 - 3) \bmod 23$

$\quad = 12 + 21 * 9 \bmod 23$

$\quad = 12 + 5 \bmod 23$

$\quad = 17$

$y^2 = x^3 + 7x + 11$ over F_{23}

27 solutions

$2P = R = (3, 17)$.

Example of point doubling

As shown on the right side in the preceding graph, the calculation that finds the R after P is added into itself (point doubling). There is no Q as shown here, and the same point P is used for doubling. Note that in the calculation, l is used to depict the tangent line going through P.

In the next section, an introduction to the discrete logarithm problem will be presented.

Discrete logarithm problem in ECC

The discrete logarithm problem in ECC is based on the idea that, under certain conditions, all points on an elliptic curve form a cyclic group.

On an elliptic curve, the public key is a random multiple of the generator point, whereas the private key is a randomly chosen integer used to generate the multiple. In other words, a private key is a randomly selected integer, whereas the public key is a point on the curve. The discrete logarithm problem is used to find the private key (an integer) where that integer falls within all points on the elliptic curve. The following equation shows this concept more precisely.

Consider an elliptic curve E, with two elements P and T. The discrete logarithmic problem is to find the integer d, where $1 <= d <= \#E$, such that:

$$P + P + \cdots + P = d\,P = T$$

Here, T is the public key (a point on the curve), and d is the private key. In other words, the public key is a random multiple of the generator, whereas the private key is the integer that is used to generate the multiple. $\#E$ represents the order of the elliptic curve, which means the number of points that are present in the cyclic group of the elliptic curve. A **cyclic group** is formed by a combination of points on the elliptic curve and point of infinity.

A key pair is linked with the specific domain parameters of an elliptic curve. Domain parameters include field size, field representation, two elements from the field a and b, two field elements Xg and Yg, order n of point G that is calculated as $G = (Xg, Yg)$, and the cofactor $h = \#E(Fq)/n$. A practical example using OpenSSL will be described later in this section.

Various parameters are recommended and standardized to use as curves with ECC. An example of `secp256k1` specifications is shown here. This is the specification that is used in Bitcoin:

The elliptic curve domain parameters over $\mathbb{F}_p$ associated with a Koblitz curve `secp256k1` are specified by the sextuple $T = (p, a, b, G, n, h)$ where the finite field $\mathbb{F}_p$ is defined by:

p = FFFFFFFF FFFFFFFF FFFFFFFF FFFFFFFF FFFFFFFF FFFFFFFF FFFFFFFE FFFFFC2F

= $2^{256} - 2^{32} - 2^9 - 2^8 - 2^7 - 2^6 - 2^4 - 1$

The curve $E: y^2 = x^3 + ax + b$ over $\mathbb{F}_p$ is defined by:

a = 00000000 00000000 00000000 00000000 00000000 00000000 00000000 00000000

b = 00000000 00000000 00000000 00000000 00000000 00000000 00000000 00000007

The base point G in compressed form is:

G = 02 79BE667E F9DCBBAC 55A06295 CE870B07 029BFCDB 2DCE28D9 59F2815B 16F81798

and in uncompressed form is:

G = 04 79BE667E F9DCBBAC 55A06295 CE870B07 029BFCDB 2DCE28D9 59F2815B 16F81798 483ADA77 26A3C465 5DA4FBFC 0E1108A8 FD17B448 A6855419 9C47D08F FB10D4B8

Finally the order n of G and the cofactor are:

n = FFFFFFFF FFFFFFFF FFFFFFFF FFFFFFFE BAAEDCE6 AF48A03B BFD25E8C D0364141

h = 01

Specification of secp256k1 taken from http://www.secg.org/sec2-v2.pdf

An explanation of all of these values in the sextuple is as follows:

- *P* is the prime *p* that specifies the size of the finite field.
- *a* and *b* are the coefficients of the elliptic curve equation.
- *G* is the base point that generates the required subgroup, also known as the *generator*. The base point can be represented in either compressed or uncompressed form. There is no need to store all points on the curve in a practical implementation. The compressed generator works because the points on the curve can be identified using only the *x* coordinate and the least significant bit of the *y* coordinate.
- *n* is the order of the subgroup.
- *h* is the cofactor of the subgroup.

In the following section, two examples of using OpenSSL are shown to help you understand the practical aspects of RSA and ECC cryptography.

RSA using OpenSSL

The following example illustrates how RSA public and private key pairs can be generated using the OpenSSL command line.

RSA public and private key pair

First, how the RSA private key can be generated using OpenSSL is shown in the following subsection.

Private key

Execute the following command to generate the private key:

```
$ openssl genpkey -algorithm RSA -out privatekey.pem -pkeyopt \
rsa_keygen_bits:1024
.............................++++++
....................++++++
```

 The backslash (\) used in the commands are for continuation

After executing the command, a file named `privatekey.pem` is produced, which contains the generated private key as follows:

```
$ cat privatekey.pem
-----BEGIN PRIVATE KEY-----
MIICdgIBADANBgkqhkiG9w0BAQEFAASCAmAwggJcAgEAAoGBAKJOFBzPy2vOd6em
Bk/UGrzDy7TvgDYnYxBfiEJId/r+EyMt/F14k2fDTOVwxXaXTxiQgD+BKuiey/69
9itnrqW/xy/pocDMvobj8QCngEntOdNoVSaN+t0f9nRM3iVM94mz3/C/v4vXvoac
PyPkr/0jhIV0woCurXGTghgqIbHRAgMBAAECgYEA1B3s/N4lJh0l1TkOSYunWtzT
6isnNkR7g1WrY9H+rG9xx4kP5b1DyE3SvxBLJA6xgB1e8JVQMzm3sKJrJPFZzzT5
NNNnugCxairxcF1mPzJAP3aqpcSjxKpTv4qgqYevwgW1A0R3xKQZzBKU+bTO2hXV
D1oHxu75mDY3xCwqSAECQQDUYV04wNSEjEy9tYJ0zaryDAcvd/VG2/U/6qiQGajB
eSpSqoEESigbusKku+wVtRYgWWEomL/X58t+K01eMMZZAkEAw6PUR9YLebsm/Sji
iOShV4AKuFdi7t7DYWE5U1b1uqP/i28zN/ytt4BXKIs/KcFykQGeAC6LDHZyycyc
ntDIOQJAVqrE1/wYvV5jkqcXbYLgV5YA+KYDOb9Y/ZRM5UETVKCVXNanf5CjfW1h
MMhfNxyGwvy2YVK0Nu8oY3xYPi+5QQJAUGcmORe4w6Cs12JUJ5p+zG0s+rG/URhw
B7djTXm7p6b6wR1EWYAZDM9MArenj8uXAA1AGCcIsmiDqHfU71gz0QJAe9mOdNGW
7qRppgmOE5nuEbxkDSQI7OqHYbOLuwfCjHzJBrSgqyi6pj9/9CbXJrZPgNDwdLEb
GgpDKtZs9gLv3A==
-----END PRIVATE KEY-----
```

Public key

As the private key is mathematically linked to the public key, it is also possible to generate or derive the public key from the private key. Using the example of the preceding private key, the public key can be generated as shown here:

```
$ openssl rsa -pubout -in privatekey.pem -out publickey.pem

writing RSA key
```

The public key can be viewed using a file reader or any text viewer:

```
$ cat publickey.pem
-----BEGIN PUBLIC KEY-----
MIGfMA0GCSqGSIb3DQEBAQUAA4GNADCBiQKBgQCiThQcz8trznenpgZP1Bq8w8u0
74A2J2MQX4hCSHf6/hMjLfxdeJNnw0z1cMV2108YkIA/gSronsv+vfYrZ661v8cv
6aHAzL6G4/EAp4BJ7TnTaFUmjfrdH/Z0TN41TPeJs9/wv7+L176GnD8j5K/9I4SF
dMKArq1xk4IYKiGx0QIDAQAB
-----END PUBLIC KEY-----
```

In order to see more details of the various components, such as the modulus, prime numbers that are used in the encryption process, or exponents and coefficients of the generated private key, the following command can be used (only partial output is shown here as the actual output is very long):

```
$ openssl rsa -text -in privatekey.pem
Private-Key: (1024 bit)
modulus:
    00:a2:4e:14:1c:cf:cb:6b:ce:77:a7:a6:06:4f:d4:
    1a:bc:c3:cb:b4:ef:80:36:27:63:10:5f:88:42:48:
    77:fa:fe:13:23:2d:fc:5d:78:93:67:c3:4c:e5:70:
    c5:76:97:4f:18:90:80:3f:81:2a:e8:9e:cb:fe:bd:
    f6:2b:67:ae:a5:bf:c7:2f:e9:a1:c0:cc:be:86:e3:
    f1:00:a7:80:49:ed:39:d3:68:55:26:8d:fa:dd:1f:
    f6:74:4c:de:25:4c:f7:89:b3:df:f0:bf:bf:8b:d7:
    be:86:9c:3f:23:e4:af:fd:23:84:85:74:c2:80:ae:
    ad:71:93:82:18:2a:21:b1:d1
publicExponent: 65537 (0x10001)
privateExponent:
    00:94:1d:ec:fc:de:25:26:1d:25:d5:39:0e:49:8b:
    a7:5a:dc:d3:ea:2b:27:36:44:7b:83:55:ab:63:d1:
    fe:ac:6f:71:c7:89:0f:e5:bd:43:c8:4d:d2:bf:10:
    4b:24:0e:b1:80:19:5e:f0:95:50:33:39:b7:b0:a2:
    6b:24:f1:59:cf:34:f9:34:d3:67:ba:00:b1:6a:2a:
    f1:70:5d:66:3f:32:40:3f:76:aa:a5:c4:a3:c4:aa:
    53:bf:8a:a0:a9:87:af:c2:05:b5:03:44:77:c4:a4:
    19:cc:12:94:f9:b4:ce:da:15:d5:0f:5a:07:c6:ee:
    f9:98:36:37:c4:2c:2a:48:01
prime1:
    00:d4:61:5d:38:c0:d4:84:8c:4c:bd:b5:82:74:cd:
    aa:f2:0c:07:2f:77:f5:46:db:f5:3f:ea:a8:90:19:
    a8:c1:79:2a:52:aa:81:04:4a:28:1b:ba:c2:a4:bb:
    ec:15:b5:16:20:59:61:28:98:bf:d7:e7:cb:7e:2b:
    4d:5e:30:c6:59
prime2:
    00:c3:a3:d4:47:d6:0b:79:bb:26:fd:28:e2:88:e4:
    a1:57:80:0a:b8:57:62:ee:de:c3:61:61:39:52:56:
    f5:ba:a3:ff:8b:6f:33:37:fc:ad:b7:80:57:28:8b:
    3f:29:c1:72:91:01:9e:00:2e:8b:0c:76:72:c9:cc:
    9c:9e:d0:c8:39
```

Exploring the public key

Similarly, the public key can be explored using the following commands. Public and private keys are base64-encoded:

```
$ openssl pkey -in publickey.pem -pubin -text
-----BEGIN PUBLIC KEY-----
MIGfMA0GCSqGSIb3DQEBAQUAA4GNADCBiQKBgQCiThQcz8trznenpgZP1Bq8w8u0
74A2J2MQX4hCSHf6/hMjLfxdeJNnw0z1cMV2108YkIA/gSronsv+vfYrZ66lv8cv
6aHAzL6G4/EAp4BJ7TnTaFUmjfrdH/Z0TN4lTPeJs9/wv7+L176GnD8j5K/9I4SF
dMKArq1xk4IYKiGx0QIDAQAB
-----END PUBLIC KEY-----
Public-Key: (1024 bit)
Modulus:
    00:a2:4e:14:1c:cf:cb:6b:ce:77:a7:a6:06:4f:d4:
    1a:bc:c3:cb:b4:ef:80:36:27:63:10:5f:88:42:48:
    77:fa:fe:13:23:2d:fc:5d:78:93:67:c3:4c:e5:70:
    c5:76:97:4f:18:90:80:3f:81:2a:e8:9e:cb:fe:bd:
    f6:2b:67:ae:a5:bf:c7:2f:e9:a1:c0:cc:be:86:e3:
    f1:00:a7:80:49:ed:39:d3:68:55:26:8d:fa:dd:1f:
    f6:74:4c:de:25:4c:f7:89:b3:df:f0:bf:bf:8b:d7:
    be:86:9c:3f:23:e4:af:fd:33:84:05:74:c2:80:ae:
    ad:71:93:82:18:2a:21:b1:d1
Exponent: 65537 (0x10001)
```

Now the public key can be shared openly, and anyone who wants to send you a message can use the public key to encrypt the message and send it to you. You can then use the corresponding private key to decrypt the file.

Encryption and decryption

In this section, an example will be presented that demonstrates how encryption and decryption operations can be performed using RSA with OpenSSL.

Encryption

Taking the private key generated in the previous example, the command to encrypt a text file `message.txt` can be constructed as shown here:

```
$ echo datatoencrypt > message.txt
$ openssl rsautl -encrypt -inkey publickey.pem -pubin  in message.txt \
  -out message.rsa
```

This will produce a file named `message.rsa`, which is in a binary format. If you open `message.rsa` in the nano editor or any other text editor of your choice, it will show some garbage as shown in the following screenshot:

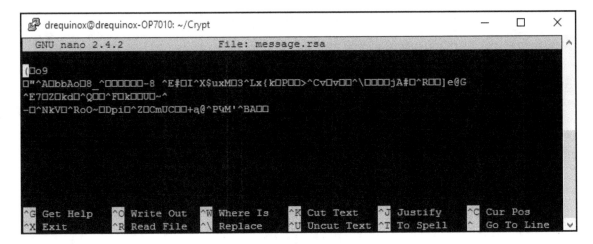

message.rsa showing garbage (encrypted) data

Decryption

In order to decrypt the RSA-encrypted file, the following command can be used:

```
$ openssl rsautl -decrypt -inkey privatekey.pem -in message.rsa \
  -out message.dec
```

Now, if the file is read using `cat`, decrypted plaintext can be seen as shown here:

```
$ cat message.dec
datatoencrypt
```

ECC using OpenSSL

OpenSSL provides a very rich library of functions to perform ECC. The following subsection shows how to use ECC functions in a practical manner in OpenSSL.

ECC private and public key pair

In this subsection, first an example is presented that demonstrates the creation of a private key using ECC functions available in the OpenSSL library.

Private key

ECC is based on domain parameters defined by various standards. You can see the list of all available standards defined and recommended curves available in OpenSSL using the following command. (Once again, only partial output is shown here, and it is truncated in the middle.):

```
$ openssl ecparam -list_curves
secp112r1 : SECG/WTLS curve over a 112 bit prime field
secp112r2 : SECG curve over a 112 bit prime field
secp128r1 : SECG curve over a 128 bit prime field
secp128r2 : SECG curve over a 128 bit prime field
secp160k1 : SECG curve over a 160 bit prime field
secp160r1 : SECG curve over a 160 bit prime field
secp160r2 : SECG/WTLS curve over a 160 bit prime field
secp192k1 : SECG curve over a 192 bit prime field
secp224k1 : SECG curve over a 224 bit prime field
secp224r1 : NIST/SECG curve over a 224 bit prime field
secp256k1 : SECG curve over a 256 bit prime field
secp384r1 : NIST/SECG curve over a 384 bit prime field
secp521r1 : NIST/SECG curve over a 521 bit prime field
prime192v1: NIST/X9.62/SECG curve over a 192 bit prime field
  .
  .
  .

brainpoolP384r1: RFC 5639 curve over a 384 bit prime field
brainpoolP384t1: RFC 5639 curve over a 384 bit prime field
brainpoolP512r1: RFC 5639 curve over a 512 bit prime field
brainpoolP512t1: RFC 5639 curve over a 512 bit prime field
```

In the following example, `secp256k1` is employed to demonstrate ECC usage.

Private key generation

To generate the private key, execute the following command:

```
$ openssl ecparam -name secp256k1 -genkey -noout -out ec-privatekey.pem
$ cat ec-privatekey.pem
-----BEGIN EC PRIVATE KEY-----
MHQCAQEEIJHUIm9NZAgfpUrSxUk/iINq1ghM/ewn/RLNreuR52h/oAcGBSuBBAAK
oUQDQgAE0G33mCZ4PKbg5EtwQjk6ucv9Qc9DTr8JdcGXYGxHdzr0Jt1NInaYE0GG
ChFMT5pK+wfvSLkY15ulUoczwWKjng==
-----END EC PRIVATE KEY-----
```

The file named `ec-privatekey.pem` now contains the **Elliptic Curve (EC)** private key that is generated based on the `secp256k1` curve. In order to generate a public key from a private key, issue the following command:

```
$ openssl ec -in ec-privatekey.pem -pubout -out ec-pubkey.pem
read EC key
writing EC key
```

Reading the file produces the following output, displaying the generated public key:

```
$ cat ec-pubkey.pem
-----BEGIN PUBLIC KEY-----
MFYwEAYHKoZIzj0CAQYFK4EEAAoDQgAE0G33mCZ4PKbg5EtwQjk6ucv9Qc9DTr8J
dcGXYGxHdzr0Jt1NInaYE0GGChFMT5pK+wfvSLkY15ul0oczwWKjng==
-----END PUBLIC KEY-----
```

Now the `ec-pubkey.pem` file contains the public key derived from `ec-privatekey.pem`. The private key can be further explored using the following command:

```
$ openssl ec -in ec-privatekey.pem -text -noout
read EC key
Private-Key: (256 bit)
priv:
    00:91:d4:22:6f:4d:64:08:1f:a5:4a:d2:c5:49:3f:
    88:83:6a:d6:08:4c:fd:ec:27:fd:12:cd:ad:eb:91:
    e7:68:7f
pub:
    04:d0:6d:f7:98:26:78:3c:a6:e0:e4:4b:70:42:39:
    3a:b9:cb:fd:41:cf:43:4e:bf:09:75:c1:97:60:6c:
    47:77:3a:f4:26:dd:4d:22:76:98:13:41:86:0a:11:
    4c:4f:9a:4a:fb:07:ef:48:b9:18:97:9b:a5:d2:87:
    33:c1:62:a3:9e
ASN1 OID: secp256k1
```

Similarly, the public key can be further explored with the following command:

```
$ openssl ec -in ec-pubkey.pem -pubin -text -noout
read EC key
Private-Key: (256 bit)
pub:
    04:d0:6d:f7:98:26:78:3c:a6:e0:e4:4b:70:42:39:
    3a:b9:cb:fd:41:cf:43:4e:bf:09:75:c1:97:60:6c:
    47:77:3a:f4:26:dd:4d:22:76:98:13:41:86:0a:11:
    4c:4f:9a:4a:fb:07:ef:48:b9:18:97:9b:a5:d2:87:
    33:c1:62:a3:9e
ASN1 OID: secp256k1
```

It is also possible to generate a file with the required parameters, in this case, `secp256k1`, and then explore it further to understand the underlying parameters:

```
$ openssl ecparam -name secp256k1 -out secp256k1.pem
$ cat secp256k1.pem
-----BEGIN EC PARAMETERS-----
BgUrgQQACg==
-----END EC PARAMETERS-----
```

The file now contains all the `secp256k1` parameters, and it can be analyzed using the following command:

```
$ openssl ecparam -in secp256k1.pem -text -param_enc explicit -noout
```

This command will produce the output similar to the one shown here:

```
Field Type: prime-field
Prime:
    00:ff:ff:ff:ff:ff:ff:ff:ff:ff:ff:ff:ff:ff:
    ff:ff:ff:ff:ff:ff:ff:ff:ff:ff:ff:ff:fe:ff:
    ff:fc:2f
A:   0
B:   7 (0x7)
Generator (uncompressed):
    04:79:be:66:7e:f9:dc:bb:ac:55:a0:62:95:ce:87:
    0b:07:02:9b:fc:db:2d:ce:28:d9:59:f2:81:5b:16:
    f8:17:98:48:3a:da:77:26:a3:c4:65:5d:a4:fb:fc:
    0e:11:08:a8:fd:17:b4:48:a6:85:54:19:9c:47:d0:
    8f:fb:10:d4:b8
Order:
    00:ff:ff:ff:ff:ff:ff:ff:ff:ff:ff:ff:ff:ff:ff:
    ff:fe:ba:ae:dc:e6:af:48:a0:3b:bf:d2:5e:8c:d0:
    36:41:41
Cofactor:  1 (0x1)
```

The preceding example shows the prime number used and values of A and B, with the generator, order, and cofactor of the `secp256k1` curve domain parameters.

With the preceding example, our introduction to public key cryptography from encryption and decryption perspective is complete. Other relevant constructs like digital signatures will be discussed later in the chapter.

In the next section, we will look at another category of cryptographic primitives, hash functions. Hash functions are not used to encrypt data; instead, they produce a fixed-length digest of the data that is provided as input to the hash function.

Hash functions

Hash functions are used to create fixed-length digests of arbitrarily-long input strings. Hash functions are keyless, and they provide the data integrity service. They are usually built using iterated and dedicated hash function construction techniques.

Various families of hash functions are available, such as MD, SHA-1, SHA-2, SHA-3, RIPEMD, and Whirlpool. Hash functions are commonly used for digital signatures and **Message Authentication Codes** (**MACs**), such as HMACs. They have three security properties, namely preimage resistance, second preimage resistance, and collision resistance. These properties are explained later in this section.

Hash functions are also typically used to provide data integrity services. These can be used both as one-way functions and to construct other cryptographic primitives, such as MACs and digital signatures. Some applications use hash functions as a means for generating **Pseudo-random Numbers Generator** (**PRNGs**). There are two practical and three security properties of hash functions that must be met depending on the level of integrity required. These properties are discussed in the following subsections.

Compression of arbitrary messages into fixed-length digest

This property relates to the fact that a hash function must be able to take an input text of any length and output a fixed-length compressed message. Hash functions produce a compressed output in various bit sizes, usually between 128-bits and 512-bits.

Easy to compute

Hash functions are efficient and fast one-way functions. It is required that hash functions be very quick to compute regardless of the message size. The efficiency may decrease if the message is too big, but the function should still be fast enough for practical use.

In the following section, security properties of hash functions are discussed.

Preimage resistance

This property can be explained by using the simple equation shown as follows:

$$h(x) = y$$

Here, h is the hash function, x is the input, and y is the hash. The first security property requires that y cannot be reverse-computed to x. x is considered a preimage of y, hence the name **preimage resistance**. This is also called a one-way property.

Second preimage resistance

The **second preimage resistance** property requires that given x and $h(x)$, it is almost impossible to find any other message m, where $m \mathrel{!=} x$ and *hash of m = hash of x* or $h(m) = h(x)$. This property is also known as **weak collision resistance**.

Collision resistance

The **collision resistance** property requires that two different input messages should not hash to the same output. In other words, $h(x) \mathrel{!=} h(z)$. This property is also known as **strong collision resistance**.

All these properties are shown in the following diagram:

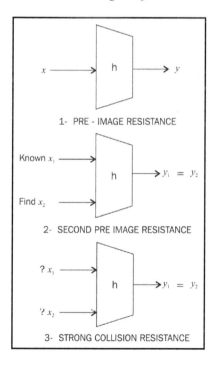

Three security properties of hash functions

Due to their very nature, hash functions will always have some collisions. This is where two different messages hash to the same output. However, they should be computationally impractical to find. A concept known as the **avalanche effect** is desirable in all hash functions. The avalanche effect specifies that a small change, even a single character change in the input text, will result in an entirely different hash output.

Hash functions are usually designed by following an iterated hash functions approach. With this method, the input message is compressed in multiple rounds on a block-by-block basis in order to produce the compressed output. A popular type of iterated hash function is **Merkle-Damgard construction**. This construction is based on the idea of dividing the input data into equal block sizes and then feeding them through the compression functions in an iterative manner. The collision resistance of the property of compression functions ensures that the hash output is also collision-resistant. Compression functions can be built using block ciphers. In addition to Merkle-Damgard, there are various other constructions of compression functions proposed by researchers, for example, Miyaguchi-Preneel and Davies-Meyer.

Multiple categories of hash function are introduced in the following subsections.

Message Digest

Message Digest (MD) functions were prevalent in the early 1990s. MD4 and MD5 fall into this category. Both MD functions were found to be insecure and are not recommended for use anymore. MD5 is a 128-bit hash function that was commonly used for file integrity checks.

Secure Hash Algorithms

The following list describes the most common **Secure Hash Algorithms (SHAs)**:

- **SHA-0**: This is a 160-bit function introduced by NIST in 1993.
- **SHA-1**: SHA-1 was introduced in 1995 by NIST as a replacement for SHA-0. This is also a 160-bit hash function. SHA-1 is used commonly in SSL and TLS implementations. It should be noted that SHA-1 is now considered insecure, and it is being deprecated by certificate authorities. Its usage is discouraged in any new implementations.
- **SHA-2**: This category includes four functions defined by the number of bits of the hash: SHA-224, SHA-256, SHA-384, and SHA-512.

- **SHA-3**: This is the latest family of SHA functions. SHA-3-224, SHA-3-256, SHA-3-384, and SHA-3-512 are members of this family. SHA-3 is a NIST-standardized version of Keccak. Keccak uses a new approach called **sponge construction** instead of the commonly used Merkle-Damgard transformation.
- **RIPEMD**: RIPEMD is the acronym for **RACE Integrity Primitives Evaluation Message Digest**. It is based on the design ideas used to build MD4. There are multiple versions of RIPEMD, including 128-bit, 160-bit, 256-bit, and 320-bit.
- **Whirlpool**: This is based on a modified version of the Rijndael cipher known as W. It uses the Miyaguchi-Preneel compression function, which is a type of one-way function used for the compression of two fixed-length inputs into a single fixed-length output. It is a single block length compression function.

Hash functions have many practical applications ranging from simple file integrity checks and password storage to use in cryptographic protocols and algorithms. They are used in hash tables, distributed hash tables, bloom filters, virus fingerprinting, peer-to-peer file sharing, and many other applications.

Hash functions play a vital role in blockchain. Especially, The PoW function in particular uses SHA-256 twice in order to verify the computational effort spent by miners. RIPEMD 160 is used to produce Bitcoin addresses. This will be discussed further in later chapters.

In the next section, the design of the SHA algorithm is introduced.

Design of Secure Hash Algorithms

In the following section, you will be introduced to the design of SHA-256 and SHA-3. Both of these are used in Bitcoin and Ethereum, respectively. Ethereum does not use NIST Standard SHA-3, but Keccak, which is the original algorithm presented to NIST. NIST, after some modifications, such as an increase in the number of rounds and simpler message padding, standardized Keccak as SHA-3.

Design of SHA-256

SHA-256 has the input message size $< 2^{64}$-bits. Block size is 512-bits, and it has a word size of 32-bits. The output is a 256-bit digest.

The compression function processes a 512-bit message block and a 256-bit intermediate hash value. There are two main components of this function: the compression function and a message schedule.

The algorithm works as follows, in eight steps:

1. **Preprocessing**:

    1. Padding of the message is used to adjust the length of a block to 512-bits if it is smaller than the required block size of 512-bits.
    2. Parsing the message into message blocks, which ensures that the message and its padding is divided into equal blocks of 512-bits.
    3. Setting up the initial hash value, which consists of the eight 32-bit words obtained by taking the first 32-bits of the fractional parts of the square roots of the first eight prime numbers. These initial values are randomly chosen to initialize the process, and they provide a level of confidence that no backdoor exists in the algorithm.

2. **Hash computation**:

    1. Each message block is then processed in a sequence, and it requires 64 rounds to compute the full hash output. Each round uses slightly different constants to ensure that no two rounds are the same.
    2. The message schedule is prepared.
    3. Eight working variables are initialized.
    4. The intermediate hash value is calculated.
    5. Finally, the message is processed, and the output hash is produced:

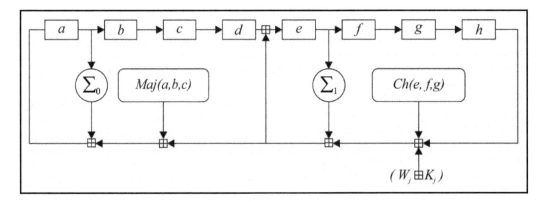

One round of a SHA-256 compression function

In the preceding diagram, **a, b, c, d, e, f, g,** and **h** are the registers. *Maj* and *Ch* are applied bitwise. Σ_0 and Σ_1 performs bitwise rotation. Round constants are $\mathbf{W_j}$ and $\mathbf{K_j}$, which are added, *mod 2^{32}*.

Design of SHA-3 (Keccak)

The structure of SHA-3 is very different from that of SHA-1 and SHA-2. The key idea behind SHA-3 is based on unkeyed permutations, as opposed to other typical hash function constructions that used keyed permutations. Keccak also does not make use of the Merkle-Damgard transformation that is commonly used to handle arbitrary-length input messages in hash functions. A newer approach called **sponge and squeeze construction** is used in Keccak. It is a random permutation model. Different variants of SHA-3 have been standardized, such as SHA-3-224, SHA-3-256, SHA-3-384, SHA-3-512, SHAKE-128, and SHAKE-256. SHAKE-128 and SHAKE-256 are **Extendable Output Functions** (XOFs), which are also standardized by NIST. XOFs allow the output to be extended to any desired length.

The following diagram shows the sponge and squeeze model, which is the basis of SHA-3 or Keccak. Analogous to a sponge, the data is first absorbed into the sponge after applying padding. There it is then changed into a subset of permutation state using XOR, and then the output is squeezed out of the sponge function that represents the transformed state. The rate is the input block size of a sponge function, while capacity determines the general security level:

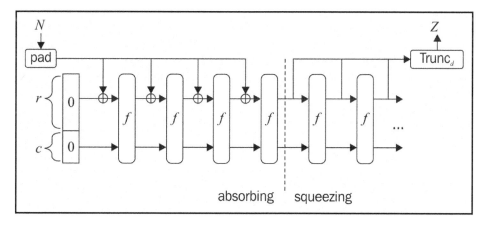

SHA-3 absorbing and squeezing function

OpenSSL example of hash functions

The following command will produce a hash of 256-bits of the `Hello` messages using the SHA-256 algorithm:

```
$ echo -n 'Hello' | openssl dgst -sha256
(stdin)= 185f8db32271fe25f561a6fc938b2e264306ec304eda518007d1764826381969
```

Note that even a small change in the text, such as changing the case of the letter H, results in a big change in the output hash. This is known as the avalanche effect, as discussed earlier:

```
$ echo -n 'hello' | openssl dgst -sha256
(stdin)= 2cf24dba5fb0a30e26e83b2ac5b9e29e1b161e5c1fa7425e73043362938b9824
```

Note that both outputs are completely different:

```
Hello:
18:5f:8d:b3:22:71:fe:25:f5:61:a6:fc:93:8b:2e:26:43:06:ec:30:4e:da:51:80:07:
d1:76:48:26:38:19:69
hello:
2c:f2:4d:ba:5f:b0:a3:0e:26:e8:3b:2a:c5:b9:e2:9e:1b:16:1e:5c:1f:a7:42:5e:73:
04:33:62:93:8b:98:24
```

Usually, hash functions do not use a key. Nevertheless, if they *are* used with a key, then they can be used to create another cryptographic construct called MACs.

Message Authentication Codes

MACs are sometimes called **keyed hash functions**, and they can be used to provide message integrity and authentication. More specifically, they are used to provide data origin authentication. These are symmetric cryptographic primitives that use a shared key between the sender and the receiver. MACs can be constructed using block ciphers or hash functions.

MACs using block ciphers

With this approach, block ciphers are used in the **Cipher Block Chaining** (**CBC**) mode in order to generate a MAC. Any block cipher, for example AES in the CBC mode, can be used. The MAC of the message is, in fact, the output of the last round of the CBC operation. The length of the MAC output is the same as the block length of the block cipher used to generate the MAC.

MACs are verified simply by computing the MAC of the message and comparing it to the received MAC. If they are the same, then the message integrity is confirmed; otherwise, the message is considered altered. It should also be noted that MACs work like digital signatures, however they cannot provide non-repudiation service due to their symmetric nature.

Hash-based MACs

Similar to the hash function, **Hash-based MACs** (**HMACs**) produce a fixed-length output and take an arbitrarily long message as the input. In this scheme, the sender signs a message using the MAC and the receiver verifies it using the shared key. The key is hashed with the message using either of the two methods known as **secret prefix** or the **secret suffix**. With the secret prefix method, the key is concatenated with the message; that is, the key comes first and the message comes afterwards, whereas with the secret suffix method, the key comes after the message, as shown in the following equations:

$$Secret\ prefix:\ M = MACk(x) = h(k||x)$$

$$Secret\ suffix:\ M=MACk(x) = h(x||k)$$

There are pros and cons to both methods. Some attacks on both schemes have occurred. There are HMAC constructions schemes that use various techniques, such as **ipad** and **opad** (inner padding and outer padding) that have been proposed by cryptographic researchers. These are considered secure with some assumptions:

Operation of a MAC function

There are various powerful applications of hash functions used in peer-to-peer networks and blockchain technology. Some noticeable examples, such as Merkle trees, Patricia trees, and **Distributed Hash Table** (**DHT**), are discussed in the following subsections.

Merkle trees

The concept of Merkle tree was introduced by Ralph Merkle. A diagram of Merkle tree is shown here. **Merkle trees** enable secure and efficient verification of large datasets.

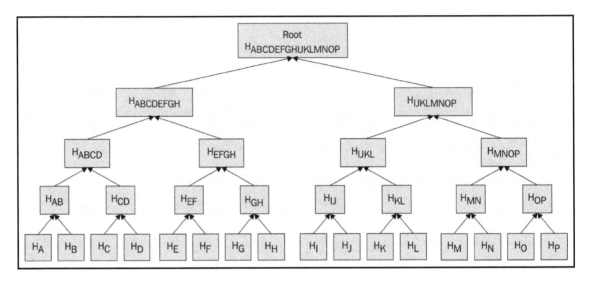

A Merkle tree

A Merkle tree is a binary tree in which the inputs are first placed at the leaves (node with no children), and then the values of pairs of child nodes are hashed together to produce a value for the parent node (internal node) until a single hash value known as **Merkle root** is achieved.

Patricia trees

To understand Patricia trees, you will first be introduced to the concept of a **trie**. A trie, or a digital tree, is an ordered tree data structure used to store a dataset.

Practical Algorithm to Retrieve Information Coded in Alphanumeric (Patricia), also known as *Radix tree*, is a compact representation of a trie in which a node that is the only child of a parent is merged with its parent.

A **Merkle-Patricia tree**, based on the definitions of Patricia and Merkle, is a tree that has a root node which contains the hash value of the entire data structure.

Distributed Hash Tables

A hash table is a data structure that is used to map keys to values. Internally, a hash function is used to calculate an index into an array of buckets from which the required value can be found. Buckets have records stored in them using a hash key and are organized into a particular order.

With the definition provided earlier in mind, one can think of a DHT as a data structure where data is spread across various nodes, and nodes are equivalent to buckets in a peer-to-peer network.

The following diagram shows how a DHT works. Data is passed through a hash function, which then generates a compact key. This key is then linked with the data (values) on the peer-to-peer network. When users on the network request the data (via the filename), the filename can be hashed again to produce the same key, and any node on the network can then be requested to find the corresponding data. DHT provides decentralization, fault tolerance, and scalability:

Distributed hash tables

Another application of hash functions is in digital signatures, where they can be used in combination with asymmetric cryptography. This concept is discussed in detail in the examples provided in the following subsections.

Digital signatures

Digital signatures provide a means of associating a message with an entity from which the message has originated. Digital signatures are used to provide data origin authentication and non-repudiation.

Digital signatures are used in blockchain where the transactions are digitally signed by senders using their private key before broadcasting the transaction to the network. This digital signing, proves they are the rightful owner of the asset, for example, bitcoins. These transactions are verified again by other nodes on the network to ensure that the funds indeed belong to the node (user) who claims to be the owner. We will discuss these concepts in more detail in chapters dedicated to Bitcoin and Ethereum in this book.

Digital signatures are calculated in two steps. As an example, the high-level steps of an RSA digital signature scheme follow.

RSA digital signature algorithm

The following is the RSA digital signature algorithm:

1. **Calculate the hash value of the data packet**: This will provide the data integrity guarantee as the hash can be computed at the receiver's end again and matched with the original hash to check whether the data has been modified in transit. Technically, message signing can work without hashing the data first, but is not considered secure.
2. **Signs the hash value with the signer's private key**: As only the signer has the private key, the authenticity of the signature and the signed data is ensured.

Digital signatures have some important properties, such as authenticity, unforgeability, and nonreusability. **Authenticity** means that the digital signatures are verifiable by a receiving party. The **unforgeability** property ensures that only the sender of the message can use the signing functionality using the private key. In other words, no one else can produce the signed message produced by a legitimate sender. **Nonreusability** means that the digital signature cannot be separated from a message and used again for another message.

The operation of a generic digital signature function is shown in the following diagram:

Digital signing (left) and verification process (right) (Example of RSA digital signatures)

If a sender wants to send an authenticated message to a receiver, there are two methods that can be used: sign then encrypt and encrypt then sign. These two approaches to using digital signatures with encryption are as follows.

Sign then encrypt

With this approach, the sender digitally signs the data using the private key, appends the signature to the data, and then encrypts the data and the digital signature using the receiver's public key. This is considered a more secure scheme as compared to the *encrypt then sign* scheme described next.

Encrypt then sign

With this method, the sender encrypts the data using the receiver's public key and then digitally signs the encrypted data.

 In practice, a digital certificate that contains the digital signature is issued by a **Certificate Authority** (**CA**) that associates a public key with an identity.

Various schemes, such as RSA, **Digital Signature Algorithm** (**DSA**), and ECDSA-based digital signature schemes are used in practice. RSA is the most commonly used; however, with the traction of ECC, ECDSA-based schemes are also becoming quite popular. This is beneficial in blockchains because ECC provides same level of security that RSA does, but it uses less space. Also, generation of keys is much faster in ECC as compared to RSA, therefore it helps with overall performance of the system. The following table shows that ECC is able to provide the same level of cryptographic strength as an RSA based system with smaller key sizes:

RSA key sizes (bits)	Elliptic curve key sizes (bits)
1024	160
2048	224
3072	256
7680	384
15360	521

Comparison of RSA and Elliptic curve key sizes providing the same level of security

The ECDSA scheme is described in detail in following subsection.

Elliptic Curve Digital Signature Algorithm

In order to sign and verify using the ECDSA scheme, first key pair needs to be generated:

1. First, define an elliptic curve E:

   - With modulus P

- Coefficients *a* and *b*
- Generator point *A* that forms a cyclic group of prime order *q*

2. An integer *d* is chosen randomly so that $0 < d < q$.
3. Calculate public key *B* so that $B = d\ A$.

The public key is the sextuple in the form shown here:

$$Kpb = (p,a,b,q,A,B)$$

The private key, *d* is randomly chosen in step 2:

$$Kpr = d$$

Now the signature can be generated using the private and public key.

4. First, an ephemeral key K_e is chosen, where $0 < K_e < q$. It should be ensured that K_e is truly random and that no two signatures have the same key; otherwise, the private key can be calculated.
5. Another value *R* is calculated using $R = K_e\ A$; that is, by multiplying *A* (the generator point) and the random ephemeral key.
6. Initialize a variable *r* with the *x* coordinate value of point *R* so that $r = xR$.
7. The signature can be calculated as follows:

$$S = \left(h(m) + dr\right)K_{e^{-1}} \bmod q$$

Here, *m* is the message for which the signature is being computed, and *h(m)* is the hash of the message *m*.

Signature verification is carried out by following this process:

1. Auxiliary value *w* is calculated as $w = s\text{-}1\ mod\ q$.
2. Auxiliary value $u1 = w.\ h(m)\ mod\ q$.
3. Auxiliary value $u2 = w.\ r\ mod\ q$.
4. Calculate point *P*, $P - u1A + u2B$.

5. Verification is carried out as follows:

r, s is accepted as a valid signature if the x coordinate of point P calculated in step 4 has the same value as the signature parameter $r \bmod q$; that is:

$$Xp = r \bmod q \text{ means valid signature}$$

$$Xp \mathrel{!=} r \bmod q \text{ means invalid signature}$$

Various practical examples are shown in the following subsections, which demonstrate how the RSA digital signature can be generated, used, and verified using OpenSSL.

How to generate a digital signature using OpenSSL

The first step is to generate a hash of the message file:

```
$ openssl dgst -sha256 message.txt
SHA256(message.txt)=
eb96d1f89812bf4967d9fb4ead128c3b787272b7be21dd2529278db1128d559c
```

Both hash generation and signing can be done in a single step, as shown here. Note that `privatekey.pem` is generated in the steps provided previously:

```
$ openssl dgst -sha256 -sign privatekey.pem -out signature.bin message.txt
```

Now, let's display the directory showing the relevant files:

```
$ ls -ltr
total 36
-rw-rw-r-- 1 drequinox drequinox  14 Sep 21 05:54 message.txt
-rw-rw-r-- 1 drequinox drequinox  32 Sep 21 05:57 message.bin
-rw-rw-r-- 1 drequinox drequinox  45 Sep 21 06:00 message.b64
-rw-rw-r-- 1 drequinox drequinox  32 Sep 21 06:16 message.ptx
-rw-rw-r-- 1 drequinox drequinox 916 Sep 21 06:28 privatekey.pem
-rw-rw-r-- 1 drequinox drequinox 272 Sep 21 06:30 publickey.pem
-rw-rw-r-- 1 drequinox drequinox 128 Sep 21 06:43 message.rsa
-rw-rw-r-- 1 drequinox drequinox  14 Sep 21 06:49 message.dec
-rw-rw-r-- 1 drequinox drequinox 128 Sep 21 07:05 signature.bin
```

Let's look at the contents of `signature.bin` by executing the following command:

```
$ cat signature.bin
```

Executing this command will give the following output:

```
V   _[ h] h t      +_T~Ol  s { Cq"# A Q U, uf   p* □ *7    T'  u eAy
$ x  <$ a      : L qWh  uG    = $   :~/Crypt$
```

In order to verify the signature, the following operation can be performed:

```
$ openssl dgst -sha256 -verify publickey.pem -signature \
  signature.bin message.txt
Verified OK
```

Similarly, if some other signature file which is not valid is used, the verification will fail, as shown here:

```
$ openssl dgst -sha256 -verify publickey.pem -signature
someothersignature.bin message.txt
Verification Failure
```

Next, an example is presented that shows how OpenSSL can be used to perform ECDSA-related operations.

ECDSA using OpenSSL

First, the private key is generated using the following commands:

```
$ openssl ecparam -genkey -name secp256k1 -noout -out eccprivatekey.pem
$ cat eccprivatekey.pem
-----BEGIN EC PRIVATE KEY-----
MHQCAQEEIMVmyrnEDOs7SYxS/AbXoIwqZqJ+gND9Z2/nQyzcpaPBoAcGBSuBBAAK
oUQDQgAEEKKS4E4+TATIeBX8o2J6PxKkjcoWrXPwNRo/k4Y/CZA4pXvlyTgH5LYm
QbU0qUtPM7dAEzOsaoXmetqB+6cM+Q==
-----END EC PRIVATE KEY-----
```

Next, the public key is generated from the private key:

```
$ openssl ec -in eccprivatekey.pem -pubout -out eccpublickey.pem
read EC key
writing EC key
$ cat eccpublickey.pem
-----BEGIN PUBLIC KEY-----
MFYwEAYHKoZIzj0CAQYFK4EEAAoDQgAEEKKS4E4+TATIeBX8o2J6PxKkjcoWrXPw
NRo/k4Y/CZA4pXvlyTgH5LYmQbU0qUtPM7dAEzOsaoXmetqB|6cM+Q==
-----END PUBLIC KEY-----
```

Now, suppose a file named `testsign.txt` needs to be signed and verified. This can be achieved as follows:

1. Create a test file:

```
$ echo testing > testsign.txt
$ cat testsign.txt
testing
```

2. Run the following command to generate a signature using a private key for the `testsign.txt` file:

```
$ openssl dgst -ecdsa-with-SHA1 -sign eccprivatekey.pem \
   testsign.txt > ecsign.bin
```

3. Finally, the command for verification can be run as shown here:

```
$ openssl dgst -ecdsa-with-SHA1 -verify eccpublickey.pem \
   -signature ecsign.bin testsign.txt
Verified OK
```

A certificate can also be produced by using the private key generated earlier by using the following command:

```
$ openssl req -new -key eccprivatekey.pem -x509 -nodes -days 365 \
   -out ecccertificate.pem
```

This command will produce the output similar to the one shown here. Enter the appropriate parameters to generate the certificate:

```
You are about to be asked to enter information that will be incorporated
into your certificate request.
What you are about to enter is what is called a Distinguished Name or a DN.
There are quite a few fields but you can leave some blank
For some fields there will be a default value,
If you enter '.', the field will be left blank.
-----
Country Name (2 letter code) [AU]:GB
State or Province Name (full name) [Some-State]:Cambridge
Locality Name (eg, city) []:Cambridge
Organization Name (eg, company) [Internet Widgits Pty Ltd]:Dr.Equinox!
Organizational Unit Name (eg, section) []:NA
Common Name (e.g. server FQDN or YOUR name) []:drequinox
Email Address []:drequinox@drequinox.com
```

The certificate can be explored using the following command:

```
$ openssl x509 -in ecccertificate.pem -text -noout
```

The following output shows the certificate:

X509 certificate that uses ECDSA algorithm with SHA-256

There following topics in cryptography are presented because of their relevance to blockchain, or their potential use in future blockchain ecosystems.

Homomorphic encryption

Usually, public key cryptosystems, such as RSA, are multiplicative homomorphic or additive homomorphic, such as the Paillier cryptosystem, and are called **Partially Homomorphic Encryption** (PHE) systems. Additive PHEs are suitable for e-voting and banking applications.

Until recently, there has been no system that supported both operations, but in 2009, a **Fully Homomorphic Encryption (FHE)** system was discovered by Craig Gentry. As these schemes enable the processing of encrypted data without the need for decryption, they have many different potential applications, especially in scenarios where maintaining privacy is required, but data is also mandated to be processed by potentially untrusted parties, for example, cloud computing and online search engines. Recent development in homomorphic encryption have been very promising, and researchers are actively working to make it efficient and more practical. This is of particular interest in blockchain technology, as described later in this book, as it can solve the problem of confidentiality and privacy in the blockchain.

Signcryption

Signcryption is a public key cryptography primitive that provides all of the functions of a digital signature and encryption. Yuliang Zheng invented signcryption, and it is now an ISO standard, ISO/IEC 29150:2011. Traditionally, sign then encrypt or encrypt then sign schemes are used to provide unforgeability, authentication, and non-repudiation, but with signcryption, all services of digital signatures and encryption are provided at a cost that is less than that of the sign then encrypt scheme.

Signcryption enables *Cost (signature & encryption) << Cost (signature) + Cost (Encryption)* in a single logical step.

Zero-Knowledge Proofs

Zero-Knowledge Proofs (ZKPs) were introduced by Goldwasser, Micali, and Rackoff in 1985. These proofs are used to prove the validity of an assertion without revealing any information whatsoever about the assertion. There are three properties of ZKPs that are required: completeness, soundness, and zero-knowledge property.

Completeness ensures that if a certain assertion is true, then the verifier will be convinced of this claim by the prover. The **soundness** property makes sure that if an assertion is false, then no dishonest prover can convince the verifier otherwise. The **zero-knowledge property**, as the name implies, is the key property of ZKPs whereby it is ensured that absolutely nothing is revealed about the assertion except whether it is true or false.

ZKPs have sparked a special interest among researchers in the blockchain space due to their privacy properties, which are very much desirable in financial and many other fields, including law and medicine. A recent example of the successful implementation of a ZKP mechanism is the Zcash cryptocurrency. In Zcash, a specific type of ZKP, known as **Zero-Knowledge Succinct Non-Interactive Argument of Knowledge (ZK-SNARK)**, is implemented. This will be discussed in detail in `Chapter 10`, *Alternative Coins*.

Blind signatures

Blind signatures were introduced by David Chaum in 1982. They are based on public key digital signature schemes, such as RSA. The key idea behind blind signatures is to get the message signed by the signer without actually revealing the message. This is achieved by disguising or blinding the message before signing it, hence the name *blind signatures*. This blind signature can then be verified against the original message just like a normal digital signature. Blind signatures were introduced as a mechanism to allow the development of digital cash schemes.

Encoding schemes

Other than cryptographic primitives, binary-to-text **encoding schemes** are also used in various scenarios. The most common use is to convert binary data into text so that it can either be processed, saved, or transmitted via a protocol that does not support the processing of binary data. For example, sometimes, images are stored in the database as base64 encoding, which allows a text field to be able to store a picture. A commonly-used encoding scheme is base64. Another encoding named base58 was popularized by its use in Bitcoin.

Cryptography is a vast field, and this section has merely introduced the basic concepts that are essential to understanding cryptography in general and specifically from the blockchain and cryptocurrency point of view. In the next section, basic financial market concepts will be presented.

The section describes general terminology related to trading, exchanges, and the trade life cycle. More detailed information will be provided in later chapters, where specific use cases are discussed.

Financial markets and trading

Financial markets enable trading of financial securities such as bonds, equities, derivatives and currencies. There are broadly three types of markets: money markets, credit markets, and capital markets:

- **Money markets**: These are short-term markets where money is lent to companies or banks to do interbank lending. Foreign exchange or FX is another category of money markets where currencies are traded.
- **Credit markets**: These consist mostly of retail banks where they borrow money from central banks and loan it to companies or households in the form of mortgages or loans.
- **Capital markets**: These facilitate the buying and selling of financial instruments, mainly stocks and bonds. Capital markets can be divided into two types: primary and secondary markets. Stocks are issued directly by the companies to investors in primary markets, whereas in secondary markets, investors resell their securities to other investors via stock exchanges. Various electronic trading systems are used by exchanges today to facilitate the trading of financial instruments.

Trading

A market is a place where parties engage in exchange. It can be either a physical location or an electronic or virtual location. Various financial instruments, including equities, stocks, foreign exchange, commodities, and various types of derivatives are traded at these marketplaces. Recently, many financial institutions have introduced software platforms to trade various types of instruments from different asset classes.

Trading can be defined as an activity in which traders buy or sell various financial instruments to generate profit and hedge risk. Investors, borrowers, hedgers, asset exchangers, and gamblers are a few types of traders. Traders have a short position when they owe something, in other words, if they have sold a contract they have a short position and have a long position when they buy a contract. There are various ways to transact trades, such as through brokers or directly on an exchange or **Over-The-Counter** (OTC) where buyers and sellers trade directly with each other instead of using an exchange. **Brokers** are agents who arrange trades for their customers. Brokers act on a client's behalf to deal at a given price or the best possible price.

Exchanges

Exchanges are usually considered to be a very safe, regulated, and reliable place for trading. During the last decade, electronic trading has gained more popularity as compared to traditional floor-based trading. Now traders send orders to a central electronic order book from which the orders, prices, and related attributes are published to all associated systems using communications networks, thus in essence creating a virtual marketplace. Exchange trades can be performed only by members of the exchange. To trade without these limitations, the counterparties can participate in OTC trading directly.

Orders and order properties

Orders are instructions to trade, and they are the main building blocks of a trading system. They have the following general attributes:

- The instrument name
- Quantity to be traded
- Direction (buy or sell)
- The type of the order that represents various conditions, for example, limit orders and stop orders are orders to buy or sell once the price hits the price specified in the order, for example, Google shares for 200 GBP. Limit order allows selling or buying of stock at a specific price or better than the specified price in the order. For example, sell Microsoft shares if price is 100 USD or better.

Orders are traded by bid prices and offer prices. Traders show their intention to buy or sell by attaching bid and offer prices to their orders. The price at which a trader will buy is known as the **bid price**. The price at which a trader is willing to sell is known as the **offer price**.

Order management and routing systems

Order routing systems routes and delivers orders to various destinations depending on the business logic. Customers use them to send orders to their brokers, who then send these orders to dealers, clearing houses, and exchanges.

There are different types of orders. The two most common ones are markets orders and limit order.

A **market order** is an instruction to trade at the best price currently available in the market. These orders get filled immediately at spot prices. On the other hand, a **limit order** is an instruction to trade at the best price available, but only if it is not lower than the limit price set by the trader. This can also be higher depending on the direction of the order: either to sell or buy. All of these orders are managed in an **order book**, which is a list of orders maintained by exchange, and it records the intention of buying or selling by the traders.

A **position** is a commitment to sell or buy a number of financial instruments, including securities, currencies, or commodities for a given price. The contracts, securities, commodities, and currencies that traders buy or sell are commonly known as **trading instruments**, and they come under the broad umbrella of **asset classes**. The most common classes are real assets, financial assets, derivative contracts, and insurance contracts.

Components of a trade

A **trade ticket** is the combination of all of the details related to a trade. However, there is some variation depending on the type of the instrument and the asset class. These elements are described in the following subsections.

The underlying instrument

The **underlying instrument** is the basis of the trade. It can be a currency, a bond, interest rate, commodity, or equities.

The attributes of financial instruments are discussed in the following subsection.

General attributes

This includes the general identification information and essential features associated with every trade. Typical attributes include a unique ID, instrument name, type, status, trade date, and time.

Economics

Economics are features related to the value of the trade, for example, buy or sell value, ticker, exchange, price, and quantity.

Sales

Sales refer to the sales-characteristic related details, such as the name of the salesperson. It is just an informational field, usually without any impact on the trade life cycle.

Counterparty

The **counterparty** is an essential component of a trade as it shows the other side (the other party involved in the trade) of the trade, and it is required to settle the trade successfully. The normal attributes include counterparty name, address, payment type, any reference IDs, settlement date, and delivery type.

Trade life cycle

A general **trade life cycle** includes the various stages from order placement to execution and settlement. This life cycle is described step-by-step as follows:

- **Pre-execution**: An order is placed at this stage.
- **Execution and booking**: When the order is matched and executed, it converts it into a trade. At this stage, the contract between counterparties is matured.
- **Confirmation**: This is where both counterparties agree to the particulars of the trade.
- **Post booking**: This stage is concerned with various scrutiny and verification processes required to ascertain the correctness of the trade.
- **Settlement**: This is the most vital part of trade life cycle. At this stage, the trade is final.
- **Overnight (end-of-day processing)**: End-of-day processes include report generation, profit and loss calculations, and various risk calculations.

This life cycle is also shown in the following screenshot:

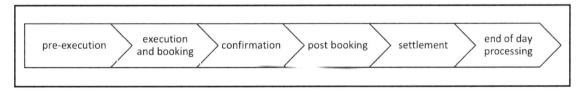

Trade life cycle

In all the aforementioned processes, many people and business functions are involved. Most commonly, these functions are divided into functions such as front office, middle office, and back office.

In the following section, you are introduced to some concepts that are essential to understanding the strict and necessary rules and regulations that govern the financial industry. Some concepts are described here and then again in later chapters when specific use cases are discussed. These ideas will help you understand the scenarios described.

Order anticipators

Order anticipators try to make a profit before other traders can carry out trading. This is based on the anticipation of a trader who knows how trading activities of other trades will affect prices. Frontrunners, sentiment-oriented technical traders, and squeezers are some examples of order anticipators.

Market manipulation

Market manipulation is strictly illegal in many countries. Fraudulent traders can spread false information in the market, which can then result in price movements thus enabling illegal profiteering. Usually, manipulative market conduct is trade-based, and it includes generalized and time-specific manipulations. Actions that can create an artificial shortage of stock, an impression of false activity, and price manipulation to gain criminal benefits are included in this category.

Both of the terms discussed here are relevant to the financial crime. However, there is a possibility of developing blockchain-based systems that can thwart market abuse due to its transparency and security properties.

Summary

We started this chapter with the introduction of asymmetric key cryptography. We discussed various constructs such as RSA and ECC. We also performed some experiments using OpenSSL to see that how theoretical concepts can be implemented practically. After this, we discussed hash functions in detail along with its properties and usage. Next, we covered concepts such as Merkle trees, which are used extensively in blockchain and, in fact, are at its core. We also presented other concepts such as Patricia trees and hash tables.

Getting Started with web3.js 7

In this chapter, we will learn web3.js and how to import, connect to geth, and use it in Node.js or client-side JavaScript. We will also learn how to build a web client using web3.js.

In this chapter, we'll cover the following topics:

- Importing web3.js in Node.js and client-side JavaScript
- Connecting to geth
- Exploring the various things that can be done using web3.js
- Discovering various most used APIs of web3.js
- Building a Node.js application for an ownership contract

Introduction to web3.js

web3.js provides us with JavaScript APIs to communicate with geth. It uses JSON-RPC internally to communicate with geth. web3.js can also communicate with any other kind of Ethereum node that supports JSON-RPC. It exposes all JSON-RPC APIs as JavaScript APIs; that is, it doesn't just support all the Ethereum-related APIs; it also supports APIs related to Whisper and Swarm.

You will learn more and more about web3.js as we build various projects, but for now, let's go through some of the most used APIs of web3.js and then we will build a frontend for our ownership smart contract using web3.js.

At the time of writing this, the latest version of web3.js is 0.16.0. We will learn everything with respect to this version.

web3.js is hosted at `https://github.com/ethereum/web3.js` and the complete documentation is hosted at `https://github.com/ethereum/wiki/wiki/JavaScript-API`.

Importing web3.js

To use web3.js in Node.js, you can simply run `npm install web3` inside your project directory, and in the source code, you can import it using `require("web3");`.

To use web3.js in client-side JavaScript, you can enqueue the `web3.js` file, which can be found inside the `dist` directory of the project source code. Now you will have the `Web3` object available globally.

Connecting to nodes

web3.js can communicate with nodes using HTTP or IPC. We will use HTTP to set up communication with nodes. web3.js allows us to establish connections with multiple nodes. An instance of `web3` represents a connection with a node. The instance exposes the APIs.

When an app is running inside Mist, it automatically makes an instance of `web3` available that's connected to the mist node. The variable name of the instance is `web3`.

Here is the basic code to connect to a node:

```
if (typeof web3 !== 'undefined') {
  web3 = new Web3(new
Web3.providers.HttpProvider("http://localhost:8545"));
}
```

At first, we check here whether the code is running inside mist by checking whether `web3` is `undefined` or not. If `web3` is defined, then we use the already available instance; otherwise, we create an instance by connecting to our custom node. If you want to connect to the custom node regardless of whether the app is running inside mist or not, then remove the `if` condition form the preceding code. Here, we are assuming that our custom node is running locally on port number `8545`.

The `Web3.providers` object exposes constructors (called providers in this context) to establish connection and transfer messages using various protocols. `Web3.providers.HttpProvider` lets us establish an HTTP connection, whereas `Web3.providers.IpcProvider` lets us establish an IPC connection.

The web3.currentProvider property is automatically assigned to the current provider instance. After creating a web3 instance, you can change its provider using the web3.setProvider() method. It takes one argument, that is, the instance of the new provider.

 Remember that geth has HTTP-RPC disabled by default. So enable it by passing the --rpc option while running geth. By default, HTTP-RPC runs on port 8545.

web3 exposes a isConnected() method, which can be used to check whether it's connected to the node or not. It returns true or false depending on the connection status.

The API structure

web3 contains an eth object (web3.eth) specifically for Ethereum blockchain interactions and an shh object (web3.shh) for whisper interaction. Most APIs of web3.js are inside these two objects.

All the APIs are synchronous by default. If you want to make an asynchronous request, you can pass an optional callback as the last parameter to most functions. All callbacks use an error-first callback style.

Some APIs have an alias for asynchronous requests. For example, web3.eth.coinbase() is synchronous, whereas web3.eth.getCoinbase() is asynchronous.

Here is an example:

```
//sync request
try
{
  console.log(web3.eth.getBlock(48));
}
catch(e)
{
  console.log(e);
}

//async request
web3.eth.getBlock(48, function(error, result){
    if(!error)
        console.log(result)
    else
```

```
            console.error(error);
    })
```

`getBlock` is used to get information on a block using its number or hash. Or, it can take a string such as `"earliest"` (the genesis block), `"latest"` (the top block of the blockchain), or `"pending"` (the block that's being mined). If you don't pass an argument, then the default is `web3.eth.defaultBlock`, which is assigned to `"latest"` by default.

All the APIs that need a block identification as input can take a number, hash, or one of the readable strings. These APIs use `web3.eth.defaultBlock` by default if the value is not passed.

BigNumber.js

JavaScript is natively poor at handling big numbers correctly. Therefore, applications that require you to deal with big numbers and need perfect calculations use the `BigNumber.js` library to work with big numbers.

web3.js also depends on BigNumber.js. It adds it automatically. web3.js always returns the `BigNumber` object for number values. It can take JavaScript numbers, number strings, and `BigNumber` instances as input.

Here is an example to demonstrate this:

```
web3.eth.getBalance("0x27E829fB34d14f3384646F938165dfcD30cFfB7c").toString(
);
```

Here, we use the `web3.eth.getBalance()` method to get the balance of an address. This method returns a `BigNumber` object. We need to call `toString()` on a `BigNumber` object to convert it into a number string.

`BigNumber.js` fails to correctly handle numbers with more than 20 floating point digits; therefore, it is recommended that you store the balance in a wei unit and while displaying, convert it to other units. web3.js itself always returns and takes the balance in wei. For example, the `getBalance()` method returns the balance of the address in the wei unit.

Unit conversion

web3.js provides APIs to convert the wei balance into any other unit and any other unit balance into wei.

The `web3.fromWei()` method is used to convert a wei number into any other unit, whereas the `web3.toWei()` method is used to convert a number in any other unit into wei. Here is example to demonstrate this:

```
web3.fromWei("1000000000000000000", "ether");
web3.toWei("0.000000000000000001", "ether");
```

In the first line, we convert wei into ether, and in the second line, we convert ether into wei. The second argument in both methods can be one of these strings:

- kwei/ada
- mwei/babbage
- gwei/shannon
- szabo
- finney
- ether
- kether/grand/einstein
- mether
- gether
- tether

Retrieving gas price, balance, and transaction details

Let's take a look at the APIs to retrieve the gas price, the balance of an address, and information on a mined transaction:

```
//It's sync. For async use getGasPrice
console.log(web3.eth.gasPrice.toString());

console.log(web3.eth.getBalance("0x407d73d8a49eeb85d32cf465507dd71d507100c1
", 45).toString());

console.log(web3.eth.getTransactionReceipt("0x9fc76417374aa880d4449a1f7f31e
c597f00b1f6f3dd2d66f4c9c6c445836d8b"));
```

The output will be of this form:

```
20000000000
30000000000
{
   "transactionHash":
"0x9fc76417374aa880d4449a1f7f31ec597f00b1f6f3dd2d66f4c9c6c445836d8b ",
   "transactionIndex": 0,
   "blockHash":
"0xef95f2f1ed3ca60b048b4bf67cde2195961e0bba6f70bcbea9a2c4e133e34b46",
   "blockNumber": 3,
   "contractAddress": "0xa94f5374fce5edbc8e2a8697c15331677e6ebf0b",
   "cumulativeGasUsed": 314159,
   "gasUsed": 30234
}
```

Here is how the preceding method works:

- `web3.eth.gasPrice()`: Determines the gas price by the x latest blocks' median gas price.
- `web3.ethgetBalance()`: Returns the balance of any given address. All the hashes should be provided as hexadecimal strings to the web3.js APIs, not as hexadecimal literals. The input for the solidity `address` type should also be hexadecimal strings.
- `web3.eth.getTransactionReceipt()`: This is used to get details about a transaction using its hash. It returns a transaction receipt object if the transaction was found in the blockchain; otherwise, it returns null. The transaction receipt object contains the following properties:
  - `blockHash`: The hash of the block where this transaction was
  - `blockNumber`: The block number where this transaction was
  - `transactionHash`: The hash of the transaction
  - `transactionIndex`: The integer of the transactions' index position in the block
  - `from`: The address of the sender
  - `to`: The address of the receiver; `null` when it's a contract creation transaction
  - `cumulativeGasUsed`: The total amount of gas used when this transaction was executed in the block
  - `gasUsed`: The amount of gas used by this specific transaction alone

- `contractAddress`: The contract address created if the transaction was a contract creation; otherwise, null
- `logs`: The array of log objects that this transaction generated

Sending ether

Let's look at how to send ether to any address. To send ether, you need to use the `web3.eth.sendTransaction()` method. This method can be used to send any kind of transaction but is mostly used to send ether because deploying a contract or calling a method of contract using this method is cumbersome as it requires you to generate the data of the transaction rather than automatically generating it. It takes a transaction object that has the following properties:

- `from`: The address for the sending account. Uses the `web3.eth.defaultAccount` property if not specified.
- `to`: This is optional. It's the destination address of the message and is left undefined for a contract-creation transaction.
- `value`: This is optional. The value is transferred for the transaction in wei as well as the endowment if it's a contract-creation transaction.
- `gas`: This is optional. It's the amount of gas to use for the transaction (unused gas is refunded). If not provided, then it's automatically determined.
- `gasPrice`: This is optional. It's the price of gas for this transaction in wei, and it defaults to the mean network gas price.
- `data`: This is optional. It's either a byte string containing the associated data of the message, or in the case of a contract-creation transaction, the initialization code.
- `nonce`: This is optional. It's an integer. Every transaction has a nonce associated with it. A nonce is a counter that indicates the number of transactions sent by the sender of the transaction. If not provided, then it is automatically determined. It helps prevent replay attacks. This nonce is not the nonce associated with a block. If we are using a nonce greater than the nonce the transaction should have, then the transaction is put in a queue until the other transactions arrive. For example, if the next transaction nonce should be 4 and if we set the nonce to 10, then geth will wait for the middle six transactions before broadcasting this transaction. The transaction with nonce 10 is called a queued transaction, and it's not a pending transaction.

Let's look at an example of how to send ether to an address:

```
var txnHash = web3.eth.sendTransaction({
  from: web3.eth.accounts[0],
  to: web3.eth.accounts[1],
  value: web3.toWei("1", "ether")
});
```

Here, we send one ether from account number 0 to account number 1. Make sure that both the accounts are unlocked using the `unlock` option while running geth. In the geth interactive console, it prompts for passwords, but the web3.js API outside of the interactive console will throw an error if the account is locked. This method returns the transaction hash of the transaction. You can then check whether the transaction is mined or not using the `getTransactionReceipt()` method.

You can also use the `web3.personal.listAccounts()`, `web3.personal.unlockAccount(addr, pwd)`, and `web3.personal.newAccount(pwd)` APIs to manage accounts at runtime.

Working with contracts

Let's learn how to deploy a new contract, get a reference to a deployed contract using it's address, send ether to a contract, send a transaction to invoke a contract method, and estimate the gas of a method call.

To deploy a new contract or to get a reference to an already deployed contract, you need to first create a contract object using the `web3.eth.contract()` method. It takes the contract ABI as an argument and returns the contract object.

Here is the code to create a contract object:

```
var proofContract =
web3.eth.contract([{"constant":false,"inputs":[{"name":"fileHash","type":"s
tring"}],"name":"get","outputs":[{"name":"timestamp","type":"uint256"},{"na
me":"owner","type":"string"}],"payable":false,"type":"function"},{"constant
":false,"inputs":[{"name":"owner","type":"string"},{"name":"fileHash","type
":"string"}],"name":"set","outputs":[],"payable":false,"type":"function"},{
"anonymous":false,"inputs":[{"indexed":false,"name":"status","type":"bool"}
,{"indexed":false,"name":"timestamp","type":"uint256"},{"indexed":false,"na
me":"owner","type":"string"},{"indexed":false,"name":"fileHash","type":"str
ing"}],"name":"logFileAddedStatus","type":"event"}]);
```

Once you have the contract, you can deploy it using the `new` method of the contract object or get a reference to an already deployed contract that matches the ABI using the `at` method.

Let's take a look at an example of how to deploy a new contract:

```
var proof = proofContract.new({
    from: web3.eth.accounts[0],
    data: "0x606060405261068...",
    gas: "4700000"
    },
    function (e, contract){
    if(e)
    {
    console.log("Error " + e);
}
else if(contract.address != undefined)
    {
      console.log("Contract Address: " + contract.address);
    }
else
    {
      console.log("Txn Hash: " + contract.transactionHash)
    }
})
```

Here, the `new` method is called asynchronously, so the callback is fired twice if the transaction was created and broadcasted successfully. The first time, it's called after the transaction is broadcasted, and the second time, it's called after the transaction is mined. If you don't provide a callback, then the `proof` variable will have the `address` property set to `undefined`. Once the contract is mined, the `address` property will be set.

In the `proof` contract, there is no constructor, but if there is a constructor, then the arguments for the constructor should be placed at the beginning of the `new` method. The object we passed contains the from address, the byte code of the contract, and the maximum gas to use. These three properties must be present; otherwise, the transaction won't be created. This object can have the properties that are present in the object passed to the `sendTransaction()` method, but here, `data` is the contract byte code and the `to` property is ignored.

You can use the `at` method to get a reference to an already deployed contract. Here is the code to demonstrate this:

```
var proof = proofContract.at("0xd45e541ca2622386cd820d1d3be74a86531c14a1");
```

Now let's look at how to send a transaction to invoke a method of a contract. Here is an example to demonstrate this:

```
proof.set.sendTransaction("Owner Name",
"e3b0c44298fc1c149afbf4c8996fb92427ae41e4649b934ca495991b7852b855", {

from: web3.eth.accounts[0],
}, function(error, transactionHash){

if (!err)

console.log(transactionHash);
})
```

Here, we call the `sendTransaction` method of the object of the method namesake. The object passed to this `sendTransaction` method has the same properties as `web3.eth.sendTransaction()`, except that the `data` and `to` properties are ignored.

If you want to invoke a method on the node itself instead of creating a transaction and broadcasting it, then you can use `call` instead of `sendTransaction`. Here is an example to demonstrate this:

```
var returnValue =
proof.get.call("e3b0c44298fc1c149afbf4c8996fb92427ae41e4649b934ca495991b785
2b855");
```

Sometimes, it is necessary to find out the gas that would be required to invoke a method so that you can decide whether to invoke it or not. `web3.eth.estimateGas` can be used for this purpose. However, using `web3.eth.estimateGas()` directly requires you to generate the data of the transaction; therefore, we can use the `estimateGas()` method of the object of the method namesake. Here is an example to demonstrate this:

```
var estimatedGas =
proof.get.estimateGas("e3b0c44298fc1c149afbf4c8996fb92427ae41e4649b934ca495
991b7852b855");
```

> If you want to just send some ether to a contract without invoking any method, then you can simply use the `web3.eth.sendTransaction` method.

Retrieving and listening to contract events

Now let's look at how to watch for events from a contract. Watching for events is very important because the result of method invocations by transactions are usually returned by triggering events.

 Before we get into how to retrieve and watch for events, we need to learn indexed parameters of events. A maximum of three parameters of an event can have the `indexed` attribute. This attribute is used to signal the node to index it so that the app client can search for events with matching return values. If you don't use the indexed attribute, then it will have to retrieve all the events from the node and filter the ones needed. For example, you can write the `logFileAddedStatus` event this way:

```
event logFileAddedStatus(bool indexed status, uint indexed timestamp,
string owner, string indexed fileHash);
```

Here is an example to demonstrate how to listen to contract events:

```
var event = proof.logFileAddedStatus(null, {
fromBlock: 0,
toBlock: "latest"
});
event.get(function(error, result){
if(!error)
{
  console.log(result);
}
else
{
  console.log(error);
}
})
event.watch(function(error, result){
if(!error)
{
  console.log(result.args.status);
}
else
{
  console.log(error);
}
})
setTimeout(function(){
event.stopWatching();
}, 60000)
```

```
  var events = proof.allEvents({
fromBlock: 0,
 toBlock: "latest"
});
events.get(function(error, result){
if(!error)
{
  console.log(result);
}
else
{
  console.log(error);
}
})
events.watch(function(error, result){
if(!error)
{
  console.log(result.args.status);
}
else
{
  console.log(error);
}
})
setTimeout(function(){
events.stopWatching();
}, 60000)
```

This is how the preceding code works:

1. At first, we get the event object by calling the method of the event namesake on a contract instance. This method takes two objects as arguments, which are used to filter events:
   - The first object is used to filter events by indexed return values: for example, {'valueA': 1, 'valueB': [myFirstAddress, mySecondAddress]}. By default, all filter values are set to null. This means that they will match any event of a given type sent from this contract.
   - The next object can contain three properties: fromBlock (the earliest block; by default, it is "latest"), toBlock (the latest block; by default, it is "latest"), and address (a list of addresses to only get logs from; by default, the contract address).

2. The `event` object exposes three methods: `get`, `watch`, and `stopWatching`. `get` is used to get all the events in the block range. `watch` is like `get` but it watches for changes after getting the events. And `stopWatching` can be used to stop watching for changes.

3. Then, we have the `allEvents` method of the contract instance. It is used to retrieve all the events of a contract.

4. Every event is represented by an object that contains the following properties:
   - `args`: An object with the arguments from the event
   - `event`: A string representing the event name
   - `logIndex`: An integer representing the log index position in the block
   - `transactionIndex`: An integer representing the transactions the index position log was created from
   - `transactionHash`: A string representing the hash of the transactions this log was created from
   - `address`: A string representing the address from which this log originated
   - `blockHash`: A string representing the hash of the block where this log was in; `null` when its pending
   - `blockNumber`: The block number where this log was in; `null` when its pending

web3.js provides a `web3.eth.filter` API to retrieve and watch for events. You can use this API, but the earlier method's way of handling events is much easier. You can learn more about it at `https://github.com/ethereum/wiki/wiki/JavaScript-API#web3ethfilter er`.

Building a client for an ownership contract

Now, it's time to build a client for our smart contract so that users can use it easily.

We will build a client where a user selects a file and enters owner details and then clicks on **Submit** to broadcast a transaction to invoke the contract's set method with the file hash and the owner's details. Once the transaction is successfully broadcasted, we will display the transaction hash. The user will also be able to select a file and get the owner's details from the smart contract. The client will also display the recent set transactions mined in real time.

We will use sha1.js to get the hash of the file on the frontend, jQuery for DOM manipulation, and Bootstrap 4 to create a responsive layout. We will use express.js and web3.js on the backend. We will use socket.io so that the backend pushes recently mined transactions to the frontend without the frontend requesting for data after every equal interval of time.

web3.js can be used in the frontend. But for this application, it will be a security risk; that is, we are using accounts stored in geth and exposing the geth node URL to the frontend, which will put the ether stored in those accounts at risk.

The project structure

In the exercise files of this chapter, you will find two directories: Final and Initial. Final contains the final source code of the project, whereas Initial contains the empty source code files and libraries to get started with building the application quickly.

To test the Final directory, you will need to run npm install inside it and replace the hardcoded contract address in app.js with the contract address you got after deploying the contract. Then, run the app using the node app.js command inside the Final directory.

In the Initial directory, you will find a public directory and two files named app.js and package.json. package.json contains the backend dependencies of our app, and app.js is where you will place the backend source code.

The public directory contains files related to the frontend. Inside public/css, you will find bootstrap.min.css, which is the Bootstrap library; inside public/html, you will find index.html, where you will place the HTML code of our app; and in the public/js directory, you will find JS files for jQuery, sha1, and socket.io. Inside public/js, you will also find a main.js file, where you will place the frontend JS code of our app.

Building the backend

Let's first build the backend of the app. First of all, run `npm install` inside the `Initial` directory to install the required dependencies for our backend. Before we get into coding the backend, make sure geth is running with rpc enabled. If you are running geth on a private network, then make sure mining is also enabled. Finally, make sure that account 0 exists and is unlocked. You can run geth on a private network with rpc and mining enabled and also unlocking account 0:

```
geth --dev --mine --rpc --unlock=0
```

One final thing you need to do before getting started with coding is deploy the ownership contract using the code we saw in the `Chapter 4`, Smart Contracts and copy the contract address.

Now let's create a single server, which will serve the HTML to the browser and also accept `socket.io` connections:

```
var express = require("express");
var app = express();
var server = require("http").createServer(app);
var io = require("socket.io")(server);
server.listen(8080);
```

Here, we are integrating both the `express` and `socket.io` servers into one server running on port `8080`.

Now let's create the routes to serve the static files and also the home page of the app. Here is the code to do this:

```
app.use(express.static("public"));
app.get("/", function(req, res){
  res.sendFile(__dirname + "/public/html/index.html");
})
```

Here, we are using the `express.static` middleware to serve static files. We are asking it to find static files in the `public` directory.

Now let's connect to the `geth` node and also get a reference to the deployed contract so that we can send transactions and watch for events. Here is the code to do this:

```
var Web3 = require("web3");

web3 = new Web3(new Web3.providers.HttpProvider("http://localhost:8545"));

var proofContract =
web3.eth.contract([{"constant":false,"inputs":[{"name":"fileHash","type":"s
tring"}],"name":"get","outputs":[{"name":"timestamp","type":"uint256"},{"na
me":"owner","type":"string"}],"payable":false,"type":"function"},{"constant
":false,"inputs":[{"name":"owner","type":"string"},{"name":"fileHash","type
":"string"}],"name":"set","outputs":[],"payable":false,"type":"function"},{
"anonymous":false,"inputs":[{"indexed":false,"name":"status","type":"bool"}
,{"indexed":false,"name":"timestamp","type":"uint256"},{"indexed":false,"na
me":"owner","type":"string"},{"indexed":false,"name":"fileHash","type":"str
ing"}],"name":"logFileAddedStatus","type":"event"}]);

var proof = proofContract.at("0xf7f02f65d5cd874d180c3575cb8813a9e7736066");
```

The code is self-explanatory. Just replace the contract address with the one you got.

Now let's create routes to broadcast transactions and get information about a file. Here is the code to do this:

```
app.get("/submit", function(req, res){
var fileHash = req.query.hash;
var owner = req.query.owner;
proof.set.sendTransaction(owner, fileHash, {
from: web3.eth.accounts[0],
}, function(error, transactionHash){
if (!error)
{
  res.send(transactionHash);
}
else
{
  res.send("Error");
}
})
})
app.get("/getInfo", function(req, res){
var fileHash = req.query.hash;
var details = proof.get.call(fileHash);
res.send(details);
})
```

Here, the /submit route is used to create and broadcast transactions. Once we get the transaction hash, we send it to the client. We are not doing anything to wait for the transaction to mine. The /getInfo route calls the get method of the contract on the node itself instead of creating a transaction. It simply sends back whatever response it got.

Now let's watch for the events from the contract and broadcast it to all the clients. Here is the code to do this:

```
proof.logFileAddedStatus().watch(function(error, result){
if(!error)
{
  if(result.args.status == true)
  {
    io.send(result);
  }
}
})
```

Here, we check whether the status is true, and if it's true, only then do we broadcast the event to all the connected socket.io clients.

Building the frontend

Let's begin with the HTML of the app. Put this code in the index.html file:

```
<!DOCTYPE html>
<html lang="en">
    <head>
        <meta name="viewport" content="width=device-width, initial-scale=1,
shrink-to-fit=no">
        <link rel="stylesheet" href="/css/bootstrap.min.css">
    </head>
    <body>
        <div class="container">
            <div class="row">
                <div class="col-md-6 offset-md-3 text-xs-center">
                    <br>
                    <h3>Upload any file</h3>
                    <br>
                    <div>
                        <div class="form-group">
                            <label class="custom-file text-xs-left">
                                <input type="file" id="file" class="custom-
file-input">
                                <span class="custom-file-control"></span>
```

```
                                </label>
                            </div>
                            <div class="form-group">
                                <label for="owner">Enter owner name</label>
                                <input type="text" class="form-control"
id="owner">
                            </div>
                            <button onclick="submit()" class="btn btn-
primary">Submit</button>
                            <button onclick="getInfo()" class="btn btn-
primary">Get Info</button>
                            <br><br>
                            <div class="alert alert-info" role="alert"
id="message">
                                You can either submit file's details or get
information about it.
                            </div>
                        </div>
                    </div>
                </div>
                <div class="row">
                    <div class="col-md-6 offset-md-3 text-xs-center">
                        <br>
                        <h3>Live Transactions Mined</h3>
                        <br>
                        <ol id="events_list">No Transaction Found</ol>
                    </div>
                </div>
            </div>
            <script type="text/javascript" src="/js/sha1.min.js"></script>
            <script type="text/javascript" src="/js/jquery.min.js"></script>
            <script type="text/javascript" src="/js/socket.io.min.js"></script>
            <script type="text/javascript" src="/js/main.js"></script>
    </body>
</html>
```

Here is how the code works:

1. At first, we display Bootstrap's file input field so that the user can select a file.
2. Then, we display a text field where the user can enter the owner's details.
3. Then, we have two buttons. The first one is to store the file hash and the owner's details in the contract, and the second button is to get information on the file from the contract. Clicking on the **Submit** button triggers the submit() method, whereas clicking on the **Get Info** button triggers the getInfo() method.

4. Then, we have an alert box to display messages.

5. Finally, we display an ordered list to display the transactions of the contract that gets mined while the user is on the page.

Now let's write the implementation for the `getInfo()` and `submit()` methods, establish a `socket.io` connect with the server, and listen for `socket.io` messages from the server. Here is the code to this. Place this code in the `main.js` file:

```javascript
function submit()
{
  var file = document.getElementById("file").files[0];
  if(file)
  {
  var owner = document.getElementById("owner").value;
  if(owner == "")
  {
  alert("Please enter owner name");
  }
else
{
 var reader = new FileReader();
 reader.onload = function (event) {
 var hash = sha1(event.target.result);
 $.get("/submit?hash=" + hash + "&owner=" + owner, function(data){
 if(data == "Error")
 {
   $("#message").text("An error occured.");
 }
 else
 {
   $("#message").html("Transaction hash: " + data);
 }
 });
 };
 reader.readAsArrayBuffer(file);
  }
}
  else
  {
    alert("Please select a file");
  }
}
function getInfo()
{
  var file = document.getElementById("file").files[0];
  if(file)
  {
```

```
      var reader = new FileReader();
      reader.onload = function (event) {
      var hash = sha1(event.target.result);
      $.get("/getInfo?hash=" + hash, function(data){
      if(data[0] == 0 && data[1] == "")
      {
        $("#message").html("File not found");
      }
      else
      {
        $("#message").html("Timestamp: " + data[0] + " Owner: " + data[1]);
      }
    });
  };
  reader.readAsArrayBuffer(file);
  }
  else
    {
      alert("Please select a file");
    }
  }
  var socket = io("http://localhost:8080");
  socket.on("connect", function () {
  socket.on("message", function (msg) {
  if($("#events_list").text() == "No Transaction Found")
  {
      $("#events_list").html("<li>Txn Hash: " + msg.transactionHash +
  "nOwner: " + msg.args.owner + "nFile Hash: " + msg.args.fileHash +
  "</li>");
  }
  else
  {
    $("#events_list").prepend("<li>Txn Hash: " + msg.transactionHash +
  "nOwner: " + msg.args.owner + "nFile Hash: " + msg.args.fileHash +
  "</li>");
  }
    });
  });
```

This is how the preceding code works:

1. At first, we defined the `submit()` method. In the `submit` method, we make sure that a file is selected and the text field is not empty. Then, we read the content of the file as an array buffer and pass the array buffer to the `sha1()` method exposed by sha1.js to get the hash of content inside the array buffer. Once we have the hash, we use jQuery to make an AJAX request to the `/submit` route and then we display the transaction hash in the alert box.

2. We define the `getInfo()` method next. It first makes sure that a file is selected. Then, it generates the hash like the one it generated earlier and makes a request to the `/getInfo` endpoint to get information about that file.

3. Finally, we establish a `socket.io` connection using the `io()` method exposed by the `socket.io` library. Then, we wait for the connect event to the trigger, which indicates that a connection has been established. After the connection is established, we listen for messages from the server and display the details about the transactions to the user.

 We aren't storing the file in the Ethereum blockchain because storing files is very expensive as it requires a lot of gas. For our case, we actually don't need to store files because nodes in the network will be able to see the file; therefore, if the users want to keep the file content secret, then they won't be able to. Our application's purpose is just to prove ownership of a file, not to store and serve the file like a cloud service.

Testing the client

Now run the `app.js` node to run the application server. Open you favorite browser and visit `http://localhost:8080/`. You will see this output in the browser:

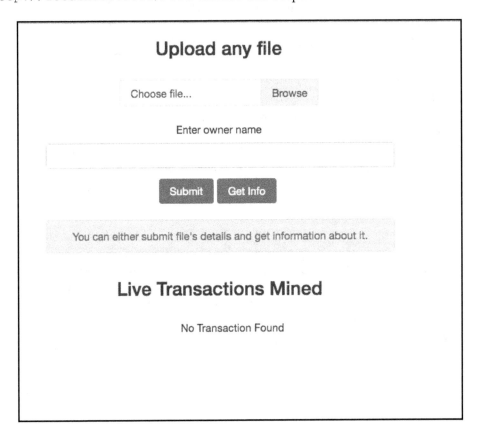

Now select a file and enter the owner's name and click on **Submit**. The screen will change to this:

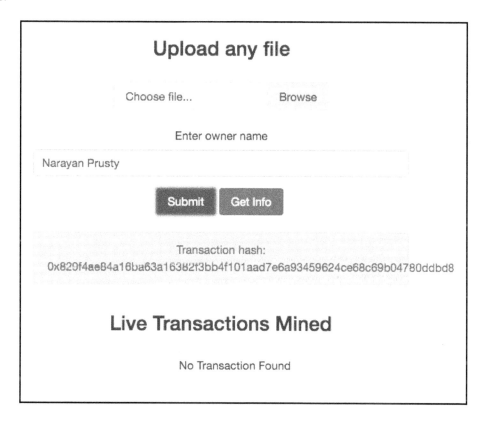

Here, you can see that the transaction hash is displayed. Now wait until the transaction is mined. Once the transaction is mined, you will be able to see the transaction in the live transactions list. Here is how the screen would look:

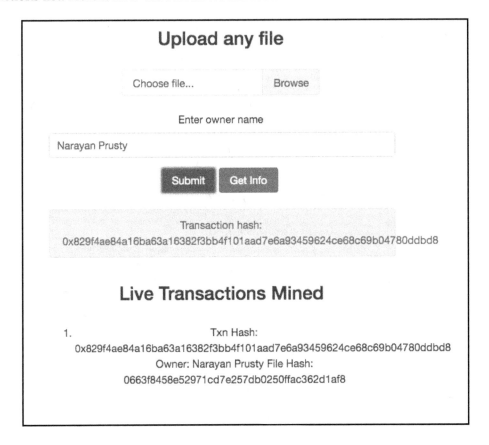

Now select the same file again and click on the **Get Info** button. You will see this output:

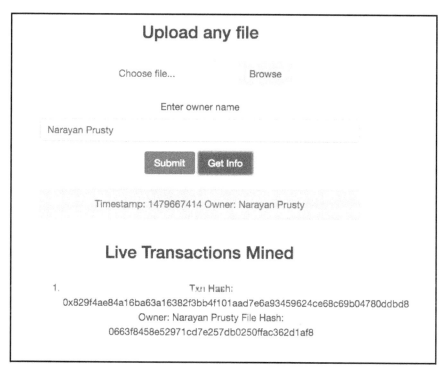

Here, you can see the timestamp and the owner's details. Now we have finished building the client for our first DApp.

Summary

In this chapter, we first learned about the fundamentals of web3.js with examples. We learned how to connect to a node, basic APIs, sending various kinds of transactions, and watching for events. Finally, we built a proper production use client for our ownership contract. Now you will be comfortable with writing smart contracts and building UI clients for them in order to ease their use.

In the `Chapter 9`, we will build a wallet service, where users can create and manage Ethereum Wallets easily, and that too is offline. We will specifically use the LightWallet library to achieve this.

8
Introducing Bitcoin

Bitcoin is the first application of blockchain technology. In this chapter, you will be introduced to Bitcoin technology in detail.

Bitcoin has started a revolution with the introduction of the very first fully decentralized digital currency, and the one that has proven to be extremely secure and stable from a network and protocol point of view. As a currency bitcoin is quite unstable and highly volatile, albeit valuable. We will explain this later in the chapter. This has also sparked a great interest in academic and industrial research and introduced many new research areas.

Since its introduction in 2008 by Satoshi Nakamoto, Bitcoin has gained massive popularity, and it is currently the most successful digital currency in the world with billions of dollars invested in it. The current market cap, at the time of writing, for this currency is $149, 984, 293, 122. Its popularity is also evident from the high number of users and investors, increasing bitcoin price, everyday news related to Bitcoin, and the number of start-ups and companies that are offering bitcoin-based online exchanges, and it's now also traded as *Bitcoin Futures* on **Chicago Mercantile Exchange** (**CME**).

 Interested readers can read more about *Bitcoin Futures* at http://www. cmegroup.com/trading/bitcoin-futures.html.

The name of the Bitcoin inventor *Satoshi Nakamoto* is believed to be a pseudonym, as the true identity of Bitcoin inventor is unknown. It is built on decades of research in the field of cryptography, digital cash, and distributed computing. In the following section, a brief history is presented in order to provide the background required to understand the foundations behind the invention of Bitcoin.

Digital currencies have always been an active area of research for many decades. Early proposals to create digital cash go as far back as the early 1980s. In 1982, David Chaum, a computer scientist, and cryptographer proposed a scheme that used blind signatures to build untraceable digital currency. This research was published in a research paper, *Blind Signatures for Untraceable Payments*.

 Interested readers can read the original research paper which David Chaum describes his invention of the cryptographic primitive of blind signatures at `http://www.hit.bme.hu/~buttyan/courses/BMEVIHIM219/2009/Chaum.Bl indSigForPayment.1982.PDF`.

In this scheme, a bank would issue digital money by signing a blind and random serial number presented to it by the user. The user could then use the digital token signed by the bank as currency. The limitation of this scheme was that the bank had to keep track of all used serial numbers. This was a central system by design and required to be trusted by the users.

Later on, in 1988, David Chaum and others proposed a refined version named e-cash that not only used a blinded signature, but also some private identification data to craft a message that was then sent to the bank.

 Original research paper for this is available at `http://citeseerx.ist.psu.edu/viewdoc/summary?doi=10.1.1.26.5759`.

This scheme allowed the detection of double spending but did not prevent it. If the same token was used at two different locations, then the identity of the double spender would be revealed. e-cash could only represent a fixed amount of money.

Adam Back, a cryptographer and now CEO of Blockstream, who is involved in blockchain development, introduced *hashcash* in 1997. It was originally proposed to thwart email spam. The idea behind hashcash was to solve a computational puzzle that was easy to verify but comparatively difficult to compute. The idea was that for a single user and a single email, the extra computational effort was negligible, but someone sending a large number of spam emails would be discouraged as the time and resources required to run the spam campaign would increase substantially.

In 1998, B-money was proposed by Wei Dai, a computer engineer who used to work for Microsoft, which introduced the idea of using **Proof of Work** (**PoW**) to create money. The term *Proof of Work* emerged and got popular later with Bitcoin, but in Wei Dai's B-money a scheme of creating money was introduced by providing a solution to a previously unsolved computational problem. It was referred in the paper as *solution to a previously unsolved computational problem*. This concept is similar to PoW, where money is created by broadcasting a solution to a previously unsolved computational problem.

The original paper is available at `http://www.weidai.com/bmoney.txt`.

A major weakness in the system was that an adversary with higher computational power could generate unsolicited money without allowing the network to adjust to an appropriate difficulty level. The system lacked details on the consensus mechanism between nodes and some security issues such as Sybil attacks were also not addressed. At the same time, Nick Szabo, a computer scientist introduced the concept of BitGold, which was also based on the PoW mechanism but had the same problems as B-money with the exception that the network difficulty level was adjustable. Tomas Sander and Amnon Ta-Shma from the **International Computer Science Institute** (**ICSI**), Berkley introduced an e-cash scheme under a research paper named *Auditable, Anonymous Electronic Cash* in 1999. This scheme, for the first time, used Merkle trees to represent coins and **Zero-Knowledge Proofs** (**ZKPs**) to prove the possession of coins.

The original research paper called *Auditable, Anonymous Electronic Cash* is available at:
`http://www.cs.tau.ac.il/~amnon/Papers/ST.crypto99.pdf`.

In this scheme, a central bank was required that kept a record of all used serial numbers. This scheme allowed users to be fully anonymous. This was a theoretical design which was not practical to implement due to inefficient proof mechanisms.

Reusable Proof of Work (RPoW) was introduced in 2004 by Hal Finney, a computer scientist, developer and first person to receive Bitcoin from Satoshi Nakamoto. It used the hashcash scheme by Adam Back as a proof of computational resources spent to create the money. This was also a central system that kept a central database to keep track of all used PoW tokens. This was an online system that used remote attestation made possible by a trusted computing platform (TPM hardware).

All the previously mentioned schemes are intelligently designed but were weak from one aspect or another. Specifically, all these schemes rely on a central server that is required to be trusted by the users.

Bitcoin

In 2008, Bitcoin was introduced through a paper called, *Bitcoin: A Peer-to-Peer Electronic Cash System*.

 This paper is available at `https://bitcoin.org/bitcoin.pdf`.

It was written by Satoshi Nakamoto, which is believed to be a pseudonym, as the true identity of Bitcoin inventor is unknown and subject of much speculation. The first key idea introduced in the paper was of a purely peer-to-peer electronic cash that does need an intermediary bank to transfer payments between peers.

Bitcoin is built on decades of cryptographic research such as the research in Merkle trees, hash functions, public key cryptography, and digital signatures. Moreover, ideas such as BitGold, B-money, hashcash, and cryptographic time stamping provided the foundations for bitcoin invention. All these technologies are cleverly combined in Bitcoin to create the world's first decentralized currency. The key issue that has been addressed in Bitcoin is an elegant solution to the Byzantine Generals' Problem along with a practical solution of the double-spend problem. Recall, that both of these concepts are explained in Chapter 1, *Blockchain 101*.

The value of bitcoin has increased significantly since 2011, and then since March 2017 as shown in the following graph:

Bitcoin price since March 2017

The regulation of Bitcoin is a controversial subject and as much as it is a libertarian's dream, law enforcement agencies, governments and banks are proposing various regulations to control it, such as BitLicense issued by New York's state department of financial services. This is a license issued to businesses that perform activities related to virtual currencies. Due to high cost and very strict regulatory requirements pertaining to BitLicense many companies have withdrawn their services from New York.

For people with a libertarian ideology, Bitcoin is a platform which can be used instead of banks for business but they think that because of regulations, Bitcoin may become another institution which is not trusted. The original idea behind Bitcoin was to develop an e-cash system which requires no trusted third party and users can be anonymous. If regulations require **Know Your Customer** (**KYC**) checks and detailed information about business transactions to facilitate regulatory process then it might be too much information to share and as a result Bitcoin may not be attractive anymore to some.

There are now many initiatives being taken to regulate Bitcoin, cryptocurrencies and related activities such as ICOs. **Securities and Exchange Commission** (**SEC**) has recently announced that digital tokens, coins and relevant activities such as **Initial Coin Offerings** (**ICOs**) fall under the category of securities. This means that any digital currency trading platforms will need to be registered with SEC and will have all relevant securities laws and regulations applicable to them. This impacted the Bitcoin price directly and it fell almost 10% on the day this announcement was made.

Interested readers can read more about the regulation of Bitcoin and other relevant activities at `https://www.coindesk.com/category/regulation/`.

The growth of Bitcoin is also due to so-called **network effect**. Also called demand-side economies of scale, it is a concept that basically means more users who use the network, the more valuable it becomes. Over time, an exponential increase has been seen in the Bitcoin network growth. This increase in the number of users is largely financial gain driven. Also, the scarcity of Bitcoin and built-in inflation control mechanism gives it value as there are only 21 million bitcoins that can ever be mined and in addition the miner reward halves every four years. Even though the price of bitcoin fluctuates a lot, it has increased significantly over the last few years. Currently (at the time of writing this), bitcoin price is 9,250 U.S Dollars (USD).

Bitcoin definition

Bitcoin can be defined in various ways; it's a protocol, a digital currency, and a platform. It is a combination of peer-to-peer network, protocols, software that facilitate the creation and usage of the digital currency named bitcoin. Nodes in this peer-to-peer network talk to each other using the Bitcoin protocol.

Note that Bitcoin with a capital B is used to refer to the Bitcoin protocol, whereas bitcoin with a lowercase b is used to refer to bitcoin, the currency.

Decentralization of currency was made possible for the first time with the invention of bitcoin. Moreover, the double spending problem was solved in an elegant and ingenious way in bitcoin. Double spending problem arises when, for example, a user sends coins to two different users at the same time and they are verified independently as valid transactions. The double spending problem is resolved in Bitcoin by using a distributed ledger (blockchain) where every transaction is recorded permanently and by implementing transaction validation and confirmation mechanism. This process will be explained later in the chapter where we introduce the concept of *mining*.

Bitcoin – a bird's-eye view

In this section, we will see how the Bitcoin network looks from a user's point of view. How a transaction is made, how it propagates from a user to the network, how transactions are verified, and finally accumulated in blocks. We will look at what are the various actors and components of the Bitcoin network. Finally, some discussion on how all actors and components interact with each other to form the Bitcoin network will also be provided.

First, let us see that what the main components of a Bitcoin network are. Bitcoin is composed of the elements listed here. We will further expand on these elements as we progress through the chapter.

- Digital keys
- Addresses
- Transactions
- Blockchain
- Miners
- The Bitcoin network
- Wallets (client software)

Now, we will see that how a user will use the Bitcoin network. The following example will help you understand that how the Bitcoin network looks like from an end user's perspective. We will see that what actors and components are involved in a Bitcoin transaction. One of the most common transactions is sending money to someone else, therefore in the following example we will see that how a payment can be sent from one user to another on the Bitcoin network.

Sending a payment to someone

This example will demonstrate that how money can be sent using Bitcoin network from one user to another. There are several steps that are involved in this process. As an example, we are using Blockchain wallet for mobile devices.

The steps are described here:

1. First, either the payment is requested from a user by sending his Bitcoin address to the sender via email or some other means such as SMS, chat applications or in fact any appropriate communication mechanism. The sender can also initiate a transfer to send money to another user. In both cases, the address of beneficiary is required. As an example, the Blockchain wallet is shown here where a payment request is created:

bitcoin payment request (using Blockchain wallet)

2. The sender either enters the receiver's address or scans the QR code that has the Bitcoin address, amount and optional description encoded in it. The wallet application recognizes this QR code and decodes it into something like `Please send <Amount> BTC to the Bitcoin address <receiver's Bitcoin address>`.

3. This will look like as shown here with values: `Please send 0.00033324 BTC to the Bitcoin address 1JzouJCVmMQBmTcd8K4Y5BP36gEFNn1ZJ3`.

4. This is also shown in the screenshot presented here:

Please send 0.00033324 BTC to the Bitcoin address 1JzouJCVmMQBmTcd8K4Y5BP36g EFNn1ZJ3.

bitcoin://
1JzouJCVmMQBmTcd8K4Y5BP36g
EFNn1ZJ3?amount=0.00033324

Bitcoin payment QR code

 The QR code shown in the preceding screenshot is decoded to `bitcoin://1JzouJCVmMQBmTcd8K4Y5BP36gEFNn1ZJ3?amount=0.000 33324` which can be opened as a URL in Bitcoin wallet.

5. In the wallet application of the sender, this transaction is constructed by following some rules and broadcasted to the Bitcoin network. This transaction is digitally signed using the private key of the sender before broadcasting it. How the transaction is created, digitally signed, broadcasted, validated and added to the block will become clear in the following sections. From a user's point of view, once the QR code is decoded the transaction will appear similar to what is shown in the following screenshot:

Send BTC using Blockchain wallet

Note that in the preceding screenshot there are a number of fields such as **From, To, BTC**, and **Fee**. While other fields are self-explanatory, it's worth noting that **Fee** is calculated based on the size of the transaction and a fee rate is a value that depends on the volume of the transaction in the network. This is represented in Satoshis/byte. Fee in Bitcoin network ensures that your transaction will be included by miners in the block.

Recently the Bitcoin fees were so high that even for smaller transactions a high amount of fee was charged. This was due to the fact that miners are free to choose which transactions they pick to verify and add in a block, and they select the ones with higher fees. The high number of users creating thousands of transactions also played a role in causing this situation of high fees because transactions were competing with each other to be picked up first and miners picked up the ones with highest fees. This fee is also usually estimated and calculated by the Bitcoin wallet software automatically before sending the transactions. The higher the transaction fee the more chances are that your transaction will be picked up at priority and included in the block. This task is performed by the miners. Mining and miners is a concept that we will look at a bit later in this chapter in the context of Bitcoin mining.

Once the transaction is sent it will appear as shown here in the Blockchain wallet software:

Transaction sent

6. At this stage, the transaction has been constructed, signed and sent out to the Bitcoin network. This transaction will be picked up by miners to be verified and included in the block. Also note that in the preceding screenshot, confirmation is pending for this transaction. These confirmations will start to appear as soon as the transaction is verified, included in the block, and mined. Also, the appropriate fee will be deducted from the original value to be transferred and will be paid to the miner who has included it in the block for mining.

This flow is shown in the following diagram, where a payment of 0.001267 BTC (approximately 11 USD) is originated from the sender's address and been paid to receiver's address (starting with 1Jz). The fee of 0.00010622 (approximately 95 cents) is also deducted from the transaction as mining fee.

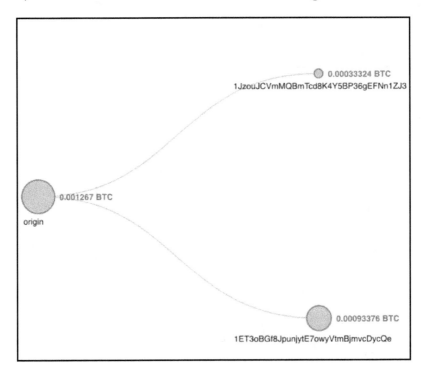

Transaction flow visualization (Blockchain.info)

The preceding screenshot visually shows how the transaction flowed on the network from origin (sender) to receivers on the right-hand side.

A summary view of various attributes of the transaction is shown here:

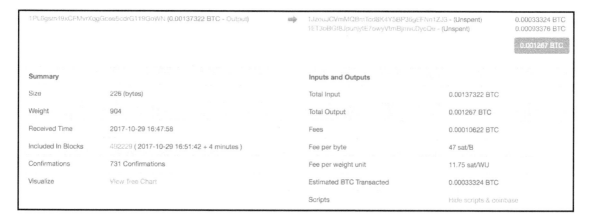

Snapshot of the transaction taken from Blockchain.info

Looking at the preceding screenshot there are a number of fields that contain various values. Important fields are listed here with their purpose and explanation:

- **Size**: This is the size of the transaction in bytes.
- **Weight**: This is the new metric given for block and transaction size since the introduction of **Segregated Witness (SegWit)** version of Bitcoin.
- **Received Time**: This is the time when the transaction is received.
- **Included In Blocks**: This shows the block number on the blockchain in which the transaction is included.
- **Confirmations**: This is the number of confirmations by miners for this transaction.
- **Total Input**: This is the number of total inputs in the transaction.
- **Total Output**: This is the number of total outputs in the transaction.
- **Fees**: This is the total fees charged.
- **Fee per byte**: This field represents the total fee divided by the number of bytes in a transaction. For example 10 Satoshis per byte.
- **Fee per weight unit**: For legacy transaction it is calculated using *total number of bytes * 4*. For SegWit transactions it is calculated by combining SegWit marker, flag, and witness field as one weight unit and each byte of other fields as four weight units.

Transaction ID of this transaction on the Bitcoin network is
`d28ca5a59b2239864eac1c96d3fd1c23b747f0ded8f5af0161bae8a616b56a1d` and can
be further explored using the `https://blockchain.info/tx/`
`d28ca5a59b2239864eac1c96d3fd1c23b747f0ded8f5af0161bae8a616b56a1d` link via services
provided by `https://blockchain.info/`. This transaction ID is available in the wallet
software after transaction is sent to the network. From there it can be further explored using
one of many Bitcoin blockchain explorers available online. We are using `https://`
`blockchain.info/` as an example.

Bitcoin transactions are serialized for transmission over the network and encoded in
hexadecimal format. As an example, the preceding transaction, is also shown here. We will
see later in the *Transactions* section that how this hexadecimal encoded transaction can be
decoded and what fields make up a transaction.

```
01000000017d3876b14a7ac16d8d550abc78345b6571134ff173918a096ef90ff0430e12408
b0000006b483045022100de6fd8120d9f142a82d5da9389e271caa3a757b01757c8e4fa7afb
f92e74257c02202a78d4fbd52ae9f3a0083760d76f84643cf8ab80f5ef971e3f98ccba2c717
58d012102c16942555f5e633645895c9affcb994ea7910097b7734a6c2d25468622f25e12ff
ffffff022c820000000000001976a914c568ffeb46c6a9362e44a5a49deaa6eab05a619a88a
cc06c0100000000001976a9149386c8c880488e80a6ce8f186f788f3585f74aee88ac000000
00
```

In summary, the payment transaction in the Bitcoin network can be divided into the
following steps:

1. Transaction starts with a sender signing the transaction with their private key
2. Transaction is serialized so that it can be transmitted over the network
3. Transaction is broadcasted to the network
4. Miners listening for the transactions picks up the transaction
5. Transaction are verified for their validity by the miners
6. Transaction are added to the candidate/proposed block for mining
7. Once mined, the result is broadcasted to all nodes on the Bitcoin network

Mining, transaction and other relevant concepts will become clearer in the following
sections in the chapter. Now in the next section various denominations of bitcoin are
presented.

The bitcoin currency, being digital has various denominations which are shown in the following table. A sender or receiver can request any amount. The smallest bitcoin denomination is the Satoshi. The bitcoin currency units are described as follows:

DENOMINATION ⇕	ABBREVIATION ⇕	FAMILIAR NAME ⇕	VALUE IN BTC ⇕
Satoshi	SAT	Satoshi	0.00000001 BTC
Microbit	µBTC (uBTC)	Microbitcoin or Bit	0.000001 BTC
Millibit	mBTC	Millibitcoin	0.001 BTC
Centibit	cBTC	Centibitcoin	0.01 BTC
Decibit	dBTC	Decibitcoin	0.1 BTC
Bitcoin	BTC	Bitcoin	1 BTC
DecaBit	daBTC	Decabitcoin	10 BTC
Hectobit	hBTC	Hectobitcoin	100 BTC
Kilobit	kBTC	Kilobitcoin	1000 BTC
Megabit	MBTC	Megabitcoin	1000000 BTC

bitcoin denominations

Now you will be introduced to the building blocks of Bitcoin one by one. First, we will look at the keys and addresses which are used to represent the ownership and transfer of value on the Bitcoin network.

Digital keys and addresses

On the Bitcoin network, possession of bitcoins and transfer of value via transactions is reliant upon private keys, public keys, and addresses. In `Chapter 6`, *Public Key Cryptography*, we have already covered these concepts, and here we will see that how private and public keys are used in the Bitcoin network.

Elliptic Curve Cryptography (ECC) is used to generate public and private key pairs in the Bitcoin network.

Private keys in Bitcoin

Private keys are required to be kept safe and normally resides only on the owner's side. Private keys are used to digitally sign the transactions proving the ownership of the bitcoins.

Private keys are fundamentally 256-bit numbers randomly chosen in the range specified by the `secp256k1` ECDSA curve recommendation. Any randomly chosen 256-bit number from `0x1` to `0xFFFF FFFF FFFF FFFF FFFF FFFF FFFF FFFE BAAE DCE6 AF48 A03B BFD2 5E8C D036 4140` is a valid private key.

Private keys are usually encoded using **Wallet Import Format** (**WIF**) in order to make them easier to copy and use. It is a way to represent the full size private key in a different format. WIF can be converted into a private key and vice versa. The steps are described here.

The following is an example of a private key:

`A3ED7EC8A03667180D01FB4251A546C2B9F2FE33507C68B7D9D4E1FA5714195201`

When it is converted into WIF format it looks like this:

`L2iN7umV7kbr6LuCmgM27rBnptGbDVc8g4ZBm6EbgTPQXnj1RCZP`

Interested readers can do some experimentation using the tool available at the following website:
`http://gobittest.appspot.com/PrivateKey`

Also, **mini private key format** is sometimes used to create the private key with a maximum of up to 30 characters in order to allow storage where physical space is limited, for example, etching on physical coins or encoding in damage-resistant QR codes. The QR code becomes more damage resistant because more dots can be used for error correction and less for encoding the private key. The private key encoded using mini private key format is also sometimes called **minikey**. The first character of mini private key is always uppercase letter S. A mini private key can be converted into a normal size private key but an existing normal size private key cannot be converted into a mini private key. This format was used in Casascius physical bitcoins.

Interested readers can find more information here
`https://en.bitcoin.it/wiki/Casascius_physical_bitcoins.`

A Casascius physical bitcoin's security hologram paper with minikey and QR code

The Bitcoin core client also allows the encryption of the wallet that contains the private keys.

Public keys in Bitcoin

Public keys exist on the blockchain and all network participants can see it. Public keys are derived from private keys due to their special mathematical relationship with the private keys. Once a transaction signed with the private key is broadcasted on the Bitcoin network, public keys are used by the nodes to verify that the transaction has indeed been signed with the corresponding private key. This process of verification proves the ownership of the bitcoin.

Bitcoin uses ECC based on the `secp256k1` standard. More specifically it makes use of ECDSA to ensure that funds remain secure and can only be spent by the legitimate owner. If you need to refresh the relevant cryptography concepts, you can refer to Chapter 6, *Public Key Cryptography* where ECC was explained. A public key is 256-bits in length. Public keys can be represented in an uncompressed or compressed format. Public keys are fundamentally *x* and *y* coordinates on an elliptic curve. In an uncompressed format public keys are presented with a prefix of `0x4` in a hexadecimal format. The *x* and *y* coordinates are both 32-bit in length. In total, the compressed public key is 33-bytes long as compared to 65-bytes in the uncompressed format. The compressed version of public keys includes only the *x* part, since the *y* part can be derived from it.

The reason why the compressed version of public keys works is that if the ECC graph is visualized, it reveals that the y coordinate can be either below the x axis or above the x axis and as the curve is symmetric, only the location in the prime field is required to be stored. If y is even then it is above the x axis and if it is odd then it is below the x axis. This means that instead of storing both x and y as the public key only x can be stored with the information that if y is even or odd.

Initially, Bitcoin client used uncompressed keys, but starting from Bitcoin core client 0.6, compressed keys are used as standard. This resulted in almost 50% reduction of space used to store public keys in the blockchain.

Keys are identified by various prefixes, described as follows:

- Uncompressed public keys use `0x04` as the prefix
- Compressed public key starts with `0x03` if the y 32-bit part of the public key is odd
- Compressed public key starts with `0x02` if the y 32-bit part of the public key is even

Addresses in Bitcoin

A bitcoin address is created by taking the corresponding public key of a private key and hashing it twice, first with the SHA-256 algorithm and then with RIPEMD-160. The resultant 160-bit hash is then prefixed with a version number and finally encoded with a Base58Check encoding scheme. The bitcoin addresses are 26-35 characters long and begin with digit `1` or `3`.

A typical bitcoin address looks like a string shown here:

`1ANAguGG8bikEv2fYsTBnRUmx7QUcK58wt`

This is also commonly encoded in a QR code for easy distribution. The QR code of the preceding bitcoin address is shown in the following screenshot:

QR code of a bitcoin address 1ANAguGG8bikEv2fYsTBnRUmx7QUcK58wt

Currently, there are two types of addresses, the commonly used P2PKH and another P2SH type, starting with number 1 and 3, respectively. In the early days, Bitcoin used direct Pay to Pubkey, which is now superseded by P2PKH. These types will be explained later in the chapter. However, direct Pay to Pubkey is still used in Bitcoin for coinbase addresses. Addresses should not be used more than once; otherwise, privacy and security issues can arise. Avoiding address reuse circumvents anonymity issues to an extent, Bitcoin has some other security issues as well, such as transaction malleability, Sybil attacks, race attacks and selfish mining which require different approaches to resolve.

Transaction malleability has been resolved with so-called *Segregated Witness* soft fork upgrade of the Bitcoin protocol. This concept will be explained later in the chapter.

From bitaddress.org, private key and bitcoin address in a paper wallet

Base58Check encoding

Bitcoin addresses are encoded using the Base58Check encoding. This encoding is used to limit the confusion between various characters, such as 0OIl as they can look the same in different fonts. The encoding basically takes the binary byte arrays and converts them into human-readable strings. This string is composed by utilizing a set of 58 alphanumeric symbols. More explanation and logic can be found in the `base58.h` source file (`https://github.com/bitcoin/bitcoin/blob/master/src/base58.h`) in the bitcoin source code:

```
/**
 * Why base-58 instead of standard base-64 encoding?
 * - Don't want 0OIl characters that look the same in some fonts and
 * could be used to create visually identical looking data.
 * - A string with non-alphanumeric characters is not as easily accepted as
 input.
 * - E-mail usually won't line-break if there's no punctuation to break at.
 * - Double-clicking selects the whole string as one word if it's all
 alphanumeric.
 */
```

Vanity addresses

As bitcoin addresses are based on base-58 encoding, it is possible to generate addresses that contain human-readable messages. An example is shown as follows:

1BasHiry2VoCQCdX6X
64oxvKRuf7fW6qGr

Vanity public address encoded in QR

Vanity addresses are generated using a purely brute-force method. An example of a paper wallet with vanity address is shown in the following screenshot:

Vanity address generated from https://bitcoinvanitygen.com/

In the preceding screenshot, on the right-hand bottom corner the public vanity address with QR code is displayed. The paper wallets can be stored physically as an alternative to electronic storage of private keys.

Multisignature addresses

As the name implies, these addresses require multiple private keys. In practical terms, it means that in order to release the coins a certain set of signatures is required. This is also known as **M-of-N MultiSig**. Here M represents threshold or the minimum number of signatures required from N number of keys to release the bitcoins.

Transactions

Transactions are at the core of the bitcoin ecosystem. Transactions can be as simple as just sending some bitcoins to a bitcoin address, or it can be quite complex depending on the requirements. Each transaction is composed of at least one input and output. Inputs can be thought of as coins being spent that have been created in a previous transaction and outputs as coins being created. If a transaction is minting new coins, then there is no input and therefore no signature is needed. If a transaction is to send coins to some other user (a bitcoin address), then it needs to be signed by the sender with their private key and a reference is also required to the previous transaction in order to show the origin of the coins. Coins are, in fact, unspent transaction outputs represented in Satoshis.

Transactions are not encrypted and are publicly visible in the blockchain. Blocks are made up of transactions and these can be viewed using any online blockchain explorer.

The transaction life cycle

The following steps describe the transaction life cycle:

1. A user/sender sends a transaction using wallet software or some other interface.
2. The wallet software signs the transaction using the sender's private key.
3. The transaction is broadcasted to the Bitcoin network using a flooding algorithm.
4. Mining nodes (miners) who are listening for the transactions verify and include this transaction in the next block to be mined. Just before the transaction are placed in the block they are placed in a special memory buffer called **transaction pool**. The purpose of the transaction pool is explained in the next section.
5. Mining starts, which is a process by which the blockchain is secured and new coins are generated as a reward for the miners who spend appropriate computational resources. This concept is explained in more detail later in this chapter.
6. Once a miner solves the PoW problem it broadcasts the newly mined block to the network. PoW is explained in detail later in this chapter.
7. The nodes verify the block and propagate the block further, and confirmations start to generate.

8. Finally, the confirmations start to appear in the receiver's wallet and after approximately three confirmations, the transaction is considered finalized and confirmed. However, three to six is just a recommended number; the transaction can be considered final even after the first confirmation. The key idea behind waiting for six confirmations is that the probability of double spending is virtually eliminated after three confirmations.

Transaction fee

Transaction fees are charged by the miners. The fee charged is dependent upon the size and weight of the transaction. Transaction fees are calculated by subtracting the sum of the inputs and the sum of the outputs.

A simple formula can be used:

$$fee = sum(inputs) - sum(outputs)$$

The fees are used as an incentive for miners to encourage them to include a user transaction in the block the miners are creating. All transactions end up in the memory pool, from where miners pick up transactions based on their priority to include them in the proposed block. The calculation of priority is introduced later in this chapter; however, from a transaction fee point of view, a transaction with a higher fee will be picked up sooner by the miners.

There are different rules based on which fee is calculated for various types of actions, such as sending transactions, inclusion in blocks, and relaying by nodes. Fees are not fixed by the Bitcoin protocol and are not mandatory; even a transaction with no fee will be processed in due course but may take a very long time. This is however no longer practical due to the high volume of transactions and competing investors on the Bitcoin network, therefore it is advisable to provide a fee always. The time for transaction confirmation usually ranges from 10 minutes to over 12 hours in some cases. Transaction time is dependent on transaction fees and network activity. If the network is very busy then naturally transactions will take longer to process and if you pay a higher fee then your transaction is more likely to be picked by miners first due to additional incentive of the higher fee.

Transaction pools

Also known as memory pools, these pools are basically created in local memory (computer RAM) by nodes in order to maintain a temporary list of transactions that are not yet confirmed in a block. Transactions are included in a block after passing verification and based on their priority.

The transaction data structure

A transaction at a high level contains metadata, inputs, and outputs. Transactions are combined to create a block.

The transaction data structure is shown in the following table:

Field	Size	Description
Version number	4 bytes	Used to specify rules to be used by the miners and nodes for transaction processing.
Input counter	1-9 bytes	The number (positive integer) of inputs included in the transaction.
List of inputs	Variable	Each input is composed of several fields, including `Previous Tx hash`, `Previous Txout-index`, `Txin-script length`, `Txin-script`, and optional sequence number. The first transaction in a block is also called a coinbase transaction. It specifies one or more transaction inputs.
Output counter	1-9 bytes	A positive integer representing the number of outputs.
List of outputs	Variable	Outputs included in the transaction.
Lock time	4 bytes	This field defines the earliest time when a transaction becomes valid. It is either a Unix timestamp or block height.

A sample transaction is shown as follows. This is the decoded transaction from the first example of a payment transaction provided at the start of this chapter.

```
{
    "lock_time":0,
    "size":226,
    "inputs":[
        {
            "prev_out":{
                "index":139,
        "hash":"40120e43f00ff96e098a9173f14f1371655b3478bc0a558d6dc17a4ab176387d"
```

```
        },
    "script":"483045022100de6fd8120d9f142a82d5da9389e271caa3a757b01757c8e4fa7af
bf92e74257c02202a78d4fbd52ae9f3a0083760d76f84643cf8ab80f5ef971e3f98ccba2c71
758d012102c16942555f5e633645895c9affcb994ea7910097b7734a6c2d25468622f25e12"
        }
    ],
    "version":1,
    "vin_sz":1,
    "hash":"d28ca5a59b2239864eac1c96d3fd1c23b747f0ded8f5af0161bae8a616b56a1d",
    "vout_sz":2,
    "out":[
        {
            "script_string":"OP_DUP OP_HASH160
c568ffeb46c6a9362e44a5a49deaa6eab05a619a OP_EQUALVERIFY OP_CHECKSIG",
            "address":"1JzouJCVmMQBmTcd8K4Y5BP36gEFNn1ZJ3",
            "value":33324,
            "script":"76a914c568ffeb46c6a9362e44a5a49deaa6eab05a619a88ac"
        },
        {
            "script_string":"OP_DUP OP_HASH160
9386c8c880488e80a6ce8f186f788f3585f74aee OP_EQUALVERIFY OP_CHECKSIG",
            "address":"1ET3oBGf8JpunjytE7owyVtmBjmvcDycQe",
            "value":93376,
            "script":"76a9149386c8c880488e80a6ce8f186f788f3585f74aee88ac"
        }
    ]
}
```

As shown in the preceding code, there are a number of structures that make up the transaction. All these elements are described in the following subsections.

Metadata

This part of the transaction contains some values such as the size of the transaction, the number of inputs and outputs, the hash of the transaction, and a lock_time field. Every transaction has a prefix specifying the version number. These fields are shown in the preceding example: lock_time, size, and version.

Inputs

Generally, each input spends a previous output. Each output is considered as **Unspent Transaction Output** (**UTXO**) until an input consumes it. UTXO is an unspent transaction output that can be spent as an input to a new transaction.

Transaction input data structure is shown in the following table:

Field	Size	Description
Transaction hash	32 bytes	This is the hash of the previous transaction with UTXO.
Output index	4 bytes	This is the previous transactions output index, that is, UTXO to be spent.
Script length	1-9 bytes	This is the size of the unlocking script.
Unlocking script	Variable	Input script (`ScriptSig`) which satisfies the requirements of the locking script.
Sequence number	4 bytes	Usually disabled or contains lock time. Disabled is represented by `'0xFFFFFFFF'`.

In the preceding example the inputs are defined under `"inputs"` : [section.

Outputs

Outputs have three fields, and they contain instructions for sending bitcoins. The first field contains the amount of Satoshis whereas the second field contains the size of the locking script. Finally, the third field contains a locking script that holds the conditions that need to be met in order for the output to be spent. More information on transaction spending using locking and unlocking scripts and producing outputs is discussed later in this section.

Transaction output data structure is shown here:

Field	Size	Description
Value	8 bytes	Total number in positive integers of Satoshis to be transferred
Script size	1-9 bytes	Size of the locking script
Locking script	Variable	Output script (`ScriptPubKey`)

In the preceding example two outputs are shown under `"OUT"` : [section.

Verification

Verification is performed using Bitcoin's scripting language which is described in the next section in detail.

The script language

Bitcoin uses a simple stack-based language called **script** to describe how bitcoins can be spent and transferred. It is not Turing complete and has no loops to avoid any undesirable effects of long-running/hung scripts on the Bitcoin network. This scripting language is based on a Forth programming language like syntax and uses a reverse polish notation in which every operand is followed by its operators. It is evaluated from the left to the right using a **Last In, First Out** (**LIFO**) stack.

Scripts use various opcodes or instructions to define their operation. Opcodes are also known as words, commands, or functions. Earlier versions of the Bitcoin node had a few opcodes that are no longer used due to bugs discovered in their design.

The various categories of the scripting opcodes are constants, flow control, stack, bitwise logic, splice, arithmetic, cryptography, and lock time.

A transaction script is evaluated by combining ScriptSig and ScriptPubKey. ScriptSig is the unlocking script, whereas ScriptPubKey is the locking script. This is how a transaction to be spent is evaluated:

1. First, it is unlocked and then it is spent
2. ScriptSig is provided by the user who wishes to unlock the transaction
3. ScriptPubkey is part of the transaction output and specifies the conditions that need to be fulfilled in order to spend the output
4. In other words, outputs are locked by ScriptPubKey that contains the conditions, when met will unlock the output, and coins can then be redeemed

Commonly used opcodes

All opcodes are declared in the script.h file in the Bitcoin reference client source code.

This can be accessed from the link at
https://github.com/bitcoin/bitcoin/blob/master/src/script/script
.h under the following comment:
/** Script opcodes */

A description of the most commonly used opcodes is listed here. This table is taken from the Bitcoin developer's guide:

Opcode	Description
OP_CHECKSIG	This takes a public key and signature and validates the signature of the hash of the transaction. If it matches, then TRUE is pushed onto the stack; otherwise, FALSE is pushed.
OP_EQUAL	This returns 1 if the inputs are exactly equal; otherwise, 0 is returned.
OP_DUP	This duplicates the top item in the stack.
OP_HASH160	The input is hashed twice, first with SHA-256 and then with RIPEMD-160.
OP_VERIFY	This marks the transaction as invalid if the top stack value is not true.
OP_EQUALVERIFY	This is the same as OP_EQUAL, but it runs OP_VERIFY afterwards.
OP_CHECKMULTISIG	This takes the first signature and compares it against each public key until a match is found and repeats this process until all signatures are checked. If all signatures turn out to be valid, then a value of 1 is returned as a result; otherwise, 0 is returned.

Types of transactions

There are various scripts available in Bitcoin to handle the value transfer from the source to the destination. These scripts range from very simple to quite complex depending upon the requirements of the transaction. Standard transaction types are discussed here. Standard transactions are evaluated using IsStandard() and IsStandardTx() tests and only standard transactions that pass the test are generally allowed to be mined or broadcasted on the Bitcoin network. However, nonstandard transactions are valid and allowed on the network.

The following are the standard transaction types:

- **Pay to Public Key Hash** (**P2PKH**): P2PKH is the most commonly used transaction type and is used to send transactions to the bitcoin addresses. The format of the transaction is shown as follows:

```
    ScriptPubKey: OP_DUP OP_HASH160 <pubKeyHash> OP_EQUALVERIFY
OP_CHECKSIG
    ScriptSig: <sig> <pubKey>
```

  The `ScriptPubKey` and `ScriptSig` parameters are concatenated together and executed. An example will follow shortly in this section, where this is explained in more detail.

- **Pay to Script Hash** (**P2SH**): P2SH is used in order to send transactions to a script hash (that is, the addresses starting with 3) and was standardized in BIP16. In addition to passing the script, the redeem script is also evaluated and must be valid. The template is shown as follows:

```
    ScriptPubKey: OP_HASH160 <redeemScriptHash> OP_EQUAL
    ScriptSig: [<sig>...<sign>] <redeemScript>
```

- **MultiSig** (**Pay to MultiSig**): M-of-N MultiSig transaction script is a complex type of script where it is possible to construct a script that required multiple signatures to be valid in order to redeem a transaction. Various complex transactions such as escrow and deposits can be built using this script. The template is shown here:

```
    ScriptPubKey: <m> <pubKey> [<pubKey> . . . ] <n> OP_CHECKMULTISIG
    ScriptSig: 0 [<sig > . . . <sign>]
```

  Raw multisig is obsolete, and multisig is usually part of the P2SH redeem script, mentioned in the previous bullet point.

- **Pay to Pubkey**: This script is a very simple script that is commonly used in coinbase transactions. It is now obsolete and was used in an old version of bitcoin. The public key is stored within the script in this case, and the unlocking script is required to sign the transaction with the private key.

  The template is shown as follows:

```
    <PubKey> OP_CHECKSIG
```

- **Null data/OP_RETURN**: This script is used to store arbitrary data on the blockchain for a fee. The limit of the message is 40 bytes. The output of this script is unredeemable because OP_RETURN will fail the validation in any case. ScriptSig is not required in this case.

  The template is very simple and is shown as follows:

  ```
  OP_RETURN <data>
  ```

A P2PKH script execution is shown in the following diagram:

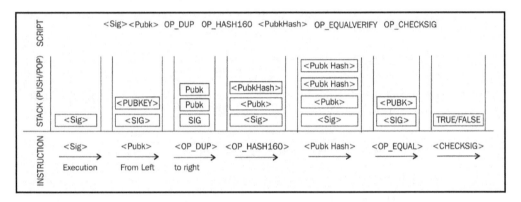

P2PKH script execution

All transactions are eventually encoded into the hexadecimal format before transmitting over the Bitcoin network. A sample transaction is shown here in hexadecimal format that is retrieved using bitcoin-cli on the Bitcoin node running on mainnet:

```
$ bitcoin-cli getrawtransaction
"d28ca5a59b2239864eac1c96d3fd1c23b747f0ded8f5af0161bae8a616b56a1d"
{
  "result":
"01000000017d3876b14a7ac16d8d550abc78345b6571134ff173918a096ef90ff0430e1240
8b0000006b483045022100de6fd8120d9f142a82d5da9389e271caa3a757b01757c8e4fa7af
bf92e74257c02202a78d4fbd52ae9f3a0083760d76f84643cf8ab80f5ef971e3f98ccba2c71
758d012102c16942555f5e633645895c9affcb994ea7910097b7734a6c2d25468622f25e12f
ffffffff022c820000000000001976a914c568ffeb46c6a9362e44a5a49deaa6eab05a619a88
acc06c0100000000001976a9149386c8c880488e80a6ce8f186f788f3585f74aee88ac00000
000",
  "error": null,
  "id": null
}
```

Note that this is the same transaction that was presented as an example at the start of this chapter.

Coinbase transactions

A coinbase transaction or generation transaction is always created by a miner and is the first transaction in a block. It is used to create new coins. It includes a special field, also called `coinbase`, which acts as an input to the coinbase transaction. This transaction also allows up to 100 bytes of arbitrary data that can be used to store arbitrary data. In the genesis block, this transaction included the most famous comment taken from *The Times* newspaper:

> *"The Times 03/Jan/2009 Chancellor on brink of second bailout for banks."*

This message is a proof that the genesis block was not mined earlier than January 3, 2009. This is because first Bitcoin block (genesis block) was created on January 3, 2009 and this news excerpt was taken from that day's newspaper.

A coinbase transaction input has the same number of fields as usual transaction input, but the structure contains coinbase data size and coinbase data fields instead of unlocking script size and unlocking script fields. Also, it does not have a reference pointer to the previous transaction. This structure is shown in the following table:

Field	Size	Description
Transaction hash	32 bytes	Set to all zeroes as no hash reference is used
Output index	4 bytes	Set to `0xFFFFFFFF`
Coinbase data length	1-9 bytes	2 bytes-100 bytes
Data	Variable	Any data
Sequence number	4 bytes	Set to `0xFFFFFFFF`

Contracts

As defined in the Bitcoin core developer guide, contracts are basically transactions that use the Bitcoin system to enforce a financial agreement. This is a simple definition but has far-reaching consequences as it allows users to design complex contracts that can be used in many real world scenarios. Contracts allow the development of a completely decentralized, independent, and reduced risk platform.

Various contracts, such as escrow, arbitration, and micropayment channels, can be built using the Bitcoin scripting language. The current implementation of a script is very limited, but various types of contracts are still possible to develop. For example, the release of funds only if multiple parties sign the transaction or perhaps the release of funds only after a certain time has elapsed. Both of these scenarios can be realized using multisig and transaction lock time options.

Transaction verification

This verification process is performed by Bitcoin nodes. The following is described in the Bitcoin developer guide:

1. Check the syntax and ensure that the syntax and data structure of the transaction conforms to the rules provided by the protocol.
2. Verify that no transaction inputs and outputs are empty.
3. Check whether the size in bytes is less than the maximum block size.
4. The output value must be in the allowed money range (0 to 21 million BTC).
5. All inputs must have a specified previous output, except for coinbase transactions, which should not be relayed.
6. Verify that nLockTime must not exceed 31-bits. (nLockTime specifies the time before which transaction will not be included in the block.)
7. For a transaction to be valid, it should not be less than 100 bytes.
8. The number of signature operations in a standard transaction should be less than or not more than two.
9. Reject nonstandard transactions; for example, ScriptSig is allowed to only push numbers on the stack. ScriptPubkey not passing the isStandard() checks. The isStandard() checks specify that only standard transactions are allowed.
10. A transaction is rejected if there is already a matching transaction in the pool or in a block in the main branch.
11. The transaction will be rejected if the referenced output for each input exists in any other transaction in the pool.
12. For each input, there must exist a referenced output unspent transaction.
13. For each input, if the referenced output transaction is the coinbase, it must have at least 100 confirmations; otherwise, the transaction will be rejected.

14. For each input, if the referenced output does not exist or has been spent already, the transaction will be rejected.

15. Using the referenced output transactions to get input values, verify that each input value, as well as the sum, is in the allowed range of 0-21 million BTC. Reject the transaction if the sum of input values is less than the sum of output values.

16. Reject the transaction if the transaction fee would be too low to get into an empty block.

17. Each input unlocking script must have corresponding valid output scripts.

Transaction malleability

Transaction malleability in Bitcoin was introduced due to a bug in the bitcoin implementation. Due to this bug, it became possible for an adversary to change the transaction ID of a transaction, thus resulting in a scenario where it would appear that a certain transaction has not been executed. This can allow scenarios where double deposits or withdrawals can occur. In other words, this bug allows the changing of the unique ID of a Bitcoin transaction before it is confirmed. If the ID is changed before confirmation, it would seem that the transaction did not occur at all which can then allow these attacks.

Blockchain

Blockchain is a public ledger of a timestamped, ordered, and immutable list of all transactions on the Bitcoin network. Each block is identified by a hash in the chain and is linked to its previous block by referencing the previous block's hash.

In the following table structure of a block is presented, followed by a detailed diagram that provides a detailed view of the blockchain structure.

The structure of a block

The following table shows the structure of a block:

Field	Size	Description
Block size	4 bytes	This is the size of the block.
Block header	80 bytes	This includes fields from the block header described in the next section.

Transaction counter	Variable	This field contains the total number of transactions in the block, including the coinbase transaction. Size ranges from 1-9 bytes
Transactions	Variable	All transactions in the block.

The structure of a block header

The following table depicts the structure of a block header:

Field	Size	Description
Version	4 bytes	The block version number that dictates the block validation rules to follow.
Previous block's header hash	32 bytes	This is a double SHA-256 hash of the previous block's header.
Merkle root hash	32 bytes	This is a double SHA-256 hash of the Merkle tree of all transactions included in the block.
Timestamp	4 bytes	This field contains the approximate creation time of the block in the Unix epoch time format. More precisely, this is the time when the miner has started hashing the header. (The time from the miner's point of view.)
Difficulty target	4 bytes	This is the current difficulty target of the network/block.
Nonce	4 bytes	This is an arbitrary number that miners change repeatedly to produce a hash that is lower than the difficulty target.

As shown in the following diagram, blockchain is a chain of blocks where each block is linked to its previous block by referencing the previous block header's hash. This linking makes sure that no transaction can be modified unless the block that records it and all blocks that follow it are also modified. The first block is not linked to any previous block and is known as the genesis block.

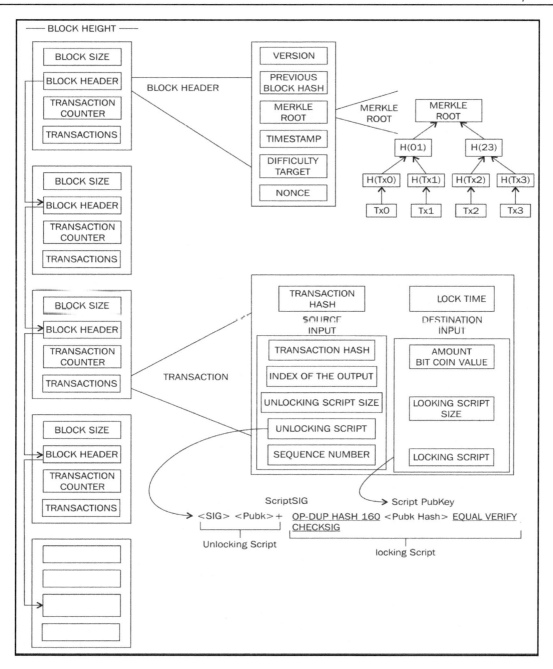

A visualization of the blockchain, block, block header, transactions and scripts

The preceding diagram shows a high-level overview of the Bitcoin blockchain. On the left-hand side blocks are shown starting from top to bottom. Each block contains transactions and block headers which are further magnified on the right-hand side. On the top, first, block header is expanded to show various elements within the block header. Then on the right-hand side the Merkle root element of the block header is shown in magnified view which shows that how Merkle root is calculated. We have discussed Merkle trees in detail previously, you can refer to Chapter 5, *Symmetric Cryptography* if you need to revise the concept. Further down transactions are also magnified to show the structure of a transaction and the elements that it contains. Also, note that transactions are then further elaborated by showing that what locking and unlocking scripts look like. This diagram shows a lot of components, we will discuss all these in this chapter.

The genesis block

This is the first block in the Bitcoin blockchain. The genesis block was hardcoded in the bitcoin core software. It is in the chainparams.cpp file (https://github.com/bitcoin/bitcoin/blob/master/src/chainparams.cpp):

```
static CBlock CreateGenesisBlock(uint32_t nTime, uint32_t nNonce, uint32_t
nBits, int32_t nVersion, const CAmount& genesisReward)
{
    const char* pszTimestamp = "The Times 03/Jan/2009 Chancellor on brink of
second bailout for banks";
    const CScript genesisOutputScript = CScript() <<
ParseHex("04678afdb0fe5548271967f1a67130b7105cd6a828e03909a67962e0ea1f61deb
649f6bc3f4cef38c4f35504e51ec112de5c384df7ba0b8d578a4c702b6bf11d5f") <<
OP_CHECKSIG;
    return CreateGenesisBlock(pszTimestamp, genesisOutputScript, nTime,
nNonce,
    nBits, nVersion, genesisReward);
}
```

Bitcoin provides protection against double spending by enforcing strict rules on transaction verification and via mining. Transactions and blocks are added in the blockchain only after strict rule checking explained earlier in the *Transaction verification* section and successful PoW solution. Block height is the number of blocks before a particular block in the blockchain. The current height (as of March 6, 2018) of the blockchain is 512,328 blocks. PoW is used to secure the blockchain. Each block contains one or more transactions, out of which the first transaction is a coinbase transaction. There is a special condition for coinbase transactions that prevent them from being spent until at least 100 blocks in order to avoid a situation where the block may be declared stale later on.

Stale blocks are created when a block is solved and every other miner who is still working to find a solution to the hash puzzle is working on that block. Mining and hash puzzles will be discussed later in the chapter in detail. As the block is no longer required to be worked on, this is considered a stale block.

Orphan blocks are also called detached blocks and were accepted at one point in time by the network as valid blocks but were rejected when a proven longer chain was created that did not include this initially accepted block. They are not part of the main chain and can occur at times when two miners manage to produce the blocks at the same time.

The latest block version is version 4, which was proposed with BIP65 and has been used since bitcoin core client 0.11.2 since the implementation of BIP9 bits in the `nVersion` field are being used to indicate soft fork changes.

Because of the distributed nature of bitcoin, network forks can occur naturally. In cases where two nodes simultaneously announce a valid block can result in a situation where there are two blockchains with different transactions. This is an undesirable situation but can be addressed by the Bitcoin network only by accepting the longest chain. In this case, the smaller chain will be considered orphaned. If an adversary manages to gain 51% control of the network hash rate (computational power), then they can impose their own version of transaction history.

Forks in blockchain can also occur with the introduction of changes in the Bitcoin protocol. In case of a *soft fork*, a client which chooses not to upgrade to the latest version supporting the updated protocol will still be able to work and operate normally. In this case, previous and new blocks are both acceptable, thus making soft fork backwards compatible.

In case of a soft fork, only miners are required to upgrade to the new client software in order to make use of the new protocol rules. Planned upgrades do not necessarily create forks because all users should have updated already. A hard fork, on the other hand, invalidates previously valid blocks and requires all users to upgrade. New transaction types are sometimes added as a soft fork, and any changes such as block structure change or major protocol changes results in a hard fork. The current size of the bitcoin blockchain as of October 29, 2017, stands at approximately 139 GB.

The following diagram shows the size increase of blockchain as a function of time:

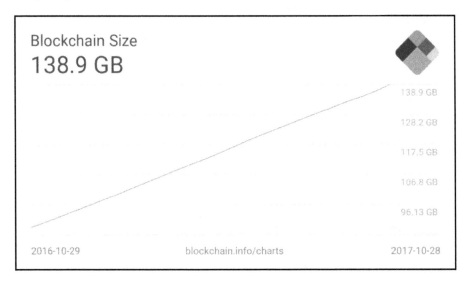

Blockchain Size
138.9 GB

138.9 GB

128.2 GB

117.5 GB

106.8 GB

96.13 GB

2016-10-29   blockchain.info/charts   2017-10-28

Current size of blockchain as of 29/10/2017

New blocks are added to the blockchain approximately every 10 minutes and network difficulty is adjusted dynamically every 2016 blocks in order to maintain a steady addition of new blocks to the network.

Network difficulty is calculated using the following equation:

*Target = Previous target * Time/2016 * 10 minutes*

Difficulty and target are interchangeable and represent the same thing. Previous target represents the old target value, and time is the time spent to generate previous 2016 blocks. Network difficulty basically means how hard it is for miners to find a new block, that is, how difficult the hashing puzzle is now.

In the next section, mining is discussed, which will explain how the hashing puzzle is solved.

Mining

Mining is a process by which new blocks are added to the blockchain. Blocks contain transactions that are validated via the mining process by mining nodes on the Bitcoin network. Blocks, once mined and verified are added to the blockchain which keeps the blockchain growing. This process is resource-intensive due to the requirements of PoW where miners compete in order to find a number which is less than the difficulty target of the network. This difficulty in finding the correct value (also called sometimes the mathematical puzzle) is there to ensure that the required resources have been spent by miners before a new proposed block can be accepted. New coins are minted by the miners by solving the PoW problem, also known as partial hash inversion problem. This process consumes a high amount of resources including computing power and electricity. This process also secures the system against frauds and double spending attacks while adding more virtual currency to the Bitcoin ecosystem.

Roughly one new block is created (mined) every 10 minutes to control the frequency of generation of bitcoins. This frequency needs to be maintained by the Bitcoin network and is encoded in the bitcoin core clients in order to control the *money supply*. Miners are rewarded with new coins if and when they discover new blocks by solving PoW. Miners are paid transaction fees in return for including transactions in their proposed blocks. New blocks are created at an approximate fixed rate of every 10 minutes. The rate of creation of new bitcoins decreases by 50%, every 210,000 blocks, roughly every 4 years. When bitcoin was initially introduced, the block reward was 50 bitcoins; then in 2012, this was reduced to 25 bitcoins. In July 2016, this was further reduced to 12.5 coins (12 coins) and the next reduction is estimated to be on July 4, 2020. This will reduce the coin reward further down to approximately six coins.

Approximately 144 blocks, that is, 1,728 bitcoins are generated per day. The number of actual coins can vary per day; however, the number of blocks remains at 144 per day. Bitcoin supply is also limited and in 2140, almost 21 million bitcoins will be finally created and no new bitcoins can be created after that. Bitcoin miners, however, will still be able to profit from the ecosystem by charging transaction fees.

Tasks of the miners

Once a node connects to the bitcoin network, there are several tasks that a bitcoin miner performs:

1. **Synching up with the network**: Once a new node joins the bitcoin network, it downloads the blockchain by requesting historical blocks from other nodes. This is mentioned here in the context of the bitcoin miner; however, this not necessarily a task only for a miner.

2. **Transaction validation**: Transactions broadcasted on the network are validated by full nodes by verifying and validating signatures and outputs.

3. **Block validation**: Miners and full nodes can start validating blocks received by them by evaluating them against certain rules. This includes the verification of each transaction in the block along with verification of the nonce value.

4. **Create a new block**: Miners propose a new block by combining transactions broadcasted on the network after validating them.

5. **Perform Proof of Work**: This task is the core of the mining process and this is where miners find a valid block by solving a computational puzzle. The block header contains a 32-bit nonce field and miners are required to repeatedly vary the nonce until the resultant hash is less than a predetermined target.

6. **Fetch reward**: Once a node solves the hash puzzle (PoW), it immediately broadcasts the results, and other nodes verify it and accept the block. There is a slight chance that the newly minted block will not be accepted by other miners on the network due to a clash with another block found at roughly the same time, but once accepted, the miner is rewarded with 12.5 bitcoins and any associated transaction fees.

Mining rewards

When Bitcoin started in 2009 the mining reward used to be 50 bitcoins. After every 210,000 blocks, the block reward halves. In November 2012 it halved down to 25 bitcoins. Currently, it is 12.5 BTC per block since July 2016. Next halving is on Friday, 12 June 2020 after which the block reward will be reduced down to 6.25 BTC per block. This mechanism is hardcoded in Bitcoin to regulate, control inflation and limit the supply of bitcoins.

Proof of Work (PoW)

This is a proof that enough computational resources have been spent in order to build a valid block. PoW is based on the idea that a random node is selected every time to create a new block. In this model, nodes compete with each other in order to be selected in proportion to their computing capacity. The following equation sums up the PoW requirement in bitcoin:

$$H\ (\ N\ ||\ P\_hash\ ||\ Tx\ ||\ Tx\ ||\ \dots\ Tx) < Target$$

Where N is a nonce, P_hash is a hash of the previous block, Tx represents transactions in the block, and $Target$ is the target network difficulty value. This means that the hash of the previously mentioned concatenated fields should be less than the target hash value.

The only way to find this nonce is the brute force method. Once a certain pattern of a certain number of zeroes is met by a miner, the block is immediately broadcasted and accepted by other miners.

The mining algorithm

The mining algorithm consists of the following steps.

1. The previous block's header is retrieved from the bitcoin network.
2. Assemble a set of transactions broadcasted on the network into a block to be proposed.
3. Compute the double hash of the previous block's header combined with a nonce and the newly proposed block using the SHA-256 algorithm.
4. Check if the resultant hash is lower than the current difficulty level (target) then PoW is solved. As a result of successful PoW the discovered block is broadcasted to the network and miners fetch the reward.
5. If the resultant hash is not less than the current difficulty level (target), then repeat the process after incrementing the nonce.

   As the hash rate of the bitcoin network increased, the total amount of 32-bit nonce was exhausted too quickly. In order to address this issue, the extra nonce solution was implemented, whereby the coinbase transaction is used as a source of extra nonce to provide a larger range of nonce to be searched by the miners.

This process can be visualized by using the following flowchart:

Mining process

Mining difficulty increased over time and bitcoins that could be mined by single CPU laptop computers now require dedicated mining centers to solve the hash puzzle. The current difficulty level can be queried using the Bitcoin command-line interface using the following command:

```
$ bitcoin-cli getdifficulty
1452839779145
```

This number represents the difficulty level of the Bitcoin network. Recall from previous sections that miners compete to find a solution to a problem. This number, in fact shows, that how difficult it is to find a hash which is lower than the network difficulty target. All successfully mined blocks must contain a hash that is less than this target number. This number is updated every 2 weeks or 2016 blocks to ensure that on average 10-minute block generation time is maintained.

Bitcoin network difficulty has increased exponentially, the following graph shows this difficulty level over a period of one year:

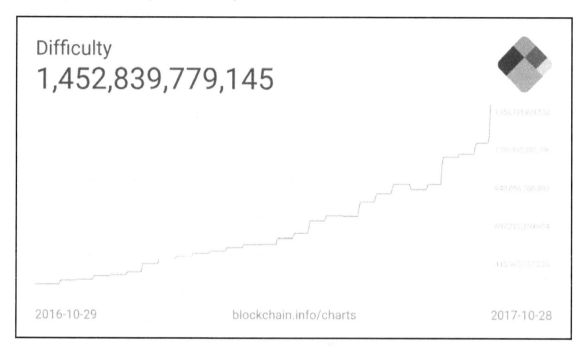

Mining difficulty over the last year

The preceding graph shows the difficulty of the Bitcoin network over a period of last year and it has increased quite significantly. The reason why mining difficulty increases is because in Bitcoin, the block generation time has to be always around 10 minutes. This means that if blocks are being mined too quickly by fast hardware then the difficulty increases so that the block generation time can remain at roughly 10 minutes per block. This is also true in reverse if blocks are not mined every 10 minutes than the difficulty is decreased. Difficulty, is calculated every 2016 blocks (in two weeks) and adjusted accordingly. If the previous set of 2016 blocks were mined in less than a period of two weeks then difficulty will be increased. Similarly, if 2016 blocks were found in more than two weeks (If blocks are mined every 10 minutes then 2016 blocks take 2 weeks to be mined) then the difficulty is decreased.

The hash rate

The hashing rate basically represents the rate of calculating hashes per second. In other words, this is the speed at which miners in the Bitcoin network are calculating hashes to find a block. In early days of bitcoin, it used to be quite small as CPUs were used. However, with dedicated mining pools and ASICs now, this has gone up exponentially in the last few years. This has resulted in increased difficulty of the Bitcoin network. The following hash rate graph shows the hash rate increase over time and is currently measured in Exa hashes. This means that in 1 second, the Bitcoin network miners are computing more than 24,000,000,000,000,000,000 hashes per second.

Hashing rate (measured in Exa-hashes) as of March 2018, shown over a period of 1 year

Mining systems

Over time, bitcoin miners have used various methods to mine bitcoins. As the core principle behind mining is based on the double SHA-256 algorithm, overtime experts have developed sophisticated systems to calculate the hash faster and faster. The following is a review of the different types of mining methods used in bitcoin and how they evolved with time.

CPU

CPU mining was the first type of mining available in the original bitcoin client. Users could even use laptop or desktop computers to mine bitcoins. CPU mining is no longer profitable and now more advanced mining methods such as ASIC-based mining is used. CPU mining only lasted for around just over a year since the introduction of Bitcoin and soon other methods were explored and tried by the miners.

GPU

Due to the increased difficulty of the bitcoin network and the general tendency of finding faster methods to mine, miners started to use GPUs or graphics cards available in PCs to perform mining. GPUs support faster and parallelized calculations that are usually programmed using the OpenCL language. This turned out to be a faster option as compared to CPUs. Users also used techniques such as overclocking to gain maximum benefit of the GPU power. Also, the possibility of using multiple graphics cards increased the popularity of graphics cards' usage for bitcoin mining. GPU mining, however, has some limitations, such as overheating and the requirement for specialized motherboards and extra hardware to house multiple graphics cards. From another angle, graphics cards have become quite expensive due to increased demand and this has impacted gamers and graphic software users.

FPGA

Even GPU mining did not last long, and soon miners found another way to perform mining using FPGAs. **Field Programmable Gate Array** (**FPGA**) is basically an integrated circuit that can be programmed to perform specific operations. FPGAs are usually programmed in **Hardware Description Languages** (**HDLs**), such as Verilog and VHDL. Double SHA-256 quickly became an attractive programming task for FPGA programmers and several open source projects started too. FPGA offered much better performance as compared to GPUs; however, issues such as accessibility, programming difficulty, and the requirement for specialized knowledge to program and configure FPGAs resulted in a short life of the FPGA era for bitcoin mining.

The arrival of ASICs resulted in quickly phased out FPGA- based systems for mining. Mining hardware such as X6500 miner, Ztex, and Icarus were developed during the time when FPGA mining was profitable. Various FPGA manufacturers, such as Xilinx and Altera, produce FPGA hardware and development boards that can be used to program mining algorithms. It should be noted that GPU mining is still profitable for some other cryptocurrencies to some extent such as Zcoin (https://zcoin.io/guide-on-how-to-mine-zcoin-xzc/), but not Bitcoin, because network difficulty of Bitcoin is so high that only ASICs (specialized hardware) running in parallel can produce some reasonable profit.

ASICs

Application Specific Integrated Circuit (**ASIC**) was designed to perform the SHA-256 operation. These special chips were sold by various manufacturers and offered a very high hashing rate. This worked for some time, but due to the quickly increasing mining difficulty level, single-unit ASICs are no longer profitable.

Currently, mining is out of the reach of individuals as vast amounts of energy and money is needed to be spent in order to build a profitable mining platform. Now professional mining centers using thousands of ASIC units in parallel are offering mining contracts to users to perform mining on their behalf. There is no technical limitation, a single user can run thousands of ASICs in parallel but it will require dedicated data centers and hardware, therefore, cost for a single individual can become prohibitive. The following are the four types of mining hardware:

CPU

GPU

FPGA

ASIC

Mining pools

A mining pool forms when group of miners work together to mine a block. The pool manager receives the coinbase transaction if the block is successfully mined, which is then responsible for distributing the reward to the group of miners who invested resources to mine the block. This is profitable as compared to solo mining, where only one sole miner is trying to solve the partial hash inversion function (hash puzzle) because, in mining pools, the reward is paid to each member of the pool regardless of whether they (more specifically, their individual node) solved the puzzle or not.

There are various models that a mining pool manager can use to pay to the miners, such as the **Pay Per Share** (**PPS**) model and the proportional model. In the PPS model, the mining pool manager pays a flat fee to all miners who participated in the mining exercise, whereas in the proportional model, the share is calculated based on the amount of computing resources spent to solve the hash puzzle.

Many commercial pools now exist and provide mining service contracts via the cloud and easy-to-use web interfaces. The most commonly used ones are AntPool (`https://www. antpool.com`), BTC (`https://btc.com`), and BTC TOP (`http://www.btc.top`). A comparison of hashing power for all major mining pools is shown in the following diagram:

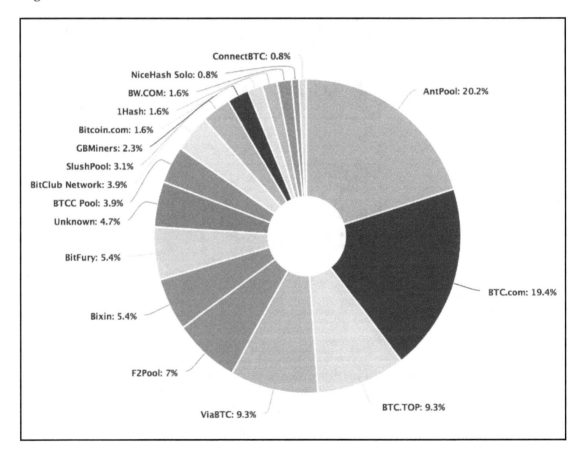

Mining pools and their hashing power (hash rate) as of 28/10/2017

Source: https://blockchain.info/pools

Mining centralization can occur if a pool manages to control more than 51% of the network by generating more than 51% hash rate of the Bitcoin network.

As discussed earlier in the introduction section, a 51% attack can result in successful double-spending attacks, and it can impact consensus and in fact impose another version of transaction history on the Bitcoin network.

This event has happened once in the Bitcoin history when GHash.IO, a large mining pool, managed to acquire more than 51% of the network capacity. Theoretical solutions, such as two-phase PoW (`http://hackingdistributed.com/2014/06/18/how-to-disincentivize-large-bitcoin-mining-pools/`), have been proposed in academia to disincentivize large mining pools. This scheme introduces a second cryptographic puzzle that results in mining pools to either reveal their private keys or provide a considerable portion of the hash rate of their mining pool, thus reducing the overall hash rate of the pool.

Various types of hardware are commercially available for mining purposes. Currently, the most profitable one is ASIC mining, and specialized hardware is available from a number of vendors such as Antminer, AvalonMiner and Whatsminer. Solo mining is not much profitable now unless a vast amount of money and energy is spent to build your own mining rig or even a data center. With the current difficulty factor (March 2018), if a user manages to produce a hash rate of 12 TH/s, they can hope to make 0.0009170 BTC (around $6) per day, which is very low as compared to the investment required to source the equipment that can produce 12 TH. Including running costs such as electricity, this turns out to be not very profitable.

For example, Antminer S9, is an efficient ASIC miner which produces hash power of 13.5 TH/s and it seems that it can produce some profit per day, which is true but a single Antminer S9 costs around 1700 GBP and combining it with electricity cost the return on investment is almost after a year's mining when it produces around 0.3 BTC. It may seem still OK, to invest but also think about the fact that the Bitcoin network difficulty keeps going up with time and during a year it will become more difficult to mine and the mining hardware will run out its utility in a few months.

Summary

We started this chapter by introducing Bitcoin and how a transaction works from a user's point of view. Then, we presented an introduction to transactions from a technical point of view. Later we discussed public and private keys that are used in Bitcoin.

In the following section, we presented addresses and its different types, following it with a discussion on transactions, its types, and usage. Next, we looked at blockchain with a detailed explanation regarding how blockchain works and what various components are included in the Bitcoin blockchain.

In the last few sections of the chapter, we presented the mining process and relevant concepts.

Building a Wallet Service

9

A wallet service is used to send and receive funds. Major challenges for building a wallet service are security and trust. Users must feel that their funds are secure and the administrator of the wallet service doesn't steal their funds. The wallet service we will build in this chapter will tackle both these issues.

In this chapter, we'll cover the following topics:

- Difference between online and offline wallets
- Using hooked-web3-provider and ethereumjs-tx to make it easier to create and sign transactions using accounts not managed by an Ethereum node
- Understanding what a HD wallet is and also its uses
- Creating an HD wallet and a transaction signer using `lightwallet.js`
- Building a wallet service

Difference between online and offline wallets

A wallet is a collection of accounts, and an account is a combination of an address and its associated private key.

A wallet is said to be an online wallet when it is connected to the Internet. For example, wallets stored in geth, any website/database, and so on are called online wallets. Online wallets are also called hot wallets, web wallets, hosted wallets, and so on. Online wallets are not recommended at least when storing large amounts of ether or storing ether for a long time because they are risky. Also, depending on where the wallet is stored, it may require trusting a third party.

For example, most of the popular wallet services store the private keys of the wallets with themselves and allow you to access the wallet via an e-mail and password, so basically, you don't have actual access to the wallet, and if they want, they can steal the funds in the wallets.

A wallet is said to be an offline wallet when it is not connected to the Internet. For example, wallets stored in pen drives, papers, text files, and so on. Offline wallets are also called cold wallets. Offline wallets are more secure than online wallets because to steal funds, someone will need physical access to the storage. The challenges with offline storage is that you need to find a location that you won't delete accidentally or forget, or nobody else can have access to. Many people store the wallet in paper and keep the paper in a safe locker if they want to hold some funds safely for a very long time. If you want to frequently send funds from your account, then you can store it in a password-protected pen drive and also in a safe locker. It is a little risker to store wallets in a digital device only because digital devices can corrupt anytime and you may lose access to your wallet; that's why along with storing in a pen drive, you should also put it in a safe locker. You can also find a better solution depending on your needs, but just make sure it's safe and that you accidentally don't lose access to it.

hooked-web3-provider and ethereumjs-tx libraries

Until now, all the examples of Web3.js library's `sendTransaction()` method we saw were using the `from` address that's present in the Ethereum node; therefore, the Ethereum node was able to sign the transactions before broadcasting. But if you have the private key of a wallet stored somewhere else, then geth cannot find it. Therefore, in this case, you will need to use the `web3.eth.sendRawTransaction()` method to broadcast transactions.

`web3.eth.sendRawTransaction()` is used to broadcast raw transactions, that is, you will have to write code to create and sign raw transactions. The Ethereum node will directly broadcast it without doing anything else to the transaction. But writing code to broadcast transactions using `web3.eth.sendRawTransaction()` is difficult because it requires generating the data part, creating raw transactions, and also signing the transactions.

The Hooked-Web3-Provider library provides us with a custom provider, which communicates with geth using HTTP; but the uniqueness of this provider is that it lets us sign the `sendTransaction()` calls of contract instances using our keys. Therefore, we don't need to create data part of the transactions anymore. The custom provider actually overrides the implementation of the `web3.eth.sendTransaction()` method. So basically, it lets us sign both the `sendTransaction()` calls of contract instances and also the `web3.eth.sendTransaction()` calls. The `sendTransaction()` method of contract instances internally generate data of the transaction and calls `web3.eth.sendTransaction()` to broadcast the transaction.

EthereumJS is a collection of those libraries related to Ethereum. ethereumjs-tx is one of those that provide various APIs related to transactions. For example, it lets us create raw transactions, sign the raw transactions, check whether transactions are signed using proper keys or not, and so on.

Both of these libraries are available for Node.js and client-side JavaScript. Download the Hooked-Web3-Provider from `https://www.npmjs.com/package/hooked-web3-provider`, and download ethereumjs-tx from `https://www.npmjs.com/package/ethereumjs-tx`.

At the time of writing this book, the latest version of Hooked-Web3-Provider is 1.0.0 and the latest version of ethereumjs-tx is 1.1.4.

Let's see how to use these libraries together to send a transaction from an account that's not managed by geth.

```
var provider = new HookedWeb3Provider({
 host: "http://localhost:8545",
 transaction_signer: {
  hasAddress: function(address, callback){
   callback(null, true);
  },
  signTransaction: function(tx_params, callback){
   var rawTx = {
          gasPrice: web3.toHex(tx_params.gasPrice),
          gasLimit: web3.toHex(tx_params.gas),
          value: web3.toHex(tx_params.value)
          from: tx_params.from,
          to: tx_params.to,
          nonce: web3.toHex(tx_params.nonce)
       };

   var privateKey =
EthJS.Util.toBuffer('0x1a56e47492bf3df9c9563fa7f66e4e032c661de9d68c3f36f358
e6bc9a9f69f2', 'hex');
   var tx = new EthJS.Tx(rawTx);
```

```
    tx.sign(privateKey);

    callback(null, tx.serialize().toString('hex'));
    }
  }
});

var web3 = new Web3(provider);

web3.eth.sendTransaction({
  from: "0xba6406ddf8817620393ab1310ab4d0c2deda714d",
  to: "0x2bdbec0ccd70307a00c66de02789e394c2c7d549",
  value: web3.toWei("0.1", "ether"),
  gasPrice: "20000000000",
  gas: "21000"
}, function(error, result){
  console.log(error, result)
})
```

Here is how the code works:

1. At first, we created a `HookedWeb3Provider` instance. This is provided by the Hooked-Web3-Provider library. This constructor takes an object that has two properties, which must be provided. `host` is the HTTP URL of the node and `transaction_signer` is an object that the custom provider communicates with to get the transaction signed.

2. The `transaction_signer` object has two properties: `hasAddress` and `signTransaction`. `hasAddress` is invoked to check whether the transaction can be signed, that is, to check whether the transaction signer has the private key of the `from` address account. This method receives the address and a callback. The callback should be called with the first argument as an error message and the second argument as `false` if the private key of the address is not found. And if the private key is found, the first argument should be `null`, and the second argument should be `true`.

3. If the private key for the address is found, then the custom provider invokes the `signTransaction` method to get the transaction signed. This method has two parameters, that is, the transactions parameters and a callback. Inside the method, at first, we convert the transaction parameters to raw transaction parameters, that is, the raw transaction parameters values are encoded as hexadecimal strings. Then we create a buffer to hold the private key. The buffer is created using the `EthJS.Util.toBuffer()` method, which is part of the `ethereumjs-util` library. The `ethereumjs-util` library is imported by the `ethereumjs-tx` library. We then create a raw transaction and sign it, after which we serialize and convert it to hexadecimal strings. Finally, we need to provide the hexadecimal string of the signed raw transaction to the custom provider using the callback. In case there is an error inside the method, then the first argument of the callback should be an error message.

4. Now the custom provider takes the raw transactions and broadcasts it using `web3.eth.sendRawTransaction()`.

5. Finally, we call the `web3.eth.sendTransaction` function to send some ether to another account. Here, we need to provide all the transaction parameters except `nonce` because the custom provider can calculate nonce. Earlier, many of these were optional because we were leaving it to the Ethereum node to calculate them, but now as we are signing it ourselves, we need to provide all of them. The `gas` is always 21,000 when the transaction doesn't have any data associated with it.

What about the public key?

In the preceding code, nowhere did we mention anything about the public key of the signing address. You must be wondering how a miner will verify the authenticity of a transaction without the public key. Miners use a unique property of ECDSA, which allows you to calculate the public key from the message and signature. In a transaction, the message indicates the intention of the transaction, and the signature is used to find whether the message is signed using the correct private key. This is what makes ECDSA so special. ethereumjs-tx provides an API to verify transactions.

What is a hierarchical deterministic wallet?

A hierarchical deterministic wallet is a system of deriving addresses and keys from a single starting point called a seed. Deterministic indicates that for the same seed, the same addresses and keys will be generated, and hierarchical indicates that the addresses and keys will be generated in the same order. This makes it easier to back up and store multiple accounts, as you just have to store the seed, not the individual keys and addresses.

Why will users need multiple accounts?

You must be wondering why users will need multiple accounts. The reason is to hide their wealth. The balance of accounts is available publicly in the blockchain. So, if user A shares an address with user B to receive some ether, then user B can check how much ether is present in that address. Therefore, users usually distribute their wealth across various accounts.

There are various types of HD wallets, which differ in terms of seed format and the algorithm to generate addresses and keys, for instance, BIP32, Armory, Coinkite, Coinb.in, and so on.

What are BIP32, BIP44, and BIP39?

A **Bitcoin Improvement Proposal (BIP)** is a design document providing information to the Bitcoin community, or describing a new feature for Bitcoin or its processes or environment. The BIP should provide a concise technical specification of the feature and a rationale for the feature. At the time of writing this book, there are 152 BIPS (Bitcoin Improvement Proposals). BIP32 and BIP39 provide information about an algorithm to implement an HD wallet and mnemonic seed specification respectively. You can learn more about these at `https://github.com/bitcoin/bips`.

Introduction to key derivation functions

Asymmetric cryptography algorithms define the nature of their keys and how the keys should be generated because the keys need to be related. For example, the RSA key generation algorithm is deterministic.

Symmetric cryptography algorithms only define key sizes. It's up to us to generate the keys. There are various algorithms to generate these keys. One such algorithm is KDF.

A **key derivation function** (**KDF**) is a deterministic algorithm to derive a symmetric key from some secret value (such as master key, password, or passphrase). There are various types of KDFs, such as bcrypt, crypt, PBKDF2, scrypt, HKDF, and so on. You can learn more about KDFs at `https://en.wikipedia.org/wiki/Key_derivation_function`.

To generate multiple keys from a single secret value, you can concatenate a number and increment it.

A password-based key derivation function takes a password and generates a symmetric key. Due to the fact that users usually use weak passwords, password-based key derivation functions are designed to be slower and take a lot of memory to make it difficult to launch brute force attacks and other kinds of attacks. Password-based key derivation functions are used widely because it's difficult to remember secret keys, and storing them somewhere is risky as it can be stolen. PBKDF2 is an example of a password-based key derivation function.

A master key or passphrase is difficult to be cracked using a brute force attack; therefore, in case you want to generate a symmetric key from a master key or passphrase, you can use a non-password-based key derivation function, such as HKDF. HKDF is much faster compared to PBKDF2.

Why not just use a hash function instead of KDFs?
The output of hash functions can be used as symmetric keys. So you must be wondering what is the need for KDFs. Well, if you are using a master key, passphrase, or a strong password, you can simply use a hash function. For example, HKDF simply uses a hash function to generate the key. But if you cannot guarantee that users will use a strong password, it's better to use a password derived hash function.

Introduction to LightWallet

LightWallet is an HD wallet that implements BIP32, BIP39, and BIP44. LightWallet provides APIs to create and sign transactions or encrypt and decrypt data using the addresses and keys generated using it.

LightWallet API is divided into four namespaces, that is, `keystore`, `signing`, `encryption`, and `txutils`. `signing`, `encrpyion`, and `txutils` provide APIs to sign transactions, asymmetric cryptography, and create transactions respectively, whereas a `keystore` namespace is used to create a `keystore`, generated seed, and so on. `keystore` is an object that holds the seed and keys encrypted. The `keystore` namespace implements transaction signer methods that requires signing the `we3.eth.sendTransaction()` calls if we are using Hooked-Web3-Provider. Therefore the `keystore` namespace can automatically create and sign transactions for the addresses that it can find in it. Actually, LightWallet is primarily intended to be a signing provider for the Hooked-Web3-Provider.

A `keystore` instance can be configured to either create and sign transactions or encrypt and decrypt data. For signing transactions, it uses the `secp256k1` parameter, and for encryption and decryption, it uses the `curve25519` parameter.

The seed of LightWallet is a 12-word mnemonic, which is easy to remember yet difficult to hack. It cannot be any 12 words; instead, it should be a seed generated by LightWallet. A seed generated by LightWallet has certain properties in terms of selection of words and other things.

HD derivation path

The HD derivation path is a string that makes it easy to handle multiple crypto currencies (assuming they all use the same signature algorithms), multiple blockchains, multiple accounts, and so on.

HD derivation path can have as many parameters as needed, and using different values for the parameters, we can produce different group of addresses and their associated keys.

By default, LightWallet uses the `m/0'/0'/0'` derivation path. Here, `/n'` is a parameter, and `n` is the parameter value.

Every HD derivation path has a `curve`, and `purpose`. `purpose` can be either `sign` or `asymEncrypt`. `sign` indicates that the path is used for signing transactions, and `asymEncrypt` indicates that the path is used for encryption and decryption. `curve` indicates the parameters of ECC. For signing, the parameter must be `secp256k1`, and for asymmetric encryption, the curve must be `curve25591` because LightWallet forces us to use these paramters due to their benefits in those purposes.

Building a wallet service

Now we have learned enough theory about LightWallet, it's time to build a wallet service using LightWallet and hooked-web3-provider. Our wallet service will let users generate a unique seed, display addresses and their associated balance, and finally, the service will let users send ether to other accounts. All the operations will be done on the client side so that users can trust us easily. Users will either have to remember the seed or store it somewhere.

Prerequisites

Before you start building the wallet service, make sure that you are running the geth development instance, which is mining, has the HTTP-RPC server enabled, allows client-side requests from any domain, and finally has account 0 unlocked. You can do all these by running this:

```
geth --dev --rpc --rpccorsdomain "*" --rpcaddr "0.0.0.0" --rpcport
"8545" --mine --unlock=0
```

Here, `--rpccorsdomain` is used to allow certain domains to communicate with geth. We need to provide a list of domains space separated, such as `"http://localhost:8080 https://mySite.com *"`. It also supports the * wildcard character. `--rpcaddr` indicates to which IP address the geth server is reachable. The default for this is `127.0.0.1`, so if it's a hosted server, you won't be able to reach it using the public IP address of the server. Therefore, we changed it's value to `0.0.0.0`, which indicates that the server can be reached using any IP address.

Project structure

In the exercise files of this chapter, you will find two directories, that is, `Final` and `Initial`. `Final` contains the final source code of the project, whereas `Initial` contains the empty source code files and libraries to get started with building the application quickly.

 To test the `Final` directory, you will need to run `npm install` inside it and then run the app using the `node app.js` command inside the `Final` directory.

In the `Initial` directory, you will find a `public` directory and two files named `app.js` and `package.json`. `package.json` contains the backend dependencies. Our app, `app.js`, is where you will place the backend source code.

The `public` directory contains files related to the frontend. Inside `public/css`, you will find `bootstrap.min.css`, which is the bootstrap library. Inside `public/html`, you will find `index.html`, where you will place the HTML code of our app, and finally, in the `public/js` directory, you will find `.js` files for Hooked-Web3-Provider, web3js, and LightWallet. Inside `public/js`, you will also find a `main.js` file where you will place the frontend JS code of our app.

Building the backend

Let's first build the backend of the app. First of all, run `npm install` inside the initial directory to install the required dependencies for our backend.

Here is the complete backend code to run an express service and serve the `index.html` file and static files:

```
var express = require("express");
var app = express();

app.use(express.static("public"));

app.get("/", function(req, res){
 res.sendFile(__dirname + "/public/html/index.html");
})

app.listen(8080);
```

The preceding code is self-explanatory.

Building the frontend

Now let's build the frontend of the app. The frontend will consists of the major functionalities, that is, generating seed, displaying addresses of a seed, and sending ether.

Now let's write the HTML code of the app. Place this code in the `index.html` file:

```
<!DOCTYPE html>
 <html lang="en">
     <head>
```

```
        <meta charset="utf-8">
        <meta name="viewport" content="width=device-width, initial-
scale=1, shrink-to-fit=no">
        <meta http-equiv="x-ua-compatible" content="ie=edge">
        <link rel="stylesheet" href="/css/bootstrap.min.css">
    </head>
    <body>
        <div class="container">
            <div class="row">
                <div class="col-md-6 offset-md-3">
                    <br>
                    <div class="alert alert-info" id="info" role="alert">
                        Create or use your existing wallet.
                    </div>
                    <form>
                        <div class="form-group">
                            <label for="seed">Enter 12-word seed</label>
                            <input type="text" class="form-control"
id="seed">
                        </div>
                        <button type="button" class="btn btn primary"
onclick="generate_addresses()">Generate Details</button>
                        <button type="button" class="btn btn-primary"
onclick="generate_seed()">Generate New Seed</button>
                    </form>
                    <hr>
                    <h2 class="text-xs-center">Address, Keys and Balances
of the seed</h2>
                    <ol id="list">
                    </ol>
                    <hr>
                    <h2 class="text-xs-center">Send ether</h2>
                    <form>
                        <div class="form-group">
                            <label for="address1">From address</label>
                            <input type="text" class="form-control"
id="address1">
                        </div>
                        <div class="form-group">
                            <label for="address2">To address</label>
                            <input type="text" class="form-control"
id="address2">
                        </div>
                        <div class="form-group">
                            <label for="ether">Ether</label>
                            <input type="text" class="form-control"
id="ether">
                        </div>
```

```
                            <button type="button" class="btn btn-primary"
    onclick="send_ether()">Send Ether</button>
                        </form>
                    </div>
                </div>
            </div>

            <script src="/js/web3.min.js"></script>
            <script src="/js/hooked-web3-provider.min.js"></script>
        <script src="/js/lightwallet.min.js"></script>
        <script src="/js/main.js"></script>
    </body>
</html>
```

Here is how the code works:

1. At first, we enqueue a Bootstrap 4 stylesheet.
2. Then we display an information box, where we will display various messages to the user.
3. And then we have a form with an input box and two buttons. The input box is used to enter the seed, or while generating new seed, the seed is displayed there.
4. The **Generate Details** button is used to display addresses and **Generate New Seed** is used to generate a new unique seed. When **Generate Details** is clicked, we call the `generate_addresses()` method, and when the **Generate New Seed** button is clicked, we call the `generate_seed()` method.
5. Later, we have an empty ordered list. Here, we will dynamically display the addresses, their balances, and associated private keys of a seed when a user clicks on the **Generate Details** button.
6. Finally, we have another form that takes a from address and a to address and the amount of ether to transfer. The from address must be one of the addresses that's currently displayed in the unordered list.

Now let's write the implementation of each of the functions that the HTML code calls. At first, let's write the code to generate a new seed. Place this code in the `main.js` file:

```
function generate_seed()
{
 var new_seed = lightwallet.keystore.generateRandomSeed();

 document.getElementById("seed").value = new_seed;

 generate_addresses(new_seed);
}
```

The `generateRandomSeed()` method of the `keystore` namespace is used to generate a random seed. It takes an optional parameter, which is a string that indicates the extra entropy.

 Entropy is the randomness collected by an application for use in some algorithm or somewhere else that requires random data. Usually, entropy is collected from hardware sources, either pre-existing ones such as mouse movements or specially provided randomness generators.

To produce a unique seed, we need really high entropy. LightWallet is already built with methods to produce unique seeds. The algorithm LightWallet uses to produce entropy depends on the environment. But if you feel you can generate better entropy, you can pass the generated entropy to the `generateRandomSeed()` method, and it will get concatenated with the entropy generated by `generateRandomSeed()` internally.

After generating a random seed, we call the `generate_addresses` method. This method takes a seed and displays addresses in it. Before generating addresses, it prompts the user to ask how many addresses they want.

Here is the implementation of the `generate_addresses()` method. Place this code in the `main.js` file:

```
var totalAddresses = 0;

function generate_addresses(seed)
{
 if(seed == undefined)
 {
  seed = document.getElementById("seed").value;
 }

 if(!lightwallet.keystore.isSeedValid(seed))
 {
  document.getElementById("info").innerHTML = "Please enter a valid seed";
  return;
 }

 totalAddresses = prompt("How many addresses do you want to generate");

 if(!Number.isInteger(parseInt(totalAddresses)))
 {
  document.getElementById("info").innerHTML = "Please enter valid number of
addresses";
  return;
 }
```

```
   var password = Math.random().toString();

lightwallet.keystore.createVault({
 password: password,
   seedPhrase: seed
}, function (err, ks) {
   ks.keyFromPassword(password, function (err, pwDerivedKey) {
     if(err)
     {
      document.getElementById("info").innerHTML = err;
     }
     else
     {
      ks.generateNewAddress(pwDerivedKey, totalAddresses);
      var addresses = ks.getAddresses();

      var web3 = new Web3(new
Web3.providers.HttpProvider("http://localhost:8545"));

      var html = "";

      for(var count = 0; count < addresses.length; count++)
      {
     var address = addresses[count];
     var private_key = ks.exportPrivateKey(address, pwDerivedKey);
     var balance = web3.eth.getBalance("0x" + address);

     html = html + "<li>";
     html = html + "<p><b>Address: </b>0x" + address + "</p>";
     html = html + "<p><b>Private Key: </b>0x" + private_key + "</p>";
     html = html + "<p><b>Balance: </b>" + web3.fromWei(balance, "ether") +
" ether</p>";
        html = html + "</li>";
      }

      document.getElementById("list").innerHTML = html;
     }
   });
 });
}
```

Here is how the code works:

1. At first, we have a variable named `totalAddresses`, which holds a number indicating the total number of addresses the user wants to generate.

2. Then we check whether the `seed` parameter is defined or not. If it's undefined, we fetch the seed from the input field. We are doing this so that the `generate_addressess()` method can be used to display the information seed while generating a new seed and also if the user clicks on the **Generate Details** button.

3. Then we validate the seed using the `isSeedValid()` method of the `keystore` namespace.

4. We then ask for the user's input regarding how many addresses they want to generate and display. And then we validate the input.

5. The private keys in the `keystore` namespace are always stored encrypted. While generating keys, we need to encrypt them, and while signing transactions, we need to decrypt the keys. The password for deriving a symmetric encryption key can be taken as input from the user or by supplying a random string as a password. For better user experience, we generate a random string and use it as the password. The symmetric key is not stored inside the `keystore` namespace; therefore, we need to generate the key from the password whenever we do operations related to the private key, such as generating keys, accessing keys, and so on.

6. Then we use the `createVault` method to create a `keystore` instance. `createVault` takes an object and a callback. The object can have four properties: `password`, `seedPharse`, `salt`, and `hdPathString`. `password` is compulsory, and everything else is optional. If we don't provide a `seedPharse`, it will generate and use a random seed. `salt` is concatenated to the password to increase the security of the symmetric key as the attacker has to also find the salt along with the password. If the salt is not provided, it's randomly generated. The `keystore` namespace holds the salt unencrypted. `hdPathString` is used to provide the default derivation path for the `keystore` namespace, that is, while generating addresses, signing transactions, and so on. If we don't provide a derivation path, then this derivation path is used. If we don't provide `hdPathString`, then the default value is `m/0'/0'/0'`. The default purpose of this derivation path is `sign`. You can create new derivation paths or overwrite the purpose of derivation paths present using the `addHdDerivationPath()` method of a `keystore` instance. You can also change the default derivation path using the `setDefaultHdDerivationPath()` method of a `keystore` instance. Finally, once the `keystore` namespace is created, the instance is returned via the callback. So here, we created a `keystore` using a password and seed only.

7. Now we need to generate the number of addresses and their associated keys the user needs. As we can generate millions of addresses from a seed, `keystore` doesn't generate any address until we want it to because it doesn't know how many addresses we want to generate. After creating the `keystore`, we generate the symmetric key from the password using the `keyFromPassword` method. And then we call the `generateNewAddress()` method to generate addresses and their associated keys.

8. `generateNewAddress()` takes three arguments: password derived key, number of addresses to generate, and derivation path. As we haven't provided a derivation path, it uses the default derivation path of the keystore. If you call `generateNewAddress()` multiple times, it resumes from the address it created in the last call. For example, if you call this method twice, each time generating two addresses, you will have the first four addresses.

9. Then we use `getAddresses()` to get all the addresses stored in the `keystore`.

10. We decrypt and retrieve private keys of the addresses using the `exportPrivateKey` method.

11. We use `web3.eth.getBalance()` to get balances of the address.

12. And finally, we display all the information inside the unordered list.

Now we know how to generate the address and their private keys from a seed. Now let's write the implementation of the `send_ether()` method, which is used to send ether from one of the addresses generated from the seed.

Here is the code for this. Place this code in the `main.js` file:

```
function send_ether()
{
 var seed = document.getElementById("seed").value;

 if(!lightwallet.keystore.isSeedValid(seed))
 {
  document.getElementById("info").innerHTML = "Please enter a valid seed";
  return;
 }

 var password = Math.random().toString();

 lightwallet.keystore.createVault({
  password: password,
    seedPhrase: seed
 }, function (err, ks) {
    ks.keyFromPassword(password, function (err, pwDerivedKey) {
```

```
    if(err)
    {
     document.getElementById("info").innerHTML = err;
    }
    else
    {
     ks.generateNewAddress(pwDerivedKey, totalAddresses);

     ks.passwordProvider = function (callback) {
        callback(null, password);
     };

     var provider = new HookedWeb3Provider({
     host: "http://localhost:8545",
     transaction_signer: ks
   });

     var web3 = new Web3(provider);

     var from = document.getElementById("address1").value;
    var to = document.getElementById("address2").value;
     var value = web3.toWei(document.getElementById("ether").value,
"ether");

     web3.eth.sendTransaction({
      from: from,
      to: to,
      value: value,
      gas: 21000
     }, function(error, result){
      if(error)
      {
       document.getElementById("info").innerHTML = error;
      }
      else
      {
       document.getElementById("info").innerHTML = "Txn hash: " + result;
      }
     })
    }
   });
  });
 }
```

Here, the code up and until generating addresses from the seed is self explanatory. After that, we assign a callback to the `passwordProvider` property of `ks`. This callback is invoked during transaction signing to get the password to decrypt the private key. If we don't provide this, LightWallet prompts the user to enter the password. And then, we create a `HookedWeb3Provider` instance by passing the `keystore` as the transaction signer. Now when the custom provider wants a transaction to be signed, it calls the `hasAddress` and `signTransactions` methods of `ks`. If the address to be signed is not among the generated addresses, `ks` will give an error to the custom provider. And finally, we send some ether using the `web3.eth.sendTransaction` method.

Testing

Now that we have finished building our wallet service, let's test it to make sure it works as expected. First, run `node app.js` inside the initial directory, and then visit `http://localhost:8080` in your favorite browser. You will see this screen:

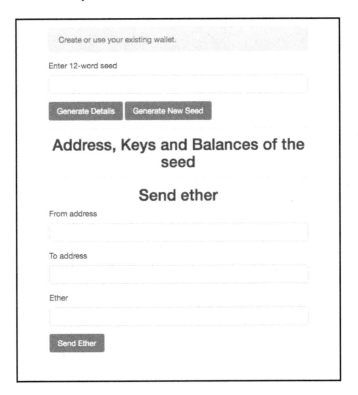

Now click on the **Generate New Seed** button to generate a new seed. You will be prompted to enter a number indicating the number of addresses to generate. You can provide any number, but for testing purposes, provide a number greater than 1. Now the screen will look something like this:

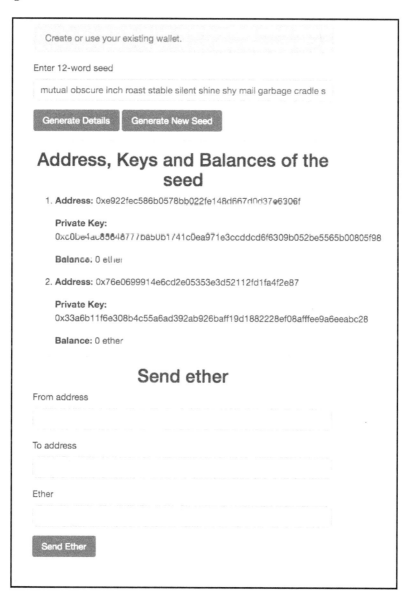

Now to test sending ether, you need to send some ether to one of the generated addresses from the coinbase account. Once you have sent some ether to one of the generated addresses, click on the **Generate Details** button to refresh the UI, although it's not necessary to test sending ether using the wallet service. Make sure the same address is generated again. Now the screen will look something like this:

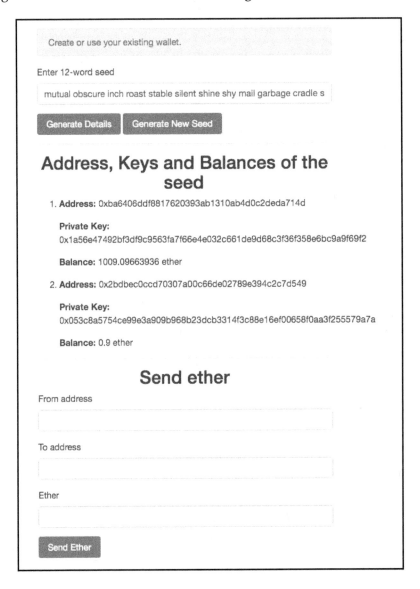

Now in the from address field, enter the account address from the list that has the balance in the `from` address field. Then enter another address in the to address field. For testing purposes, you can enter any of the other addresses displayed. Then enter some ether amount that is less than or equal to the ether balance of the from address account. Now your screen will look something like this:

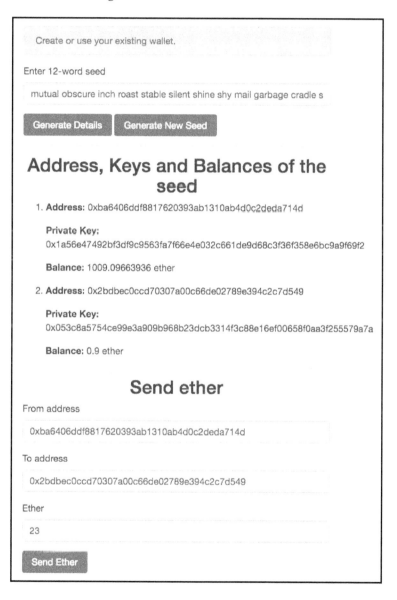

Now click on the **Send Ether** button, and you will see the transaction hash in the information box. Wait for sometime for it to get mined. Meanwhile, you can check whether the transactions got mined or not by clicking on the **Generate Details** button in a very short span of time. Once the transaction is mined, your screen will look something like this:

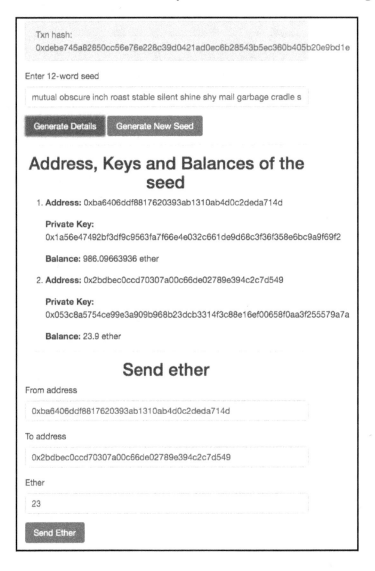

If everything goes the same way as explained, your wallet service is ready. You can actually deploy this service to a custom domain and make it available for use publicly. It's completely secure, and users will trust it.

Summary

In this chapter, you learned about three important Ethereum libraries: Hooked-Web3-Provider, ethereumjs-tx, and LightWallet. These libraries can be used to manage accounts and sign transactions outside of the Ethereum node. While developing clients for most kinds of DApps, you will find these libraries useful.

And finally, we created a wallet service that lets users manage their accounts that share private keys or any other information related to their wallet with the backend of the service..

10
Alternative Coins

Since the initial success of Bitcoin, many alternative currency projects have been launched. Bitcoin was released in 2009, and the first alternative coin project (named Namecoin) was introduced in 2011. In 2013 and 2014, the **alternative coins (altcoin)** market grew exponentially, and many different types of alternative coin project were started.

A few of those became a success, whereas many were unpopular due to less interest and as a result, they did not succeed. A few were *pump and dump* scams that surfaced for some time but soon disappeared. Alternative approaches to bitcoin can be divided broadly into two categories, based on the primary purpose of their development. If the primary goal is to build a decentralized blockchain platform, they are called alternative chains; if the sole purpose of the alternative project is to introduce a new virtual currency, it is called an altcoin.

Alternative blockchains will be discussed in detail in Chapter 14, *Alternative Blockchains.*

This chapter is mainly dedicated to altcoins whose primary purpose is to introduce a new virtual currency (coin) although some material will also be presented on the topic of alternative protocols built on top of bitcoin to provide various services. These include concepts such as Namecoin, where the primary purpose is to provide decentralized naming and identity services instead of currency.

Currently, as of late 2018, there are hundreds of altcoins on the market, and they hold some monetary value such as Namecoin, Zcash, Primecoin, and many others. We will examine some of these later in this chapter. Zcash is a more successful altcoin introduced in 2016. On the other hand, Primecoin did not gain much popularity however it is still used. Many of these alternative projects are direct forks of Bitcoin source code although some of those have been written from scratch. Some altcoins set out to address Bitcoin limitations such as privacy. Some others offer different types of mining, changes in block times, and distribution schemes.

By definition, an altcoin is generated in the case of a hard fork. If bitcoin has a hard fork then the other, older chain is effectively considered another coin. However, there is no established rule as to which chain becomes the altcoin. This has happened with Ethereum, where a hard fork caused a new currency **Ethereum Classic** (**ETC**) to come into existence in addition to the **Ethereum** (**ETH**) currency. Ethereum classic is the old chain and Ether is the new chain after the fork. Such a contentious hard fork is not desirable for some reasons. First it is against the true spirit of decentralization as the Ethereum foundation, a central entity, decided to go ahead with the hard fork even though not everyone agreed to the proposition; second, it also splits the user community due to disagreement over the hard fork. Although a hard fork, in theory, generates an altcoin, it is limited in what it can offer because, even if the change results in a hard fork, usually there are no drastic changes around the fundamental parameters of the coin. They typically remain the same. For this reason, it is desirable to either write a new coin from scratch or fork the bitcoin (or another coin's source code) to create a new currency with the desired parameters and features.

Altcoins must be able to attract new users, trades, and miners otherwise the currency will have no value. Currency gains its value, especially in the virtual currency space, due to the network effect and its acceptability by the community. If a coin fails to attract enough users then soon it will be forgotten. Users can be attracted by providing an initial amount of coins and can be achieved by using various methods. There is, however, a risk that if the new coin does not perform well than their initial investment may be lost. Methods of providing an initial number of altcoins are discussed as follows:

- **Create a new blockchain**: Altcoins can create a new blockchain and allocate coins to initial miners, but this approach is now unpopular due to many scam schemes or *pump and dump* schemes where initial miners made a profit with the launch of a new currency and then disappeared.

- **Proof of Burn (PoB)**: Another approach to allocating initial funds to a new altcoin is PoB, also called a one-way peg or price ceiling. In this method users permanently destroy a certain quantity of bitcoins in proportion to the quantity of altcoins to be claimed. For example, if ten bitcoins were destroyed then altcoins can have a value no greater than some bitcoins destroyed. This means that bitcoins are being converted into altcoins by burning them.

- **Proof of ownership**: Instead of permanently destroying bitcoins, an alternative method is to prove that users own a certain number of bitcoins. This proof of ownership can be used to claim altcoins by tethering altcoin blocks to Bitcoin blocks. For example, this can be achieved by merged mining in which effectively bitcoin miners can mine altcoin blocks while mining for bitcoin without any extra work. Merged mining is explained later in the chapter.

- **Pegged sidechains**: Sidechains, as the name suggests, are blockchains separate from the bitcoin network but bitcoins can be transferred to them. Altcoins can also be transferred back to the bitcoin network. This concept is called a **two-way peg**.

Investing and trading these alternative coins is also a big business, albeit not as big as bitcoin but enough to attract new investors and traders and provide liquidity to the market. Combined altcoin market capitalization is shown as follows:

 The graph is generated from `https://coinmarketcap.com/`.

This graph shows that at the time of writing the Combined Altcoin Market Capitalization is more than 200 billion US Dollars

Current market cap (as of March, 2018) of the top 10 coins is shown as follows:

Name	Market Cap	Price USD
Bitcoin	$151,388,873,045	$8,951.83
Ethereum	$68,472,253,587	$697.94
Ripple	$31,340,920,806	$0.801723
Bitcoin Cash	$17,182,167,856	$1,010.08
Litecoin	$9,952,905,688	$179.11
NEO	$5,638,100,000	$86.74
Cardano	$5,450,310,987	$0.210217
Stellar	$5,438,720,268	$0.294010
EOS	$4,347,501,290	$6.04
Monero	$4,211,690,257	$266.40

The data is taken from `https://coinmarketcap.com/`.

There are various factors and new concepts introduced with alternative coins. Many concepts were invented even before bitcoin but with bitcoin were not only new concepts, such as a solution to the Byzantine Generals' Problem, introduced but also previous ideas such as hashcash and **Proof of Work** (**PoW**) were used ingeniously and came into the limelight.

Since then, with the introduction of alternative coin projects, various new techniques and concepts have been developed and introduced. To appreciate the current landscape of alternative cryptocurrencies, it is essential to understand some theoretical concepts first.

Theoretical foundations

In this section, various theoretical concepts are introduced to the reader that has been developed with the introduction of different altcoins in the past few years.

Alternatives to Proof of Work

The PoW scheme in the context of cryptocurrency was first used in Bitcoin and served as a mechanism to provide assurance that a miner had completed the required amount of work to find a block. This process in return provided decentralization, security, and stability for the blockchain. This is the primary vehicle in Bitcoin for providing decentralized distributed consensus. PoW schemes are required to have a much-desired property called **progress freeness**, which means that the reward for consuming computational resources should be random and proportional to the contribution made by the miners. In this case, some chance of winning the block reward is given to even those miners who have comparatively less computational power.

The term progress freeness was introduced by Arvind Narayanan and others in the book *Bitcoin and Cryptocurrency Technologies*. Other requirements for mining computational puzzles include adjustable difficulty and quick verification. Adjustable difficulty ensures that the difficulty target for mining on the blockchain is regulated in response to increased hashing power and the number of users.

Quick verification is a property which means that mining computational puzzles should be easy and quick to verify. Another aspect of the PoW scheme, especially the one used in Bitcoin (Double SHA-256), is that since the introduction of ASICs the power is shifting towards miners or mining pools who can afford to operate large-scale ASIC farms. This power shift challenges the core philosophy of the decentralization of Bitcoin.

There are a few alternatives that have been proposed such as ASIC-resistant puzzles and are designed in such a way that building ASICs for solving this puzzle is infeasible and does not result in a major performance gain over commodity hardware. A common technique used for this purpose is to apply a class of computationally hard problems called **memory hard computational puzzles**. The core idea behind this method is that as puzzle solving requires a large amount of memory, it is not feasible to be implemented on ASIC-based systems.

This technique was initially used in Litecoin and Tenebrix where the Scrypt hash function was used as an ASIC-resistant PoW scheme. Even though this scheme was initially advertised as ASIC resistant, recently Scrypt ASICs have now become available, disproving the original claim by Litecoin. This happened because Scrypt is a memory intensive mechanism and initially it was thought that building ASICs with large memories is difficult due to technical and cost limitations. This is no longer the case, because memory is increasingly becoming cheaper and with the ability to produce nanometer scale circuits it is possible to build ASICs that can run Scrypt algorithm.

Another approach to ASIC resistance is where multiple hash functions are required to be calculated to provide PoW. This is also called a **chained hashing scheme**. The rationale behind this idea is that designing multiple hash functions on an ASIC is not very feasible. The most common example is the X11 memory hard function implemented in Dash. X11 comprises 11 SHA-3 contestants where one algorithm outputs the calculated hash to the next algorithm until all 11 algorithms are used in a sequence. These algorithms include BLAKE, BMW, Groestl, JH, Keccak, Skein, Luffa, CubeHash, SHAvite, SIMD, and ECHO.

This approach did provide some resistance to ASIC development initially, but now ASIC miners are available commercially and support mining of X11 and similar schemes. A recent example is ASIC Baikal Miner, which supports X11, X13, X14, and X15 mining. Other examples include miners such as iBeLink DM384M X11 miner and PinIdea X11 ASIC miner.

Perhaps another approach could be to design self-mutating puzzles that intelligently or randomly change the PoW scheme or its requirements as a function of time. This strategy will make it almost impossible to be implemented in ASICs as it will require multiple ASICs to be designed for each function and also randomly changing schemes would be almost impossible to handle in ASICs. At the moment, it is unclear how this can be achieved practically.

PoW does have various drawbacks, and the biggest of all is energy consumption. It is estimated that the total electricity consumed by Bitcoin miners currently is more than that of Bangladesh at 54.69 **Terawatt hash** (**TWh**). This is huge, and all that power is in a way wasted; in fact, no useful purpose is served except mining. Environmentalists have raised real concerns about this situation. In addition to electricity consumption, the carbon footprint is also very high currently estimated at around 387 kg of CO_2 per transaction.

The following graph shows the scale of Bitcoin energy consumption as compared to other countries. This is only expected to grow and it is estimated that by the end of year 2018, the energy consumption can reach approximately 125 TWh per year.

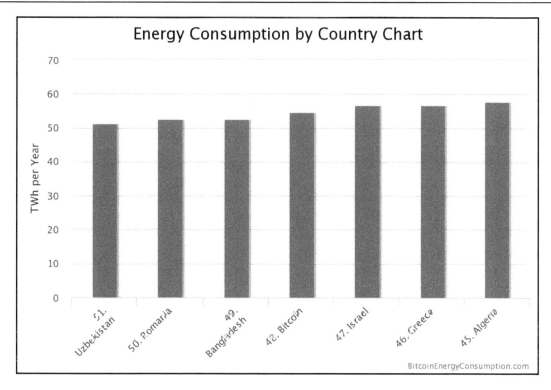

Energy consumption by country

The preceding graph shown is taken from the website which tracks this subject. It is available at `https://digiconomist.net/bitcoin-energy-consumption`.

It has been proposed that PoW puzzles can be designed in such a way that they serve two purposes. First, their primary purpose is in consensus mechanisms and second to perform some useful scientific computation. This way not only can the schemes be used in mining but they can also help to solve other scientific problems too potentially. This proof of useful work has been recently put into practice by Primecoin where the requirement is to find special prime number chains known as Cunningham chains and bi-twin chains. As the study of prime number distribution has special significance in scientific disciplines such as physics, by mining Primecoin miners not only achieve the block reward but also help in finding the special prime numbers.

Proof of Storage

Also known as proof of retrievability, this is another type of proof of useful work that requires storage of a large amount of data. Introduced by Microsoft Research, this scheme provides a useful benefit of distributed storage of archival data. Miners are required to store a pseudo, randomly-selected subset of large data to perform mining.

Proof of Stake (PoS)

This proof is also called virtual mining. This is another type of mining puzzle that has been proposed as an alternative to traditional PoW schemes. It was first proposed in Peercoin in August 2012. In this scheme, the idea is that users are required to demonstrate possession of a certain amount of currency (coins) thus proving that they have a stake in the coin. The simplest form of the stake is where mining is made comparatively easier for those users who demonstrably own larger amounts of digital currency. The benefits of this scheme are twofold; first acquiring large amounts of digital currency is relatively difficult as compared to buying high-end ASIC devices and second it results in saving computational resources. Various forms of stake have been proposed and are briefly discussed in the following subsection.

Various stake types

Different type of stakes will now be introduced in the following subsections.

Proof of coinage

The age of a coin is the time since the coins were last used or held. This is a different approach from the usual form of PoS where mining is made easier for users who have the highest stake in the altcoin. In the coin-age-based approach, the age of the coin (coinage) is reset every time a block is mined. The miner is rewarded for holding and not spending coins for a period of time. This mechanism has been implemented in Peercoin combined with PoW in a creative way.

The difficulty of mining puzzles (PoW) is inversely proportional to the coinage, meaning that if miners consume some coinage using coin-stake transactions, then the PoW requirements are relieved.

Proof of Deposit (PoD)

The core idea behind this scheme is that newly minted blocks by miners are made unspendable for a certain period. More precisely the coins get locked for a set number of blocks during the mining operation. The scheme works by allowing miners to perform mining at the cost of freezing a certain number of coins for some time. This is a type of PoS.

Proof of Burn

As an alternate expenditure to computing power, PoB, in fact, destroys a certain number of bitcoins to get equivalent altcoins. This is commonly used when starting up a new coin projects as a means to provide a fair initial distribution. This can be considered an alternative mining scheme where the value of the new coins comes from the fact that previously a certain number of coins have been destroyed.

Proof of Activity (PoA)

This scheme is a hybrid of PoW and PoS. In this scheme, blocks are initially produced using PoW, but then each block randomly assigns three stakeholders that are required to digitally sign it. The validity of subsequent blocks is dependent on the successful signing of previously randomly chosen blocks.

There is, however, a possible issue known as the nothing at stake problem where it would be trivial to create a fork of the blockchain. This is possible because in PoW appropriate computational resources are required to mine whereas in PoS there is no such requirement; as a result, an attacker can try to mine on multiple chains using the same coin.

Nonoutsourceable puzzles

The key motivation behind this puzzle is to develop resistance again the development of mining pools. Mining pools as previously discussed offer rewards to all participants in proportion to the computing power they consume. However, in this model the mining pool operator is a central authority to whom all the rewards go and who can enforce specific rules. Also, in this model, all miners only trust each other because they are working towards a common goal together in the hope of the pool manager getting the reward. Nonoutsourceable puzzles are a scheme that allows miners to claim rewards for themselves; consequently, pool formation becomes unlikely due to inherent mistrust between anonymous miners.

There are also various other alternatives to PoW, some of which have been described in Chapter 1, *Blockchain 101* and some will be explained later in this book in Chapter 13, *Hyperledger* and Chapter 16, *Scalability and Other Challenges*. As this is an ongoing area of research, new alternatives will keep emerging as blockchain technology grows.

Difficulty adjustment and retargeting algorithms

Another concept that has been introduced with the advent of bitcoin and altcoins is difficulty in retargeting algorithms. In bitcoin, a difficulty target is calculated simply by the following equation; however other coins have either developed their algorithms or implemented modified versions of the bitcoin difficulty algorithm:

$$T = Time\ previous * time\ actual\ /\ 2016 * 10\ min$$

The idea behind difficulty regulation in bitcoin is that a generation of 2016 blocks should take roughly around two weeks (inter-block time should be around 10 minutes). If it takes longer than two weeks to mine 2016 blocks, then the difficulty is decreased, and if it takes less than two weeks to mine 2016 blocks, then the difficulty is increased. When ASICs were introduced due to a high block generation rate, the difficulty increased exponentially, and that is one drawback of PoW algorithms that are not ASIC resistant. This leads to mining power centralization.

This also poses another problem; if a new coin starts now with the same PoW based on SHA-256 as bitcoin uses, then it would be easy for a malicious user to just simply use an ASIC miner and control the entire network. This attack would be more practical if there is less interest in the new altcoin and someone decides to take over the network by consuming adequately high computing resources. This may not be a possible attack if other miners with similar computing power also join the altcoin network because then miners will be competing with each other.

Also, multipools pose a more significant threat where a group of miners can automatically switch to the currency that is becoming profitable. This phenomenon is known as **pool hopping** and can adversely affect a blockchain, and consequently the growth of the altcoin. Pool hopping impacts the network adversely because pool hoppers join the network only when the difficulty is low and they can gain quick rewards; the moment difficulty goes up (or is readjusted) they hop off and then come back again when the difficulty is adjusted back.

For example, if a multipool consumes its resources in quickly mining a new coin, the difficulty will increase very quickly; when the multipool leaves the currency network; it becomes almost unusable because of the fact that now the difficulty has increased to such a level that it is no longer profitable for solo miners and can no longer be maintained. The only fix for this problem is to initiate a hard fork which is usually undesirable for the community.

There are a few algorithms that have come into existence to address this issue and are discussed later in this chapter. All these algorithms are based on the idea of readjusting various parameters in response to hash rate changes; these parameters include the number of previous blocks, the difficulty of previous blocks, the ratio of adjustment, and the number by which the difficulty can be readjusted back or up.

In the following section, readers will be introduced to the few difficulty algorithms being used in and proposed for various altcoins.

Kimoto Gravity Well

This algorithm is used in various altcoins to regulate difficulty. This method was first introduced in Megacoin and used to adjust the difficulty of the network every block adaptively. The logic of the algorithm is shown as follows:

$$KGW = 1 + (0.7084 * pow((double(PastBlocksMass)/double(144)), -1.228))$$

The algorithm runs in a loop that goes through a set of predetermined blocks (*PastBlockMass*) and calculates a new readjustment value. The core idea behind this algorithm is to develop an adaptive difficulty regulation mechanism that can readjust the difficulty in response to rapid spikes in hash rates. **Kimoto Gravity Well** (**KGW**) ensures that the time between blocks remains approximately the same. In Bitcoin, the difficulty is adjusted every 2016 blocks, but in KGW the difficulty is adjusted at every block.

This algorithm is vulnerable to time warp attacks, which, allow an attacker to enjoy less difficulty in creating new blocks temporarily. This attack allows a time window where the difficulty becomes low, and the attacker can quickly generate many coins at a fast rate.

More information can be found at the link `https://cryptofrenzy.` `wordpress.com/2014/02/09/multipools-vs-gravity-well/.`

Dark Gravity Wave

Dark Gravity Wave (**DGW**) is a new algorithm designed to address certain flaws such as the time warp attack in the KGW algorithm. This concept was first introduced in Dash, previously known as Darkcoin. It makes use of multiple exponential moving averages and simple move averages to achieve a smoother readjustment mechanism. The formula is shown as follows:

$$2222222/ ((((Difficulty+2600)/9)^2)$$

This formula is implemented in Dash coin, Bitcoin SegWit2X and various other altcoins as a mechanism to readjust difficulty.

DGW version 3.0 is the latest implementation of DGW algorithm and allows improved difficulty retargeting as compared to KGW.

 More information can be found at `https://dashpay.atlassian.net/wiki/spaces/DOC/pages/1146926/Dark+Gravity+Wave`.

DigiShield

This is another difficulty retargeting algorithm that has recently been used in Zcash with slight variations and after adequate experimentation. This algorithm works by going through a fixed number of previous blocks to calculate the time they took to be generated and then readjusts the difficulty to the difficulty of the previous block by dividing the actual time span by averaging the target time. In this scheme, the retargeting is calculated much more rapidly, and also the recovery from a sudden increase or decrease in hash rate is quick. This algorithm protects against multipools, which can result in rapid hash rate increases.

The network difficulty is readjusted every block or every minute depending on the implementation. The key innovation is faster readjusting times as compared to KGW.

Zcash uses DigiShield v3.0 which uses the following formula for difficulty adjustment:

(New difficulty) = (previous difficulty) x SQRT [(150 seconds) / (last solve time)

There is detailed discussion available on it at `https://github.com/zcash/zcash/issues/147#issuecomment-245140908`.

MIDAS

Multi-Interval Difficulty Adjustment System (**MIDAS**) is an algorithm that is comparatively more complex than the algorithms discussed previously due to number of parameters it uses. This method responds much more rapidly to abrupt changes in hash rates. This algorithm also protects against time warp attacks.

The original post about this is now available via web archive at `https://web.archive.org/web/20161005171345/http://dillingers.com/blog/2015/04/21/altcoin-difficulty-adjustment-with-midas/`.

The interested readers can read more about this at the preceding location.

This concludes our introduction to various difficulty adjustment algorithms.

Many alternative cryptocurrencies and protocols have emerged as an attempt to address various limitations in Bitcoin.

Bitcoin limitations

Various limitations in Bitcoin have also sparked some interest in altcoins, which were developed specifically to address limitations in Bitcoin. The most prominent and widely discussed limitation is the lack of anonymity in Bitcoin. We will now discuss some of the limitations of Bitcoin.

Privacy and anonymity

As the blockchain is a public ledger of all transactions and is openly available, it becomes trivial to analyze it. Combined with traffic analyses, transactions can be linked back to their source IP addresses, thus possibly revealing a transaction's originator. This is a big concern from a privacy point of view.

Even though in Bitcoin it is a recommended and common practice to generate a new address for every transaction, thus allowing some level of unlinkability, this is not enough, and various techniques have been developed and successfully used to trace the flow of transactions throughout the network and link them back to their originator. These techniques analyze blockchains by using transaction graphs, address graphs and entity graphs which facilitate linking users back to the transactions, thus raising privacy concerns. The techniques mentioned earlier in the preceding analysis can be further enriched by using publicly available information about transactions and linking them to the actual users. There are open source block parsers available that can be used to extract transaction information, balances, and scripts from the blockchain database.

 A parser available at `https://github.com/mikispag/rusty-blockparser` is written in Rust language and provides advanced blockchain analysis capabilities.

Various proposals have been made to address the privacy issue in Bitcoin. These proposals fall into three categories: mixing protocols, third-party mixing networks, and inherent anonymity.

A brief discussion of each category is presented as follows.

Mixing protocols

These schemes are used to provide anonymity to bitcoin transactions. In this model, a mixing service provider (an intermediary or a shared wallet) is used. Users send coins to this shared wallet as a deposit, and then, the shared wallet can send some other coins (of the same value deposited by some other users) to the destination. Users can also receive coins that were sent by others via this intermediary. This way the link between outputs and inputs is no longer there and transaction graph analysis will not be able to reveal the actual relationship between senders and receivers.

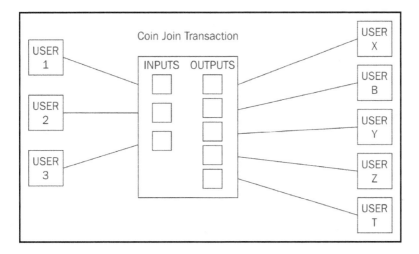

CoinJoin transaction with three users joining their transaction into a single larger CoinJoin transaction

CoinJoin is one example of mixing protocols, where two transactions are joined together to form a single transaction while keeping the inputs and outputs unchanged. The core idea behind CoinJoin is to build a shared transaction that is signed by all participants. This technique improves privacy for all participants involved in the transactions.

Third-party mixing protocols

Various third-party mixing services are available, but if the service is centralized, then it poses the threat of tracing the mapping between senders and receivers because the mixing service knows about all inputs and outputs. In addition to this, fully centralized miners even pose the risk of the administrators of the service stealing the coins.

Various services, with varying degrees of complexity, such as CoinShuffle, Coinmux, and Darksend in Dash (coin) are available that are based on the idea of CoinJoin (mixing) transactions. CoinShuffle is a decentralized alternative to traditional mixing services as it does not require a trusted third party.

CoinJoin-based schemes, however, have some weaknesses, most prominently the possibility of launching a denial of service attack by users who committed to signing the transactions initially but now are not providing their signature, thus delaying or stopping joint transaction altogether.

Inherent anonymity

This category includes coins that support privacy inherently and is built into the design of the currency. The most popular is Zcash, which uses **Zero-Knowledge Proofs** (**ZKP**) to achieve anonymity. It is discussed in detail later in the chapter. Other examples include Monero, which makes use of ring signatures to provide anonymous services.

The next section introduces various enhancements that have been made or are proposed, to extend the Bitcoin protocol.

Extended protocols on top of Bitcoin

Several protocols, discussed in the following sections, have been proposed and implemented on top of Bitcoin to enhance and extend the Bitcoin protocol and use for various other purposes instead of just as a virtual currency.

Colored coins

Colored coins are a set of methods that have been developed to represent digital assets on the Bitcoin blockchain. Coloring a bitcoin refers colloquially to updating it with some metadata representing a digital asset (smart property). The coin still works and operates as a bitcoin but additionally carries some metadata that represents some assets. This can be some information related to the asset, some calculations related to transactions or any arbitrary data. This mechanism allows issuing and tracking specific bitcoins. Metadata can be recorded using the bitcoins OP_RETURN opcode or optionally in multisignature addresses. This metadata can also be encrypted if required to address any privacy concerns. Some implementations also support storage of metadata on publicly available torrent networks which means that virtually unlimited amounts of metadata can be stored. Usually these are JSON objects representing various attributes of the colored coin. Moreover, smart contracts are also supported. One example of such implementation is Colu, which can be found at, http://colu.co/.

Colored coins can be used to represent a multitude of assets including, but not limited to commodities, certificates, shares, bonds, and voting. It should also be noted that to work with colored coins, a wallet that interprets colored coins is necessary and normal Bitcoin wallets will not work. Normal Bitcoin wallets will not work, because they cannot differentiate between *colored coins* and *not colored coins*.

Colored coin wallets can be set up online using a service available at `https://www.coinprism.com/`. By using this service, any digital asset can be created and issued via a colored coin.

The idea of colored coins is very appealing as it does not require any modification to the existing Bitcoin protocol and can make use of the already existing secure Bitcoin network. In addition to the traditional representation of digital assets, there is also the possibility of creating smart assets that behave according to the parameters and conditions defined for them. These parameters include time validation, restrictions on transferability, and fees.

A significant use case can be the issuance of financial instruments on the blockchain. This will ensure low transaction fees, valid and mathematically secure proof of ownership, fast transferability without requiring some intermediary, and instant dividend payouts to the investors.

A rich API is available for colored coins at `http://coloredcoins.org/`.

Counterparty

This is another service that can be used to create custom tokens that act as a cryptocurrency and can be used for various purposes such as issuing digital assets on top of bitcoin blockchain. This is quite a robust platform and runs on bitcoin blockchains at their core but has developed its client and other components to support issuing digital assets. The architecture consists of a counterparty server, counter block, counter wallet, and `armory_utxsvr`. Counterparty works based on the same idea as colored coins by embedding data into regular bitcoin transactions but provides a much more productive library and set of powerful tools to support the handling of digital assets. This embedding is also called **embedded consensus** because the counterparty transactions are embedded within bitcoin transactions. The method of embedding the data is by using `OP_RETURN` opcode in bitcoin.

The currency produced and used by Counterparty is known as XCP and is used by smart contracts as the fee for running the contract. At the time of writing its price is 2.78 USD. XCPs were created by using the PoB method discussed previously.

Counterparty allows the development of smart contracts on Ethereum using solidity language and allows interaction with bitcoin blockchain. To achieve this, BTC Relay is used as a means to provide interoperability between Ethereum and Bitcoin. This is a clever concept where Ethereum contracts can talk to bitcoin blockchain and transactions through BTC Relay. The relayers (nodes that are running BTC Relay) fetch the bitcoin block headers and relay them to a smart contract on the Ethereum network that verifies the PoW. This process verifies that a transaction has occurred on the bitcoin network.

 This is available at `http://btcrelay.org/`.

Technically, this is an Ethereum contract that is capable of storing and verifying bitcoin block headers just like bitcoin simple payment verification lightweight clients do by using bloom filters. SPV clients were discussed in detail in the previous chapters. The idea can be visualized with the following diagram:

BTC relay concept

 Counterparty is available at `http://counterparty.io/`.

Development of altcoins

Altcoin projects can be started very quickly from a coding point of view by simply forking the bitcoin or another coin's source code, but this probably is not enough. When a new coin project is started, several things need to be considered to ensure a successful launch and the coin's longevity. Usually, the code base is written in C++ as was the case with bitcoin, but almost any language can be used to develop coin projects, for example, Golang or Rust.

Writing code or forking the code for an existing coin is the trivial part, the challenging issue is how to start a new currency so that investors and users can be attracted to it. Generally, the following steps are taken in order to start a new coin project.

From a technical point of view, in the case of forking the code of another coin, for example, bitcoin, there are various parameters that can be changed to effectively create a new coin. These parameters are required to be tweaked or introduced in order to create a new coin. These parameters can include but are not limited to the following.

Consensus algorithms

There is a choice of consensus algorithms available, for example PoW used in Bitcoin or PoS, used in Peercoin. There are also other algorithms available such as **Proof of Capacity (PoC)** and few others, but PoW and PoS are the most common choices.

Hashing algorithms

This is either SHA-256, Scrypt, X11, X13, X15, or any other hashing algorithm that is adequate for use as a consensus algorithm.

Difficulty adjustment algorithms

Various options are available in this category to provide difficulty retargeting mechanisms. The most prominent examples are KGW, DGW, Nite's Gravity Wave, and DigiShield. Also, all these algorithms can be tweaked based on requirements to produce different results; therefore, many variants are possible.

Inter-block time

This is the time elapsed between the generation of each block. For bitcoin the blocks are generated every 10 minutes, for litecoin it's 2.5 minutes. Any value can be used but an appropriate value is usually between a few minutes; if the generation time is too fast it might destabilize the blockchain, if it's too slow it may not attract many users.

Block rewards

A block reward is for the miner who solves the mining puzzle and is allowed to have a coinbase transaction that contains the reward. This used to be 50 coins in bitcoin initially and now many altcoins set this parameter to a very high number; for example, in Dogecoin it is 10,000, currently.

Reward halving rate

This is another important factor; in bitcoin, it is halved every 4 years and now is set to 12.5 bitcoins. It's a variable number that can be set to any time period or none at all depending on the requirements.

Block size and transaction size

This is another important factor that determines how high or low the transaction rate can be on the network. Block sizes in bitcoin are limited to 1 MB but in altcoins, it can vary depending on the requirements.

Interest rate

This property applies only to PoS systems where the owner of the coins can earn interest at a rate defined by the network in return for some coins that are held on the network as a stake to protect the network. This interest rate keeps inflation under control. If interest rate is too low then it can cause hyperinflation.

Coinage

This parameter defines how long the coin has to remain unspent in order for it to become eligible to be considered stake worthy.

Total supply of coins

This number sets the total limit of the coins that can ever be generated. For example, in Bitcoin the limit is 21 million, whereas in Dogecoin it's unlimited. This limit is fixed by the block reward and halving schedule discussed earlier.

There are two options to create your own virtual currency: forking existing established cryptocurrency source code or writing a new one from scratch. The latter option is less popular but the first option is easier and has allowed the creation of many virtual currencies over the last few years. Fundamentally, the idea is that first a cryptocurrency source code is forked and then appropriate changes are made at different strategic locations in the source code to effectively create a new currency. NEM coin is one of the newly created coins that have their code written entirely from scratch.

In the next section, readers are introduced to some altcoin projects. It is not possible to cover all alternative currencies in this chapter, but a few selected coins are discussed in the following section. Selection is based on longevity, market cap, and innovation. Each coin is discussed from different angles such as theoretical foundations, trading, and mining.

Namecoin

Namecoin is the first fork of the Bitcoin source code. The key idea behind Namecoin is not to produce an altcoin but instead to provide improved decentralization, censorship resistance, privacy, security, and faster-decentralized naming. Decentralized naming services are intended to respond to inherent limitations such as slowness and centralized control in the traditional **Domain Name System** (**DNS**) protocols used on the internet. Namecoin is also the first solution to Zooko's triangle, which was briefly discussed in Chapter 1, *Blockchain 101*.

Namecoin is used to essentially provide a service to register a key/value pair. One major use case of Namecoin is that it can provide a decentralized **Transport Layer Security** (**TLS**) certificate validation mechanism, driven by blockchain-based distributed and decentralized consensus.

It is based on the same technology introduced with bitcoin, but with its own blockchain and wallet software.

 The source code for the Namecoin core is available at
https://github.com/namecoin/namecoin-core.

In summary, Namecoin provides the following three services:

- Secure storage and transfer of names (keys)
- Attachment of some value to the names by attaching up to 520 bytes of data
- Production of a digital currency (Namecoin)

Namecoin also for the first time introduced merged mining, which allows a miner to mine on more than one chain simultaneously. The idea is simple but very effective: miners create a Namecoin block and produce a hash of that block. Then the hash is added to a Bitcoin block and miners solve that block at equal to or greater than the Namecoin block difficulty to prove that enough work has been contributed towards solving the Namecoin block.

The coinbase transaction is used to include the hash of the transactions from Namecoin (or any other altcoin if merged mining with that coin). The mining task is to solve Bitcoin blocks whose coinbase `scriptSig` contains a hash pointer to Namecoin (or any other altcoin) block. This is shown in the following diagram:

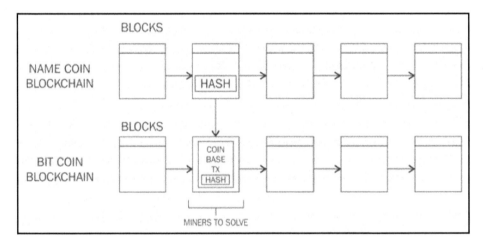

Merged mining visualization

If a miner manages to solve a hash at the bitcoin blockchain difficulty level, the bitcoin block is built and becomes part of the Bitcoin network. In this case, the Namecoin hash is ignored by the bitcoin blockchain. On the other hand, if a miner solves a block at Namecoin blockchain difficulty level a new block is created in the Namecoin blockchain. The core benefit of this scheme is that all the computational power spent by the miners contributes towards securing both Namecoin and Bitcoin.

Trading Namecoins

The current market cap of Namecoin is $29,143,884 USD as per `https://coinmarketcap.com/` in March, 2018. It can be bought and sold at various exchanges such as:

- `https://cryptonit.net/`
- `https://bisq.network`
- `https://www.evonax.com`
- `https://bter.com`

Obtaining Namecoins

Even though Namecoins can be mined independently, they are usually mined as part of bitcoin mining by utilizing the merged mining technique as explained earlier. This way Namecoin can be mined as a by-product of bitcoin mining. Solo mining is no longer profitable as is evident from the following difficulty graph; instead, it is recommended to use merged mining, use a mining pool, or even use a cryptocurrency exchange to buy Namecoin.

Namecoin difficulty as shown at: https://bitinfocharts.com/comparison/difficulty-nmc.html (since December, 2016)

Various mining pools such as `https://slushpool.com` also offer the option of merged mining. This allows a miner to mine primarily bitcoin but also, as a result, earn Namecoin too.

Another method that can be used to quickly get some Namecoins is to swap your existing coins with Namecoins, for example, if you already have some bitcoins or another cryptocurrency that can be used to exchange with Namecoin.

An online service, `https://shapeshift.io/`, is available that provides this service. This service allows conversion from one cryptocurrency to another, using a simple user-friendly interface.

For example, paying BTC to receive NMC is shown as follows:

1. First the deposit coin is selected, which in this case is bitcoin and coin to be received is selected, which is Namecoin in this case. In the top editbox, the Namecoin address where you want to receive the exchanged Namecoin is entered. In the second editbox, at the bottom the bitcoin refund address is entered, where the coins will be returned to in case the transaction fails for any reason.

2. The exchange rate and miner fee are calculated instantly as soon as the deposit and exchange currency are chosen. Exchange rate is driven by the market conditions whereas miner fee is calculated algorithmically based on the target currency chosen and what the target network's miner would charge.

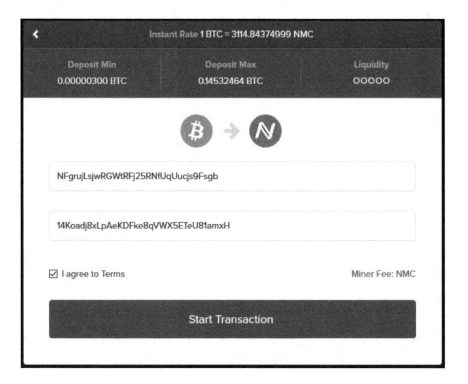

Bitcoin to Namecoin exchange

3. Once **Start Transaction** is clicked, the transaction starts and instructs the user to send the bitcoins to a specific bitcoin address. When the user sends the required amount, the conversion process starts as shown in the following screenshot. This whole process takes few minutes:

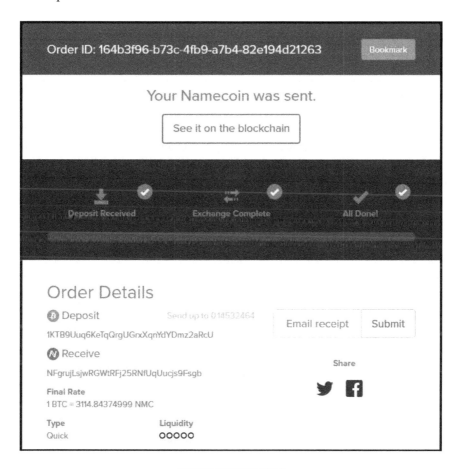

Notification of Namecoin delivery

The preceding screenshot shows that after sending the deposit the exchange occurs and finally **All Done!** message is displayed indicating that the exchange has been successful.

A few other order details are displayed on the page such as what currency was deposited and what was received after exchange. In this case it is Bitcoin to Namecoin exchange. It's also worth noting that relevant addresses are also displayed under each coin icon. There are few other option such **Email receipt** which can be invoked to receive an email receipt of the transaction.

When the process completes, the transactions can be viewed in the Namecoin wallet as shown here:

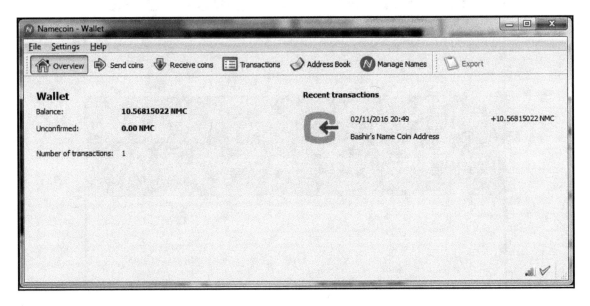

Namecoin wallet

It may take some time (usually around 1 hour) to confirm the transactions; until that time, it is not possible to use the Namecoins to manage names. Once Namecoins are available in the wallet, the **Manage Names** option can be used to generate Namecoin records.

Generating Namecoin records

Namecoin records are in the form of key and value pairs. A name is a lowercase string of the form `d/examplename` whereas a value is a case-sensitive, UTF-8 encoded JSON object with a maximum of 520 bytes. The name should be RFC1035 (`https://tools.ietf.org/html/rfc1035`)-compliant.

A general Namecoin name can be an arbitrary binary string up to 255 bytes long with, 1024-bits of associated identifying information. A record on a Namecoin chain is only valid for around 200 days or 36,000 blocks after which it needs to be renewed. Namecoin also introduced .bit top-level domains that can be registered using Namecoin and can be browsed using specialized Namecoin-enabled resolvers. Namecoin wallet software as shown in the following screenshot can be used to register .bit domain names.

The name is entered and, after the **Submit** button is pressed, it will ask for configuration information such as DNS, IP, or identity:

Namecoin wallet: domain name configuration

As shown in the following screenshot, `masteringblockchain` will register as `masteringblockchain.bit` on the Namecoin blockchain:

Namecoin wallet: showing registered name

Litecoin

Litecoin is a fork of the bitcoin source code released in 2011. It uses Scrypt as PoW, originally introduced in the Tenebrix coin. Litecoin allows for faster transactions as compared to bitcoin due to its faster block generation time of 2.5 minutes. Also, difficulty readjustment is achieved every 3.5 days roughly due to faster block generation time. The total coin supply is 84 million.

Scrypt is a sequentially memory hard function that is the first alternative to the SHA-256-based PoW algorithm. It was originally proposed as a **Password-Based Key Derivation Function (PBKDF)**. The key idea is that if the function requires a significant amount of memory to run then custom hardware such as ASICs will require more VLSI area, which would be infeasible to build. The Scrypt algorithm requires a large array of pseudorandom bits to be held in memory and a key is derived from this in a pseudorandom fashion.

The algorithm is based on a phenomenon called **Time-Memory Trade-Off** (**TMTO**). If memory requirements are relaxed, then it results in increased computational cost. Put another way, TMTO shortens the running time of a program if more memory is given to it. This trade-off makes it unfeasible for an attacker to gain more memory because it is expensive and difficult to implement on custom hardware, or if the attacker chooses not to increase memory, then it results in the algorithm running slowly due to high processing requirements. This means that ASICs are difficult to build for this algorithm.

Scrypt uses the following parameters to generate a derived key (*Kd*):

- **Passphrase**: This is a string of characters to hash
- **Salt**: This is a random string that is provided to Scrypt functions (generally all hash functions) in order to provide a defense against brute-force dictionary attacks using rainbow tables
- **N**: This is a memory/CPU cost parameter that must be a power of $2 > 1$
- **P**: This is the parallelization parameter
- **R**: This is the block size parameter
- **dkLen**: This is the intended length of the derived key in bytes

Formally, this function can be written as follows:

$$Kd = scrypt\ (P,\ S,\ N,\ P,\ R,\ dkLen)$$

Before applying the core Scrypt function, the algorithm takes *P* and *S* as input and applies PBKDF2 and SHA-256-based HMAC. Then the output is fed to an algorithm called ROMix, which internally uses the Blockmix algorithm using the Salsa20/8 core stream cipher to fill up the memory which requires large memory to operate, thus enforcing the sequentially memory hard property.

The output from this step of the algorithm is finally fed to the PBKDF2 function again in order to produce a derived key. This process is shown in the following diagram:

Scrypt algorithm

Scrypt is used in Litecoin mining with specific parameters where *N= 1024, R = 1, P=1,* and *S = random 80 bytes* producing a 256-bit output.

It appears that, due to the selection of these parameters, the development of ASICs for Scrypt for Litecoin mining turned out to be not very difficult. In an ASIC for Litecoin mining, a sequential logic can be developed that takes the data and nonce as input and applies the PBKDF2 algorithm with HMAC-SHA256; then the resultant bit stream is fed into the SALSA20/8 function which produces a hash that again is fed down to the PBKDF2 and HMAC-256 functions to produce a 256-bit hash output. As is the case with bitcoin PoW, in Scrypt also if the output hash is less than the target hash (already passed as input at the start, stored in memory, and checked with every iteration) then the function terminates; otherwise, the nonce is incremented and the process is repeated again until a hash is found that is lower than the difficulty target.

Scrypt ASIC design simplified flowchart

- **Trading litecoin**: As with other coins, trading litecoin is easily carried out on various online exchanges. The current market cap of litecoin is $10,448,974,615. The current price (as of March, 2018) of litecoin is $188.04/LTC.
- **Mining**: Litecoin mining can be carried out solo or in pools. At the moment, ASICs for Scrypt are available that are commonly used to mine Litecoin.

Litecoin mining on a CPU is no longer profitable as is the case with many other digital currencies now. There are online cloud mining providers and ASIC miners available that can be used to mine Litecoin. Litecoin mining started from the CPU, progressed through GPU mining rigs, and eventually now has reached a point where specialized ASIC miners, such as ASIC Scrypt Miner Wolf are available from Ehsminer are now required to be used in the hope of being able to make some coins. Generally, it is true that even with ASICs it is better to mine in pools instead of solo as solo mining is not as profitable as mining in pools due to the proportional rewards scheme used by mining pools. These miners are capable of producing a hashing rate of 2 Gh/s for Scrypt algorithms.

- **Software source code and wallet**: The source code for litecoin is available at `https://github.com/litecoin-project/litecoin`. The Litecoin wallet can be downloaded from `https://litecoin.org/` and can be used just like the Bitcoin core client software.

Primecoin

Primecoin is the first digital currency on the market that introduced a useful PoW, as opposed to Bitcoin's SHA256-based PoW. Primecoin uses searching prime numbers as a PoW. Not all types of prime number meet the requirements to be selected as PoW. Three types of prime numbers (known as Cunningham chain of the first kind, Cunningham chain of the second kind, and bi-twin chains) meet the requirements of a PoW algorithm to be used in cryptocurrencies.

The difficulty is dynamically adjusted via a continuous difficulty evaluation scheme in Primecoin blockchain. The efficient verification of PoW based on prime numbers is also of high importance, because if verification is slow, then PoW is not suitable. Therefore, prime chains are selected as a PoW because finding prime chains gets difficult as the chain increases in length whereas verification remains quick enough to warrant being used as an efficient PoW algorithm.

It is also important that once a PoW has been verified on a block, it must not be reusable on another block. This is accomplished in Primecoin by a combination of PoW certificates and hashing it with the header of the parent block in the child block.

The PoW certificate is produced by linking the prime chain to the block header hash. It also requires that the block header's origin be divisible by the block header hash. If it is, it is divided and after division, the quotient is used as a PoW certificate. Another property of the adjustable difficulty of PoW algorithms is met by introducing difficulty adjustment every block instead of every 2,016, as is the case with bitcoin. This is a smoother approach as compared to bitcoin and allows readjustment in the case of sudden increases in hash power. Also, the total number of coins generated is community-driven, and there is no definite limit on the number of coins Primecoin can generate.

Trading Primecoin

Primecoins can be traded on major virtual currency trading exchanges. The current market cap of Primecoin is $17,482,507 at the time of writing (March, 2018). It is not very large but, because Primecoin is based on a novel idea and there is a dedicated community behind it, this continues to hold some market share.

A graph, showing some statistics related to Primecoin

Data sourced from: https://coinmarketcap.com/currencies/primecoin/

Mining guide

The first step is to download a wallet. Primecoin supports native mining within the wallet, just like original Bitcoin clients, but also can be mined on the cloud via various online cloud service providers.

A quick Windows guide is presented as follows, Linux client is also available at `http://primecoin.io/downloads.php`.

1. The first step is to download the Primecoin wallet from `http://primecoin.io/index.php`.

2. Once the wallet is installed and synced with the network, mining can be started by following the next step. A debug window can be opened in the Primecoin wallet by clicking on the **Help menu** and selecting the **Debug window** menu item. Additional help can be invoked through typing `help` in the **Console** window of **Debug window** used to enable the Primecoin mining function:

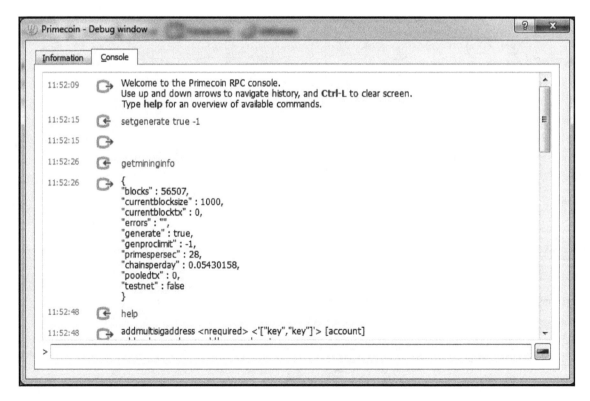

Primecoin mining

3. Once the preceding commands are successfully executed mining will start in solo mode. This may not be very fast and profitable if you have an entry level PC with slower CPU but as this is a CPU mined cryptocurrency the miner can use PCs with powerful CPUs. As an alternative cloud services can be used which host powerful server hardware:

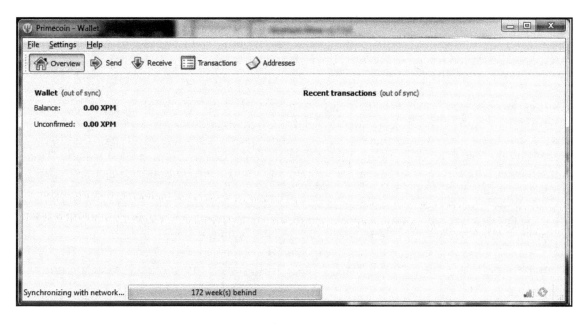

Primecoin wallet software, synching with the network

 The Primecoin source code is available at `https://github.com/primecoin/primecoin`.

Primecoin is a novel concept and the PoW that it has introduced have great scientific significance. It is still in use with a market cap of $17,034,198 USD but it appears that no active development is being carried out to further develop Primecoin as is evident from GitHub inactivity.

 Readers can further explore Primecoin by reading the Primecoin whitepaper by Sunny King (pseudonym) at: `http://primecoin.io/bin/primecoin-paper.pdf`.

Zcash

Zcash was launched on October 28, 2016. This is the first currency that uses a specific type of ZKPs known as **Zero-Knowledge Succinct Non-Interactive Arguments of Knowledge (ZK-SNARKs)** to provide complete privacy to the user. These proofs are concise and easy to verify; however, setting up the initial public parameters is a complicated process. The latter include two keys: the proving key and verifying key. The process requires sampling some random numbers to construct the public parameters. The issue is that these random numbers, also called toxic waste, must be destroyed after the parameter generation in order to prevent counterfeiting of Zcash.

For this purpose, the Zcash team came up with a multi-party computation protocol to generate the required public parameters collaboratively from independent locations to ensure that toxic waste is not created. Because these public parameters are required to be created by the Zcash team, it means that the participants in the ceremony are trusted. This is the reason why the ceremony was very open and conducted by making use of a multi-party computation mechanism.

This mechanism has a property whereby all of the participants in the ceremony will have to be compromised to compromise the final parameters. When the ceremony is completed all participants physically destroyed the equipment used for private key generation. This action eliminates any trace of the participants' part of the private key on the equipment.

ZK-SNARKs must satisfy the properties for completeness, soundness, succinctness, and non- interactivity. Completeness means that there is a definite strategy for a prover to satisfy a verifier that an assertion is true. On the other hand, soundness means that no prover can convince the verifier that a false statement is true. Succinctness means that messages passed between the prover and verifier are tiny in size.

Finally, the property non-interactive means that the verification of correctness of an assertion can be carried out without any interaction or very little interaction. Also, being a ZKP, the property of zero-knowledge (discussed in `Chapter 6`, *Public Key Cryptography*) needs to be met too.

Zcash developers have introduced the concept of a **Decentralized Anonymous Payment scheme (DAP scheme)** that is used in the Zcash network to enable direct and private payments. The transactions reveal no information about the origin, destination, and amount of the payments. There are two types of addresses available in Zcash, Z address and T address. Z addresses are based on ZKPs and provide privacy protection whereas T addresses are similar to those of bitcoin. A snapshot of various attributes of Zcash (after an initial slow start) is shown as follows:

Attribute	Value
Name	Zcash
Launch date	28/10/16
Main purpose	Currency
Currency Code	ZEC
Maximum coins	21 million
Block time	10 minutes
Consensus facilitation algorithm	Proof of Work (equihash)
Difficulty adjustment algorithm	DigiShield V3 (modified)
Mining hardware	CPU, GPU
Difficulty adjustment period	1 block

Zcash attributes summary

Zcash uses an efficient PoW scheme named asymmetric PoW (Equihash), which is based on the *Generalized Birthday Problem*. It allows very efficient verification. It is a memory-hard and ASIC-resistant function. A novel idea (initial slow mining) has been introduced with Zcash, which means that the block reward increases gradually over a period until it reaches the 20,000th block. This allows for initial scaling of the network and experimentation by early miners, and adjustment by Zcash developers if required. The slow start did have an impact on price due to scarcity as the price of ZEC on its first day of launch reached roughly 25,000 USD. A slightly modified version of the DigiShield difficulty adjustment algorithm has been implemented in Zcash. The formula is shown as follows:

(Next difficulty) = (last difficulty) x SQRT [(150 seconds) / (last solve time)]

Trading Zcash

Zcash can be bought on major digital currency sellers and exchanges such as CryptoGo (`https://cryptogo.com`). Another exchange where Zcash can be bought or sold is Crypto Robot 365 (`https://cryptorobot365.com`). When Zcash was introduced its price was very high. As shown in the following graph, the price soared as high as approximately ten bitcoins per Zcash. Some exchanges carried out orders as high as 2,500 BTC per ZEC. Price of ZEC is around 311 USD at the time writing (March, 2018):

Zcash market cap and price

Mining guide

There are multiple methods to mine Zcash. Currently, CPU and GPU mining are possible. Various commercial cloud mining pools also offer contracts for mining Zcash. To perform solo mining using a CPU, the following steps can be followed on Ubuntu Linux:

1. The first step is to install prerequisites using the following command:

```
$ sudo apt-get install \
  build-essential pkg-config libc6-dev m4 g++-multilib \
  autoconf libtool ncurses-dev unzip git python \
  zlib1g-dev wget bsdmainutils automake
```

If the prerequisites are already installed, a message will display indicating that components are already the newest version. If not already installed or older than the latest package, then the installation will continue, the required packages will be downloaded, and the installation will be completed.

2. Next, run the commands to clone Zcash from Git as shown in the following screenshot:

```
$ git clone https://github.com/zcash/zcash.git
```

Note that if you are running `git` for the first time then you may have to accept a few configuration changes, which will automatically be done for you, but you may have to do this interactively.

This command will clone the Zcash Git repository locally. The output is shown in the following screenshot:

```
drequinox@drequinox-OP7010:~$ git clone https://github.com/zcash/zcash.git
Cloning into 'zcash'...
remote: Counting objects: 56593, done.
remote: Total 56593 (delta 0), reused 0 (delta 0), pack-reused 56593
Receiving objects: 100% (56593/56593), 42.78 MiB | 2.11 MiB/s, done.
Resolving deltas: 100% (43020/43020), done.
Checking connectivity... done.
drequinox@drequinox-OP7010:~$ cd zcash/
drequinox@drequinox-OP7010:~/zcash$ git checkout v1.0.0
Note: checking out 'v1.0.0'.

You are in 'detached HEAD' state. You can look around, make experimental
changes and commit them, and you can discard any commits you make in this
state without impacting any branches by performing another checkout.

If you want to create a new branch to retain commits you create, you may
do so (now or later) by using -b with the checkout command again. Example:

  git checkout -b <new-branch-name>

HEAD is now at 1feaefa... Update network magics for 1.0.0 💙
```

Cloning the Zcash Git repository

3. The next step is to download proving and verifying keys, by using the following commands:

```
$ ./zcutil/fetch-param.sh
```

This command will produce the output similar to the one shown here:

```
drequinox@drequinox-OP7010:~/zcash$ ./zcutil/fetch-params.sh
Zcash - fetch-params.sh

This script will fetch the Zcash zkSNARK parameters and verify their
integrity with sha256sum.

The parameters are currently just under 911MB in size, so plan accordingly
for your bandwidth constraints. If the files are already present and
have the correct sha256sum, no networking is used.

Creating params directory. For details about this directory, see:
/home/drequinox/.zcash-params/README

Retrieving: https://z.cash/downloads/sprout-proving.key
--2016-10-28 21:46:21--  https://z.cash/downloads/sprout-proving.key
Resolving z.cash (z.cash)... 104.236.171.172
Connecting to z.cash (z.cash)|104.236.171.172|:443... connected.
HTTP request sent, awaiting response... 301 Moved Permanently
Location: https://s3.amazonaws.com/zcashfinalmpc/sprout-proving.key [following]
--2016-10-28 21:46:22--  https://s3.amazonaws.com/zcashfinalmpc/sprout-proving.key
Resolving s3.amazonaws.com (s3.amazonaws.com)... 54.231.40.114
Connecting to s3.amazonaws.com (s3.amazonaws.com)|54.231.40.114|:443... connected.
HTTP request sent, awaiting response... 200 OK
Length: 910173851 (868M) [application/octet-stream]
Saving to: '/home/drequinox/.zcash-params/sprout-proving.key.dl'

    0K ........ ........ ........ ........  3% 2.71M 5m8s
32768K ........ ........ ........ ........  7% 3.58M 4m20s
65536K ........ ........ ........ ........ 11% 2.53M 4m28s
98304K ........ ........ ........ ........ 14% 1.75M 4m59s
131072K ........ ........ ........
```

Zcash setup fetching ZK-SNARK parameters

4. Once this command runs, it will download around 911 MBs of keys into the `~/.zcash-params/` directory. The directory contains files for proving and verifying keys:

```
$ pwd
/home/drequinox/.zcash-params
$ ls -ltr
sprout-verifying.key
sprout-proving.key
```

5. Once the preceding commands are completed successfully, the source code can be built using the following command:

```
$ ./zcutil/build.sh -j$(nproc)
```

This will produce a very long output; if everything goes well it will produce a zcashd binary file. Note that this command takes nproc as the parameter, which is basically a command that finds the number of cores or processors in the system and displays that number. If you don't have that command then replace nproc with the number of processors in your system.

6. Once the build is completed, the next step is to configure Zcash. This is achieved by creating a configuration file with the name zcash.conf in the ~/.zcash/ directory.

A sample configuration file is shown as follows:

```
addnode=mainnet.z.cash
rpcuser=drequinox
rpcpassword=xxxxxxxoJNo4o5c(F6E(J4P2C1D5izizIKPZJhTzdW5A=
gen=1
genproclimit=8
equihashsolver=tromp
```

The preceding configuration enables various features. The first line adds the mainnet node and enables mainnet connectivity. rpcuser and rpcpassword are the username and password for the RPC interface. gen = 1 is used to enable mining. genproclimit is the number of processors that can be used for mining. The last line enables a faster mining solver; this is not required if you want to use standard CPU mining.

7. Now Zcash can be started using the following command:

```
$ ./zcashd --daemon
```

Once started this will allow interaction with the RPC interface via the zcash-cli command-line interface. This is almost the same as the bitcoin command-line interface. Once the Zcash daemon is up-and-running, various commands can be run to query different attributes of Zcash. Transactions can be viewed locally by using the CLI or via a blockchain explorer.

A blockchain explorer for Zcash is available at:
`https://explorer.zcha.in/`.

Address generation

New Z addresses can be generated using the following command:

```
$ ./zcash-cli z_getnewaddress
zcPDBKuuwHJ4gqT5Q59zAMXDHhFoihyTC1aLE5Kz4GwgUXfCBWG6SDr45SFLUsZhpcdvHt7nFmC
3iQcn37rKBcVRa93DYrA
```

Running the `zcash-cli` command with the `getinfo` parameter produces the output shown in the following screenshot. It displays valuable information such as `blocks`, `difficulty`, and `balance`:

```
drequinox@drequinox-OP7010:~/zcash/src$ ./zcash-cli getinfo
{
    "version" : 1000050,
    "protocolversion" : 170002,
    "walletversion" : 60000,
    "balance" : 0.00000000,
    "blocks" : 601,
    "timeoffset" : 0,
    "connections" : 8,
    "proxy" : "",
    "difficulty" : 13748.56014152,
    "testnet" : false,
    "keypoololdest" : 1477688856,
    "keypoolsize" : 101,
    "paytxfee" : 0.00000000,
    "relayfee" : 0.00005000,
    "errors" : "WARNING: abnormally high number of blocks generated, 190 blocks received in the last 4 hours (96 expected)"
}
drequinox@drequinox-OP7010:~/zcash/src$
```

Screenshot displaying the output of getinfo

New T addresses can be generated using the following command:

```
$ ./zcash-cli getnewaddress
t1XRCGMAw36yPVCcxDUrxv2csAAuGdS8Nny
```

GPU mining

Other than CPU mining, a GPU mining option is also available. There is no official GPU miner yet; however open source developers have produced various proofs of concepts and working miners. The Zcash Company held an open competition to encourage developers to build and submit CPU and GPU miners. No winning entry has been announced as of the time of writing.

 Readers can get more information by visiting the website, https://zcashminers.org/.

There is another mining: using cloud mining contracts available from various online cloud mining providers. The cloud mining service providers perform mining on the customers' behalf. In addition to cloud mining contracts, miners can use their own equipment to mine via mining pools using stratum or other protocols. One key example is Zcash pool by NiceHash available at: https://www.nicehash.com. Using this pool, miners can sell their hash power.

An example of building and using a CPU miner on a Zcash mining pool is shown as follows.

Downloading and compiling nheqminer

The following steps can be used to download and compile nheqminer on an Ubuntu Linux distribution:

```
$ sudo apt-get install cmake build-essential libboost-all-dev git clone
https://github.com/nicehash/nheqminer.git
$ cd nheqminer/nheqminer
$ mkdir build
$ cd build
$ cmake .. make
```

Once all the steps are completed successfully, `nhequminer` can be run using the following command:

```
$ ./nhequminer -l eu -u <btc address> -t <number of threads>
```

 `nhequminer` releases are available for Windows and Linux at the following link: https://github.com/nicehash/nheqminer/releases

`nheqminer` takes several parameters such as location (`-l`), username (`-u`), and the number of threads to be used for mining (`-t`).

A sample run of Linux miner `nheqminer` for Zcash is shown as follows. In this screenshot the payout is being made to a Bitcoin address for selling hash power:

```
drequinox@drequinox-OP7010:~/nheqminer/nheqminer/build$ ./nheqminer -l eu -u 1PL6gsm49xCFMvrXqgGcee5cdrG119GoWN.worker1 -t 6 -od 0
Equihash CPU Miner for NiceHash v0.1c
Thanks to Zcash developers for providing most of the code
Special thanks to tromp for providing optimized CPU equihash solver

Setting log level to 2
[09:28:53][0x00007f51009cd700] stratum | Connecting to stratum server equihash.eu.nicehash.com:3357
[09:28:53][0x00007f51009cd700] stratum | Connected!
[09:28:53][0x00007f51009cd700] stratum | Starting miner
[09:28:53][0x00007f50fafce700] miner#1 | Starting thread #1
[09:28:53][0x00007f50fb7cf700] miner#0 | Starting thread #0
[09:28:53][0x00007f50f8fca700] miner#5 | Starting thread #5
[09:28:53][0x00007f50fa7cd700] miner#2 | Starting thread #2
[09:28:53][0x00007f50f97cb700] miner#4 | Starting thread #4
[09:28:53][0x00007f50f9fcc700] miner#3 | Starting thread #3
[09:28:54][0x00007f51009cd700] stratum | Subscribed to stratum server
[09:28:54][0x00007f51009cd700] miner | Extranonce is 5000e5b80000000000000005000e5b9ab
[09:28:54][0x00007f51009cd700] stratum | Authorized worker 1PL6gsm49xCFMvrXqgGcee5cdrG119GoWN.worker1
[09:28:54][0x00007f51009cd700] stratum | Target set to 01e1e1e1e0000000000000000000000000000000000000000000000000000000
[09:28:54][0x00007f51009cd700] stratum | Received new job #000000329b82d287
[09:28:55][0x00007f50fa7cd700] stratum | Submitting share #4, nonce 02000000000000000000000000000000
[09:28:55][0x00007f51009cd700] stratum | Accepted share #4
[09:28:55][0x00007f51009cd700] stratum | Ignoring non-clean job #000000329b82d2cc
[09:28:57][0x00007f50fafce700] stratum | Submitting share #5, nonce 01000000000000000000000000000001
[09:28:57][0x00007f51009cd700] stratum | Accepted share #5
[09:28:59][0x00007f50f97cb700] stratum | Submitting share #6, nonce 04000000000000000000000000000005
```

Using the BTC address to receive payouts for selling hash power

The screenshot, shown here, shows a sample run of `nheqminer` on Windows with payouts being made to a Zcash T address for selling hash power:

```
C:\nheqminer_v0.3a>nheqminer_zcash.exe -l eu -u t1YiNeyxoLZcjDHnaMtq5WLEbKquTY11gK8.miner1 -t 6 -od 0
================== www.nicehash.com ==================
            Equihash CPU&GPU Miner for NiceHash v0.3a
    Thanks to Zcash developers for providing base of the code.
        Special thanks to tromp and xenoncat for providing
            optimized CPU and CUDA equihash solvers.
================== www.nicehash.com ==================
Setting log level to 2
[2016-10-29 22:37:18.196024][0x00001404]: Using SSE2: YES
[2016-10-29 22:37:18.203024][0x00001404]: Using AVX: YES
[2016-10-29 22:37:18.207025][0x00001404]: Using AVX2: YES
[2016-10-29 22:37:18.222026][0x00001590]: stratum | Starting miner
[2016-10-29 22:37:18.228026][0x00001c4]: miner#0 | Starting thread #0 (CPU-XENONCAT-AVX2)
[2016-10-29 22:37:18.228026][0x0000524]: miner#1 | Starting thread #1 (CPU-XENONCAT-AVX2)
[2016-10-29 22:37:18.243027][0x00000b20]: miner#3 | Starting thread #3 (CPU-XENONCAT-AVX2)
[2016-10-29 22:37:18.243027][0x00001570]: miner#2 | Starting thread #2 (CPU-XENONCAT-AVX2)
[2016-10-29 22:37:20.354147][0x00001330]: miner#5 | Starting thread #5 (CPU-XENONCAT-AVX2)
[2016-10-29 22:37:20.354147][0x000015f8]: miner#4 | Starting thread #4 (CPU-XENONCAT-AVX2)
[2016-10-29 22:37:20.354147][0x00001590]: stratum | Connecting to stratum server stratum.eu.zcash.nicehash.com:3357
[2016-10-29 22:37:20.354147][0x00001108]: miner#6 | Starting thread #6 (OCL_XMP) TODO
<info> found 1 devices
Using device 0 as GPU 0
<info> compiling ...
<info> source: 41162 bytes
[2016-10-29 22:37:28.796630][0x00001590]: stratum | Connected!
[2016-10-29 22:37:28.892636][0x00001590]: stratum | Subscribed to stratum server
[2016-10-29 22:37:28.899636][0x00001590]: miner | Extranonce is 1ffff7da00000000000000001ffff7d9
[2016-10-29 22:37:28.999642][0x00001590]: stratum | ←[35mTarget set to 03c3c3cUUUUUU0000000000000000000000000000000000000000000000000- [0m
[2016-10-29 22:37:29.016643][0x00001590]: stratum | ←[36mReceived new job #6←[0m
[2016-10-29 22:37:29.290659][0x00001590]: stratum | Authorized worker t1YiNeyxoLZcjDHnaMtq5WLEbKquTY11gK8.miner1
[2016-10-29 22:37:22.211889][0x00001404]: ←[33mSpeed [300 sec]: 0.154357 I/s, 0.231535 Sols/s←[0m
[2016-10-29 22:37:40.476298][0x0000524]: stratum | Submitting share #4, nonce 01000000000000000000000000000004
[2016-10-29 22:37:40.605306][0x00001590]: stratum | ←[32mAccepted share #4←[0m
[2016-10-29 22:37:43.411466][0x00001404]: ←[33mSpeed [300 sec]: 0.824045 I/s, 1.43124 Sols/s←[0m
```

Using Zcash T address to receive payouts for selling hash power

Zcash has used ZKPs in an innovative way and they pave the way for future applications that require inherent privacy, such as banking, medicine, or the law.

This section completes the introduction to Zcash; readers can explore more about Zcash online at `https://z.cash`.

Initial Coin Offerings (ICOs)

ICOs are comparable to the **Initial Public Offering** (IPO). Just as an IPO is launched to raise capital by a firm similarly, ICOs are launched to generate money for a start-up project. The critical difference is that IPOs are regulated and fall under the umbrella of securities market (shares in the company) whereas ICOs are unregulated and do not fall under any strict category of already established market structures.

However, there are few suggestions that ICOs should be treated as securities in the light of some scam ICO schemes launched in the last few months and growing concerns around investor protection. Recently the **Securities and Exchange Commission** (**SEC**) suggested that all coins, ICOS, digital assets fall under the definition of *security*. This means that same laws would be applicable to ICOs, Bitcoin and other digital coins that are in applicable to securities. Also, an introduction of formal **Know Your Customer** (**KYC**) and **Anti Money Laundering** (**AML**) is also being recommended to addresses issues related to money laundering. Experts are recommending *Howey Test* as some criteria for any ICO to be considered a security.

Another difference is that ICOs by design usually require investors to invest using cryptocurrencies and payouts are paid using cryptocurrencies, most commonly this is the new token (a new cryptocurrency) introduced by the ICO. This can also be Fiat currency, but most commonly cryptocurrency is used. For example, in the Ethereum crowdfunding campaign a new token, Ether was introduced. The name token sale for crowdfunding is also quite popular and both terms are used interchangeably. ICO are also called crowd sales.

When a new blockchain based application or organization is launched, a new token can be launched with it as a token to access and use the application and also to gain incentives that are paid in the very same token that has been introduced by the ICO. This token is released to the public in exchange of some already established cryptocurrency (for example, Bitcoin or Ethereum) or Fiat currency. The advantage is that when the usage of the application or product launched increases the value of the new token also increases with it. This way the investors who invested initially gain a good incentive.

In the year 2017, ICOs have become a leading tool for raising capital for new start-ups. The first successful ICO was that of Ethereum which raised 18 million USD in 2014. A recent success is Tezos which made 232 million USD in a few weeks' time. Another example is Filecoin which raised more than 250 million USD.

The process of creating a new token has been standardized on Ethereum blockchain thus making it relatively easy to launch an ICO and issue new tokens in exchange of Ether, Bitcoin or some other cryptocurrency. This standard is called ECR20 and is described in the next section. It's worth noting that using ECR20 is not a requirement and a completely new cryptocurrency can be invented on a new blockchain to start an ICO, but ERC20 has been used in various ICOs recently and provides a comparatively easier way to build a token for an ICO.

Recently ICOs have also been offered via platforms other than Ethereum, such as NEM (`https://nem.io`) and Stellar (`https://www.stellar.org`).

ERC20 tokens

ERC20 token is an interface which defines various functions dictating the requirements of the token. It does not, however, provide implementation details and has been left to the implementer to decide. ERC is basically an abbreviation of **Ethereum Request for Comments** which is equivalent to Bitcoin's BIPs for suggesting improvements in Ethereum blockchain.

 This is defined under EIP 20, which you can read more about here https://github.com/ethereum/EIPs/blob/master/EIPS/eip-20-token-standard.md.

Ethereum is becoming a platform for choice for ICOs due to its ability to create new tokens and with ERC20 standard, it has become even more accessible.

ECR20 token standard defines various functions which describe various properties, rules, and attributes of the new token. These include total supply of the coins, total balance of holders, transfer function, approval and allowance functions.

 There are other standards such as ERC223, ERC777 and extension of ERC20 called ERC827 are also under development. You can refer to the followings links to learn more:

- https://github.com/ethereum/EIPs/issues/827
- https://github.com/ethereum/EIPs/issues/223
- https://github.com/ethereum/EIPs/issues/777

Summary

In this chapter, we introduced you to the overall cryptocurrency landscape. We discussed a number of altcoins in detail, especially Zcash and Namecoin. Cryptocurrencies are a very active area for research, especially around scalability, privacy, and security aspects. Some research has also been conducted to invent new difficulty retargeting algorithms to thwart the threat of centralization in cryptocurrencies.

Further research needs to be carried out in the areas of privacy and especially scalability of blockchain.

Now you should be able to appreciate the concept of altcoins and various motivations behind them. We also discussed few practical aspects, such as mining and starting a new currency project, which hopefully will give you a strong foundation, enabling you to explore these areas further. Altcoins are a fascinating field of research and they open many possibilities for a decentralized future.

11
Development Tools and Frameworks

This chapter is an introduction to development tools, languages, and frameworks used for Ethereum smart contract development. We will examine different methods of developing smart contracts for the Ethereum blockchain. We will discuss various constructs of Solidity language in detail, which is currently the most popular development language for smart contract development on Ethereum.

In this chapter we will cover the following topics:

- Development tools, IDEs, and clients
    - Remix
    - Ganache
    - EthereumJS
    - TestRPC
    - MetaMask
    - Truffle
- Prerequisites
    - Node
    - Node Package Manager (NPM)
- Other tools and utilities

There are a number of tools available for Ethereum development. The following diagram shows the taxonomy of various development tools, clients, IDEs, and development frameworks for Ethereum:

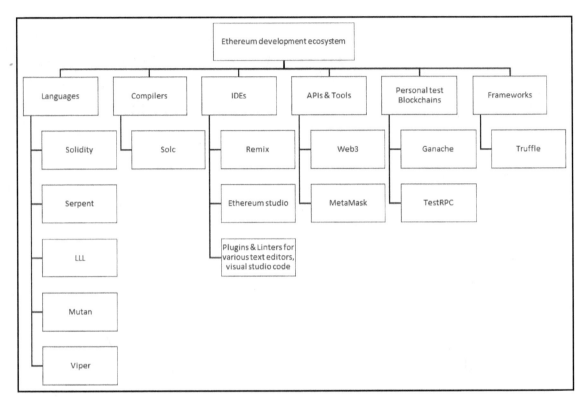

Taxonomy of Ethereum development ecosystem components

The preceding taxonomy does not include all frameworks and tools that are out there for development on Ethereum. It shows most commonly used tools and frameworks and also the ones that we will use in our examples throughout this chapter.

 There are number of resources available related to development tools for Ethereum at the address
http://ethdocs.org/en/latest/contracts-and-transactions/develope
r-tools.html#developer-tools.

In this chapter, the main focus will be on Geth, Remix IDE, Solidity, Ganache, MetaMask, solc, and Truffle. The rest of the elements such as prerequisites (Node) will also be discussed briefly.

Languages

Smart contracts can be programmed in a variety of languages for Ethereum blockchain. There are five languages that can be used in order to write contracts:

- **Mutan**: This is a Go-style language, which was deprecated in early 2015 and is no longer used.
- **LLL**: This is a **Low-level Lisp-like Language**, hence the name LLL. This is also not used anymore.
- **Serpent**: This is a simple and clean Python-like language. It is not used for contract development anymore and not supported by the community anymore.
- **Solidity**: This language has now become almost a standard for contract writing for Ethereum. This language is the focus of this chapter and is discussed in detail in later sections.
- **Vyper**: This language is a Python-like experimental language that is being developed to bring security, simplicity, and auditability to smart contract development.

Compilers

Compilers are used to convert high-level contract source code into the format that the Ethereum execution environment understands. The Solidity compiler is the most common one in use and is discussed here.

Solidity compiler (solc)

solc converts from a high-level solidity language into **Ethereum Virtual Machine** (**EVM**) bytecode so that it can be executed on the blockchain by EVM.

Installation on Linux

solc can be installed on a Linux Ubuntu operating system using the following commands:

```
$ sudo apt-get install solc
```

If PPAs are not already installed, those can be installed by running the following command:

```
$ sudo add-apt-repository ppa:ethereum/ethereum
$ sudo apt-get update
```

In order to verify the existing version of the solc and verify that it is installed, the following command can be used:

```
$ solc --version
solc, the solidity compiler commandline interface
Version: 0.4.19+commit.c4cbbb05.Darwin.appleclang
```

Installation on macOS

To install solc on macOS, execute the following commands:

```
$ brew tap ethereum/ethereum
$ brew install solidity
$ brew linkapps solidity
```

solc supports a variety of functions. A few examples are shown as follows:

- Display contract in a binary format:

    ```
    $ solc --bin Addition.sol
    ```

    This command will produce an output similar to the following. This shows the binary translation of the Addition.sol contract code:

```
imrans-MacBook-Pro:~ drequinox$ solc --bin Addition.sol

======= Addition.sol:Addition =======
Binary:
6060604052341561000f57600080fd5b61010b8061001e6000396000f30060606040526004361060495760003 57c01000000
000000000000000000000000000000000000000000000000900463ffffffff16806336718d8014604e578063ac04e0a014
607d575b600080fd5b3415605857600080fd5b607b600480803560ff1690602001909190803560ff16906020019091905050
60a9565b005b3415608757600080fd5b608d60c9565b604051808260ff1660ff168152602001915050604051809103905 0f35b
8082016000806101000a81548160ff021916908360ff16021790555050565b60008060009054906101000a900460ff1690
50905600a165627a7a7230582037bbf1721ae442876d01fa64f7feee6baac85d550db40825cf6dea392487369e0029
imrans-MacBook-Pro:~ drequinox$ ▊
```

Solidity compiler binary output

- Estimate gas:

    ```
    $ solc --gas Addition.sol
    ```

This will give the following output:

```
imrans-MacBook-Pro:~ drequinox$ solc --gas Addition.sol

======= Addition.sol:Addition =======
Gas estimation:
construction:
   100 + 53400 = 53500
external:
   addx(uint8,uint8):   20475
   retrievex(): 464
imrans-MacBook-Pro:~ drequinox$
```

Gas estimation using solc

- Generate ABI:

  $ solc --abi Addition.sol

  The following are the contents of Addition.abi:

  ```
  ======= Addition.sol:Addition =======
  Contract JSON ABI
  [{"constant":false,"inputs":[{"name":"y","type":"uint8"},
  {"name":"z","type":"uint8"}],"name":"addx","outputs":
  [],"payable":false,"stateMutability":"nonpayable","type":"function"},{"cons
  tant":true,"inputs":
      [],"name":"retrievex","outputs":
  [{"name":"","type":"uint8"}],"payable":false,"stateMutability":"view","type
  ":"function"}]
  ```

- Compilation:

  Another useful command to compile and produce a binary compiled file along with an ABI is shown here:

  $ solc --bin --abi --optimize -o bin Addition.sol

  This command will produce two files in the output directory bin:

    - Addition.abi: This contains the Application Binary Interface of the smart contract in JSON format
    - Addition.bin: This contains the hex representation of binary of the smart contract code

The output of both files is shown in the following screenshot:

```
imrans-MacBook-Pro:bin drequinox$ cat Addition.abi
[{"constant":false,"inputs":[{"name":"y","type":"uint8"},{"name":"z","type":"uint8"}],"name":"addx","outputs":[]
,"payable":false,"stateMutability":"nonpayable","type":"function"},{"constant":true,"inputs":[],"name":"retrieve
x","outputs":[{"name":"","type":"uint8"}],"payable":false,"stateMutability":"view","type":"function"}]imrans-Mac
Book-Pro:bin drequinox$
imrans-MacBook-Pro:bin drequinox$
imrans-MacBook-Pro:bin drequinox$ cat Addition.bin
6060604052341561000f57600080fd5b60da8061001d6000396000f30060606040526004361060485763ffffffff7c010000000000000000
0000000000000000000000000000000000006000350416633671d808114604d578063ac04e0a014606b575b600080fd5b3415605757
600080fd5b606960ff60043581169060243516609156b005b3415607557600080fd5b607b60a5565b60405160ff909116815260200160 40
5180910390f35b6000805460ff19169190920160ff16179055565b60005460ff16905600a165627a7a72305820f7ca91776882f1c97964c8
29324591eb96e72adb62b5548a67f4ea22e9daf2b80029imrans-MacBook-Pro:bin drequinox$
imrans-MacBook-Pro:bin drequinox$
imrans-MacBook-Pro:bin drequinox$
```

ABI and binary output of solidity compiler

ABI is the abbreviation of **Application Binary Interface**. ABI encodes information about smart contract's functions and events. It acts as an interface between EVM level bytecode and high level smart contract program code. To interact with a smart contract deployed on the Ethereum blockchain, external programs require ABI and address of the smart contract.

solc is a very powerful command and further options can be explored using `-- help` flag which will display detailed options. However, the preceding commands used for compilation, ABI generation and gas estimation should be sufficient for most development and deployment requirements.

Integrated Development Environments (IDEs)

There are various IDEs available for Solidity development. Most of the IDEs are available online and are presented via web interfaces. Remix (formerly browser Solidity) is the most commonly used IDE for building and debugging smart contracts. It is discussed here.

Remix

Remix is the web-based environment for the development and testing of contracts using Solidity. It is a feature-rich IDE which does not run on live blockchain; in fact, it is a simulated environment in which contracts can be deployed, tested, and debugged.

It is available at https://remix.ethereum.org.

An example interface is shown as follows:

Remix IDE

On the left-hand side, there is a code editor with syntax highlighting and code formatting, and on the right-hand side, there are a number of tools available that can be used to deploy, debug, test, and interact with the contract.

Various features, such as transaction interaction, options to connect to JavaScript VM, configuration of execution environment, debugger, formal verification, and static analysis, are available. They can be configured to connect to execution environments such as JavaScript VM, injected Web3—where Mist, MetaMask, or a similar environment has provided the execution environment—or Web3 provider, which allows connection to the locally running Ethereum client (for example, `geth`) via IPC or RPC over HTTP (Web3 provider endpoint).

Remix also has a debugger for EVM which is very powerful and can be used to perform detailed level tracing and analysis of the EVM bytecode. An example is shown here:

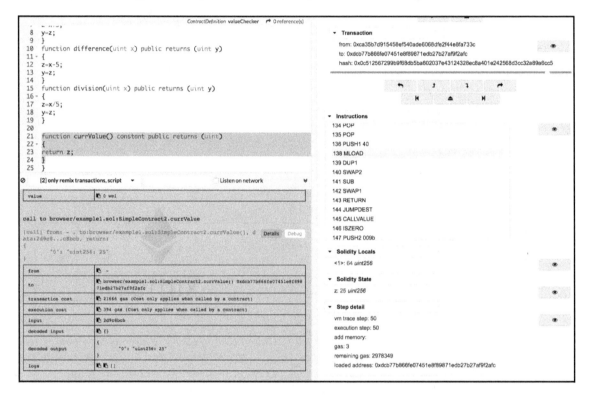

Remix IDE, debugging

The preceding screenshot shows different elements of the Remix IDE. On the top left-hand side, the source code is shown. Below that is the output log which shows informational messages and data related to compilation and execution of the contract.

The following screenshot shown shows the Remix debugger in more detail. It has the source code decoded into EVM instructions. The user can step through the instructions one by one and can examine what the source code does when executed:

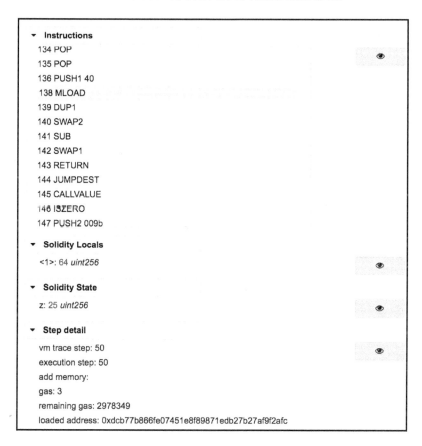

Remix Debugger

Tools and libraries

There are various tools and libraries available for Ethereum. The most common ones are discussed here.

In this section, we will first install prerequisites that are required for developing applications for Ethereum. First requirement is Node, which will see next.

Node version 7

As Node is required for most of the tools and libraries, it can be installed using the following commands:

```
$ curl -sL https://deb.nodesource.com/setup_7.x | sudo -E bash - sudo apt-
get install -y nodejs
```

EthereumJS

At times, it is not possible to test on the testnet and mainnet is obviously not a place to test the contracts. Private net can be time-consuming to set up at times. EthereumJS' TestRPC comes in handy when quick testing is required and no proper testnet is available. It uses EthereumJS to simulate the Ethereum `geth` client behavior and allows for faster development testing. TestRPC is available via `npm` as a Node package.

Before installing TestRPC, Node should already have been installed and the `npm` package manager should also be available.

TestRPC can be installed using this command:

```
$ npm install -g ethereumjs-testrpc
```

In order to start `testrpc`, simply issue this command and keep it running in the background and open another Terminal to work on contracts:

```
$ testrpc
```

When TestRPC runs, it will display the output similar to the one shown in the following screenshot. It will automatically generate ten accounts and private keys, along with HD wallet. It will start to listen for incoming connection on TCP port `8545`.

```
EthereumJS TestRPC v6.0.3 (ganache-core: 2.0.2)

Available Accounts
==================
(0) 0x6ca19d903eb53e00bb73622d275c965f2abad3d8
(1) 0x1f192daefa61ae050332e6a965e71fcf4621e887
(2) 0x97c0b2ea19a5b496e314e55d1e5a3a5d41b5ad21
(3) 0x3a04fbc6f8eb34b89918628a5a5fde4267e32e28
(4) 0x43e03d85a8a9328f510732be594993ac7011335c
(5) 0x6dfe1a7059df7a625c1ffaed0e97c42384b68446
(6) 0xb9992f167e68dc4bd4a1ce79c07b6193c4e72f37
(7) 0x46243dfcfb6d2d4ec60aa97ebbceac0f96aa33ab
(8) 0xe5b9c05dcb55ad987a504da7fb3dde4281d73bc4
(9) 0x37f6576fd633d95cbc29db28bbae4a272fe5594c

Private Keys
==================
(0) c82c6a860eeb57c8eedbd2e8bc59dc7c800f99118b7f1ef5540c41cdb10805dc
(1) 144271a65d21c59bd6f321659798b42e3d1a22feeb45c2c44f823db0477f330d
(2) d2a55f4406b23c8c18c55a6d30f4b4982ab17a01a6125f0d091e0d4807346905
(3) 1c16608a159b52ba84a0ae170d7642f31667125146934981e09640dccf4cae8b9
(4) b7dea27d5bd105bb3e4fbf69598b561563557d343d4c89ea2d7d689f5a160554
(5) 10d6467570c50e103ade3694ef85cf9ae0f14cf331ddcd9faaae1f752ed766c5
(6) 7571ece88840db22a09d8e6062292c1e3d106c9e9d5d634f05d4524c76bfa50a
(7) 15e215703ba63d52c870392086f3474b78b5a1b0b6f276fe48c9aae6061f478d
(8) 5dd1fd136b3ba917922b011daafbbce2b5fd3e332a1f0d09ad5bef664190bdb
(9) 30e1850a76ee65fcfd565caf81fa7310ff239679816be51f0b04149afe4407e1

HD Wallet
==================
Mnemonic:      prepare flavor identify liquid twice tip bullet blanket vast vivid hunt now
Base HD Path:  m/44'/60'/0'/0/{account_index}

Listening on localhost:8545
```

TestRPC

Ganache

Ganache is the latest addition to the plethora of development tools and libraries developed for Ethereum. This is, in a way a replacement of TestRPC and uses a user-friendly graphical user interface to see transaction and blocks and relevant details. This is fully working Byzantium enabled personal blockchain which is used to provide a local testing environment for blockchains.

Ganache is based on a JavaScript implementation of the Ethereum blockchain, with built-in block explorer and mining, making testing locally on the system very easy.

As shown in the following screenshot you can view transaction, blocks, and addresses in detail on the frontend:

Ganache, A personal Ethereum blockchain

Ganache can be downloaded from `http://truffleframework.com/ganache/`.

MetaMask

MetaMask allows interaction with Ethereum blockchain via Firefox and Chrome browsers. It injects a `web3` object within the running websites' JavaScript context which allows immediate interface capability for DApps. This *injection* allows DApps to interact directly with the blockchain.

It is available at `https://metamask.io/`.

MetaMask also allows account management. This acts as a verification method before any transaction is executed on the blockchain. The user is shown a secure interface to review the transaction for approval or rejection before it can reach the target blockchain.

It is available at `https://github.com/MetaMask/metamask-plugin`.

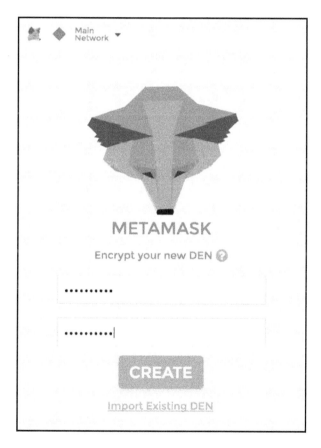

MetaMask

It allows connectivity with various Ethereum networks as shown in the following screenshot. This is the screenshot of the MetaMask, where it allows users to select the network of their choice:

MetaMask networks as shown in the MetaMask user interface

An interesting feature to note is that MetaMask can connect to any custom RPC too which allows you to run your own blockchain, such as private nets locally or even remotely and allows your browser to connect to it. It can also be used to connect to a locally running blockchain like Ganache and TestRPC.

MetaMask allows account management and also records all transactions for these accounts. This is shown in the following screenshot:

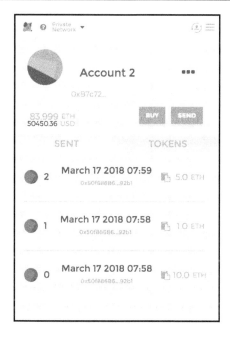

MetaMask accounts and transactions view

Truffle

Truffle (available at `http://truffleframework.com/`) is a development environment that makes it easier and simpler to test and deploy Ethereum contracts. Truffle provides contract compilation and linking along with an automated testing framework using Mocha and Chai. It also makes it easier to deploy the contracts to any private net, public, or testnet Ethereum blockchain. Also, asset pipeline is provided, which makes it easier for all JavaScript files to be processed, making them ready for use by a browser.

Installation

Before installation, it is assumed that `node` is available, which can be queried as shown here. If the `node` is not available, then the installation of `node` is required first in order to install `truffle`:

```
$ node —version
v7.2.1
```

The installation of `truffle` is very simple and can be done using the following command via **Node Package Manager** (**npm**):

```
$ sudo npm install -g truffle
```

This will take a few minutes; once it is installed, the `truffle` command can be used to display help information and verify that it is installed correctly:

```
$ sudo npm install -g truffle
Password:
/us/local/bin/truffle ->
/usr/local/lib/node_modules/truffle/build/cli.bundled.js
/usr/local/lib
└── truffle@4.0.1
```

Type `truffle` at Terminal to display usage help:

```
$ truffle
```

This will display the following output:

```
Truffle v4.0.1 - a development framework for Ethereum

Usage: truffle <command> [options]

Commands:
  init       Initialize new Ethereum project with example contracts and tests
  compile    Compile contract source files
  migrate    Run migrations to deploy contracts
  deploy     (alias for migrate)
  build      Execute build pipeline (if configuration present)
  test       Run Mocha and Solidity tests
  debug      Interactively debug any transaction on the blockchain (experimental)
  opcode     Print the compiled opcodes for a given contract
  console    Run a console with contract abstractions and commands available
  develop    Open a console with a local TestRPC
  create     Helper to create new contracts, migrations and tests
  install    Install a package from the Ethereum Package Registry
  publish    Publish a package to the Ethereum Package Registry
  networks   Show addresses for deployed contracts on each network
  watch      Watch filesystem for changes and rebuild the project automatically
  serve      Serve the build directory on localhost and watch for changes
  exec       Execute a JS module within this Truffle environment
  unbox      Unbox Truffle project
  version    Show version number and exit

See more at http://truffleframework.com/docs
```

Truffle help

Alternatively, the repository is available at `https://github.com/ConsenSys/truffle`, which can be cloned locally to install `truffle`. **Git** can be used to clone the repository using the following command:

```
$ git clone https://github.com/ConsenSys/truffle.git
```

Contract development and deployment

There are various steps that need to be taken in order to develop and deploy the contracts. Broadly, these can be divided into four steps: writing, testing, verification and deployment. After deployment, the next optional step is to create the user interface and present it to the end users via a web server. Web interface is sometimes not needed in the contracts where no human input or monitoring is required, but usually there is a requirement to create web interface to interact with the contract.

Writing

The writing step is concerned with writing the contract source code in Solidity. This can be done in any text editor. There are various plugins and add-ons available for Vim in Linux, Atom, and other editors that provide syntax highlighting and formatting for Solidity source code.

Visual studio code has become quite popular and is used commonly for Solidity development. There is a Solidity plugin available that allows syntax highlighting, formatting, and intelligence. It can be installed via **Extensions** option in Visual Studio Code.

Visual studio code

Testing

Testing is usually performed by automated means. Earlier in the chapter, you were introduced to Truffle, which uses the Mocha framework to test contracts. However, manual functional testing can be performed as well by using Remix and running functions manually and validating results.

In the next section, you will be introduced to language Solidity. This is a brief introduction to Solidity, which should provide the base knowledge required in order to write the contracts. The syntax is very similar to C and JavaScript, and it is quite easy to program.

Solidity language

Solidity is a domain-specific language of choice for programming contracts in Ethereum. There are, however, other languages that can be used, such as Serpent, Mutan, and LLL but Solidity is the most popular at the time of writing this. Its syntax is closer to both JavaScript and C.

Solidity has evolved into a mature language over the last few years and is quite easy to use, but it still has a long way to go before it can become advanced, standardized, and feature-rich like other well-established languages such as Java, C or C Sharp. Nevertheless, this is the most widely used language available for programming contracts currently.

It is a statically typed language, which means that variable type checking in Solidity is carried out at compile time. Each variable, either state or local, must be specified with a type at compile time. This is beneficial in the sense that any validation and checking is completed at compile time and certain types of bugs, such as interpretation of data types, can be caught earlier in the development cycle instead of at runtime, which could be costly, especially in the case of the blockchain / smart contracts paradigm. Other features of the language include inheritance, libraries, and the ability to define composite data types.

Solidity is also called a contract-oriented language. In Solidity, contracts are equivalent to the concept of classes in other object-oriented programming languages.

Types

Solidity has two categories of data types: **value types** and **reference types**.

Value types

These are explained in detail here:

Boolean

This data type has two possible values, `true` or `false`, for example:

```
bool v = true;
bool v = false;
```

This statement assigns the value `true` to `v`.

Integers

This data type represents integers. The following table shows various keywords used to declare integer data types:

Keyword	Types	Details
int	Signed integer	`int8` to `int256`, which means that keywords are available from `int8` up to `int256` in increments of 8, for example, `int8`, `int16`, `int24`.
uint	Unsigned integer	`uint8`, `uint16`, ... to `uint256`, unsigned integer from 8 bits to 256 bits. The usage is dependent on the requirements that how many bits are required to be stored in the variable.

For example, in this code, note that `uint` is an alias for `uint256`:

```
uint256 x;
uint y;
uint256 z;
```

These types can also be declared with the `constant` keyword, which means that no storage slot will be reserved by the compiler for these variables. In this case, each occurrence will be replaced with the actual value:

```
uint constant z=10+10;
```

State variables are declared outside the body of a function, and they remain available throughout the contract depending on the accessibility assigned to them and as long as the contract persists.

Address

This data type holds a 160-bit long (20 byte) value. This type has several members that can be used to interact with and query the contracts. These members are described here:

- **Balance**: The `balance` member returns the balance of the address in Wei.
- **Send**: This member is used to send an amount of ether to an address (Ethereum's 160-bit address) and returns `true` or `false` depending on the result of the transaction, for example, the following:

```
address to = 0x6414cc08d148dce9ebf5a2d0b7c220ed2d3203da; address from
= this;
    if (to.balance < 10 && from.balance > 50) to.send(20);
```

- **Call functions**: The `call`, `callcode`, and `delegatecall` calls are provided in order to interact with functions that do not have ABI. These functions should be used with caution as they are not safe to use due to the impact on type safety and security of the contracts.
- **Array value types (fixed size and dynamically sized byte arrays)**: Solidity has fixed size and dynamically sized byte arrays. Fixed size keywords range from `bytes1` to `bytes32`, whereas dynamically sized keywords include `bytes` and `string`. The `bytes` keyword is used for raw byte data and `string` is used for strings encoded in UTF-8. As these arrays are returned by the value, calling them will incur gas cost. `length` is a member of array value types and returns the length of the byte array.

  An example of a static (fixed size) array is as follows:

```
bytes32[10] bankAccounts;
```

  An example of a dynamically sized array is as follows:

```
bytes32[] trades;
```

Get length of trades by using the following code:

```
trades.length;
```

Literals

These used to represent a fixed value. There are different types of literals that are described in the following subsections.

Integer literals

Integer literals are a sequence of decimal numbers in the range of 0-9. An example is shown as follows:

```
uint8 x = 2;
```

String literals

String literals specify a set of characters written with double or single quotes. An example is shown as follows:

```
'packt' "packt"
```

Hexadecimal literals

Hexadecimal literals are prefixed with the keyword `hex` and specified within double or single quotation marks. An example is shown as follows:

```
(hex'AABBCC');
```

Enums

This allows the creation of user-defined types. An example is shown as follows:

```
enum Order {Filled, Placed, Expired };
Order private ord;
ord=Order.Filled;
```

Explicit conversion to and from all integer types is allowed with enums.

Function types

There are two function types: internal and external functions.

Internal functions

These can be used only within the context of the current contract.

External functions

External functions can be called via external function calls.

A **function** in solidity can be marked as a constant. Constant functions cannot change anything in the contract; they only return values when they are invoked and do not cost any gas. This is the practical implementation of the concept of *call*.

The syntax to declare a function is shown as follows:

```
function <nameofthefunction> (<parameter types> <name of the variable>)
{internal|external} [constant] [payable] [returns (<return types> <name of
the variable>)]
```

Reference types

As the name suggests, these types are passed by reference and are discussed in the following section. These are also called **complex types**.

Arrays

Arrays represent a contiguous set of elements of the same size and type laid out at a memory location. The concept is the same as any other programming language. Arrays have two members named `length` and `push`:

```
uint[] OrderIds;
```

Structs

These constructs can be used to group a set of dissimilar data types under a logical group. These can be used to define new types, as shown in the following example:

```
pragma solidity ^0.4.0;
contract TestStruct {
  struct Trade
  {
    uint tradeid;
    uint quantity;
    uint price;
    string trader;
  }

  //This struct can be initialized and used as below

  Trade tStruct = Trade({tradeid:123, quantity:1, price:1,
trader:"equinox"});

}
```

Data location

Data location specifies where a particular complex data type will be stored. Depending on the default or annotation specified, the location can be storage or memory. This is applicable to arrays and structs and can be specified using the `storage` or `memory` keywords.

As copying between memory and storage can be quite expensive, specifying a location can be helpful to control the gas expenditure at times. **Calldata** is another memory location that is used to store function arguments.

Parameters of external functions use **calldata** memory. By default, parameters of functions are stored in **memory**, whereas all other local variables make use of **storage**. State variables, on the other hand, are required to use storage.

Mappings

Mappings are used for a key to value mapping. This is a way to associate a value with a key. All values in this map are already initialized with all zeroes, for example, the following:

```
mapping (address => uint) offers;
```

This example shows that offers is declared as a mapping. Another example makes this clearer:

```
mapping (string => uint) bids;
bids["packt"] = 10;
```

This is basically a dictionary or a hash table where string values are mapped to integer values. The mapping named `bids` has string `packt` mapped to value `10`.

Global variables

Solidity provides a number of global variables that are always available in the global namespace. These variables provide information about blocks and transactions. Additionally, cryptographic functions and address-related variables are available as well.

A subset of available functions and variables is shown as follows:

```
keccak256(...) returns (bytes32)
```

This function is used to compute the Keccak-256 hash of the argument provided to the function:

```
ecrecover(bytes32 hash, uint8 v, bytes32 r, bytes32 s) returns (address)
```

This function returns the associated address of the public key from the elliptic curve signature:

```
block.number
```

This returns the current block number.

Control structures

Control structures available in solidity language are `if...else`, `do`, `while`, `for`, `break`, `continue`, and `return`. They work exactly the same as other languages such as C-language or JavaScript.

Some examples are shown here:

- **if**: If x is equal to 0 then assign value 0 to y else assign 1 to z:

```
if (x == 0)
    y = 0;
else
    z = 1;
```

- **do**: Increment x while z is greater than 1:

```
do{
    x++;
} (while z>1);
```

- **while**: Increment z while x is greater than 0:

```
while(x > 0){
    z++;
}
```

- **for, break, and continue**: Perform some work until x is less than or equal to 10. This for loop will run 10 times, if z is 5 then break the for loop:

```
for(uint8 x=0; x<=10; x++)
{
    //perform some work
    z++
    if(z == 5) break;
}
```

It will continue the work similarly, but when the condition is met, the loop will start again.

- **return**: Return is used to stop the execution of a function and returns an optional value. For example:

```
return 0;
```

It will stop the execution and return value of 0.

Events

Events in Solidity can be used to log certain events in EVM logs. These are quite useful when external interfaces are required to be notified of any change or event in the contract. These logs are stored on the blockchain in transaction logs. Logs cannot be accessed from the contracts but are used as a mechanism to notify change of state or the occurrence of an event (meeting a condition) in the contract.

In a simple example here, the valueEvent event will return true if the x parameter passed to function Matcher is equal to or greater than 10:

```
pragma solidity ^0.4.0;
contract valueChecker
{
    uint8 price=10;
    event valueEvent(bool returnValue);
    function Matcher(uint8 x) public returns (bool)
    {
        if (x>=price)
        {
            valueEvent(true);
            return true;
        }
    }
}
```

Inheritance

Inheritance is supported in Solidity. The is keyword is used to derive a contract from another contract. In the following example, valueChecker2 is derived from the valueChecker contract. The derived contract has access to all non-private members of the parent contract:

```
pragma solidity ^0.4.0;
contract valueChecker
{
    uint8 price = 20;
    event valueEvent(bool returnValue);
    function Matcher(uint8 x) public returns (bool)
    {
        if (x>=price)
        {
            valueEvent(true);
            return true;
        }
    }
```

```
    }
contract valueChecker2 is valueChecker
{
    function Matcher2() public view returns (uint)
    {
        return price+10;
    }
}
```

In the preceding example, if the `uint8 price = 20` is changed to `uint8 private price = 20`, then it will not be accessible by the `valueChecker2` contract. This is because now the member is declared as private, it is not allowed to be accessed by any other contract. The error message that you will see in Remix is

```
browser/valuechecker.sol:20:8: DeclarationError: Undeclared identifier.
return price+10;
       ^---^
```

Libraries

Libraries are deployed only once at a specific address and their code is called via CALLCODE or DELEGATECALL opcode of the EVM. The key idea behind libraries is code reusability. They are similar to contracts and act as base contracts to the calling contracts. A library can be declared as shown in the following example:

```
library Addition
{
    function Add(uint x,uint y) returns (uint z)
    {
        return x + y;
    }
}
```

This library can then be called in the contract, as shown here. First, it needs to be imported and then it can be used anywhere in the code. A simple example is shown as follows:

```
import "Addition.sol"
function Addtwovalues() returns(uint)
{
    return Addition.Add(100,100);
}
```

There are a few limitations with libraries; for example, they cannot have state variables and cannot inherit or be inherited. Moreover, they cannot receive Ether either; this is in contrast to contracts that can receive Ether.

Functions

Functions in Solidity are modules of code that are associated with a contract. Functions are declared with a name, optional parameters, access modifier, optional `constant` keyword, and optional return type. This is shown in the following example:

```
function orderMatcher (uint x)
private constant returns(bool return value)
```

In the preceding example, `function` is the keyword used to declare the function. `orderMatcher` is the function name, `uint x` is an optional parameter, `private` is the **access modifier** or **specifier** that controls access to the function from external contracts, `constant` is an optional keyword used to specify that this function does not change anything in the contract but is used only to retrieve values from the contract and `returns (bool return value)` is the optional return type of the function.

- **How to define a function**: The syntax of defining a function is shown as follows:

```
function <name of the function>(<parameters>) <visibility specifier>
returns
(<return data type> <name of the variable>)
{
    <function body>
}
```

- **Function signature**: Functions in Solidity are identified by its signature, which is the first four bytes of the Keccak-256 hash of its full signature string. This is also visible in Remix IDE, as shown in the following screenshot. `f9d55e21` is the first four bytes of 32-byte Keccak-256 hash of the function named `Matcher`.

```
FUNCTIONHASHES

{
    "f9d55e21": "Matcher(uint8)"
}
```

Function hash as shown in Remix IDE

In this example function, `Matcher` has the signature hash of `d99c89cb`. This information is useful in order to build interfaces.

- **Input parameters of a function**: Input parameters of a function are declared in the form of `<data type>` `<parameter name>`. This example clarifies the concept where `uint` `x` and `uint` `y` are input parameters of the `checkValues` function:

```
contract myContract
{
    function checkValues(uint x, uint y)
    {
    }
}
```

- **Output parameters of a function**: Output parameters of a function are declared in the form of `<data type>` `<parameter name>`. This example shows a simple function returning a `uint` value:

```
contract myContract
{
    function getValue() returns (uint z)
    {
        z=x+y;
    }
}
```

A function can return multiple values. In the preceding example function, `getValue` only returns one value, but a function can return up to 14 values of different data types. The names of the unused return parameters can be omitted optionally.

- **Internal function calls**: Functions within the context of the current contract can be called internally in a direct manner. These calls are made to call the functions that exist within the same contract. These calls result in simple JUMP calls at the EVM bytecode level.
- **External function calls**: External function calls are made via message calls from a contract to another contract. In this case, all function parameters are copied to the memory. If a call to an internal function is made using the `this` keyword, it is also considered an external call. The `this` variable is a pointer that refers to the current contract. It is explicitly convertible to an address and all members for a contract are inherited from the address.

- **Fallback functions**: This is an unnamed function in a contract with no arguments and return data. This function executes every time Ether is received. It is required to be implemented within a contract if the contract is intended to receive Ether; otherwise, an exception will be thrown and Ether will be returned. This function also executes if no other function signatures match in the contract. If the contract is expected to receive Ether, then the fallback function should be declared with the payable **modifier**. The payable is required; otherwise, this function will not be able to receive any Ether. This function can be called using the `address.call()` method as, for example, in the following:

```
function ()
{
    throw;
}
```

In this case, if the fallback function is called according to the conditions described earlier; it will call `throw`, which will roll back the state to what it was before making the call. It can also be some other construct than `throw`; for example, it can log an event that can be used as an alert to feed back the outcome of the call to the calling application.

- **Modifier functions**: These functions are used to change the behavior of a function and can be called before other functions. Usually, they are used to check some conditions or verification before executing the function. _ (underscore) is used in the modifier functions that will be replaced with the actual body of the function when the modifier is called. Basically, it symbolizes the function that needs to be *guarded*. This concept is similar to guard functions in other languages.
- **Constructor function**: This is an optional function that has the same name as the contract and is executed once a contract is created. Constructor functions cannot be called later on by users, and there is only one constructor allowed in a contract. This implies that no overloading functionality is available.
- **Function visibility specifiers (access modifiers)**: Functions can be defined with four access specifiers as follows:
    - **External**: These functions are accessible from other contracts and transactions. They cannot be called internally unless the `this` keyword is used.
    - **Public**: By default, functions are public. They can be called either internally or using messages.

- **Internal**: Internal functions are visible to other derived contracts from the parent contract.
- **Private**: Private functions are only visible to the same contract they are declared in.

- **Function Modifiers:**
  - **pure**: This modifier prohibits access or modification to state
  - **view**: This modifier disables any modification to state
  - **payable**: This modifier allows payment of ether with a call
  - **constant**: This modifier disallows access or modification to state

- **Other important keywords/functions throw**: `throw` is used to stop execution. As a result, all state changes are reverted. In this case, no gas is returned to the transaction originator because all the remaining gas is consumed.

Layout of a Solidity source code file

In the following subsections we will look at the components of a Solidity source code file.

Version pragma

In order to address compatibility issues that may arise from future versions of the solc version, `pragma` can be used to specify the version of the compatible compiler as, for example, in the following:

```
pragma solidity ^0.5.0
```

This will ensure that the source file does not compile with versions smaller than 0.5.0 and versions starting from 0.6.0.

Import

Import in Solidity allows the importing of symbols from the existing Solidity files into the current global scope. This is similar to `import` statements available in JavaScript, as for example, in the following:

```
import "module-name";
```

Comments

Comments can be added in the Solidity source code file in a manner similar to C-language. Multiple line comments are enclosed in /* and */, whereas single line comments start with //.

An example Solidity program is as follows, showing the use of `pragma`, `import`, and comments:

```
1   pragma solidity ^0.4.0; //specify the compiler version
2   /*
3   This is a simple value checker contract that checks the value
4   provided and returns boolean value based on the condition
5   expression evaluation.
6   */
7   import "dev.oraclize.it/api.sol";
8   contract valuechecker {
9       uint price=10;
10      //This is price variable declare and initialized with value 10
11      event valueEvent(bool returnValue);
12      function Matcher (uint8 x) returns (bool)
13      {
14          if ( x >= price)
15          {
16              valueEvent(true);
17              return true;
18          }
19      }
20  }
```

Sample Solidity program as shown in Remix IDE

This completes a brief introduction to the Solidity language. The language is very rich and under constant improvement. Detailed documentation and coding guidelines are available online at http://solidity.readthedocs.io/en/latest/.

Summary

This chapter started with the introduction of development tools for Ethereum such as Remix IDE. Then we discussed some frameworks such as Truffle along with local blockchain solutions for development and testing such as Ganache, EthereumJS and TestRPC. Other tools such as MetaMask were also explored. Installation of Node was also introduced, as most of the tools are JavaScript and Node based.

12
Building a Betting App

Sometimes, it is necessary for smart contracts to access data from other dapps or from the World Wide Web. But it's really complicated to let smart contracts access outside data due to technical and consensus challenges. Therefore, currently, Ethereum smart contracts don't have native support to access outside data. But there are third-party solutions for Ethereum smart contracts to access data from some popular dapps and from the World Wide Web. In this chapter, we will learn how to use Oraclize to make HTTP requests from Ethereum smart contracts to access data from the World Wide Web. We will also learn how to access files stored in IPFS, use the strings library to work with strings, and so on. We will learn all this by building a football-betting smart contract and a client for it.

In this chapter, we'll cover the following topics:

- How does Oraclize work?
- What are Oraclize's various data sources and how do each of them work?
- How does consensus work in Oraclize?
- Integrating Oraclize in Ethereum smart contracts
- Using strings the `Solidity` library to make it easy to work with strings
- Building a football betting app

Introduction to Oraclize

Oraclize is a service that aims to enable smart contracts to access data from other blockchains and the World Wide Web. This service is currently live on bitcoin and Ethereum's testnet and mainnet. What makes Oraclize so special is that you don't need to trust it because it provides proof of authenticity of all data it provides to smart contracts.

In this chapter, our aim is to learn how Ethereum smart contracts can use the Oraclize service to fetch data from the World Wide Web.

How does it work?

Let's look at the process by which an Ethereum smart contract can fetch data from other blockchains and the World Wide Web using Oraclize.

To fetch data that exists outside of the Ethereum blockchain, an Ethereum smart contract needs to send a query to Oraclize, mentioning the data source (representing where to fetch the data from) and the input for the data source (representing what to fetch).

Sending a query to Oraclize Oraclize means sending a contract call (that is, an internal transaction) to the Oraclize contract present in the Ethereum blockchain.

The Oraclize server keeps looking for new incoming queries to its smart contract. Whenever it sees a new query, it fetches the result and sends it back to your contract by calling the `_callback` method of your contract.

Data sources

Here is a list of sources from which Oraclize lets smart contracts fetch data:

- URL: The URL data source provides you with the ability to make an HTTP GET or POST request, that is, fetch data from the WWW.
- `WolframAlpha`: The `WolframAlpha` data source provides you with the ability to submit a query to the `WolframAlpha` knowledge engine and get the answer.
- `Blockchain`: The `blockchain` data source provides you with ability to access data from other `blockchains`. Possible queries that can be submitted to the `blockchain` data source are `bitcoin blockchain height`, `litecoin hashrate`, `bitcoin difficulty`, `1NPFRDJuEdyqEn2nmLNaWMfojNksFjbL4S balance`, and so on.
- `IPFS`: The `IPFS` data source provides you with the ability to fetch the content of a file stored in `IPFS`.

- Nested: The nested data source is a metadata source; it does not provide access to additional services. It was designed to provide a simple aggregation logic, enabling a single query to leverage sub-queries based on any available data source and producing a single string as a result; for example:

```
[WolframAlpha] temperature in ${[IPFS]
QmP2ZkdsJG7LTw7jBbizTTgY1ZBeen64PqMgCAWz2koJBL}.
```

- Computation: The computation data source enables the auditable execution of a given application into a secure off-chain context; that is, it lets us fetch the result of an off-chain execution of an application. This application has to print the query result on the last line (on the standard output) before its quits. The execution context has to be described by a Dockerfile, where building and running it should start your main application straight away. The Dockerfile initialization plus your application execution should terminate as soon as possible: the maximum execution timeout is 5 minutes on an AWS t2.micro instance. Here, we are considering an AWS t2.micro instance because that's what Oraclize will use to execute the application. As the input for the data source is the IPFS multihash of a ZIP archive containing such files (Dockerfile plus any external file dependencies, and the Dockerfile has to be placed in the archive root), you should take care of preparing this archive and pushing it to IPFS beforehand.

These data sources are available at the time of writing this book. But many more data sources are likely to be available in the future.

Proof of authenticity

Although Oraclize is a trusted service, you may still want to check whether the data returned by Oraclize is authentic or not, that is, whether it was manipulated by Oraclize or someone else in transit.

Optionally, Oraclize provides the TLSNotary proof of result that's returned from the URL, blockchain, and nested and computation data sources. This proof is not available for WolframAlpha and IPFS data sources. Currently, Oraclize only supports the TLSNotary proof, but in the future, they may support some other ways to authenticate. Currently, the TLSNotary proof needs to be validated manually, but Oraclize is already working on on-chain proof verification; that is, your smart contract code can verify the TLSNotary proof on its own while receiving the data from Oraclize so that this data is discarded if the proof turns out to be invalid.

This tool (`https://github.com/Oraclize/proof-verification-tool`) is an open source tool provided by Oraclize to validate the TLSNotary proof in case you want to.

 Understanding how TLSNotary works is not required to use Oraclize or to verify the proof. The tool to validate the TLSNotary proof is open source; therefore, if it contains any malicious code, then it can easily be caught, so this tool can be trusted.

Let's look at a high-level overview of how TLSNotary works. To understand how TLSNotary works, you need to first understand how TLS works. The TLS protocol provides a way for the client and server to create an encrypted session so that no one else can read or manipulate what is transferred between the client and server. The server first sends its certificate (issued to the domain owner by a trusted CA) to the client. The certificate will contain the public key of the server. The client uses the CA's public key to decrypt the certificate so that it can verify that the certificate is actually issued by the CA and get the server's public key. Then, the client generates a symmetric encryption key and a MAC key and encrypts them using the server's public key and sends it to the server. The server can only decrypt this message as it has the private key to decrypt it. Now the client and server share the same symmetric and MAC keys and no one else knows about these keys and they can start sending and receiving data from each other. The symmetric key is used to encrypt and decrypt the data where the MAC key and the symmetric key together are used to generate a signature for the encrypted message so that in case the message is modified by an attacker, the other party can know about it.

TLSNotary is a modification of TLS, which is used by Oraclize to provide cryptography proof showing that the data they provided to your smart contract was really the one the data source gave to Oraclize at a specific time. Actually the TLSNotary protocol is an open source technology, developed and used by the PageSigner project.

TLSNotary works by splitting the symmetric key and the MAC key among three parties, that is, the server, an auditee, and an auditor. The basic idea of TLSNotary is that the auditee can prove to the auditor that a particular result was returned by the server at a given time.

So here is an overview of how exactly TLSNotary lets us achieve this. The auditor calculates the symmetric key and MAC key and gives only the symmetric key to the auditee. The MAC key is not needed by the auditee as the MAC signature check ensures that the TLS data from the server was not modified in transit. With the symmetric encryption key, the auditee can now decrypt data from the server. Because all messages are "signed" by the bank using the MAC key and only the server and the auditor know the MAC key, a correct MAC signature can serve as proof that certain messages came from the bank and were not spoofed by the auditee.

In the case of the Oraclize service, Oraclize is the auditee, while a locked-down AWS instance of a specially designed, open source Amazon machine image acts as the auditor.

The proof data they provide are the signed attestations of this AWS instance that a proper TLSnotary proof did occur. They also provide some additional proof regarding the software running in the AWS instance, that is, whether it has been modified since being initialized.

Pricing

The first Oraclize query call coming from any Ethereum address is completely free of charge. Oraclize calls are free when used on testnets! This works for moderate usage in test environments only.

From the second call onward, you have to pay in ether for queries. While sending a query to Oraclize (that is, while making an internal transaction call), a fee is deducted by transferring ether from the calling contract to the Oraclize contract. The amount of ether to deduct depends on the data source and proof type.

Here is a table that shows the number of ether that is deducted while sending a query:

Data source	Without proof	With TLSNotary proof
URL	$0.01	$0.05
Blockchain	$0.01	$0.05
WolframAlpha	$0.03	$0.03
IPFS	$0.01	$0.01

So if you are making a HTTP request and you want the TLSNotary proof too, then the calling contract must have an ether worth of $0.05; otherwise, an exception is thrown.

Getting started with the Oraclize API

For a contract to use the Oraclize service, it needs to inherit the `usingOraclize` contract. You can find this contract at `https://github.com/Oraclize/Ethereum-api`.

The usingOraclize contract acts as the proxy for the OraclizeI and OraclizeAddrResolverI contracts. Actually, usingOraclize makes it easy to make calls to the OraclizeI and OraclizeAddrResolverI contracts, that is, it provides simpler APIs. You can also directly make calls to the OraclizeI and OraclizeAddrResolverI contracts if you feel comfortable. You can go through the source code of these contracts to find all the available APIs. We will only learn the most necessary ones.

Let's look at how to set proof type, set proof storage location, make queries, find the cost of a query, and so on.

Setting the proof type and storage location

Whether you need the TLSNotary proof from Oraclize or not, you have to specify the proof type and proof storage location before making queries.

If you don't want proof, then put this code in your contract:

```
oraclize_setProof(proofType_NONE)
```

And if you want proof, then put this code in your contract:

```
oraclize_setProof(proofType_TLSNotary | proofStorage_IPFS)
```

Currently, proofStorage_IPFS is the only proof storage location available; that is, TLSNotary proof is only stored in IPFS.

You may execute any of these methods just once, for instance, in the constructor or at any other time if, for instance, you need the proof for certain queries only.

Sending queries

To send a query to Oraclize, you will need to call the oraclize_query function. This function expects at least two arguments, that is, the data source and the input for the given data source. The data source argument is not case-sensitive.

Here are some basic examples of the oraclize_query function:

```
oraclize_query("WolframAlpha", "random number between 0 and 100");

oraclize_query("URL",
"https://api.kraken.com/0/public/Ticker?pair=ETHXBT");

oraclize_query("IPFS", "QmdEJwJG1T9rzHvBD8i69HHuJaRgXRKEQCP7Bh1BVttZbU");
```

```
oraclize_query("URL", "https://xyz.io/makePayment", '{"currency": "USD",
"amount": "1"}');
```

Here is how the preceding code works:

- If the first argument is a string, it is assumed to be the data source and the second argument is assumed to be the input for the data source. In the first call, the data source is `WolframAlpha` and the search query we sent to it was `random number between 0 and 100`.
- In the second call, we make an `HTTP GET` request to the `URL` present in the second argument.
- In the third call, we fetch the content of the `QmdEJwJG1T9rzHvBD8i69HHuJaRgXRKEQCP7Bh1BVttZbU` file from `IPFS`.
- If two consecutive arguments after the data source are strings, then it's assumed to be a POST request. In the last call, we make an `HTTP POST` request to `https://xyz.io/makePayment` and the `POST` request body content is the string in the third argument. Oraclize is intelligent enough to detect the content-type header based on the string format.

Scheduling queries

If you want Oraclize to execute your query at a scheduled future time, just specify the delay (in seconds) from the current time as the first argument.

Here is an example:

```
oraclize_query(60, "WolframAlpha", "random number between 0 and 100");
```

The preceding query will be executed by Oraclize 60 seconds after it's been seen. So if the first argument is a number, then it's assumed that we are scheduling a query.

Custom gas

The transaction originating from Oraclize to your __callback function costs gas, just like any other transaction. You need to pay Oraclize the gas cost. The ether oraclize_query charges to make a query are also used to provide gas while calling the __callback function. By default, Oraclize provides 200,000 gas while calling the __callback function.

This return gas cost is actually in your control since you write the code in the __callback method and as such, can estimate it. So, when placing a query with Oraclize, you can also specify how much the gasLimit should be on the __callback transaction. Note, however, that since Oraclize sends the transaction, any unspent gas is returned to Oraclize, not you.

If the default, and minimum, value of 200,000 gas is not enough, you can increase it by specifying a different gasLimit in this way:

```
oraclize_query("WolframAlpha", "random number between 0 and 100", 500000);
```

Here, you can see that if the last argument is a number, then it's assumed to be the custom gas. In the preceding code, Oraclize will use a 500k gasLimit for the callback transaction instead of 200k. Because we are asking Oraclize to provide more gas, Oraclize will deduct more ether (depending on how much gas is required) while calling oraclize_query.

> Note that if you offer too low a gasLimit, and your __callback method is long, you may never see a callback. Also note that the custom gas has to be more than 200k.

Callback functions

Once your result is ready, Oraclize will send a transaction back to your contract address and invoke one of these three methods:

- either __callback(bytes32 myid, string result). Myid is a unique ID for every query. This ID is returned by the oraclize_query method. If you have multiple oraclize_query calls in your contract, then this is used to match the query this result is for.
- If you requested for the TLS Notary proof, this is the result:
  __callback(bytes32 myid, string result, bytes proof)
- As a last resort, if the other methods are absent, the fallback function is
  function()

Here is an example of the __callback function:

```
function __callback(bytes32 myid, string result) {
    if (msg.sender != oraclize_cbAddress()) throw; // just to be sure the
calling address is the Oraclize authorized one

    //now doing something with the result..
}
```

Parsing helpers

The result returned from an HTTP request can be HTML, JSON, XML, binary, and so on. In Solidity, it is difficult and expensive to parse the result. Due to this, Oraclize provides parsing helpers to let it handle the parsing on its servers, and you get only the part of the result that you need.

To ask Oraclize to parse the result, you need to wrap the URL with one of these parsing helpers:

- `xml(..)` and `json(..)` helpers let you ask Oraclize to only return part of the JSON or XML-parsed response; for example, take a look at the following:
    - In order to get the whole response back, you use the `URL` data source with the `api.kraken.com/0/public/Ticker?pair=ETHUSD` URL argument
    - If all you want is the last-price field, you need to use the JSON parsing call as `json(api.kraken.com/0/public/Ticker?pair=ETHUSD).result.XETHZUSD.c.0`
- The `html(..).xpath(..)` helper is useful for HTML scraping. Just specify the XPATH you want as the `xpath(..)` argument; for example, take a look at the following:
    - To fetch the text of a specific tweet, use `html(https://twitter.com/oraclizeit/status/671316655893561344).xpath(//*[contains(@class, 'tweet-text')]/text()).`
- The `binary(..)` helper is useful in getting binary files such as certificate files:
    - To fetch only a portion of the binary file, you can use `slice(offset, length)`; the first parameter is the offset, while the second one is the length of the slice you want back (both in bytes).
    - Example: Fetch only the first 300 bytes from a binary CRL, `binary(https://www.sk.ee/crls/esteid/esteid2015.crl).slice(0,300)`. The binary helper must be used with the slice option, and only binary files (not encoded) are accepted.

 If and when the server is not responding or is unreachable, we will send you an empty response. You can test queries using `http://app.Oraclize.it/home/test_query`.

Getting the query price

If you would like to know how much a query would cost before making the actual query, then you can use the `Oraclize.getPrice()` function to get the amount of wei required. The first argument it takes is the data source, and the second argument is optional, which is the custom gas.

One popular use case of this is to notify the client to add ether to the contract if there isn't enough to make the query.

Encrypting queries

Sometimes, you may not want to reveal the data source and/or the input for the data source. For example: you may not want to reveal the API key in the URL if there is any. Therefore, Oraclize provides a way to store queries encrypted in the smart contract and only Oraclize's server has the key to decrypt it.

Oraclize provides a Python tool (`https://github.com/Oraclize/encrypted-queries`), which can be used to encrypt the data source and/or the data input. It generates a non-deterministic encrypted string.

The CLI command to encrypt an arbitrary string of text is as follows:

```
python encrypted_queries_tools.py -e -p
044992e9473b7d90ca54d2886c7addd14a61109af202f1c95e218b0c99eb060c7134c4ae463
45d0383ac996185762f04997d6fd6c393c86e4325c469741e64eca9 "YOUR DATASOURCE or
INPUT"
```

The long hexadecimal string you see is the public key of Oraclize's server. Now you can use the output of the preceding command in place of the data source and/or the input for the data source.

> In order to prevent the misuse of encrypted queries (that is, replay attacks) the first contract querying Oraclize with a specific encrypted query becomes its rightful owner. Any other contract reusing the exact same string will not be allowed to use it and will receive an empty result. As a consequence, remember to always generate a newly encrypted string when redeploying contracts using encrypted queries.

Decrypting the data source

There is another data source called decrypt. It is used to decrypt an encrypted string. But this data source doesn't return any result; otherwise, anyone would have the ability to decrypt the data source and input for the data source.

It was specifically designed to be used within the nested data source to enable partial query encryption. It is its only use case.

Oraclize web IDE

Oraclize provides a web IDE, using which you can write, compile, and test Oraclize-based applications. You can find it at `http://dapps.Oraclize.it/browser-Solidity/`.

If you visit the link, then you will notice that it looks exactly the same as browser Solidity. And it's actually browser Solidity with one extra feature. To understand what that feature is, we need to understand browser Solidity more in depth.

Browser Solidity not only lets us write, compile, and generate web3.js code for our contracts, but it also lets us test those contracts there itself. Until now, in order to test our contract, we were setting up an Ethereum node and sending transactions to it. But browser Solidity can execute contracts without connecting to any node and everything happens in memory. It achieves this using ethereumjs-vm, which is a JavaScript implementation of EVM. Using ethereumjs-vm, you can create our own EVM and run byte code. If we want, we can configure browser Solidity to use the Ethereum node by providing the URL to connect to. The UI is very informative; therefore, you can try all these by yourself.

What's special about the Oraclize web IDE is that it deploys the Oraclize contract in the in-memory execution environment so that you don't have to connect to the testnet or mainnet node, but if you use browser Solidity, then you have to connect to the testnet or mainnet node to test Oraclize APIs.

 You can find more resources related to integrating Oraclize at `https://dev.Oraclize.it/`.

Working with strings

Working with strings in Solidity is not as easy as working with strings in other high-level programming languages, such as JavaScript, Python, and so on. Therefore, many Solidity programmers have come up with various libraries and contracts to make it easy to work with strings.

The `strings` library is the most popular strings utility library. It lets us join, concatenate, split, compare, and so on by converting a string to something called a slice. A slice is a struct that holds the length of the string and the address of the string. Since a slice only has to specify an offset and a length, copying and manipulating slices is a lot less expensive than copying and manipulating the strings they reference.

To further reduce gas costs, most functions on slice that need to return a slice modify the original one instead of allocating a new one; for instance, s.split(".") will return the text up to the first ".", modifying s to only contain the remainder of the string after the ".". In situations where you do not want to modify the original slice, you can make a copy with .copy(), for example, s.copy().split("."). Try and avoid using this idiom in loops; since Solidity has no memory management, it will result in allocating many short-lived slices that are later discarded.

Functions that have to copy string data will return strings rather than slices; these can be cast back to slices for further processing if required.

Let's look at a few examples of working with strings using the `strings` library:

```
pragma Solidity ^0.4.0;

import "github.com/Arachnid/Solidity-stringutils/strings.sol";

contract Contract
{
    using strings for *;

    function Contract()
    {
        //convert string to slice
        var slice = "xyz abc".toSlice();

        //length of string
        var length = slice.len();

        //split a string
        //subslice = xyz
        //slice = abc
```

```
var subslice = slice.split(" ".toSlice());

//split a string into an array
var s = "www.google.com".toSlice();
var delim = ".".toSlice();
var parts = new string[](s.count(delim));
for(uint i = 0; i < parts.length; i++) {
    parts[i] = s.split(delim).toString();
}

//Converting a slice back to a string
var myString = slice.toString();

//Concatenating strings
var finalSlice = subslice.concat(slice);

//check if two strings are equal
if(slice.equals(subslice))
{

}
        }
    }
```

The preceding code is self-explanatory.

Functions that return two slices come in two versions: a nonallocating version that takes the second slice as an argument, modifying it in place, and an allocating version that allocates and returns the second slice; for example, let's take a look at the following:

```
var slice1 = "abc".toSlice();

//moves the string pointer of slice1 to point to the next rune (letter)
//and returns a slice containing only the first rune
var slice2 = slice1.nextRune();

var slice3 = "abc".toSlice();
var slice4 = "".toSlice();

//Extracts the first rune from slice3 into slice4, advancing the slice to
point to the next rune and returns slice4.
var slice5 = slice3.nextRune(slice4);
```

 You can learn more about the strings library at https://github.com/Arachnid/Solidity-stringutils.

Building the betting contract

In our betting application, two people can choose to bet on a football match with one person supporting the home team and the other person supporting the away team. They both should bet the same amount of money, and the winner takes all the money. If the match is a draw, then they both will take back their money.

We will use the FastestLiveScores API to find out the result of matches. It provides a free API, which lets us make 100 requests per hour for free. First, go ahead and create an account and then generate an API key. To create an account, visit `https://customer.fastestlivescores.com/register`, and once the account is created, you will have the API key visible at `https://customer.fastestlivescores.com/`. You can find the API documentation at `https://docs.crowdscores.com/`.

For every bet between two people in our application, a betting contract will be deployed. The contract will contain the match ID retrieved from the `FastestLiveScores` API, the amount of wei each of the parties need to invest, and the addresses of the parties. Once both parties have invested in the contract, they will find out the result of the match. If the match is not yet finished, then they will try to check the result after every 24 hours.

Here is the code for the contract:

```
pragma Solidity ^0.4.0;

import "github.com/Oraclize/Ethereum-api/oraclizeAPI.sol";
import "github.com/Arachnid/Solidity-stringutils/strings.sol";

contract Betting is usingOraclize
{
    using strings for *;

    string public matchId;
    uint public amount;
    string public url;

    address public homeBet;
    address public awayBet;

    function Betting(string _matchId, uint _amount, string _url)
    {
        matchId = _matchId;
        amount = _amount;
        url = _url;

        oraclize_setProof(proofType_TLSNotary | proofStorage_IPFS);
```

```
}

//1 indicates home team
//2 indicates away team
function betOnTeam(uint team) payable
{

    if(team == 1)
    {
        if(homeBet == 0)
        {
            if(msg.value == amount)
            {
                homeBet = msg.sender;
                if(homeBet != 0 && awayBet != 0)
                {
                    oraclize_query("URL", url);
                }
            }
            else
            {
                throw;
            }
        }
        else
        {
            throw;
        }
    }
    else if(team == 2)
    {
        if(awayBet == 0)
        {
            if(msg.value == amount)
            {
                awayBet = msg.sender;

                if(homeBet != 0 && awayBet != 0)
                {
                    oraclize_query("URL", url);
                }
            }
            else
            {
                throw;
            }
        }
        else
```

```
                    {
                        throw;
                    }
                }
                else
                {
                    throw;
                }
            }

            function __callback(bytes32 myid, string result, bytes proof) {
                if (msg.sender != oraclize_cbAddress())
                {
                    throw;
                }
                else
                {
                    if(result.toSlice().equals("home".toSlice()))
                    {
                        homeBet.send(this.balance);
                    }
                    else if(result.toSlice().equals("away".toSlice()))
                    {
                        awayBet.send(this.balance);
                    }
                    else if(result.toSlice().equals("draw".toSlice()))
                    {
                        homeBet.send(this.balance / 2);
                        awayBet.send(this.balance / 2);
                    }
                    else
                    {
                        if (Oraclize.getPrice("URL") < this.balance)
                        {
                            oraclize_query(86400, "URL", url);
                        }
                    }
                }
            }
        }
    }
```

The contract code is self-explanatory. Now compile the preceding code using `solc.js` or browser Solidity depending on whatever you are comfortable with. You will not need to link the `strings` library because all the functions in it are set to the `internal` visibility.

In browser Solidity, when specifying to import a library or contract from the HTTP URL, make sure that it's hosted on GitHub; otherwise, it won't fetch it. In that GitHub file URL, make sure that you remove the protocol as well as `blob/{branch-name}`.

Building a client for the betting contract

To make it easy to find match's IDs, deploy, and invest in contracts, we need to build a UI client. So let's get started with building a client, which will have two paths, that is, the home path to deploy contracts and bet on matches and the other path to find the list of matches. We will let users deploy and bet using their own offline accounts so that the entire process of betting happens in a decentralized manner and nobody can cheat.

Before we start building our client, make sure that you have testnet synced because Oraclize works only on Ethereum's testnet/mainnet and not on private networks. You can switch to testnet and start downloading the testnet blockchain by replacing the `--dev` option with the `--testnet` option. For example, take a look at the following:

```
geth --testnet --rpc --rpccorsdomain "*" --rpcaddr "0.0.0.0" --rpcport
"8545"
```

Projecting the structure

In the exercise files of this chapter, you will find two directories, that is, Final and Initial. Final contains the final source code of the project, whereas Initial contains the empty source code files and libraries to get started with building the application quickly.

 To test the `Final` directory, you will need to run `npm install` inside it and then run the app using the `node app.js` command inside the Final directory.

In the `Initial` directory, you will find a `public` directory and two files named `app.js` and `package.json`. The `package.json` file contains the backend dependencies of our app, and `app.js` is where you will place the backend source code.

The `public` directory contains files related to the frontend. Inside `public/css`, you will find `bootstrap.min.css`, which is the bootstrap library. Inside `public/html`, you will find the `index.html` and `matches.ejs` files, where you will place the HTML code of our app, and in the `public/js` directory, you will find js files for web3.js, and ethereumjs-tx. Inside `public/js`, you will also find a `main.js` file, where you will place the frontend JS code of our app. You will also find the Oraclize Python tool to encrypt queries.

Building the backend

Let's first build the backend of the app. First of all, run `npm install` inside the Initial directory to install the required dependencies for our backend.

Here is the backend code to run an express service and serve the `index.html` file and static files and set the view engine:

```
var express = require("express");
var app = express();

app.set("view engine", "ejs");

app.use(express.static("public"));

app.listen(8080);

app.get("/", function(req, res) {
    res.sendFile(__dirname + "/public/html/index.html");
})
```

The preceding code is self-explanatory. Now let's proceed further. Our app will have another page, which will display a list of recent matches with matches' IDs and result if a match has finished. Here is the code for the endpoint:

```
var request = require("request");
var moment = require("moment");

app.get("/matches", function(req, res) {
request("https://api.crowdscores.com/v1/matches?api_key=7b7a988932de4eaab4e
d1b4dcdc1a82a", function(error, response, body) {
        if (!error && response.statusCode == 200) {
            body = JSON.parse(body);

            for (var i = 0; i < body.length; i++) {
             body[i].start = moment.unix(body[i].start /
                1000).format("YYYY MMM DD hh:mm:ss");
            }
```

```
            res.render(__dirname + "/public/html/matches.ejs", {
                matches: body
            });
        } else {
            res.send("An error occured");
        }
    })
})
```

Here, we are making the API request to fetch the list of recent matches and then we are passing the result to the `matches.ejs` file so that it can render the result in a user-friendly UI. The API results give us the match start time as a timestamp; therefore, we are using moment to convert it to a human readable format. We make this request from the backend and not from the frontend so that we don't expose the API key to the users.

Our backend will provide an API to the frontend, using which the frontend can encrypt the query before deploying the contract. Our application will not prompt users to create an API key, as it would be a bad UX practice. The application's developer controlling the API key will cause no harm as the developer cannot modify the result from the API servers; therefore, users will still trust the app even after the application's developer knows the API key.

Here is code for the encryption endpoint:

```
var PythonShell = require("python-shell");

app.get("/getURL", function(req, res) {
    var matchId = req.query.matchId;

    var options = {
        args: ["-e", "-p",
"044992e9473b7d90ca54d2886c7addd14a61109af202f1c95e218b0c99eb060c7134c4ae46
345d0383ac996185762f04997d6fd6c393c86e4325c469741e64eca9",
"json(https://api.crowdscores.com/v1/matches/" + matchId +
"?api_key=7b7a988932de4eaab4ed1b4dcdc1a82a).outcome.winner"],
        scriptPath: __dirname
    };

    PythonShell.run("encrypted_queries_tools.py", options, function
      (err, results) {
        if(err)
        {
            res.send("An error occured");
        }
        else
        {
            res.send(results[0]);
```

```
            }
        });
    })
```

We have already seen how to use this tool. To run this endpoint successfully, make sure that Python is installed on your system. Even if Python is installed, this endpoint may show errors, indicating that Python's cryptography and base58 modules aren't installed. So make sure you install these modules if the tool prompts you to.

Building the frontend

Now let's build the frontend of our application. Our frontend will let users see the list of recent matches, deploy the betting contract, bet on a game, and let them see information about a betting contract.

Let's first implement the `matches.ejs` file, which will display the list of recent matches. Here is the code for this:

```html
<!DOCTYPE html>
<html lang="en">
    <head>
        <meta charset="utf-8">
        <meta name="viewport" content="width=device-width, initial-scale=1, shrink-to-fit=no">
        <meta http-equiv="x-ua-compatible" content="ie=edge">
        <link rel="stylesheet" href="/css/bootstrap.min.css">
    </head>
    <body>
        <div class="container">
            <br>
            <div class="row m-t-1">
                <div class="col-md-12">
                    <a href="/">Home</a>
                </div>
            </div>
            <br>
            <div class="row">
                <div class="col-md-12">
                    <table class="table table-inverse">
                        <thead>
                          <tr>
                              <th>Match ID</th>
                              <th>Start Time</th>
                              <th>Home Team</th>
                              <th>Away Team</th>
```

```
                                  <th>Winner</th>
                              </tr>
                          </thead>
                          <tbody>
                              <% for(var i=0; i < matches.length; i++) {
%>

                                  <tr>
                                      <td><%= matches[i].dbid %></td>
                                      <% if (matches[i].start) { %>
                                       <td><%= matches[i].start %></td>
                                  <% } else { %>
                                        <td>Time not finalized</td>
                                  <% } %>
                                      <td><%= matches[i].homeTeam.name
%></td>

                                      <td><%= matches[i].awayTeam.name
%></td>

                                      <% if (matches[i].outcome) { %>
                                       <td><%= matches[i].outcome.winner
%></td>

                                  <% } else { %>
                                        <td>Match not finished</td>
                                  <% } %>
                                  </tr>
                              <% } %>
                          </tbody>
                      </table>
                  </div>
              </div>
          </div>
      </body>
  </html>
```

The preceding code is self-explanatory. Now let's write the HTML code for our home page. Our home page will display three forms. The first form is to deploy a betting contract, the second form is to invest in a betting contract, and the third form is to display information on a deployed betting contract.

Here is the HTML code for the home page. Place this code in the index.html page:

```
<!DOCTYPE html>
  <html lang="en">
      <head>
          <meta charset="utf-8">
          <meta name="viewport" content="width=device-width, initial-
  scale=1, shrink-to-fit=no">
          <meta http-equiv="x-ua-compatible" content="ie=edge">
          <link rel="stylesheet" href="/css/bootstrap.min.css">
```

```
            </head>
            <body>
                <div class="container">
                    <br>
                    <div class="row m-t-1">
                        <div class="col-md-12">
                            <a href="/matches">Matches</a>
                        </div>
                    </div>
                    <br>
                    <div class="row">
                        <div class="col-md-4">
                            <h3>Deploy betting contract</h3>
                            <form id="deploy">
                                <div class="form-group">
                                    <label>From address: </label>
                                    <input type="text" class="form-control"
id="fromAddress">
                                </div>
                                <div class="form-group">
                                    <label>Private Key: </label>
                                    <input type="text" class="form-control"
id="privateKey">
                                </div>
                                <div class="form-group">
                                    <label>Match ID: </label>
                                    <input type="text" class="form-control"
id="matchId">
                                </div>
                                <div class="form-group">
                                    <label>Bet Amount (in ether): </label>
                                    <input type="text" class="form-control"
id="betAmount">
                                </div>
                                <p id="message" style="word-wrap: break-word"></p>
                                <input type="submit" value="Deploy" class="btn
btn-primary" />
                            </form>
                        </div>
                        <div class="col-md-4">
                            <h3>Bet on a contract</h3>
                            <form id="bet">
                                <div class="form-group">
                                    <label>From address: </label>
                                    <input type="text" class="form-control"
id="fromAddress">
                                </div>
                                <div class="form-group">
```

```html
                                    <label>Private Key: </label>
                                    <input type="text" class="form-control"
id="privateKey">
                                </div>
                                <div class="form-group">
                                    <label>Contract Address: </label>
                                    <input type="text" class="form-control"
id="contractAddress">
                                </div>
                                <div class="form-group">
                                    <label>Team: </label>
                                    <select class="form-control" id="team">
                                        <option>Home</option>
                                        <option>Away</option>
                                    </select>
                                </div>
                                <p id="message" style="word-wrap: break-word"></p>
                                <input type="submit" value="Bet" class="btn btn-
primary" />
                            </form>
                        </div>
                        <div class="col md 4">
                            <h3>Display betting contract</h3>
                            <form id="find">
                                <div class="form-group">
                                    <label>Contract Address: </label>
                                    <input type="text" class="form-control"
 d="contractAddress">
                                </div>
                                <p id="message"></p>
                                <input type="submit" value="Find" class="btn btn-
primary" />
                            </form>
                        </div>
                    </div>
                </div>

        <script type="text/javascript" src="/js/web3.min.js"></script>
        <script type="text/javascript" src="/js/ethereumjs-
tx.js"></script>
        <script type="text/javascript" src="/js/main.js"></script>
    </body>
</html>
```

The preceding code is self-explanatory. Now let's write JavaScript code to actually deploy the contract, invest in contracts, and display information on contracts. Here is the code for all this. Place this code in the `main.js` file:

```
var bettingContractByteCode = "6060604...";
var bettingContractABI =
[{"constant":false,"inputs":[{"name":"team","type":"uint256"}],"name":"betO
nTeam","outputs":[],"payable":true,"type":"function"},{"constant":false,"in
puts":[{"name":"myid","type":"bytes32"},{"name":"result","type":"string"}],
"name":"__callback","outputs":[],"payable":false,"type":"function"},{"const
ant":false,"inputs":[{"name":"myid","type":"bytes32"},{"name":"result","typ
e":"string"},{"name":"proof","type":"bytes"}],"name":"__callback","outputs"
:[],"payable":false,"type":"function"},{"constant":true,"inputs":[],"name":
"url","outputs":[{"name":"","type":"string"}],"payable":false,"type":"funct
ion"},{"constant":true,"inputs":[],"name":"matchId","outputs":[{"name":"","
type":"string"}],"payable":false,"type":"function"},{"constant":true,"input
s":[],"name":"amount","outputs":[{"name":"","type":"uint256"}],"payable":fa
lse,"type":"function"},{"constant":true,"inputs":[],"name":"homeBet","outpu
ts":[{"name":"","type":"address"}],"payable":false,"type":"function"},{"con
stant":true,"inputs":[],"name":"awayBet","outputs":[{"name":"","type":"addr
ess"}],"payable":false,"type":"function"},{"inputs":[{"name":"_matchId","ty
pe":"string"},{"name":"_amount","type":"uint256"},{"name":"_url","type":"st
ring"}],"payable":false,"type":"constructor"}];

var web3 = new Web3(new
Web3.providers.HttpProvider("http://localhost:8545"));

function getAJAXObject()
{
    var request;
    if (window.XMLHttpRequest) {
        request = new XMLHttpRequest();
    } else if (window.ActiveXObject) {
        try {
            request = new ActiveXObject("Msxml2.XMLHTTP");
        } catch (e) {
            try {
                request = new ActiveXObject("Microsoft.XMLHTTP");
            } catch (e) {}
        }
    }

    return request;
}

document.getElementById("deploy").addEventListener("submit", function(e){
    e.preventDefault();
```

```
var fromAddress = document.querySelector("#deploy #fromAddress").value;
var privateKey = document.querySelector("#deploy #privateKey").value;
var matchId = document.querySelector("#deploy #matchId").value;
var betAmount = document.querySelector("#deploy #betAmount").value;

var url = "/getURL?matchId=" + matchId;

var request = getAJAXObject();

request.open("GET", url);

request.onreadystatechange = function() {
    if (request.readyState == 4) {
        if (request.status == 200) {
            if(request.responseText != "An error occured")
            {
        var queryURL = request.responseText;

        var contract = web3.eth.contract(bettingContractABI);
        var data = contract.new.getData(matchId,
          web3.toWei(betAmount, "ether"), queryURL, {
            data: bettingContract.ByteCode
             });

        var gasRequired = web3.eth.estimateGas({ data: "0x" + data
           });

    web3.eth.getTransactionCount(fromAddress, function(error, nonce){

     var rawTx = {
         gasPrice: web3.toHex(web3.eth.gasPrice),
          gasLimit: web3.toHex(gasRequired),
           from: fromAddress,
            nonce: web3.toHex(nonce),
             data: "0x" + data,
               };

    privateKey = EthJS.Util.toBuffer(privateKey, "hex");

     var tx = new EthJS.Tx(rawTx);
     tx.sign(privateKey);

    web3.eth.sendRawTransaction("0x" +
     tx.serialize().toString("hex"), function(err, hash) {
         if(!err)
             {document.querySelector("#deploy #message").
                innerHTML = "Transaction Hash: " + hash + ".
                  Transaction is mining...";
```

```
                    var timer = window.setInterval(function(){
                    web3.eth.getTransactionReceipt(hash, function(err, result){
                    if(result)
                      {window.clearInterval(timer);
           document.querySelector("#deploy #message").innerHTML =
             "Transaction Hash: " + hash + " and contract address is: " +
                result.contractAddress;}
                  })
                    }, 10000)
                      }
                  else
                {document.querySelector("#deploy #message").innerHTML = err;
                  }
                });
              })

            }
              }
          }
      };

      request.send(null);

}, false)

document.getElementById("bet").addEventListener("submit", function(e){
    e.preventDefault();

    var fromAddress = document.querySelector("#bet #fromAddress").value;
    var privateKey = document.querySelector("#bet #privateKey").value;
    var contractAddress = document.querySelector("#bet
#contractAddress").value;
    var team = document.querySelector("#bet #team").value;

    if(team == "Home")
    {
        team = 1;
    }
    else
    {
        team = 2;
    }

    var contract =
web3.eth.contract(bettingContractABI).at(contractAddress);
    var amount = contract.amount();

    var data = contract.betOnTeam.getData(team);
```

```
    var gasRequired = contract.betOnTeam.estimateGas(team, {
        from: fromAddress,
        value: amount,
        to: contractAddress
    })

    web3.eth.getTransactionCount(fromAddress, function(error, nonce){

        var rawTx = {
          gasPrice: web3.toHex(web3.eth.gasPrice),
          gasLimit: web3.toHex(gasRequired),
          from: fromAddress,
          nonce: web3.toHex(nonce),
          data: data,
          to: contractAddress,
          value: web3.toHex(amount)
        };

        privateKey = EthJS.Util.toBuffer(privateKey, "hex");

        var tx = new EthJS.Tx(rawTx);
          tx.sign(privateKey);

          web3.eth.sendRawTransaction("0x" + tx.serialize().toString("hex"),
function(err, hash) {
                if(!err)
                {
    document.querySelector("#bet #message").innerHTML = "Transaction
      Hash: " + hash;
          }
        else
          {
          document.querySelector("#bet #message").innerHTML = err;
        }
      })
    })
    }, false)

document.getElementById("find").addEventListener("submit", function(e){
    e.preventDefault();

    var contractAddress = document.querySelector("#find
      #contractAddress").value;
    var contract =
      web3.eth.contract(bettingContractABI).at(contractAddress);

    var matchId = contract.matchId();
    var amount = contract.amount();
```

```
    var homeAddress = contract.homeBet();
    var awayAddress = contract.awayBet();

    document.querySelector("#find #message").innerHTML = "Contract balance
is: " + web3.fromWei(web3.eth.getBalance(contractAddress), "ether") + ",
Match ID is: " + matchId + ", bet amount is: " + web3.fromWei(amount,
"ether") + " ETH, " + homeAddress + " has placed bet on home team and " +
awayAddress + " has placed bet on away team";
}, false)
```

This is how the preceding code works:

1. At first, we store the contract byte code and ABI in the
   bettingContractByteCode and bettingContractABI variables, respectively.
2. Then, we are create a Web3 instance, which is connected to our testnet node.
3. Then, we have the getAJAXObject function (a cross-browser compatible
   function), which returns an AJAX object.
4. Then, we attach a submit event listener to the first form, which is used to deploy
   the contract. In the event listener's callback, we make a request to the getURL
   endpoint by passing matchId to get the encrypted query string. And then, we
   generate the data to deploy the contract. Then, we find out the gasRequired. We
   use the function object's estimateGas method to calculate the gas required, but
   you can use the web3.eth.estimateGas method too. They both differ in terms of
   arguments; that is, in the preceding case, you don't need to pass the transaction
   data. Remember that estimateGas will return the block gas limit if the function
   call throws an exception. Then, we calculate the nonce. Here, we just use the
   getTransactionCount method instead of the actual procedure we learned
   earlier. We do this just for simplification of the code. Then, we create the raw
   transaction, signing it and broadcasting it. Once the transaction is mined, we
   display the contract address.

5. Then, we attach a `submit` event listener for the second form, which is used to invest in a contract. Here, we generate the `data` part of the transaction, calculating the gas required, creating the raw transaction, signing it, and broadcasting it. While calculating the gas required for the transaction, we pass the contract address from the account address and value object properties as it's a function call, and the gas differs depending on the value, the from address, and contract address. Remember that while finding the gas required to call a contract's function, you can pass the `to`, `from`, and `value` properties because gas depends on these values.

6. Finally, we have a `submit` event listener for the third form, that is, to display information on a deployed betting contract.

Testing the client

Now that we have finished building our betting platform, it's time to test it. Before testing, make sure the testnet blockchain is completely downloaded and is looking for new incoming blocks.

Now using our wallet service we built earlier, generate three account. Add one ether to each of the accounts using `http://faucet.ropsten.be:3001/`.

Then, run `node app.js` inside the `Initial` directory and then visit `http://localhost:8080/matches,` and you will see what is shown in this screenshot:

Home

Match ID	Start Time	Home Team	Away Team	Winner
123945	2017 Feb 27 04:30:00	Lokomotiv Tashkent	Al Ahli (UAE)	home
123063	2017 Feb 27 05:00:00	Home United	Courts Young Lions	home
123061	2017 Feb 27 05:00:00	Hougang United	Geylang International	home
90293	2017 Feb 27 08:30:00	Mersin İdmanyurdu	Denizlispor	draw
126758	2017 Feb 27 08:30:00	Ashanti Gold	Asante Kotoko	away
123641	2017 Feb 27 08:40:00	Al Fateh	Lekhwiya	draw
124173	2017 Feb 27 09:00:00	Al Jazira	Esteghlal Khuzestan	away
123667	2017 Feb 27 09:00:00	Esteghlal	Al Taawoun	home
126759	2017 Feb 27 09:30:00	Lyngby	Esbjerg	draw
86683	2017 Feb 27 10:30:00	Galatasaray	Beşiktaş	away
68211	2017 Feb 27 10:30:00	Ruch Chorzów	Śląsk Wrocław	home
68346	2017 Feb 27 11:30:00	Viborg	AGF Aarhus	draw
119466	2017 Feb 27 11:30:00	Melgar	USMP	home
76297	2017 Feb 28 12:45:00	St Pauli	Karlsruher	home
96417	2017 Feb 28 01:00:00	Bari	Brescia	home
91822	2017 Feb 28 01:15:00	Fiorentina	Torino	draw
67919	2017 Feb 28 01:15:00	Stade de Reims	Brest	draw
69287	2017 Feb 28 01:30:00	Leicester City	Liverpool	home
85271	2017 Feb 28 01:30:00	Arouca	Belenenses	away
119697	2017 Feb 28 02:00:00	Deportivo Lara	Portuguesa (VEN)	home
114730	2017 Feb 28 03:30:00	Deportes Valdivia	San Marcos de Arica	draw
119692	2017 Feb 28 04:30:00	Zamora	Estudiantes de Mérida	home
120929	2017 Feb 28 05:00:00	Curicó Unido	Deportivo Ñublense	draw
119470	2017 Feb 28 05:30:00	Cantolao	Alianza Atlético	away
119076	2017 Feb 28 06:15:00	Deportes Quindío	Unión Magdalena	home

Here, you can copy any match ID. Let's assume you want to test with the first match, that is, 123945. Now visit `http://localhost:8080` and you will see what is shown in this screenshot:

Now deploy the contract by filling the input fields in the first form and clicking on the **Deploy** button, as shown here. Use your first account to deploy the contract.

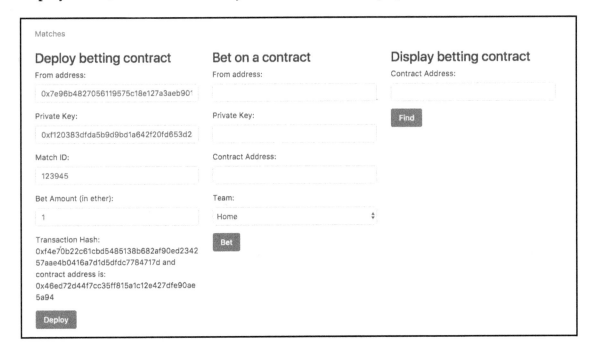

Now bet on the contract's home team from the second account and the `away team` from the third account , as shown in the following screenshot:

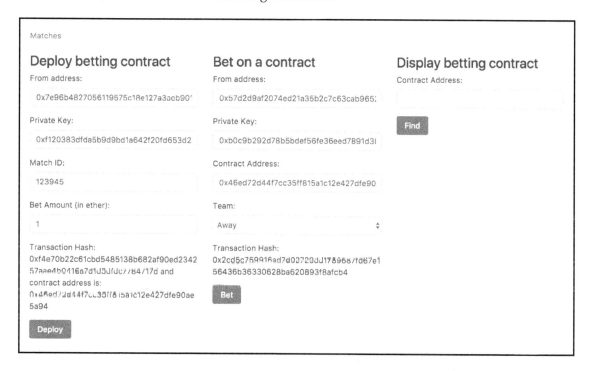

Now put the contract address on the third form and click on the **Find** button to see the details about the contract. You will see something similar to what is shown in the following screenshot:

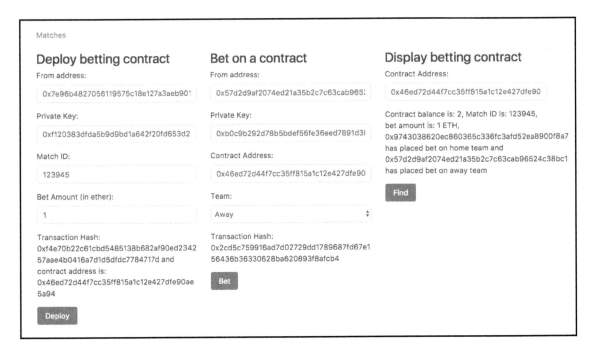

Once both the transactions are mined, check the details of the contract again, and you will see something similar to what is shown in the following screenshot:

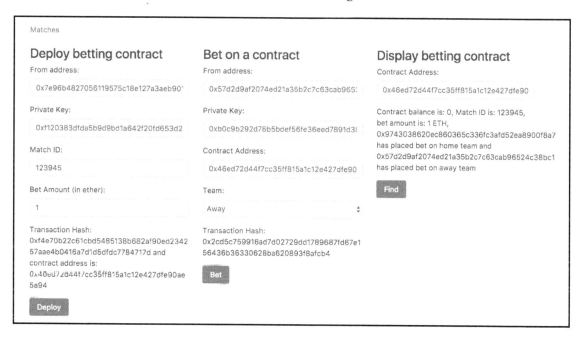

Here, you can see that the contract doesn't have any ether and all the ether was transferred to the account that put the bet on the home team.

Summary

In this chapter, we learned about Oraclize and the `strings` library in depth. We used them together to build a decentralized betting platform. Now you can go ahead and customize the contract and the client based on your requirements. To enhance the app, you can add events to the contract and display notifications on the client. The objective was to understand the basic architecture of a decentralized betting app.

13
Hyperledger

Hyperledger is not a blockchain, but it is a project that was initiated by the Linux Foundation in December 2015 to advance blockchain technology. This project is a collaborative effort by its members to build an open source distributed ledger framework that can be used to develop and implement cross-industry blockchain applications and systems. The principal focus is to develop and run platforms that support global business transactions. The project also focuses on improving the reliability and performance of blockchain systems.

Projects under Hyperledger undergo various stages of development, starting from proposal to incubation and graduating to an active state. Projects can also be deprecated or in end-of-life state where they are no longer actively developed. For a project to be able to move into the incubation stage, it must have a fully working code base along with an active community of developers.

Projects under Hyperledger

There are two categories of projects under Hyperledger. The first is **blockchain projects** and the second category is **relevant tools or modules that support these blockchains**.

Currently, there are five blockchain framework projects under the Hyperledger umbrella: **Fabric**, **Sawtooth Lake**, **Iroha**, **Burrow**, and **Indy**. Under modules, there are the **Hyperledger Cello**, **Hyperledger Composer**, **Hyperledger Explorer**, and **Hyperledger Quilt**. The Hyperledger project currently has more than 200-member organizations and is very active with many contributors, with regular meet-ups and talks organized around the globe.

A brief introduction of all these projects follows, after which we will see more details around the design, architecture, and implementation of Fabric and Sawtooth Lake.

Fabric

The fabric is a blockchain project that was proposed by **IBM** and **DAH** (**Digital Asset Holdings**). This blockchain framework implementation is intended to provide a foundation for the development of blockchain solutions with a modular architecture. It is based on a pluggable architecture where various components, such as consensus engine and membership services, can be plugged into the system as required. It also makes use of container technology which is used to run smart contracts in an isolated contained environment. Currently, its status is *active* and it's the first project to graduate from incubation to active state.

 The source code is available at `https://github.com/hyperledger/fabric`.

Sawtooth Lake

The Sawtooth Lake is a blockchain project proposed by Intel in April 2016 with some key innovations focusing on the decoupling of ledgers from transactions, flexible usage across multiple business areas using transaction families, and pluggable consensus.

Decoupling can be explained more precisely by saying that the transactions are decoupled from the consensus layer by making use of a new concept called **transaction families**. Instead of transactions being individually coupled with the ledger, transaction families are used, which allows for more flexibility, rich semantics, and open design of business logic. Transactions follow the patterns and structures defined in the transaction families.

Some of the innovative elements Intel has introduced include a novel consensus algorithm abbreviated as **PoET**, **Proof of Elapsed Time**, which makes use of **Trusted Execution Environment** (TEE) provided by **Intel Software Guard Extensions** (**Intel's SGX**) to provide a safe and random leader election process. It also supports permissioned and permission-less setups.

 This project is available at
`https://github.com/hyperledger/sawtooth-core`.

Iroha

Iroha was contributed by Soramitsu, Hitachi, NTT Data, and Colu in September 2016. Iroha is aiming to build a library of reusable components that users can choose to run on their own Hyperledger-based distributed ledgers.

Iroha's primary goal is to complement other Hyperledger projects by providing reusable components written in C++ with an emphasis on mobile development. This project has also proposed a novel consensus algorithm called **Sumeragi**, which is a chain-based Byzantine fault tolerant consensus algorithm.

 Iroha is available at https://github.com/hyperledger/iroha.

Various libraries have been proposed and are being worked on by Iroha, including but not limited to a digital signature library (ed25519), a SHA-3 hashing library, a transaction serialization library, a P2P library, an API server library, an iOS library, an Android library, and a JavaScript library.

Burrow

This project is currently in the incubation state. Hyperledger Burrow was contributed by Monax, who develop blockchain development and deployment platforms for business. Hyperledger Burrow introduces a modular blockchain platform and an **Ethereum Virtual Machine** (EVM) based smart contract execution environment. Burrow uses proof of stake, Byzantine fault tolerant Tendermint consensus mechanism. As a result, Burrow provides high throughput and transaction finality.

 The source code is available at https://github.com/hyperledger/burrow.

Indy

This project is under incubation under Hyperledger. Indy is a distributed ledger developed for building a decentralized identity. It provides tools, utility libraries, and modules which can be used to build blockchain-based digital identities. These identities can be used across multiple blockchains, domains, and applications. Indy has its own distributed ledger and uses **Redundant Byzantine Fault Tolerance (RBFT)** for consensus.

 The source code is available at
`https://github.com/hyperledger/indy-node`.

Explorer

This project aims to build a blockchain explorer for Hyperledger Fabric that can be used to view and query the transactions, blocks, and associated data from the blockchain. It also provides network information and the ability to interact with chain code.

Currently, there are few other projects that are in incubation under Hyperledger. These projects are aimed to provide tools and utilities to support blockchain networks. These projects are introduced in the following section.

 The source code is available at `https://github.com/hyperledger/`
`blockchain-explorer`.

Cello

The aim behind Cello is to allow easy deployment of blockchains. This will provide an ability to allow "as a service" deployments of blockchain service. Currently, this project is in the incubation stage.

 The source code of Cello is available at
`https://github.com/hyperledger/cello`.

Composer

This utility makes the development of blockchain solutions easier by allowing business processes to be described in a business language, while abstracting away the low-level smart contract development details.

Hyperledger composer is available at
`https://hyperledger.github.io/composer/`.

Quilt

This utility implements the Interledger protocol, which facilitates interoperability across different distributed and non-distributed ledger networks.

Quilt is available at `https://github.com/hyperledger/quilt.`

Currently, all the mentioned projects are in various stages of development.

This list is expected to grow as more and more members are joining Hyperledger project and contributing to the development of blockchain technology. Now in the next section, we will see the reference architecture of Hyperledger, which provides general principles and design philosophy which can be followed to build new Hyperledger projects.

Hyperledger as a protocol

Hyperledger is aiming to build new blockchain platforms that are driven by industry use cases. As there have been many contributions made to the Hyperledger project by the community, Hyperledger blockchain platform is evolving into a protocol for business transactions. Hyperledger is also evolving into a specification that can be used as a reference to build blockchain platforms as compared to earlier blockchain solutions that address only a specific type of industry or requirement.

In the following section, a reference architecture is presented that has been published by the Hyperledger project. As this work is under continuous and rigorous development, some changes are expected in this, but core services are expected to remain unchanged.

The reference architecture

Hyperledger has published a white paper which is available at `https://docs.google.com/document/d/1Z4M_qwILLRehPbVRUsJ3OF8Iir-gqS-ZYe7W-LE9gnE` `/edit#heading=h.m6iml6hqrnm2`.

This document presents a reference architecture that can serve as a guideline to build permissioned distributed ledgers. The reference architecture consists of various components that form a business blockchain. These high-level components are shown in the reference architecture diagram shown here:

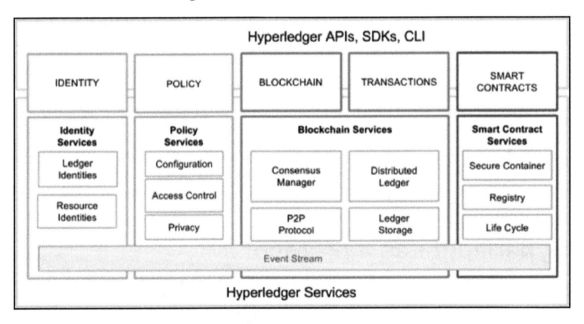

Reference architecture - source: Hyperledger whitepaper

Starting from the left we see that we have five top-level components which provide various services. We will explore all these components in detail.

First is identity, that provides authorization, identification, and authentication services under membership services.

Then is the policy component, which provides policy services.

After this, ledger and transactions come, which consists of the distributed ledger, ordering service, network protocols, and endorsement and validation services. This ledger is updateable only via consensus among the participants of the blockchain network.

Finally, we have the smart contracts layer, which provides chaincode services in Hyperledger and makes use of secure container technology to host smart contracts. We will see all these in more detail in the *Hyperledger Fabric* section shortly.

Generally, from a components point of view Hyperledger contains various elements described here:

- **Consensus layer**: These services are responsible for facilitating the agreement process between the participants on the blockchain network. The consensus is required to make sure that the order and state of transactions is validated and agreed upon in the blockchain network.
- **Smart contract layer**: These services are responsible for implementing business logic as per the requirements of the users. Transaction are processed based on the logic defined in the smart contracts that reside on the blockchain.
- **Communication layer**: This layer is responsible for message transmission and exchange between the nodes on the blockchain network.
- **Security and crypto layer**: These services are responsible for providing a capability to allow various cryptographic algorithms or modules to provide privacy, confidentiality and non-repudiations services.
- **Data stores**: This layer provides an ability to use different data stores for storing state of the ledger. This means that data stores are also pluggable and allows usage of any database backend.
- **Policy services**: This set of services provide the ability to manage different policies required for the blockchain network. This includes endorsement policy and consensus policy.
- **APIs and SDKs**: This layer allows clients and applications to interact with the blockchain. An SDK is used to provide mechanisms to deploy and execute chaincode, query blocks and monitor events on the blockchain.

There are certain requirements of a blockchain service. In the next section, we are going to discuss the design goals of Hyperledger Fabric.

Requirements and design goals of Hyperledger Fabric

There are certain requirements of a blockchain service. The reference architecture is driven by the needs and requirements raised by the participants of the Hyperledger project and after studying the industry use cases. There are several categories of requirements that have been deduced from the study of industrial use cases and are discussed in the following sections.

The modular approach

The main requirement of Hyperledger is a modular structure. It is expected that as a cross-industry fabric (blockchain), it will be used in many business scenarios. As such, functions related to storage, policy, chaincode, access control, consensus, and many other blockchain services should be modular and pluggable. The specification suggests that the modules should be plug and play and users should be able to easily remove and add a different module that meets the requirements of the business.

Privacy and confidentiality

This requirement is one of the most critical factors. As traditional blockchains are permissionless, in the permissioned model like Hyperledger Fabric, it is of utmost importance that transactions on the network are visible to only those who are allowed to view it.

Privacy and confidentiality of transactions and contracts are of absolute importance in a business blockchain. As such, Hyperledger's vision is to provide support for a full range of cryptographic protocols and algorithms. We discussed cryptography in Chapter 5, *Symmetric Cryptography* and Chapter 6, *Public Key Cryptography*.

It is expected that users will be able to choose appropriate modules according to their business requirements. For example, if a business blockchain needs to be run only between already trusted parties and performs very basic business operations, then perhaps there is no need to have advanced cryptographic support for confidentiality and privacy. Therefore, users should be able to remove that functionality (module) or replace that with a more appropriate module that suits their needs.

Similarly, if users need to run a cross-industry blockchain, then confidentiality and privacy can be of paramount importance. In this case, users should be able to plug an advanced cryptographic and access control mechanism (module) into the blockchain (fabric), which can even allow usage of **hardware of security modules** (**HSMs**).

Also, the blockchain should be able to handle sophisticated cryptographic algorithms without compromising performance. In addition to the previously mentioned scenarios, due to regulatory requirements in business, there should also be a provision to allow implementation of privacy and confidentiality policies in conformance with regulatory and compliance requirements.

Scalability

This is another major requirement which once met will allow reasonable transaction throughput, which will be sufficient for all business requirements and also a large number of users.

Deterministic transactions

This is a core requirement in any blockchain because if transactions do not produce the same result every time they are executed regardless of who and where the transaction is executed, then achieving consensus is impossible. Therefore, deterministic transactions become a key requirement in any blockchain network. We discussed these concepts in Chapter 4, *Smart Contracts*.

Identity

In order to provide privacy and confidentiality services, a flexible PKI model that can be used to handle the access control functionality is also required. The strength and type of cryptographic mechanisms is also expected to vary according to the needs and requirements of the users. In certain scenarios, it might be required for a user to hide their identity, and as such, the Hyperledger is expected to provide this functionality.

Auditability

Auditability is another requirement of Hyperledger Fabric. It is expected that an immutable audit trail of all identities, related operations, and any changes is kept.

Interoperability

Currently, there are many blockchain platforms available, but they cannot communicate with each other and this can be a limiting factor in the growth of a blockchain-based global business ecosystem. It is envisaged that many blockchain networks will operate in the business world for specific needs, but it is important that they are able to communicate with each other. There should be a common set of standards that all blockchains can follow in order to allow communication between different ledgers. It is expected that a protocol will be developed that will allow the exchange of information between many fabrics.

Portability

The portability requirement is concerned with the ability to run across multiple platforms and environments without the need to change anything at code level. Hyperledger Fabric is envisaged to be portable, not only at infrastructure level but also at code, libraries, and API levels, so that it can support uniform development across various implementations of Hyperledger.

Rich data queries

The blockchain network should allow rich queries to be run on the network. This can be used to query the current state of the ledger using traditional query languages, which will allow for wider adoption and ease of use.

All aforementioned points describe the requirements, which need to be met to develop blockchain solutions that are in line with the Hyperledger design philosophy. In the next section, we will have a look at Hyperledger Fabric, which is the first project to graduate to active status under Hyperledger.

Fabric

To understand various projects that are under development in the Hyperledger project, it is essential to understand the foundations of Hyperledger first. A few terminologies that are specific to Hyperledger need some clarification before readers are introduced to the more in-depth material.

First, there is the concept of fabric. Fabric can be defined as a collection of components providing a foundation layer that can be used to deliver a blockchain network. There are various types and capabilities of a fabric network, but all fabrics share common attributes such as immutability and are consensus-driven. Some fabrics can provide a modular approach towards building blockchain networks. In this case, the blockchain network can have multiple pluggable modules to perform a various function on the network.

For example, consensus algorithms can be a pluggable module in a blockchain network where, depending on the requirements of the network, an appropriate consensus algorithm can be chosen and plugged into the network. The modules can be based on some particular specification of the fabric and can include APIs, access control, and various other components.

Fabrics can also be designed either to be private or public and can allow the creation of multiple business networks. As an example, Bitcoin is an application that runs on top of its fabric (blockchain network). As discussed earlier in Chapter 1, *Blockchain 101*, blockchain can either be permissioned or permission-less. However, the aim of Hyperledger Fabric is to develop a permissioned distributed ledger.

Fabric is also the name given to the code contribution made by IBM to the Hyperledger foundation and is formally called Hyperledger Fabric. IBM also offers blockchain as a service (IBM Blockchain) via its *IBM Cloud service*.

 It is available at https://www.ibm.com/cloud/.

Now let's have a detailed look at Hyperledger Fabric.

Hyperledger Fabric

The fabric is the contribution made initially by IBM and Digital Assets to the Hyperledger project. This contribution aims to enable a modular, open, and flexible approach towards building blockchain networks.

Various functions in the fabric are pluggable, and it also allows the use of any language to develop smart contracts. This functionality is possible because it is based on container technology (Docker), which can host any language.

Chaincode is sandboxed in a secure container, which includes a secure operating system, chaincode language, runtime environment, and SDKs for Go, Java, and Node.js. Other languages can be supported too in future, if required, but needs some development work. Smart contracts are called chaincode in the fabric. This ability is a compelling feature compared to domain-specific languages in Ethereum, or the limited scripted language in Bitcoin. It is a permissioned network that aims to address issues such as scalability, privacy, and confidentiality. The fundamental idea behind this is modularization, which would allow for flexibility in design and implementation of the business blockchain. This can then result in achieving scalability, privacy, and other desired attributes and fine tune them according to the requirements.

Transactions in the fabric are private, confidential, and anonymous for general users, but they can still be traced and linked to the users by authorized auditors. As a permissioned network, all participants are required to be registered with the membership services to access the blockchain network. This ledger also provided auditability functionality to meet the regulatory and compliance needs required by the user.

Membership services

These services are used to provide access control capability for the users of the fabric network. The following list shows the functions that membership services perform:

- User identity verification
- User registration
- Assign appropriate permissions to the users depending on their roles

Membership services make use of **a certificate authority** in order to support identity management and authorization operations. This CA can be internal (Fabric CA), which is a default interface in Hyperledger Fabric or organization can opt to use an external certificate authority. Fabric CA issues **enrollment certificates** (**E-Certs**), which are produced by **enrollment certificate authority** (**E-CA**). Once peers are issued with an identity, they are allowed to join the blockchain network. There are also temporary certificates issued called T-Certs, which are used for one-time transactions.

All peers and applications are identified using certificate authority. Authentication service is provided by the certificate authority. MSPs can also interface with existing identity services like LDAP.

Blockchain services

Blockchain services are at the core of the Hyperledger Fabric. Components within this category are as follows.

Consensus services

A consensus service is responsible for providing the interface to the consensus mechanism. This serves as a module that is pluggable and receives the transaction from other Hyperledger entities and executes them under criteria according to the type of mechanism chosen.

Consensus in Hyperledger V1 is implemented as a peer called **orderer**, which is responsible for ordering the transactions in sequence into a block. Orderer does not hold smart contracts or ledgers. Consensus is pluggable and currently, there are two types of ordering services available in Hyperledger Fabric:

- **SOLO**: This is a basic ordering service intended to be used for development and testing purposes.
- **Kafka**: This is an implementation of Apache Kafka, which provides ordering service. It should be noted that currently Kafka only provides crash fault tolerance but does not provide byzantine fault tolerance. This is acceptable in a permissioned network where chances of malicious actors are almost none.

In addition to these mechanisms, the **Simple Byzantine Fault Tolerance** (**SBFT**) based mechanism is also under development, which will become available in the later releases of Hyperledger Fabric.

Distributed ledger

Blockchain and world state are two main elements of the distributed ledger. Blockchain is simply a cryptographically linked list of blocks (as introduced in Chapter 1, *Blockchain 101*) and world state is a key-value database. This database is used by smart contracts to store relevant states during execution by the transactions. The blockchain consists of blocks that contain transactions. These transactions contain chaincode, which runs transactions that can result in updating the world state. Each node saves the world state on disk in LevelDB or CouchDB depending on the implementation. As Fabric allows pluggable data store, you can choose any data store for storage.

A block consists of three main components called Block header, Transactions (Data) and block metadata.

The following diagram shows a typical block in the Hyperledger Fabric 1.0 with the relevant fields:

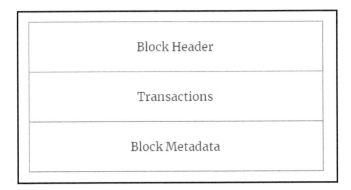

Block structure

Block Header consists of three fields, namely Number, Previous hash, and Data hash.

Transaction is made up of multiple fields such as transaction type, version, timestamp, channel ID, transaction ID, epoch, payload visibility, chaincode path, chaincode name, chaincode version, creator identity, signature, chaincode type, input, timeout, endorser identities and signatures, proposal hash, chaincode events, response status, namespace, read set, write set, start key, end key, list of read, and Merkle tree query summary.

Block Metadata consists of creator identity, relevant signatures, last configuration block number, flag for each transaction included in the block, and last offset persisted (kafka).

The peer to peer protocol

The P2P protocol in the Hyperledger Fabric is built using **google RPC (gRPC)**. It uses protocol buffers to define the structure of the messages.

Messages are passed between nodes in order to perform various functions. There are four main types of messages in Hyperledger Fabric: **discovery**, **transaction**, **synchronization**, and **consensus**. Discovery messages are exchanged between nodes when starting up in order to discover other peers on the network. Transaction messages are used to deploy, invoke, and query transactions, and consensus messages are exchanged during consensus. Synchronization messages are passed between nodes to synchronize and keep the blockchain updated on all nodes.

Ledger storage

In order to save the state of the ledger, by default, LevelDB is used which is available at each peer. An alternative is to use CouchDB which provides the ability to run rich queries.

Chaincode services

These services allow the creation of secure containers that are used to execute the chaincode. Components in this category are as follows:

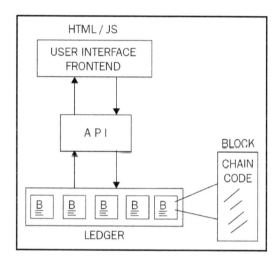

- **Secure container**: Chaincode is deployed in Docker containers that provide a locked down sandboxed environment for smart contract execution. Currently, Golang is supported as the main smart contract language, but any other mainstream languages can be added and enabled if required.
- **Secure registry:** This provides a record of all images containing smart contracts.

Events

Events on the blockchain can be triggered by endorsers and smart contracts. External applications can listen to these events and react to them if required via event adapters.

APIs and CLIs

An application programming interface provides an interface into the fabric by exposing various REST APIs. Additionally, command-line interfaces that provide a subset of REST APIs and allow for quick testing and limited interaction with the blockchain are also available.

Components of the fabric

There are various components that can be part of the Hyperledger Fabric blockchain. These components include but are not limited to the ledger, chaincode, consensus mechanism, access control, events, system monitoring and management, wallets, and system integration components.

Peers

Peers participate in maintaining the state of the distributed ledger. They also hold a local copy of the distributed ledger. Peers communicate via gossip protocol. There are three types of peers in the Hyperledger Fabric network:

- **Endorsing peers** or endorsers which simulate the transaction execution and generate a read-write set. Read is a simulation of transaction's reading of data from the ledger and write is the set of updates that would be made to the ledger if and when the transaction is executed and committed to the ledger. Endorses execute and endorse transactions. It should be noted that an endorser is also a committer too. Endorsement policies are implemented with chaincode and specify the rules for transaction endorsement.
- **Committing peers** or committers which receives transaction endorsed by endorsers, verify them and then update the ledger with the read-write set. A committer verifies the read-write set generated by the endorsers along with transaction validation.
- **Submitters** is the third type of peers which has not been implemented yet. It is on the development roadmap and will be implemented

Orderer nodes

Ordering nodes receive transactions from endorsers along with read-write sets, arrange them in a sequence, and send those to committing peers. Committing peers then perform validation and committing to the ledger.

All peers make use of certificates issued by membership services.

Clients

Clients are software that makes use of APIs to interact with the Hyperledger Fabric and propose transactions.

Channels

Channels allow the flow of confidential transactions between different parties on the network. They allow using the same blockchain network but with separate blockchains. Channels allow only members of the channel to view the transaction related to them, all other members of the network will not be able to view the transactions.

World state database

World state reflects all committed transaction on the blockchain. This is basically a key-value store which is updated as a result of transactions and chaincode execution. For this purpose, either LevelDB or CouchDB is used. LevelDB is a key-value store whereas CouchDB stores data as JSON objects which allows rich queries to run against the database.

Transactions

Transaction messages can be divided into two types: **deployment transactions** and **invocation transactions**. The former is used to deploy new chaincode to the ledger, and the latter is used to call functions from the smart contract. Transactions can be either public or confidential. Public transactions are open and available to all participants whilst confidential transactions are visible only in a channel open to its participants.

Membership Service Provider (MSP)

MSP is a modular component that is used to manage identities on the blockchain network. This provider is used to authenticate clients who want to join the blockchain network. We have discussed certificate authority is some detail earlier in this chapter. CA is used in MSP to provide identity verification and binding service.

Smart contracts

We discussed smart contracts in good detail in Chapter 4, *Smart Contracts*. In Hyperledger Fabric same concept of smart contracts is implemented but they are called chain code instead of smart contracts. They contain conditions and parameters to execute transactions and update the ledger. Chaincode is usually written in Golang and Java.

Crypto service provider

As the name suggests this is a service that provides cryptographic algorithms and standards for usage in the blockchain network. This service provides key management, signature and verification operations, and encryption-decryption mechanisms. This service is used with the membership service to provide support for cryptographic operations for elements of blockchain such as endorsers, clients, and other nodes and peers.

After this introduction to this component of Hyperledger Fabric, in the next section, we will see what an application looks like when on a Hyperledger network.

Applications on blockchain

A typical application on Fabric is simply composed of a user interface, usually written in JavaScript/HTML, that interacts with the backend chaincode (smart contract) stored on the ledger via an API layer:

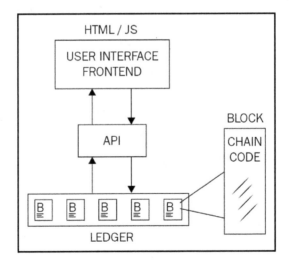

A typical Fabric application

Hyperledger provides various APIs and command-line interfaces to enable interaction with the ledger. These APIs include interfaces for identity, transactions, chaincode, ledger, network, storage, and events.

Chaincode implementation

Chaincode is usually written in Golang or Java. Chaincode can be public (visible to all on the network), confidential, or access controlled. These code files serve as a smart contract that users can interact with via APIs. Users can call functions in the chaincode that result in a state change, and consequently updates the ledger.

There are also functions that are only used to query the ledger and do not result in any state change. Chaincode implementation is performed by first creating the chaincode shim interface in the code. Shim provides APIs for accessing state variables and transaction context of chain code. It can either be in Java or Golang code.

The following four functions are required in order to implement the chaincode:

- `Init()`: This function is invoked when chaincode is deployed onto the ledger. This initializes the chaincode and results in making a state change, which accordingly updates the ledger.
- `Invoke()`: This function is used when contracts are executed. It takes a function name as parameters along with an array of arguments. This function results in a state change and writes to the ledger.
- `Query()`: This function is used to query the current state of a deployed chaincode. This function does not make any changes to the ledger.
- `4()`: This function is executed when a peer deploys its own copy of the chaincode. The chaincode is registered with the peer using this function.

The following diagram illustrates the general overview of Hyperledger Fabric, note that peers cluster at the top includes all types of nodes such as endorsers, committers, Orderers, and so on.

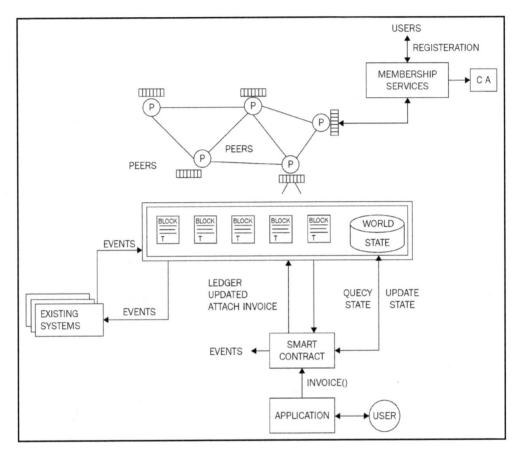

A high-level overview of Hyperledger Fabric

The preceding diagram shows that peers shown at the top middle communicate with each and each node has a copy of blockchain. On the top-right corner, the membership services are shown which validate and authenticate peers on the network by using a **certificate authority (CA)**. At the bottom of the image, a magnified view of blockchain is shown where by existing systems can produce events for the blockchain and also can listen for the blockchain events, which then can optionally trigger an action. At the bottom right-hand side, a user's interaction is shown with the application which talks to the smart contract via the `invoice()` method, and smart contracts can query or update the state of the blockchain.

The application model

Any blockchain application for Hyperledger Fabric follows the MVC-B architecture. This is based on the popular MVC design pattern. Components in this model are Model, View, Control, and Blockchain:

- **View logic**: This is concerned with the user interface. It can be a desktop, web application, or mobile frontend.
- **Control logic**: This is the orchestrator between the user interface, data model, and APIs.
- **Data model**: This model is used to manage the off-chain data.
- **Blockchain logic**: This is used to manage the blockchain via the controller and the data model via transactions.

 The IBM cloud service offers sample applications for blockchain under its blockchain as a service offering. It is available at
`https://www.ibm.com/blockchain/platform/.` This service allows users to create their own blockchain networks in an easy-to-use environment.

Consensus in Hyperledger Fabric

The consensus mechanism in Hyperledger Fabric consists of three steps:

1. **Transaction endorsement**: This process endorses the transactions by simulating the transaction execution process.
2. **Ordering**: This is a service provided by the cluster of orderers which takes endorsed transactions and decide on a sequence in which the transactions will be written to the ledger.
3. **Validation and commitment**: This process is executed by committing peers which first validates the transactions received from the orderers and then commit that transaction to the ledger.

These steps are shown in the following flowchart:

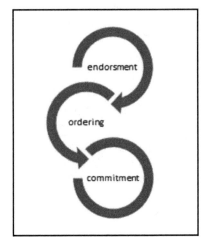

The consensus flow

The transaction life cycle in Hyperledger Fabric

There are several steps that are involved in a transaction flow in Hyperledger Fabric. These steps are shown in the following diagram below

A quick summary of the process can be visualized in the following diagram:

The transaction life cycle

The steps are described below in detail:

1. Transaction proposal by clients. This is the first step where a transaction is proposed by the clients and sent to endorsing peers on the distributed ledger network. All clients need to be enrolled via membership services before they can propose transactions.
2. The transaction is simulated by endorsers which generates a read-write (RW) set. This is achieved by executing the chaincode but instead of updating the ledger, only a read-write set depicting any reads or updates to the ledger is created.
3. The endorsed transaction is sent back to the application.
4. Submission of endorsed transactions and read-write (RW) sets to the ordering service by the application.
5. The ordering service assembles all endorsed transactions and read-write sets in order into a block, and sorts them by channel ID.
6. Ordering service broadcasts the assembled block to all committing peers.
7. Committing peers validate the transactions.
8. Committing peers update the ledger.
9. Finally, notification of success or failure of the transaction by committing peers is sent back to the clients/applications.

The following diagram represents the above-mentioned steps and Fabric architecture from transaction flow point of view:

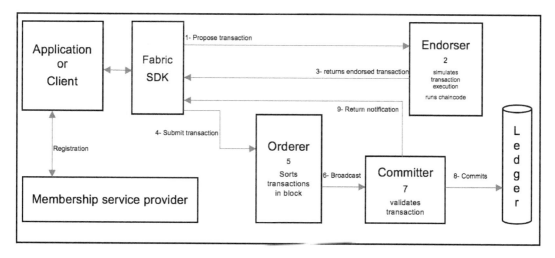

The transaction flow architecture

As seen in the preceding diagram, the first step is to propose transactions which a client does via an SDK. Before this, it is assumed that all clients and peers are registered with the Membership service provider.

With this topic, our introduction to Hyperledger Fabric is complete. In the next section, we will see another Hyperledger project named Sawtooth Lake.

Sawtooth Lake

Sawtooth Lake can run in both permissioned and non-permissioned modes. It is a distributed ledger that proposes two novel concepts: the first is the introduction of a new consensus algorithm called **Proof of Elapsed Time (PoET)**; and the second is the idea of **transaction families**.

A description of these novel proposals is given in the following sections.

PoET

PoET is a novel consensus algorithm that allows a node to be selected randomly based on the time that the node has waited before proposing a block. This concept is in contrast to other leader election and lottery-based proof of work algorithms, such as the PoW used in Bitcoin where an enormous amount of electricity and computer resources are used in order be elected as a block proposer; for example in the case of Bitcoin. PoET is a type of Proof of Work algorithm but, instead of spending computer resources, it uses a trusted computing model to provide a mechanism to fulfill the Proof of Work requirements. PoET makes use of Intel's SGX architecture (Software Guard Extensions) to provide a trusted execution environment (TEE) to ensure randomness and cryptographic security of the process.

It should be noted that the current implementation of Sawtooth Lake does not require real hardware SGX-based TEE, as it is simulated for experimental purposes only and as such should not be used in production environments. The fundamental idea in PoET is to provide a mechanism of leader election by waiting randomly to be elected as a leader for proposing new transactions.

PoET, however, has a limitation which has been highlighted by Ittay Eyal. This limitation is called the *stale chips* problem.

 The research paper is available at `https://eprint.iacr.org/2017/179.pdf`.

This limitation results in hardware wastage, which can result in the waste of resources. There is also a possibility of hacking the chip's hardware, which could result in system compromise and undue incentivizing to miners.

Transaction families

A traditional smart contract paradigm provides a solution that is based on a general-purpose instruction set for all domains. For example, in the case of Ethereum, a set of opcodes has been developed for the EVM that can be used to build smart contracts to address any type of requirements for any industry.

While this model has its merits, it is becoming clear that this approach is not very secure as it provides a single interface into the ledger with a powerful and expressive language, which potentially offers a larger attack surface for malicious code. This complexity and generic virtual machine paradigm have resulted in several vulnerabilities that were found and exploited recently by hackers. A recent example is the **DAO hack** and further **Denial of Services** (**DoS**) attacks that exploited limitations in some EVM opcodes. The DAO hack was discussed in Chapter 4, *Smart Contracts*.

A model shown in the following figure describes the traditional smart contract model, where a generic virtual machine has been used to provide the interface into the blockchain for all domains:

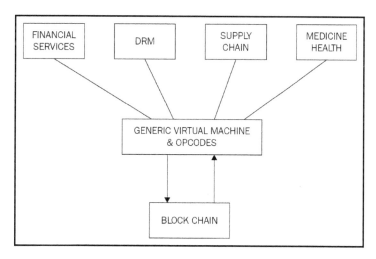

The traditional smart contract paradigm

In order to address this issue, Sawtooth Lake has proposed the idea of transaction families. A transaction family is created by decomposing the logic layer into a set of rules and a composition layer for a specific domain. The key idea is that business logic is composed within transaction families, which provides a more secure and powerful way to build smart contracts. Transaction families contain the domain-specific rules and another layer that allows for creating transactions for that domain. Another way of looking at it is that transaction families are a combination of a data model and a transaction language that implements a logic layer for a specific domain. The data model represents the current state of the blockchain (ledger) whereas the transaction language modifies the state of the ledger. It is expected that users will build their own transaction families according to their business requirements.

The following diagram represents this model, where each specific domain, like financial services, **digital rights management** (**DRM**), supply chain, and the health industry, has its own logic layer comprised of operations and services specific to that domain. This makes the logic layer both restrictive and powerful at the same time. Transaction families ensure that operations related to only the required domain are present in the control logic, thus removing the possibility of executing needless, arbitrary and potentially harmful operations:

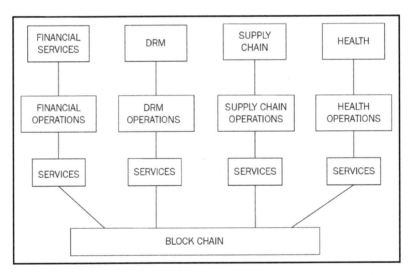

The Sawtooth (transaction families) smart contract paradigm

Intel has provided three transaction families with Sawtooth: Endpoint registry, Integerkey, and MarketPlace.

- **Endpoint registry** is used for registering ledger services
- **Integerkey** is used for testing deployed ledgers
- **MarketPlace** is used for selling, buying, and trading operations and services

Sawtooth_bond has been developed as a proof of concept to demonstrate a bond trading platform.

 It is available at `https://github.com/hyperledger/sawtooth-core/tree/master/extensions/bond`.

Consensus in Sawtooth

Sawtooth has two types of consensus mechanisms based on the choice of network. PoET, as discussed previously, is a trusted executed environment-based lottery function that elects a leader randomly based on the time a node has waited for block proposal.

There is another consensus type called **quorum voting**, which is an adaptation of consensus protocols built by Ripple and Stellar. This consensus algorithm allows instant transaction finality, which is usually desirable in permissioned networks.

The development environment – Sawtooth Lake

In this section, a quick introduction is given on how to set up a development environment for Sawtooth Lake. There are a few prerequisites that are required in order to set up the development environment.

Examples in this section assume a running Ubuntu system and the following:

- Vagrant, at least version 1.9.0, available at
  `https://www.vagrantup.com/downloads.html`.
- VirtualBox, at least 5.0.10 r104061, available at
  `https://www.virtualbox.org/wiki/Downloads`.

Once both of the prerequisites are downloaded and installed successfully, the next step is to clone the repository.

```
$ git clone https://github.com/IntelLedger/sawtooth-core.git
```

This will produce an output similar to the one shown in the following screenshot:

```
drequinox@drequinox-OP7010:~/project$ git clone https://github.com/IntelLedger/sawtooth-core.git
Cloning into 'sawtooth-core'...
remote: Counting objects: 12527, done.
remote: Compressing objects: 100% (964/964), done.
remote: Total 12527 (delta 452), reused 0 (delta 0), pack-reused 11515
Receiving objects: 100% (12527/12527), 9.26 MiB | 1.76 MiB/s, done.
Resolving deltas: 100% (8131/8131), done.
Checking connectivity... done.
```

The GitHub Sawtooth clone

Once Sawtooth is cloned correctly, the next step is to start up the environment. First, run the following command to change the directory to the correct location and then start the vagrant box:

```
$ cd sawtooth-core/tools
$ vagrant up
```

This will produce an output similar to the following screenshot:

```
drequinox@drequinox-OP7010:~/project/sawtooth-core/tools$ vagrant up
Could not determine vagrant user.
VAGRANT_BOX = ubuntu/xenial64
VAGRANT_FORWARD_PORTS = true
VAGRANT_MEMORY = 2048
VAGRANT_CPUS = 2
Proxyconf plugin not found
Install: vagrant plugin install vagrant-proxyconf
Bringing machine 'default' up with 'virtualbox' provider...
==> default: Box 'ubuntu/xenial64' could not be found. Attempting to find and install...
    default: Box Provider: virtualbox
    default: Box Version: >= 0
==> default: Loading metadata for box 'ubuntu/xenial64'
    default: URL: https://atlas.hashicorp.com/ubuntu/xenial64
==> default: Adding box 'ubuntu/xenial64' (v20161221.0.0) for provider: virtualbox
    default: Downloading: https://atlas.hashicorp.com/ubuntu/boxes/xenial64/versions/20161221.0.0/providers/virtualbox.bo
x
    default: Progress: 1% (Rate: 1709k/s, Estimated time remaining: 0:04:04)
```

The vagrant up command

If at any point vagrant needs to be stopped, the following command can be used:

```
$ vagrant halt
```

Or:

```
$ vagrant destroy
```

`halt` will stop the vagrant machine, whereas `destroy` will stop and delete vagrant machines.

Finally, the transaction validator can be started by using the following commands. First `ssh` into the vagrant Sawtooth box:

```
$ vagrant ssh
```

When the vagrant prompt is available, run the following commands. First build the Sawtooth Lake core using following command:

```
$ /project/sawtooth-core/bin/build_all
```

When the build has completed successfully, in order to run the transaction validator, issue the following commands:

```
$ /project/sawtooth-core/docs/source/tutorial/genesis.sh
```

This will create the genesis block and clear any existing data files and keys. This command should show an output similar to the following screenshot:

```
ubuntu@ubuntu-xenial:/project/sawtooth-core$ /project/sawtooth-core/docs/source/tutorial/genesis.sh
writing file: /home/ubuntu/sawtooth/keys/base000.wif
writing file: /home/ubuntu/sawtooth/keys/base000.addr
```

Genesis block and keys generation

The next step is to run the transaction validator, and change the directory as shown follows:

```
$ cd /project/saw-toothcore
```

Run the transaction validator:

```
$ ./bin/txnvalidator -v -F ledger.transaction.integer_key --config
/home/ubuntu/sawtooth/v0.json
```

```
ubuntu@ubuntu-xenial:/project/sawtooth-core$ ./bin/txnvalidator -v -F ledger.transaction.integer_key --config /home/ubuntu/sawto
oth/v0.json
[22:08:22 INFO    validator_cli] validator started with arguments: ['./bin/txnvalidator', '-v', '-F', 'ledger.transaction.intege
r_key', '--config', '/home/ubuntu/sawtooth/v0.json']
[22:08:22 INFO    validator_cli] read signing key from /home/ubuntu/sawtooth/keys/base000.wif
[22:08:24 WARNING validator_cli] validator pid is 10937
[22:08:24 INFO    gossip_core] listening on IPv4Address(UDP, '0.0.0.0', 33713)
[22:08:24 INFO    global_store_manager] create blockstore from file /home/ubuntu/sawtooth/data/base000_state.dbm with flag c
[22:08:24 INFO    validator] set administration node to None
[22:08:24 INFO    validator] starting ledger base000 with id 1K5RNedZ at network address ('127.0.0.1', 33713)
[22:08:24 INFO    web_api] listen for HTTP requests on {ip='localhost', port=8800)
[22:08:24 INFO    validator_cli] adding transaction family: ledger.transaction.integer_key
[22:08:24 INFO    journal_core] restore ledger state from persistence
[22:08:24 INFO    global_store_manager] add block 60af3ec894fa1cb0 to the queue for loading
[22:08:24 INFO    global_store_manager] load block 60af3ec894fa1cb0 from storage
[22:08:24 INFO    journal_core] commit head: 60af3ec894fa1cb0
[22:08:26 INFO    validator] ledger connections using RandomWalk topology
[22:08:26 INFO    random_walk] initiate random walk topology update
[22:08:29 INFO    validator] ledger initialization complete
[22:08:29 INFO    journal_core] process initial transactions and blocks
[22:08:29 INFO    validator] register endpoint 1K5RNedZ with name base000
[22:08:29 INFO    journal_core] build transaction block to extend 60af3ec8 with 1 transactions
[22:08:29 INFO    wait_timer] wait timer created; TIMER, 5.00, 33.69, HE2DQNJWGI2DCNJQ
```

Running transaction validator

The validator node can be stopped by pressing *Ctrl + C*. Once the validator is up and running, various clients can be started up in another terminal window to communicate with the transaction validator and submit transactions.

For example, in the following screenshot, the market client is started up to communicate with the transaction validator. Note that keys under /keys/mkt.wif are created by using the following command:

```
./bin/sawtooth keygen --key-dir validator/keys mkt
```

```
ubuntu@ubuntu-xenial:/project/sawtooth-core$ ./bin/mktclient --name market --keyfile validator/keys/mkt.wif
//UNKNOWN> help

Documented commands (type help <topic>):
========================================
EOF         dump          exit      liability    selloffer    tokenstore
account     echo          help      map          session      waitforcommit
asset       exchange      holding   offers       sleep
assettype   exchangeoffer holdings  participant  state

Miscellaneous help topics:
==========================
symbols  names

//UNKNOWN> participant reg --name market --description "the market"
transaction ff652e63dadeaf32 submitted
//market>
```

mktclient for marketplace transaction family

This completes our basic introduction to Sawtooth. The example shown above is also quite basic but demonstrates that how Sawtooth Lake works.

Sawtooth Lake is also under continuous development and therefore, it is recommended that readers keep an eye on documentation available at `http://intelledger.github.io/` to keep up with the latest developments.

 There is an excellent online page where official Sawtooth lake examples are provided. The page is available at `https://sawtooth.hyperledger.org/examples/`. Readers are encouraged to visit this page and explore these sample projects.

Now in the next section we will see an introduction to Corda. It should be noted that Corda is not yet an official project under Hyperledger; however, it may become a member very soon. Therefore, for now, this is being discussed under Hyperledger, but in the future, it may not become part of Hyperledger.

Corda

Corda is not a blockchain by definition because it does not contain blocks of bundled transactions, but it falls under the category of distributed ledgers. It provides all benefits that a blockchain can. Traditional blockchain solutions, as discussed before, have the concept of transactions that are bundled together in a block and each block is linked back cryptographically to its parent block, which provides an immutable record of transactions. This is not the case with Corda.

Corda has been designed entirely from scratch with a new model for providing all blockchain benefits, but without a traditional blockchain. It has been developed purely for the financial industry to solve issues arising from the fact that each organization manages their own ledgers and thus have their own view of *truth*, which leads to contradictions and operational risk. Moreover, data is also duplicated at each organization, which results in an increased cost of managing individual infrastructures and complexity. These are the types of problems within the financial industry that Corda aims to resolve by building a decentralized database platform.

 The Corda source code is available at `https://github.com/corda/corda`. It is written in a language called Kotlin, which is a statically typed language targeting the **Java Virtual Machine (JVM)**.

Architecture

The main components of the Corda platform include state objects, contract code, legal prose, transactions, consensus, and flows. We will now explore them in more detail.

State objects

State objects represent the smallest unit of data that represent a financial agreement. They are created or deleted as a result of a transaction execution. They refer to **contract code** and **legal prose.** Legal prose is optional and provides legal binding to the contract. However, contract code is mandatory in order to manage the state of the object. It is required in order to provide a state transition mechanism for the node according to the business logic defined in the contract code. State objects contain a data structure that represents the current state of the object. A state object can be either current (live) or historic (no longer valid).

For example, in the following diagram, a state object represents the current state of the object. In this case, it is a simple mock agreement between **Party A** and **Party B** where **Party ABC** has paid **Party XYZ 1,000 GBP**. This represents the current state of the object; however, the referred contract code can change the state via transactions. State objects can be thought of as a state machine, which are consumed by transactions in order to create updated state objects.

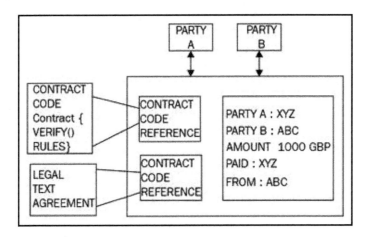

An example state object

Transactions

Transactions are used to perform transitions between different states. For example, the state object shown in the preceding diagram is created as a result of a transaction. Corda uses a Bitcoin-style UTXO-based model for its transaction processing. The concept of state transition by transactions is same as in Bitcoin. Similar to Bitcoin, transactions can have none, single, or multiple inputs, and single or multiple outputs. All transactions are digitally signed.

Moreover, Corda has no concept of mining because it does not use blocks to arrange transactions in a blockchain. Instead, notary services are used in order to provide temporal ordering of transactions. In Corda, new transaction types can be developed using JVM bytecode, which makes it very flexible and powerful.

Consensus

The consensus model in Corda is quite simple and is based on notary services that are discussed in a later section of this chapter. The general idea is that the transactions are evaluated for their uniqueness by the notary service and, if they are unique (that is, unique transaction inputs), they are signed by consensus services as valid. There can be single or multiple clustered notary services running on a Corda network. Various consensus algorithms like PBFT or Raft can be used by notaries to reach consensus.

There are two main concepts regarding consensus in Corda: **consensus over state validity** and **consensus over state uniqueness**. The first concept is concerned with the validation of the transaction, ensuring that all required signatures are available and states are appropriate. The second concept is a means to detect double-spend attacks and ensures that a transaction has not already been spent and is unique.

Flows

Flows in Corda are a novel idea that allows the development of decentralized workflows. All communication on the Corda network is handled by these flows. These are transaction-building protocols that can be used to define any financial flow of any complexity using code. Flows run as an asynchronous state machine and they interact with other nodes and users. During the execution, they can be suspended or resumed as required.

Components

The Corda network has multiple components. All these components are described in the upcoming sections.

Nodes

Nodes in a Corda network operated under a trust-less model and run by different organizations. Nodes run as part of an authenticated peer-to-peer network. Nodes communicate directly with each other using the **Advanced Message Queuing Protocol (AMQP)**, which is an approved international standard (ISO/IEC 19464) and ensures that messages across different nodes are transferred safely and securely. AMQP works over **Transport Layer Security** (**TLS**) in Corda, thus ensuring privacy and integrity of data communicated between nodes.

Nodes also make use of a local relational database for storage. Messages on the network are encoded in a compact binary format. They are delivered and managed by using the **Apache Artemis message broker** (**Active MQ**). A node can serve as a network map service, notary, Oracle, or a regular node. The following diagram shows a high-level view of two nodes communicating with each other:

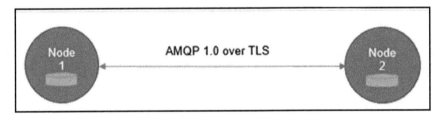

Two nodes communicating in a Corda network

In the preceding diagram, **Node 1** is communicating with **Node 2** over a TLS communication channel using the AMQP protocol, and the nodes have a local relational database for storage.

The permissioning service

A permissioning service is used to provision TLS certificates for security. In order to participate in the network, participants are required to have a signed identity issued by a root certificate authority. Identities are required to be unique on the network and the permissioning service is used to sign these identities. The naming convention used to recognize participants is based on the X.500 standard. This ensures the uniqueness of the name.

Network map service

This service is used to provide a network map in the form of a document of all nodes on the network. This service publishes IP addresses, identity certificates, and a list of services offered by nodes. All nodes announce their presence by registering to this service when they first startup, and when a connection request is received by a node, the presence of the requesting node is checked on the network map first. Put another way, this service resolves the identities of the participants to physical nodes.

Notary service

In a traditional blockchain, mining is used to ascertain the order of blocks that contain transactions. In Corda, notary services are used to provide transaction ordering and timestamping services. There can be multiple notaries in a network and they are identified by composite public keys. Notaries can use different consensus algorithms like BFT or Raft depending on the requirements of the applications. Notary services sign the transactions to indicate validity and finality of the transaction which is then persisted to the database.

Notaries can be run in a load-balanced configuration in order to spread the load across the nodes for performance reasons; and, in order to reduce latency, the nodes are recommended to be run physically closer to the transaction participants.

Oracle service

Oracle services either sign a transaction containing a fact, if it is true, or can themselves provide factual data. They allow real-world feed into the distributed ledgers. Oracles were discussed in `Chapter 4`, *Smart Contracts*.

Transactions

Transactions in a Corda network are never transmitted globally but in a semi-private network. They are shared only between a subset of participants who are related to the transaction. This is in contrast to traditional blockchain solutions like Ethereum and Bitcoin, where all transactions are broadcasted to the entire network globally. Transactions are digitally signed and either consume state(s) or create new state(s).

Transactions on a Corda network are composed of the following elements:

- **Input references**: This is a reference to the states the transaction is going to consume and use as an input.
- **Output states**: These are new states created by the transaction.
- **Attachments**: This is a list of hashes of attached ZIP files. ZIP files can contain code and other relevant documentation related to the transaction. Files themselves are not made part of the transaction, instead, they are transferred and stored separately.
- **Commands**: A command represents the information about the intended operation of the transaction as a parameter to the contract. Each command has a list of public keys, which represents all parties that are required to sign a transaction.
- **Signatures**: This represents the signature required by the transaction. The total number of signatures required is directly proportional to the number of public keys for commands.
- **Type**: There are two types of transactions namely, normal or notary changing. Notary changing transactions are used for reassigning a notary for a state.
- **Timestamp**: This field represents a bracket of time during which the transaction has taken place. These are verified and enforced by notary services. Also, it is expected that if strict timings are required, which is desirable in many financial services scenarios, notaries should be synced with an atomic clock.
- **Summaries:** This is a text description that describes the operations of the transaction.

Vaults

Vaults run on a node and are akin to the concept of wallets in bitcoin. As the transactions are not globally broadcasted, each node will have only that part of data in their vaults that is considered relevant to them. Vaults store their data in a standard relational database and as such can be queried by using standard SQL. Vaults can contain both on ledger and off ledger data, meaning that it can also have some part of data that is not on ledger.

CorDapp

The core model of Corda consists of state objects, transactions, and transaction protocols, which when combined with contract code, APIs, wallet plugins, and user interface components results in constructing a **Corda distributed application (CorDapp)**.

Smart contracts in Corda are written using Kotlin or Java. The code is targeted for JVM.

JVM has been modified slightly in order to achieve deterministic results of execution of JVM bytecode. There are three main components in a Corda smart contract as follows:

- Executable code that defines the validation logic to validate changes to the state objects.
- State objects represent the current state of a contract and either can be consumed by a transaction or produced (created) by a transaction.
- Commands are used to describe the operational and verification data that defines how a transaction can be verified.

The development environment – Corda

The development environment for Corda can be set up easily using the following steps. Required software includes the following:

- JDK 8 (8u131), which is available at
  `http://www.oracle.com/technetwork/java/javase/downloads/index.html`.
- IntelliJ IDEA Community edition, which is free and available at
  `https://www.jetbrains.com/idea/download`.
- H2 database platform independent ZIP, and is available at
  `http://www.h2database.com/html/download.html`.
- Git, which is available at `https://git-scm.com/downloads`.
- Kotlin language, which is available for IntelliJ, and more information can be found at `https://kotlinlang.org/`.

Gradle is another component that is used to build Corda. It is available at `https://gradle.org`.

Once all these tools are installed, smart contract development can be started. CorDapps can be developed by utilizing an example template available at
`https://github.com/corda/cordapp-template`.

 Detailed documentation on how to develop contract code is available at `https://docs.corda.net/`.

Corda can be cloned locally from GitHub using the following command:

```
$ git clone https://github.com/corda/corda.git
```

When the cloning is successful, you should see output similar to the following:

```
Cloning into 'corda'...
remote: Counting objects: 74695, done.
remote: Compressing objects: 100% (67/67), done.
remote: Total 74695 (delta 17), reused 0 (delta 0), pack-reused 74591
Receiving objects: 100% (74695/74695), 51.27 MiB | 1.72 MiB/s, done.
Resolving deltas: 100% (42863/42863), done.
Checking connectivity... done.
```

Once the repository is cloned, it can be opened in IntelliJ for further development. There are multiple samples available in the repository, such as a bank of Corda, interest rate swaps, demo, and traders demo. Readers can find them under the `/samples` directory under `corda` and they can be explored using IntelliJ IDEA IDE.

Summary

In this chapter, we have gone through an introduction to the Hyperledger project. Firstly, the core ideas behind the Hyperledger project were discussed, and a brief introduction to all projects under Hyperledger was provided. Three main Hyperledger projects were discussed in detail, namely Hyperledger Fabric, Sawtooth lake, and Corda. All these projects are continuously improving and changes are expected in the next releases. However, the core concepts of all the projects mentioned above are expected to remain unchanged or change only slightly. Readers are encouraged to visit the relevant links provided within the chapter to see the latest updates.

It is evident that a lot is going on in this space and projects like Hyperledger from the Linux Foundation are playing a pivotal role in the advancement of blockchain technology. Each of the projects discussed in this chapter has novel approaches towards solving the issues faced in various industries, and any current limitations within the blockchain technology are also being addressed, such as scalability and privacy. It is expected that more projects will soon be proposed to the Hyperledger project, and it is envisaged that with this collaborative and open effort blockchain technology will advance tremendously and will benefit the community as a whole.

In the next chapter, alternative blockchain solutions and platforms will be introduced. As blockchain technology is growing very fast and has attracted lot of research interest there are many new projects that have emerged recently. We will discuss those projects in the next chapter.

14
Alternative Blockchains

This chapter is intended to provide an introduction to alternative blockchain solutions. With the success of Bitcoin and subsequent realization of the potential of blockchain technology, a Cambrian explosion started that resulted in the development of various blockchain protocols, applications, and platforms. Some projects did not gain much traction, for example as an estimate 46% of ICOs have failed this year, but many have succeeded in creating a solid place in this space.

In this chapter, readers will be introduced to alternative blockchains and platforms such as Kadena, Ripple, and Stellar. We will explore the projects that either are new blockchains on their own or provide support to other existing blockchains by providing SDKs, frameworks, and tools to make development and deployment of blockchain solutions easier. The success of Ethereum and Bitcoin has resulted in various projects that spawned into existence by leveraging the underlying technologies and concepts introduced by them. These new projects add value by addressing the limitations in the current blockchains such as scalability and or enhancing the existing solutions by providing an additional layer of user-friendly tools on top of them.

Blockchains

In this section, an introduction to new blockchain solutions will be given, and later sections will cover various platforms and development kits that complement existing blockchains. For example, Kadena is a new private blockchain with novel ideas such as Scalable BFT. Various concepts such as sidechains, drivechains, and pegging have also been introduced with this growth of blockchain technologies. This chapter will cover all these technologies and related concepts in detail. Of course, it's not possible to cover all **alternative chains (altchains)** and platforms, but all those platforms have been included in this chapter that is related to blockchains, covered in the previous chapters, or are expected to gain traction soon.

We will explore Kadena, Ripple, Stellar, Quorum and various other blockchains in the section.

Kadena

Kadena is a private blockchain that has successfully addressed scalability and privacy issues in blockchain systems. A new Turing incomplete language, called Pact, has also been introduced with Kadena that allows the development of smart contracts. A key innovation in Kadena is its Scalable BFT consensus algorithm, which has the potential to scale to thousands of nodes without performance degradation.

Scalable BFT is based on the original Raft algorithm and is a successor of Tangaroa and Juno. Tangaroa, which is a name given to an implementation of Raft with fault tolerance (a BFT Raft), was developed to address the availability and safety issues that arose from the behavior of Byzantine nodes in the Raft algorithm, and Juno was a fork of Tangaroa that was developed by JPMorgan. Consensus algorithms are discussed in `Chapter 1`, *Blockchain 101* in more detail.

Both of these proposals have a fundamental limitation—they cannot scale while maintaining a high level of high performance. As such, Juno could not gain much traction. Private blockchains have the more desirable property of maintaining high performance as the number of nodes increase, but the aforementioned proposals lack this feature. Kadena solves this issue with its proprietary Scalable BFT algorithm, which is expected to scale up to thousands of nodes without any performance degradation.

Moreover, confidentiality is another significant aspect of Kadena that enables privacy of transactions on the blockchain. This security service is achieved by using a combination of key rotation, symmetric on-chain encryption, incremental hashing, and Double Ratchet protocol.

Key rotation is used as a standard mechanism to ensure the security of the private blockchain. It is used as a best practice to thwart any attacks if the keys have been compromised, by periodically changing the encryption keys. There is native support for key rotation in Pact smart contract language.

Symmetric on-chain encryption allows encryption of transaction data on the blockchain. These transactions can be automatically decrypted by the participants of a particular private transaction. Double Ratchet protocol is used to provide key management and encryption functions.

Scalable BFT consensus protocol ensures that adequate replication and consensus has been achieved before smart contract execution. The consensus is achieved by following the process described here.

This is how a transaction originates and flows in the network:

1. First, a new transaction is signed by the user and broadcasted over the blockchain network, which is picked up by a leader node that adds it to its immutable log. At this point, an incremental hash is also calculated for the log. Incremental hash is a type of hash function that allows computation of hash messages in the scenario where, if a previous original message which is already hashed is slightly changed, then the new hash message is computed from the already existing hash. This scheme is quicker and less resource intensive compared to a conventional hash function where an altogether new hash message is required to be generated even if the original message has only changed very slightly.

2. Once the transaction is written to the log by the leader node, it signs the replication and incremental hash and broadcasts it to other nodes.

3. Other nodes after receiving the transaction, verify the signature of the leader node, add the transaction into their own logs, and broadcast their own calculated incremental hashes (quorum proofs) to other nodes. Finally, the transaction is committed to the ledger permanently after an adequate number of proofs are received from other nodes.

A simplified version of this process is shown in the following diagram, where the leader node is recording the new transactions and then replicating them to the follower nodes:

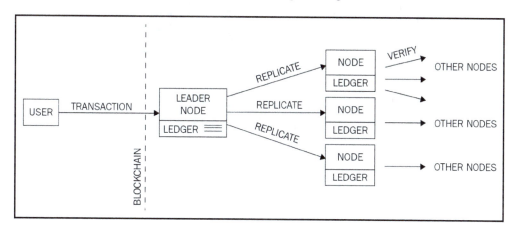

Consensus mechanism in Kadena

Once the consensus is achieved, a smart contract execution can start and takes a number of steps, as follows:

1. First, the signature of the message is verified.
2. Pact smart contract layer takes over.
3. Pact code is compiled.
4. The transaction is initiated and executes any business logic embedded within the smart contract. In case of any failures, an immediate rollback is initiated that reverts that state back to what it was before the execution started.
5. Finally, the transaction completes and relevant logs are updated.

 Pact has been open sourced by Kadena and is available for download at `http://kadena.io/pact/downloads.html`.

This can be downloaded as a standalone binary that provides a REPL for Pact language. An example is shown here where Pact is run by issuing the `./pact` command in Linux console:

```
drequinox@drequinox-OP7010:~/Downloads$ ./pact
pact> 1234
1234
pact> (+ 1 2)
3
pact> (if (= (+ 1 2) 3 "OK" "ERROR")
(interactive):1:31: error: unexpected
    EOF, expected: ")", ";", "{",
    Boolean false, Boolean true,
    Decimal literal, Integer literal,
    String literal, Symbol literal,
    list literal, pact, sexp, space
(if (= (+ 1 2) 3 "OK" "ERROR")<EOF>
                              ^
pact> (if (= (+ 1 2) 3) "OK" "ERROR")
"OK"
pact>
```

Pact REPL, showing sample commands and error output

A smart contract in Pact language is usually composed of three sections: keysets, modules, and tables. These sections are described here:

- **Keysets**: This section defines relevant authorization schemes for tables and modules.
- **Modules**: This section defines the smart contract code encompassing the business logic in the form of functions and pacts. Pacts within modules are composed of multiple steps and are executed sequentially.
- **Tables:** This section is an access-controlled construct defined within modules. Only administrators defined in the admin keyset have direct access to this table. Code within the module is granted full access, by default to the tables.

Pact also allows several execution modes. These modes include contract definition, transaction execution, and querying. These execution modes are described here:

- **Contract definition:** This mode allows a contract to be created on the blockchain via a single transaction message.
- **Transaction execution:** This mode entails the execution of modules of smart contract code that represent business logic.
- **Querying:** This mode is concerned with simply probing the contract for data and is executed locally on the nodes for performance reason. Pact uses LISP-like syntax and represents in the code exactly what will be executed on the blockchain, as it is stored on the blockchain in human-readable format. This is in contrast to Ethereum's EVM, which compiles into bytecode for execution, which makes it difficult to verify what code is in execution on the blockchain. Moreover, it is Turing incomplete, supports immutable variables, and does not allow null values, which improves the overall safety of the transaction code execution.

It is not possible to cover the complete syntax and functions of Pact in this limited length chapter; however, a small example is shown here, that shows the general structure of a smart contract written in Pact. This example shows a simple addition module that defines a function named `addition` that takes three parameters. When the code is executed it adds all three values and displays the result.

The following example has been developed using the online Pact compiler available at http://kadena.io/try-pact/.

```
 1  ;Begin transaction with optinal NAME.
 2  (begin-tx) 'testTransaction
 3  ;Set transaction data in JSON format or pact types
 4  (env-data { "keyset": {"keys": ["admin"], "pred": "keys-any"}})
 5  ;Define keyset as NAME with KEYSET
 6  (define-keyset 'admin-keyset (read-keyset "keyset"))
 7  ;Set transaction signature KEYS
 8  (env-keys ["admin"])
 9  ;define module using syntax (module NAME KEYSET [DOCSTING] DEFS . . .)
10  (module additionModule 'admin-keyset
11  ;define function that takes three arguments x y z
12  (defun addition (x y z) (+ x (+ y z))))
13  ;Commit transaction.
14  (commit-tx)
15  ;use the function addition
16  (use 'additionModule)
17  ;run the function addition and format result
18  (format "Result : {} " [(addition 100 200 300)])
```

Sample Pact code

When the code is run, it produces the output shown as follows:

```
Begin Tx Just 1
testTransaction
Setting transaction data
Keyset defined
Setting transaction keys
Loaded module "additionModule"
  , hash "eaf647f843b2e88b5009253fe4eeca6f8890a646da76b4
Commit Tx Just 1
Using "additionModule"
Result : 600
```

The output of the code

As shown in the preceding example, the execution output matches exactly with the code layout and structure, which allows for greater transparency and limits the possibility of malicious code execution.

Kadena is a new class of blockchains introducing the novel concept of **pervasive determinism** where, in addition to standard public/private key-based data origin security, an additional layer of fully deterministic consensus is also provided. It provides cryptographic security at all layers of the blockchain including transactions and consensus layer.

 Relevant documentation and source code for Pact can be found here `https://github.com/kadena-io/pact`.

Kadena has also introduced a public blockchain in January, 2018 which is another leap forward in building blockchains with massive throughput. The novel idea in this proposal is to build a PoW parallel chain architecture. This scheme works by combining individually mined chains on peers into a single network. The result is massive throughput capable of processing more than 10,000 transactions per second.

 The original research paper is available at `http://kadena.io/docs/chainweb-v15.pdf`.

Ripple

Introduced in 2012, Ripple is a currency exchange and real-time gross settlement system. In Ripple, the payments are settled without any waiting as opposed to traditional settlement networks, where it can take days for settlement.

It has a native currency called **Ripples** (**XRP**). It also supports non-XRP payments. This system is considered similar to an old traditional money transfer mechanism known as *Hawala*. This system works by making use of agents who take the money and a password from the sender, then contact the payee's agent and instruct them to release funds to the person who can provide the password. The payee then contacts the local agent, tells them the password and collects the funds. An analogy to the agent is gateway in Ripple. This is just a very simple analogy; the actual protocol is rather complex but principally it is the same.

The Ripple network is composed of various nodes that can perform different functions based on their type:

- **User nodes**: These nodes use in payment transactions and can pay or receive payments.
- **Validator nodes**: These nodes participate in the consensus mechanism. Each server maintains a set of unique nodes, which it needs to query while achieving consensus. Nodes in the **Unique Node List** (**UNL**) are trusted by the server involved in the consensus mechanism and will accept votes only from this list of unique nodes.

Ripple is sometimes not considered a truly decentralized network as there are network operators and regulators involved. However, it can be considered decentralized due to the fact that anyone can become part of the network by running a validator node. Moreover, the consensus process is also decentralized because any changes proposed to make on the ledger have to be decided by following a scheme of super majority voting. However, this is a hot topic among researchers and enthusiasts and there are arguments against and in favor of each school of thought. There are some discussions online that readers can refer to for further exploration of these ideas.

You can find these online discussions at the following links:

- https://www.quora.com/Why-is-Ripple-centralized
- https://thenextweb.com/hardfork/2018/02/06/ripple-report-bitmex-centralized/
- https://www.reddit.com/r/Ripple/comments/6c8j7b/is_ripple_centralized_and_other_related_questions/?st=jewkor7bamp;sh=e39bc635

Ripple maintains a globally distributed ledger of all transactions that are governed by a novel low-latency consensus algorithm called **Ripple Protocol Consensus Algorithm** (**RPCA**). The consensus process works by achieving an agreement on the state of an open ledger containing transactions by seeking verification and acceptance from validating servers in an iterative manner until an adequate number of votes are achieved. Once enough votes are received (a super majority, initially 50% and gradually increasing with each iteration up to at least 80%) the changes are validated and the ledger is closed. At this point, an alert is sent to the whole network indicating that the ledger is closed.

Original research paper for RPCA is available at `https://ripple.com/files/ripple_consensus_whitepaper.pdf`.

In summary, the consensus protocol is a three-phase process:

- **Collection phase**: In this phase validating nodes gather all transactions broadcasted on the network by account owners and validate them. Transactions, once accepted, are called candidate transactions and can be accepted or rejected based on the validation criteria.
- **Consensus phase**: After the collection phase the consensus process starts, and after achieving it the ledger is **closed**.
- **Ledger closing phase**: This process runs asynchronously every few seconds in rounds and, as result, the ledger is opened and closed (updated) accordingly:

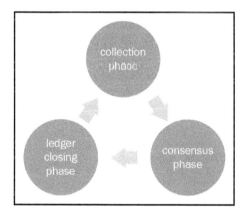

Ripple consensus protocol phases

In a Ripple network, there are a number of components that work together in order to achieve consensus and form a payment network. These components are discussed individually here:

- **Server**: This component serves as a participant in the consensus protocol. Ripple server software is required in order to be able to participate in consensus protocol.
- **Ledger**: This is the main record of balances of all accounts on the network. A ledger contains various elements such as ledger number, account settings, transactions, timestamp, and a flag that indicates the validity of the ledger.

- **Last closed ledger**: A ledger is closed once consensus is achieved by validating nodes.
- **Open ledger**: This is a ledger that has not been validated yet and no consensus has been reached about its state. Each node has its own open ledger, which contains proposed transactions.
- **Unique Node List:** This is a list of unique trusted nodes that a validating server uses in order to seek votes and subsequent consensus.
- **Proposer**: As the name suggests, this component proposes new transactions to be included in the consensus process. It is usually a subset of nodes (UNL defined in the previous point) that can propose transactions to the validating server.

Transactions

Transactions are created by the network users in order to update the ledger. A transaction is expected to be digitally signed and valid in order for it to be considered as a candidate in the consensus process. Each transaction costs a small amount of XRP, which serves as a protection mechanism against denial of service attacks caused by spamming.

There are different types of transaction in the Ripple network. A single field within the Ripple transaction data structure called `TransactionType` is used to represent the type of the transaction. Transactions are executed by using a four-step process:

1. First, transactions are prepared whereby an unsigned transaction is created by following the standards
2. The second step is signing, where the transaction is digitally signed to authorize it
3. After this, the actual submission to the network occurs via the connected server
4. Finally, the verification is performed to ensure that the transaction is validated successfully

Roughly, the transactions can be categorized into three types, namely payments related, order related, and account and security related. All these types are described in the following section.

Payments related

There are several fields in this category that result in certain actions. All these fields are described as follows:

- Payment: This transaction is most commonly used and allows one user to send funds to another.
- PaymentChannelClaim: This is used to claim Ripples (XRP) from a payment channel. A payment channel is a mechanism that allows recurring and unidirectional payments between parties. This can also be used to set the expiration time of the payment channel.
- PaymentChannelCreate: This transaction creates a new payment channel and adds XRP to it in *drops*. A single drop is equivalent to 0.000001 of an XRP.
- PaymentChannelFund: This transaction is used to add more funds to an existing channel. Similar to the PaymentChannelClaim transaction, this can also be used to modify the expiration time of the payment channel.

Order related

This type of transaction includes following two fields:

- OfferCreate: This transaction represents a limit order, which represents an intent for the exchange of currency. It results in creating an offer node in the consensus ledger if it cannot be completely fulfilled.
- OfferCancel: This is used to remove a previously created offer node from the consensus ledger, indicating withdrawal of the order.

Account and security-related

This type of transaction includes the fields listed as follows. Each field is responsible for performing a certain function:

- AccountSet: This transaction is used to modify the attributes of an account in the Ripple consensus ledger.
- SetRegularKey: This is used to change or set the transaction signing key for an account. An account is identified using a base-58 Ripple address derived from the account's master public key.
- SignerListSet: This can be used to create a set of signers for use in multisignature transactions.
- TrustSet: This is used to create or modify a trust line between accounts.

A transaction in Ripple is composed of various fields that are common to all transaction types. These fields are listed as follows with a description:

- `Account`: This is the address of the initiator of the transaction.
- `AccountTxnID`: This is an optional field which contains the hash of another transaction. It is used to chain the transaction together.
- `Fee`: This is the amount of XRP.
- `Flags`: This is an optional field specifying the flags for the transaction.
- `LastLedgerSequence`: This is the highest sequence number of the ledger in which the transaction can appear.
- `Memos`: This represents optional arbitrary information.
- `SigningPubKey`: This represents the public key.
- `Signers`: This represent signers in a multisig transaction.
- `SourceTag`: This represents either sender or reason of the transaction.
- `SourceTag`: This represents either sender or reason of the transaction.
- `TxnSignature`: This is the verification digital signature for the transaction.

Interledger

Interledger is a simple protocol that is composed of four layers: Application, Transport, Interledger, and Ledger. Each layer is responsible for performing various functions under certain protocols. These functions and protocols are described in the following section.

 The specifications of this protocol are available at: `https://interledger.org/rfcs/0003-interledger-protocol/draft-9.html`

Application layer

Protocols running on this layer govern the key attributes of a payment transaction. Examples of application layer protocols include **Simple Payment Setup Protocol** (**SPSP**) and **Open Web Payment Scheme** (**OWPS**). SPSP is an Interledger protocol that allows secure payment across different ledgers by creating connectors between them. OWPS is another scheme that allows consumer payments across different networks.

Once the protocols on this layer have run successfully, protocols from the transport layer will be invoked in order to start the payment process.

Transport layer

This layer is responsible for managing payment transactions. Protocols such as **Optimistic Transport Protocol (OTP)**, **Universal Transport Protocol (UTP)** and **Atomic Transport Protocol (ATP)** are available currently for this layer. OTP is the simplest protocol, which manages payment transfers without any escrow protection, whereas UTP provides escrow protection. ATP is the most advanced protocol, which not only provides an escrowed transfer mechanism but in addition, makes use of trusted notaries to further secure the payment transactions.

Interledger layer

This layer provides interoperability and routing services. This layer contains protocols such as **Interledger Protocol (ILP)**, **Interledger Quoting Protocol (ILQP)**, and **Interledger Control Protocol (ILCP)**. ILP packet provides the final target (destination) of the transaction in a transfer. ILQP is used in making quote requests by the senders before the actual transfer. ILCP is used to exchange data related to routing information and payment errors between connectors on the payment network.

Ledger layer

This layer contains protocols that enable communication and execution of payment transactions between connectors. **Connectors** are basically objects that implement the protocol for forwarding payments between different ledgers. It can support various protocols such as simple ledger protocol, various blockchain protocols, legacy protocols, and different proprietary protocols.

Ripple connect consists of various Plug and Play modules that allow connectivity between ledgers by using the ILP. It enables the exchange of required data between parties before the transaction, visibility, fee management, delivery confirmation, and secure communication using transport layer security. A third-party application can connect to the Ripple network via various connectors that forward payments between different ledgers.

All layers described in the preceding sections make up the architecture of Interledger Protocol. Overall, Ripple is a solution that is targeted for the financial industry and makes real-time payments possible without any settlement risk. As this is a very feature-rich platform, covering all aspects of it are not possible in this chapter.

 Ripple documentation for the platform are available at `https://ripple.com/`.

Stellar

Stellar is a payment network based on blockchain technology and a novel consensus model called **Federated Byzantine Agreement** (**FBA**). FBA works by creating quorums of trusted parties. **Stellar Consensus Protocol** (**SCP**) is an implementation of FBA.

Key issues identified in the Stellar whitepaper are the cost and complexity of current financial infrastructure. This limitation warrants the need for a global financial network that addresses these issues without compromising the integrity and security of the financial transaction. This requirement has resulted in the invention of SCP which is a provably safe consensus mechanism.

 Original research paper for SCP is available at `https://www.stellar.org/papers/stellar-consensus-protocol.pdf`.

It has four main properties, which are described here:

- **Decentralized control**: This allows participation by anyone without any central party
- **Low latency**: This addresses the much-desired requirement of fast transaction processing
- **Flexible trust**: This allows users to choose which parties they trust for a specific purpose
- **Asymptotic security**: This makes use of digital signatures and hash functions for providing the required level of security on the network

The Stellar network allows transfer and representation of the value of an asset by its native digital currency, called **Lumens,** abbreviated as **XLM**. Lumens are consumed when a transaction is broadcasted on the network, which also serves as a deterrent against denial of service attacks.

At its core, the Stellar network maintains a distributed ledger that records every transaction and is replicated on each Stellar server (node). The consensus is achieved by verifying transactions between servers and updating the ledger with updates. The Stellar ledger can also act as a distributed exchange order book by allowing users to store their offers to buy or sell currencies.

There are various tools, SDKs, and software that make up the Stellar network.

The core software is available at `https://github.com/stellar/stellar-core`.

Rootstock

Before discussing **Rootstock** (**RSK**) in detail, it's important to define and introduce some concepts that are fundamental to the design of Rootstock. These concepts include sidechains, drivechains, and two-way pegging. The concept of the sidechain was originally developed by Blockstream.

 Blockstream's online presence is at `https://blockstream.com`.

Two-way pegging is a mechanism by which value (coins) can transfer between one blockchain to another and vice versa. There is no real transfer of coin between chains. The idea revolves around the concept of locking the same amount and value of coins in a bitcoin blockchain (main chain) and unlocking the equivalent number of tokens in the secondary chain.

Bearing this definition in mind, sidechains can be defined as described in the following section.

Sidechain

This is a blockchain that runs in parallel with a main blockchain and allows transfer of value between them. This means that tokens from one blockchain can be used in the sidechain and vice versa. This is also called a pegged sidechain because it supports two-way pegged assets.

Drivechain

This is a relatively new concept, where control on unlocking the locked bitcoins (in main chain) is given to the miners who can vote when to unlock them. This is in contrast to sidechains, where consensus is validated though simple payment verification mechanism in order to transfer the coins back to the main chain.

Rootstock is a smart contract platform which has a two-way peg into bitcoin blockchain. The core idea is to increase the scalability and performance of the bitcoin system and enable it to work with smart contracts. Rootstock runs a Turing complete deterministic virtual machine called **Rootstock Virtual Machine (RVM)**. It is also compatible with the EVM and allows solidity-compiled contracts to run on Rootstock. Smart contracts can also run under the time-tested security of bitcoin blockchain. The Rootstock blockchain works by merge mining with bitcoins. This allows Rootstock blockchain to achieve the same security level as Bitcoin. This is especially true for preventing double spends and achieving settlement finality. It allows scalability, up to 400 transactions per second due to faster block times and other design considerations.

The research paper is available at, should you want to explore it further
`https://uploads.strikinglycdn.com/files/ec5278f8-218c-407a-af3c-ab71a910246d/RSK%20White%20Paper%20-%20Overview.pdf`.

RSK has released the main network called Bamboo, RSK MainNet which is a beta currently.

It is available at `http://www.rsk.co/`.

Quorum

This is a blockchain solution built by enhancing the existing Ethereum blockchain. There are several enhancements such as transaction privacy and a new consensus mechanism that has been introduced in Quorum. Quorum has introduced a new consensus model known as QuorumChain, which is based on a majority voting and time-based mechanism. Another feature called Constellation is also introduced which is a general-purpose mechanism for submitting information and allows encrypted communication between peers. Furthermore, permissions at node level is governed by smart contracts. It also provides a higher level of performance compared to public Ethereum blockchains.

Several components make up the Quorum blockchain ecosystem. These are listed in the following subsections.

Transaction manager

This component enables access to encrypted transaction data. It also manages local storage on nodes and communication with other transaction managers on the network.

Crypto Enclave

As the name suggests, this component is responsible for providing cryptographic services to ensure transaction privacy. It is also responsible for performing key management functions.

QuorumChain

This is the key innovation in Quorum. It is a BFT consensus mechanism which allows verification and circulation of votes via transactions on the blockchain network. In this scheme, a smart contract is used to manage the consensus process and nodes can be given voting rights to vote on which new block should be accepted. Once an appropriate number of votes is received by the voters, the block is considered valid. Nodes can have two roles, namely Voter or Maker. The **Voter** node is allowed to vote, whereas the **Maker** node is the one that creates a new block. By design, a node can have either right, none, or only one.

Network manager

This component provides an access control layer for the permissioned network.

A node in the quorum network can take several roles, for example, a Maker node that is allowed to create new blocks. Transaction privacy is provided using cryptography and the concept that certain transactions are meant to be viewable only by their relevant participants. This idea is similar to Corda's idea of private transactions that was discussed in Chapter 13, *Hyperledger*. As it allows both public and private transactions on the blockchain, the state database has been divided into two databases representing private and public transactions. As such, there are two separate Patricia-Merkle trees that represent the private and public state of the network. A private contract state hash is used to provide consensus evidence in private transactions between transacting parties.

Transaction in a Quorum network consists of various elements such as the recipient, the digital signature of the sender, which is used to identify the transaction originator, optional Ether amount, the optional list of participants that are allowed to see the transaction, and a field that contains a hash in case of private transactions.

A transaction goes through several steps before it can reach its destination. These steps are described as follows in detail:

1. User applications (DApps) send the transaction to the Quorum node via an API exposed by the blockchain network. This also contains the recipient address and transaction data.
2. The API then encrypts the payload and applies any other necessary cryptographic algorithm in order to ensure the privacy of the transaction and is sent to the transaction manager. The hash of the encrypted payload is also calculated at this step.
3. After receiving the transaction, the transaction manager validates the signature of the transaction sender and stores the message.
4. The hash of the previously encrypted payload is sent to the Quorum node.
5. Once the Quorum node starts to validate a block that contains the private transaction, it requests more relevant data from the transaction manager.
6. Once this request is received by the transaction manager, it sends the encrypted payload and relevant symmetric keys to the requestor Quorum node.
7. Once the Quorum node has all the data, it decrypts the payload and sends it to the EVM for execution. This is how Quorum achieves privacy with symmetric encryption on the blockchain, while it is able to use native Ethereum protocol and EVM for message transfer and execution respectively.

A similar concept, but quite different in a few aspects, has been proposed before in the form of **HydraChain**, which is based on Ethereum blockchain and allows the creation of permissioned distributed ledgers.

 Quorum is available for download at `https://github.com/ jpmorganchase/quorum`.

Tezos

Tezos is a generic self-amending cryptographic ledger, which means that it not only allows decentralized consensus on the state of the blockchain but also allows consensus on how the protocol and nodes are evolved over time. Tezos has been developed to address limitations in the Bitcoin protocol such as issues arising from hard forks, cost, and mining power centralization due to PoW, limited scripting ability, and security issues. It has been developed in a purely functional language called OCaml.

The original research paper is available at `https://www.tezos.com/static/papers/white_paper.pdf`.

The architecture of Tezos distributed ledger is divided into three layers: the network layer, consensus layer, and transaction layer. This decomposition allows the protocol to be evolved in a decentralized fashion. For this purpose, a generic network shell is implemented in Tezos that is responsible for maintaining the blockchain, which is represented by a combination of consensus and transaction layer. This shell provides an interface layer between the network and the protocol.

A concept of seed protocol has also been introduced, which is used as a mechanism to allow stakeholders on the network to approve any changes to the protocol.

Tezos blockchain starts from a seed protocol compared to a traditional blockchain that starts from a genesis block.

This seed protocol is responsible for defining procedures for amendments in the blockchain and even the amendment protocol itself. The reward mechanism in Tezos is based on a PoS algorithm, therefore there is no mining requirement.

Contract script language has been developed in Tezos for writing smart contracts, which is a stack-based Turing complete language. Smart contracts in Tezos are formally verifiable, which allows the code to be mathematically proven for its correctness.

Tezos has recently completed crowdfunding via ICO of 232 million USD. Their public network is due to be released in Q1 2018.

Tezos code is available at `https://github.com/tezos/tezos`.

Storj

Existing models for cloud-based storage are all centralized solutions, which may or may not be as secure as users expect them to be. There is a need to have a cloud storage system that is secure, highly available, and above all decentralized. Storj aims to provide blockchain based, decentralized, and distributed storage. It is a cloud shared by the community instead of a central organization. It allows execution of storage contracts between nodes that act as autonomous agents. These agents (nodes) execute various functions such as data transfer, validation, and perform data integrity checks.

The core concept is based on **Distributed Hash Tables** (**DHTs**) called **Kademlia**, however this protocol has been enhanced by adding new message types and functionalities in Storj. It also implements a peer to peer **publish/subscribe** (**pub/sub**) mechanism known as **Quasar**, which ensures that messages successfully reach the nodes that are interested in storage contracts. This is achieved via a bloom filter-based storage contract parameters selection mechanism called **topics**.

Storj stores files in an encrypted format spread across the network. Before the file is stored on the network, it is encrypted using AES-256-CTR symmetric encryption and is then stored piece by piece in a distributed manner on the network. This process of dissecting the file into pieces is called **sharding** and results in increased availability, security, performance, and privacy of the network. Also, if a node fails the shard is still available because by default a single shard is stored at three different locations on the network.

It maintains a blockchain, which serves as a shared ledger and implements standard security features such as public/private key cryptography and hash functions similar to any other blockchain. As the system is based on hard drive sharing between peers, anyone can contribute by sharing their extra space on the drive and get paid with Storj's own cryptocurrency called **Storjcoin X** (**SJCX**). SJCX was developed as a *Counterparty* asset and makes use of Counterparty (Bitcoin blockchain based) for transactions. This has been migrated to Ethereum now.

 A detailed discussion is available at `https://blog.storj.io/post/158740607128/migration-from-counterparty-to-ethereum`. Storj code is available at `https://github.com/Storj/`.

MaidSafe

This is another distributed storage system similar to Storj. Users are paid in Safecoin for their storage space contribution to the network. This mechanism of payment is governed by *proof of resource*, which ensures that the disk space committed by a user to the network is available, if not then the payment of Safecoin will drop accordingly. The files are encrypted and divided into small portions before being transmitted on to the network for storage.

Another concept of **opportunistic caching** has been introduced with MaidSafe, which is a mechanism to create copies of frequently accessed data physically closer to where the access requests are coming from, which results in high performance of the network. Another novel feature of the SAFE network is that it automatically removes any duplicate data on the network, thus resulting in reduced storage requirements.

Moreover, the concept of **churning** has also been introduced, which basically means that data is constantly moved across the network so that the data cannot be targeted by malicious adversaries. It also keeps multiple copies of data across the network to provide redundancy in case a node goes offline or fails.

BigchainDB

This is a scalable blockchain database. It is not strictly a blockchain itself but complements blockchain technology by providing a decentralized database. At its core it's a distributed database but with the added attributes of a blockchain such as decentralization, immutability, and handling of digital assets. It also allows usage of NoSQL for querying the database.

It is intended to provide a database in a decentralized ecosystem where not only processing is decentralized (blockchain) or the filesystem is decentralized (for example, IPFS) but the database is also decentralized. This makes the whole application ecosystem decentralized.

 This is available at `https://www.bigchaindb.com/`.

MultiChain

MultiChain has been developed as a platform for the development and deployment of private blockchains. It is based on bitcoin code and addresses security, scalability, and privacy issues. It is a highly configurable blockchain platform that allows users to set different blockchain parameters. It supports control and privacy via a granular permissioning layer. Installation of MultiChain is very quick.

 Link to installation files are available at `http://www.multichain.com/download-install/`.

Tendermint

Tendermint is a software that provides a BFT consensus mechanism and state machine replication functionality to an application. Its main motivation is to develop a general purpose, secure, and high-performance replicated state machine.

There are two components in Tendermint, which are described in the following section.

Tendermint Core

This is a consensus engine that enables secure replication of transactions on each node in the network.

Tendermint Socket Protocol (TMSP)

This is an application interface protocol that allows interfacing with any programming language to process transactions.

Tendermint allows decoupling of the application process and consensus process, which allows any application to benefit from the consensus mechanism.

The Tendermint consensus algorithm is a round-based mechanism where validator nodes propose new blocks in each round. A locking mechanism is used to ensure protection against a scenario where two different blocks are selected for committing at the same height of the blockchain. Each validator node maintains a full local replicated ledger of blocks that contain transactions. Each block contains a header, which consists of the previous block hash, timestamp of the proposal of block, the current block height, and the Merkle root hash of all transactions present in the block.

Tendermint has recently been used in **Cosmos** (https://cosmos.network) which is a network of blockchains that allows interoperability between different chains running on BFT consensus algorithm. Blockchains on this network are called zones. The first zone in Cosmos is called Cosmos hub, which is, in fact, a public blockchain and is responsible for providing connectivity service to other blockchains. For this purpose, the hub makes use of **Inter Blockchain Communication** (**IBC**) protocol. IBC protocol supports two types of transactions called IBCBlockCimmitTx and IBCPacketTx. The first type is used to provide proof of the most recent block hash in a blockchain to any party, whereas the latter type is used to provide data origin authentication. A packet from one blockchain to another is published by first posting a proof to the target chain. The receiving (target) chain checks this proof in order to verify that the sending chain has indeed published the packet. In addition, it has its own native currency called Atom. This scheme addresses scalability and interoperability issues by allowing multiple blockchains to connect to the hub.

Tendermint is available at https://tendermint.com/.

Platforms and frameworks

This section covers various platforms that have been developed to enhance the experience of existing blockchain solutions.

Eris

Eris is not a single blockchain, it is an open modular platform developed by Monax for development of blockchain-based ecosystem applications. It offers various frameworks, SDKs, and tools that allow accelerated development and deployment of blockchain applications.

The core idea behind the Eris application platform is to enable development and management of ecosystem applications with a blockchain backend. It allows integration with multiple blockchains and enables various third-party systems to interact with various other systems.

This platform makes use of smart contracts written in Solidity language. It can interact with blockchains such as Ethereum or Bitcoin. The interaction can include connectivity commands, start, stop, disconnection, and creation of new blockchains. Complexity related to setup and interaction with blockchains have been abstracted away in Eris. All commands are standardized for different blockchains, and the same commands can be used across the platform regardless of the blockchain type being targeted.

An ecosystem application can consist the Eris platform, enabling the API gateway to allow legacy applications to connect to key management systems, consensus engines, and application engines. The Eris platform provides various toolkits that are used to provide various services to the developers. These modules are described as follows:

- **Chains**: This allows the creation of and interaction with blockchains.
- **Packages**: This allows the development of smart contracts.
- **Keys**: This is used for key management and signing operations.
- **Files**: This allows working with distributed data management systems. It can be used to interact with filesystems such as IPFS and data lakes.
- **Services**: This exposes a set of services that allows the management and integration of ecosystem applications.

Several SDKs has also been developed by Eris that allow the development and management of ecosystem applications. These SDKs contain smart contracts that have been fully tested and address specific needs and requirements of business. For example, a finance SDK, insurance SDK, and logistics SDK. There is also a base SDK that serves as a basic development kit to manage the life cycle of an ecosystem application.

Monax has developed its own permissioned blockchain client called `eris:db`. It is a PoS-based blockchain system that allows integration with a number of different blockchain networks. The `eris:db` client consists of four components:

- **Consensus**: This is based on the Tendermint consensus mechanism, discussed before
- **Virtual machine**: Eris uses EVM, as such it supports Solidity compiled contracts
- **Permissions layer**: Being a permissioned ledger, Eris provides an access control mechanism that can be used to assign specific roles to different entities on the network

- **Interface**: This provides various command-line tools and RPC interfaces to enable interaction with the backend blockchain network

The key difference between Ethereum blockchain and `eris:db` is that `eris:db` makes use of a **Practical Byzantine Fault-Tolerance** (**PBFT**) algorithm, which is implemented as a deposit-based Proof of Stake (DPOS system) whereas Ethereum uses PoW. Moreover, `eris:db` uses the ECDSA `ed22519` curve scheme whereas Ethereum uses the `secp256k1` algorithm. Finally, it is permissioned with an access control layer on top whereas Ethereum is a public blockchain.

Eris is a feature-rich application platform that offers a large selection of toolkits and services to develop blockchain-based applications.

It is available at `https://monax.io/`.

Summary

This chapter started with the introduction of alternative blockchains and is divided into two main sections discussing blockchains and platforms. Blockchain technology is a very thriving area, as such changes are quite rapid in existing solutions and new relevant technologies or tools are being introduced almost every day. In this chapter, a careful selection of platforms and blockchains was introduced. Several solutions were considered that complement material covered in previous chapters, for example, Eris, which supports blockchain development. New blockchains such as Kadena, various new protocols such as Ripple, and concepts such as sidechains and drivechains were also discussed.

The material covered in this chapter is intended to provide a strong foundation for more in-depth research into areas that readers are interested in. As said before, blockchain is a very fast-moving field, and there are many other blockchain proposals projects such as Tau-Chain, HydraChain, Elements, CREDITS, and many more that have not been discussed in this chapter. Readers are encouraged to keep an eye on the developments in this field to keep themselves up to date with advancement in this rapidly growing area.

In the next chapter, we will explore that how blockchain can be used out of its original usage, that is, cryptocurrencies. We will cover various use cases and especially usage of blockchain in IoT.

15
Blockchain - Outside of Currencies

Digital currencies were the first-ever application of blockchain technology, arguably without realizing its real potential. With the invention of Bitcoin, the concept of blockchain was introduced for the very first time, but it was not until 2013 that the true potential of blockchain technology was realized with its possible application in many different industries, other than cryptocurrencies. Since then many use cases of blockchain technology in various industries have been proposed, including but not limited to finance, the Internet of Things, digital rights management, government, and law.

In this chapter, four main industries namely the Internet of Things, government, health, and finance, have been selected, with the aid of use cases, for discussion.

In 2010, discussion started regarding BitDNS, a decentralized naming system for domains on the internet. Then Namecoin (`https://wiki.namecoin.org/index.php?title=History`) started in April 2011 with a different vision as compared to Bitcoin whose sole purpose is to provision electronic cash. This can be considered first example of blockchain usage other than purely cryptocurrencies.
After this by 2013, many ideas emerged. Since 2013 this trend is growing exponentially.

Internet of Things

The **Internet of Things (IoT)** for short has recently gained much traction due to its potential for transforming business applications and everyday life. IoT can be defined as a network of computationally intelligent physical objects (any object such as cars, fridges, industrial sensors, and so on) that are capable of connecting to the internet, sensing real-world events or environments, reacting to those events, collecting relevant data, and communicating it over the internet.

This simple definition has enormous implications and has led to exciting concepts, such as wearables, smart homes, smart grids, smart connected cars, and smart cities, that are all based on this basic concept of an IoT device. After dissecting the definition of IoT, four functions come to light as being performed by an IoT device. These include **sensing, reacting, collecting**, and **communicating**. All these functions are performed by using various components on the IoT device.

Sensing is performed by sensors. Reacting or controlling is performed by actuators, the collection is a function of various sensors, and communication is performed by chips that provide network connectivity. One thing to note is that all these components are accessible and controllable via the internet in the IoT. An IoT device on its own is perhaps useful to some extent, but if it is part of a broader IoT ecosystem, it is more valuable.

A typical IoT can consist of many physical objects connecting with each other and to a centralized cloud server. This is shown in the following diagram:

A typical IoT network

Source: IBM

Elements of IoT are spread across multiple layers, and various reference architectures exist that can be used to develop IoT systems. A five-layer model can be used to describe IoT, which contains a physical object layer, device layer, network layer, services layer, and application layer. Each layer or level is responsible for various functions and includes multiple components. These are shown in the following diagram:

| Application Layer |
| Transportation, financial, insurance and many others |
| Management Layer |
| Data processing, analytics, security management |
| Network Layer |
| LAN, WAN, PAN, Routers |
| Device Layer |
| Sensors , Actuators, smart devices |
| Physical Objects |
| People, cars, homes etc. etc. |

IoT five-layer model

Now we will examine each layer in detail.

Physical object layer

These include any real-world physical objects. It includes people, animals, cars, trees, fridges, trains, factories, homes, and in fact anything that is required to be monitored and controlled can be connected to the IoT.

Device layer

This layer contains things that make up the IoT such as sensors, transducers, actuators, smartphones, smart devices, and **Radio-Frequency Identification** (**RFID**) tags. There can be many categories of sensors such as body sensors, home sensors, and environmental sensors based on the type of work they perform. This layer is the core of an IoT ecosystem where various sensors are used to sense real-world environments. This layer includes sensors that can monitor temperature, humidity, liquid flow, chemicals, air, pressure, and much more. Usually, an **Analog to Digital Converter** (**ADC**) is required on a device to turn the real-world analog signal into a digital signal that a microprocessor can understand.

Actuators in this layer provide the means to enable control of external environments, for example, starting a motor or opening a door. These components also require digital to analog converters to convert a digital signal into analog. This method is especially relevant when control of a mechanical component is required by the IoT device.

Network layer

This layer is composed of various network devices that are used to provide Internet connectivity between devices and to the cloud or servers that are part of the IoT ecosystem. These devices can include gateways, routers, hubs, and switches. This layer can include two types of communication.

First there is the horizontal means of communication, which includes radio, Bluetooth, Wi-Fi, Ethernet, LAN, Zigbee, and PAN and can be used to provide communication between IoT devices. Second, we have communication to the next layer, which is usually through the internet and provides communication between machines and people or other upper layers. The first layer can optionally be included in the device layer as it physically is residing on the device layer where devices can communicate with each other at the same layer.

Management layer

This layer provides the management layer for the IoT ecosystem. This includes platforms that enable processing of data gathered from the IoT devices and turn that into meaningful insights. Also, device management, security management, and data flow management are included in this layer. It also manages communication between the device and application layers.

Application layer

This layer includes applications running on top of the IoT network. This layer can consist of many applications depending on the requirements such as transportation, healthcare, financial, insurance, or supply chain management. This list, of course, is not an exhaustive list by any stretch of the imagination; there is a myriad of IoT applications that can fall into this layer.

With the availability of cheap sensors, hardware, and bandwidth, IoT has gained popularity in recent years and currently has applications in many different areas including healthcare, insurance, supply chain management, home automation, industrial automation, and infrastructure management. Moreover, advancements in technology such as the availability of IPv6, smaller and powerful processors, and better internet access have also played a vital role in the popularity of IoT.

The benefits of IoT range from cost saving to enabling businesses to make vital decisions and thus improve performance based on the data provided by the IoT devices. Even in domestic usage IoT equipped home appliances can provide valuable data for cost saving. For example, smart meters for energy monitoring can provide valuable information on how the energy is being used and can convey that back to the service provider. Raw data from millions of things (IoT devices) is analyzed and provides meaningful insights that help in making timely and efficient business decisions.

The usual IoT model is based on a centralized paradigm where IoT devices usually connect to a cloud infrastructure or central servers to report and process the relevant data back. This centralization poses certain possibilities of exploitation including hacking and data theft. Moreover, not having control of personal data on a single, centralized service provider also increases the possibility of security and privacy issues. While there are methods and techniques to build a highly secure IoT ecosystem based on the normal IoT model, there are specific much more desirable benefits that blockchain can bring to IoT. A blockchain-based IoT model differs from the traditional IoT network paradigm.

According to IBM, blockchain for IoT can help to build trust, reduce costs, and accelerate transactions. Additionally, decentralization, which is at the very core of blockchain technology, can eliminate single points of failure in an IoT network. For example, a central server perhaps is not able to cope with the amount of data that billions of IoT devices (things) are producing at high frequency. Also, the peer-to-peer communication model provided by blockchain can help to reduce costs because there is no need to build high-cost centralized data centers or implementation of complex public key infrastructure for security. Devices can communicate with each other directly or via routers.

As an estimate of various researchers and companies, by 2020 there will be roughly 22 billion devices connected to the internet. With this explosion of billions of devices connecting to the internet, it is hard to imagine that centralized infrastructures will be able to cope with the high demands of bandwidth, services, and availability without incurring excessive expenditure. Blockchain-based IoT will be able to solve scalability, privacy, and reliability issues in the current IoT model.

Blockchain enables *things* to communicate and transact with each other directly and with the availability of smart contracts, negotiation, and financial transactions can also occur directly between the devices instead of requiring an intermediary, authority, or human intervention. For example, if a room in a hotel is vacant, it can rent itself out, negotiate the rent, and can open the door lock for a human who has paid the right amount of funds. Another example could be that if a washing machine runs out of detergent, it could order it online after finding the best price and value based on the logic programmed in its smart contract.

The aforementioned five-layer IoT model can be adapted to a blockchain-based model by adding a blockchain layer on top of the network layer. This layer will run smart contracts, and provide security, privacy, integrity, autonomy, scalability, and decentralization services to the IoT ecosystem. The management layer, in this case, can consist of only software related to analytics and processing, and security and control can be moved to the blockchain layer. This model can be visualized in the following diagram:

Application Layer
Transportation, financial, insurance and many others
Management Layer
Data processing, analytics
Blockchain Layer
Security, P2P (M2M) autonomous transactions, decentralization, smart contracts
Network Layer
LAN, WAN, PAN, Routers
Device Layer
Sensors , Actuators, smart devices
Physical Objects
People, cars, homes etc. etc.

Blockchain-based IoT model

In this model, other layers would perhaps remain the same, but an additional blockchain layer will be introduced as a middleware between all participants of the IoT network.

It can also be visualized as a peer-to-peer IoT network after abstracting away all the layers mentioned earlier. This model is shown in the following diagram where all devices are communicating and negotiating with each other without a central command and control entity:

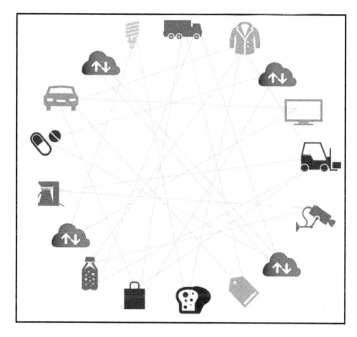

Blockchain-based direct communication model, source: IBM

It can also result in cost saving which is due to easier device management by using a blockchain based decentralized approach. The IoT network can be optimized for performance by using blockchain. In this case, there will be no need to store IoT data centrally for millions of devices because storage and processing requirements can be distributed to all IoT devices on the blockchain. This can result in completely removing the need for large data centers for processing and storing the IoT data.

Blockchain-based IoT can also thwart denial of service attacks where hackers can target a centralized server or data center more efficiently, but with blockchain's distributed and decentralized nature, such attacks are no longer possible. Additionally, if as estimated there will be billions of devices connected to the internet soon, it will become almost impossible to manage security and updates of all those devices from traditional centrally-owned servers. Blockchain can provide a solution to this problem by allowing devices to communicate with each other directly in a secure manner and even request firmware and security updates from each other. On a blockchain network, these communications can be recorded immutably and securely which will provide auditability, integrity, and transparency to the system. This mechanism is not possible with traditional peer-to-peer systems.

In summary, there are clear benefits that can be reaped with the convergence of IoT and blockchain and a lot of research and work in academia and industry are already in progress. There are various projects already proposed providing blockchain-based IoT solutions. For example, IBM Blue Horizon and IBM Bluemix are IoT platforms supporting blockchain IoT platforms. Various start-ups such as Filament have already proposed novel ideas on how to build a decentralized network that enables devices on IoT to transact with each other directly and autonomously driven by smart contracts.

In the following section, a practical example is provided on how to build a simple IoT device and connect it to the Ethereum blockchain. This IoT device is connected to the Ethereum blockchain and is used to open a door (in this case the door lock is represented by an LED) when the appropriate amount of funds is sent by a user on the blockchain. This is a simple example and requires a more rigorously-tested version to implement it in production, but it demonstrates how an IoT device can be connected, controlled, and responded to in response to certain events on an Ethereum blockchain.

IoT blockchain experiment

This example makes use of a Raspberry Pi device which is a **Single Board Computer** (**SBC**). The Raspberry Pi is a SBC developed as a low-cost computer to promote computer education but has also gained much more popularity as a tool of choice for building IoT platforms. A Raspberry Pi 3 Model B is shown in the following picture. You may be able to use earlier models too, but those have not been tested:

Raspberry Pi Model B

In the following section, an example will be discussed where a Raspberry Pi will be used as an IoT device connected to the Ethereum blockchain and will act in response to a smart contract invocation.

First, the Raspberry Pi needs to be set up. This can be done by using NOOBS which provides an easy method of installing Raspbian or any other operating system.

This can be downloaded and installed from the link `https://www.raspberrypi.org/downloads/noobs/`.
Alternatively, only Raspbian can be installed from the link `https://www.raspberrypi.org/downloads/raspbian/`.
Another alternative available at `https://github.com/debian-pi/raspbian-ua-netinst` can also be used to install a minimal non-GUI version of Raspbian OS.

For this example, NOOBS has been used to install Raspbian, as such the rest of the exercise assumes Raspbian is installed on the SD memory card of the Raspberry Pi. The command output in the following screenshot shows that which architecture the operating system is running on. In this case, it is `armv71`; therefore ARM-compatible binary for Geth will be downloaded.

The platform can be confirmed by running the command `uname -a` in a terminal window in Raspberry Pi Raspbian operating system.

```
                              pi@raspberrypi: ~
 File  Edit  Tabs  Help
pi@raspberrypi:~ $ uname -a
Linux raspberrypi 4.4.34-v7+ #930 SMP Wed Nov 23 15:20:41 GMT 2016 armv71 GNU/Linux
pi@raspberrypi:~ $ █
```

Raspberry Pi architecture

Once the Raspbian operating system is installed, the next step is to download the appropriate Geth binary for the Raspberry Pi ARM platform.

The download and installation steps are described in detail:

1. Geth download. Note that in the following example a specific version is downloaded however other versions are available which can be downloaded from `https://geth.ethereum.org/downloads/`.

   We can use `wget`, to download the `geth` client images:

   ```
   $ wget https://gethstore.blob.core.windows.net/builds/geth-linux-
   arm7-1.5.6-2a609af5.tar.gz
   ```

    Other versions are also available, but it's recommended that you download this version, as this is the one that has been used in examples in this chapter.

2. Unzip and extract into a directory. The directory named `geth-linux-arm7-1.5.6-2a609af5` will be created automatically with the `tar` command shown next:

```
$ tar -zxvf geth-linux-arm7-1.5.6-2a609af5.tar
```

This command will create a directory named `geth-linux-arm7-1.5.6-2a609af5` and will extract the Geth binary and related files into that directory. The Geth binary can be copied into `/usr/bin` or the appropriate path on Raspbian to make it available from anywhere in the operating system. When the download is finished, the next step is to create the genesis block.

3. A genesis block needs to be used . The genesis file can be copied from the other node on the network. This is shown in the following screenshot. Alternatively, an entirely new genesis block can be generated.

```
{
        "nonce": "0x0000000000000042",
        "timestamp": "0x00",
        "parentHash":
"0x0000000000000000000000000000000000000000000000000000000000000000",
        "extraData": "0x00",
        "gasLimit": "0x8000000",
        "difficulty": "0x0400",
        "mixhash":
"0x0000000000000000000000000000000000000000000000000000000000000000",
        "coinbase": "0x3333333333333333333333333333333333333333",
        "alloc": {
        },
        "config": {
            "chainId": 786,
            "homesteadBlock": 0,
            "eip155Block": 0,
            "eip158Block": 0
        }
    }
```

4. Once the `genesis.json` file is copied onto the Raspberry Pi; the following command can be run to generate the genesis block. It is important that the same genesis block is used that was generated previously otherwise the nodes will effectively be running on separate networks:

```
$ ./geth init genesis.json
```

This will show the output similar to the one shown in the following screenshot:

```
pi@raspberrypi:~/geth-linux-arm7-1.5.6-2a609af5 $ ./geth init genesis.json
I0110 23:37:15.714795 cmd/utils/flags.go:612] WARNING: No etherbase set and no accounts found as default
I0110 23:37:15.715283 ethdb/database.go:83] Allotted 128MB cache and 1024 file handles to /home/pi/.ethereum/geth/chaindata
I0110 23:37:15.794383 ethdb/database.go:176] closed db:/home/pi/.ethereum/geth/chaindata
I0110 23:37:15.794723 ethdb/database.go:83] Allotted 128MB cache and 1024 file handles to /home/pi/.ethereum/geth/chaindata
I0110 23:37:15.923300 core/genesis.go:93] Genesis block already in chain. Writing canonical number
I0110 23:37:15.923895 cmd/geth/chaincmd.go:131] successfully wrote genesis block and/or chain rule set: f2b2ffed01907a845a01d1dea21e5a
ec021e8e68b5ec9ffccb82df
```

Initialize genesis file

5. After genesis block creation, there is a need to add peers to the network. This can be achieved by creating a file named `static-nodes.json`, which contains the enode ID of the peer that `geth` on the Raspberry Pi will connect for syncing:

```
pi@raspberrypi:~/.ethereum $ cat static-nodes.json
[
"enode://44352ede5b9e792e437c1c0431c1578ce3676a87e1f588434aff1299d30325c233c8d426fc
57a25380481c8a36fb3be2787375e932fb4885885f6452f6efa77f@192.168.0.19:30301"
]
```

Static nodes configuration

This information can be obtained from the Geth JavaScript console by running the following command, and this command should be run on the peer to which Raspberry Pi is going to connect:

```
> admin.nodeInfo
```

This will show the output similar to the one shown in the following screenshot:

```
> admin.nodeInfo
{
  enode: "enode://44352ede5b9e792e437c1c0431c1578ce3676a87e1f588434aff1299d30325c233c8d426fc57a25380481c8a36fb3
87375e932fb4885885f6452f6efa77f@[::]:30301",
  id: "44352ede5b9e792e437c1c0431c1578ce3676a87e1f588434aff1299d30325c233c8d426fc57a25380481c8a36fb3be2787375e9
4885885f6452f6efa77f",
```

geth nodeInfo

After this step, further instructions presented in the following sections can be followed to connect Raspberry Pi to the other node on the private network. In the example, the Raspberry Pi will be connected to the network ID `786`. The key is to use the same genesis file created previously and different port numbers. Same genesis file will ensure that clients connect to the same network in which the genesis file originated from.

Different ports are not a strict requirement, however, if the two nodes are running under a private network and access from an environment external to the network is required then a combination of DMZ, router and port forwarding will be used. Therefore, it is recommended to use different TCP ports to allow port forwarding to work correctly. The --identity switch shown in the following command for first node set up, which hasn't been introduced previously, allows for an identifying name to be specified for the node.

First node setup

First, the `geth` client needs to be started on the first node using the following command:

```
$ geth --datadir .ethereum/privatenet/ --networkid 786 --maxpeers 5 --rpc --
 rpcapi web3,eth,debug,personal,net --rpcport 9001 --rpccorsdomain "*" --
 port 30301 --identity "drequinox"
```

This will give the output similar to the following:

```
imran@drequinox-OP7010:~$ geth --datadir .ethereum/privatenet/ --networkid 786 --maxpeers 5 --rpc --rp
capi web3,eth,debug,personal,net --rpcport 9001 --rpccorsdomain "*" --port 30301 --identity "drequinox
"
I0110 23:26:46.032878 ethdb/database.go:83] Allotted 128MB cache and 1024 file handles to /home/imran/
.ethereum/privatenet/geth/chaindata
I0110 23:26:46.072986 ethdb/database.go:176] closed db:/home/imran/.ethereum/privatenet/geth/chaindata
I0110 23:26:46.073243 node/node.go:175] instance: Geth/drequinox/v1.5.2-stable-c8695209/linux/go1.7.3
I0110 23:26:46.073258 ethdb/database.go:83] Allotted 128MB cache and 1024 file handles to /home/imran/
.ethereum/privatenet/geth/chaindata
I0110 23:26:46.082654 eth/backend.go:193] Protocol Versions: [63 62], Network Id: 786
I0110 23:26:46.083188 core/blockchain.go:214] Last header: #7991 [999c534f...] TD=11652654509
I0110 23:26:46.083203 core/blockchain.go:215] Last block: #7991 [999c534f...] TD=11652654509
I0110 23:26:46.083210 core/blockchain.go:216] Fast block: #7991 [999c534f...] TD=11652654509
I0110 23:26:46.083929 p2p/server.go:336] Starting Server
I0110 23:26:48.239776 p2p/discover/udp.go:217] Listening, enode://44352ede5b9e792e437c1c0431c1578ce367
6a87e1f588434aff1299d30325c233c8d426fc57a25380481c8a36fb3be2787375e932fb4885885f6452f6efa77f@[::]:3030
1
I0110 23:26:48.239893 p2p/server.go:604] Listening on [::]:30301
I0110 23:26:48.240913 node/node.go:340] IPC endpoint opened: /home/imran/.ethereum/privatenet/geth.ipc
I0110 23:26:48.241212 node/node.go:410] HTTP endpoint opened: http://localhost:9001
I0110 23:42:58.206205 eth/backend.go:479] Automatic pregeneration of ethash DAG ON (ethash dir: /home/
imran/.ethash)
I0110 23:42:58.206217 miner/miner.go:136] Starting mining operation (CPU=8 TOT=9)
```

geth on first node

Once this is started up, it should be kept running, and another `geth` instance should be started from the Raspberry Pi node.

Raspberry Pi node setup

On Raspberry Pi, the following command is required to be run to start `geth` and to sync it with other nodes (in this case only one node). The following is the command:

```
$ ./geth --networkid 786 --maxpeers 5 --rpc --rpcapi
web3,eth,debug,personal,net --rpccorsdomain "*" --port 30302 --identity
"raspberry"
```

This should produce the output similar to the one shown in the following screenshot. When the output contains the row displaying `Block synchronisation started` it means that the node has connected successfully to its peer.

```
pi@raspberrypi:~/geth-linux-arm7-1.5.6-2a609af5 $ ./geth  --networkid 786 --maxpeers 5 --rpc --rpcapi web3,eth,debug,personal,net --
 --rpccorsdomain "*" --port 30302 --identity "raspberry"
I0110 23:38:04.654374 cmd/utils/flags.go:612] WARNING: No etherbase set and no accounts found as default
I0110 23:38:04.654776 ethdb/database.go:83] Allotted 128MB cache and 1024 file handles to /home/pi/.ethereum/geth/chaindata
I0110 23:38:04.693111 ethdb/database.go:176] closed db:/home/pi/.ethereum/geth/chaindata
I0110 23:38:04.696937 node/node.go:176] instance: Geth/raspberry/v1.5.6-stable-2a609af5/linux/go1.7.4
I0110 23:38:04.697042 ethdb/database.go:83] Allotted 128MB cache and 1024 file handles to /home/pi/.ethereum/geth/chaindata
I0110 23:38:04.847835 eth/backend.go:191] Protocol Versions: [63 62], Network Id: 786
I0110 23:38:04.849753 eth/backend.go:219] Chain config: {ChainID: 0 Homestead: <nil> DAO: <nil> DAOSupport: false EIP150: <nil> EIP1
P158: <nil>}
I0110 23:38:04.857847 core/blockchain.go:216] Last header: #2668 [6776ef24..] TD=708187563
I0110 23:38:04.858174 core/blockchain.go:217] Last block: #2668 [6776ef24..] TD=708187563
I0110 23:38:04.858349 core/blockchain.go:218] Fast block: #2668 [6776ef24..] TD=708187563
I0110 23:38:04.866705 p2p/server.go:340] Starting Server
I0110 23:38:10.223170 p2p/discover/udp.go:227] Listening, enode://98ba36ecea7ff011803d634da45752abd25101f20a62f23427afc3f280017bc134
b195ac6ed59c3b01ca2a3f14638a52697a1bb1bf967fc84274@86.15.44.209:30302
I0110 23:38:10.224031 p2p/server.go:608] Listening on [::]:30302
I0110 23:38:10.233788 node/node.go:341] IPC endpoint opened: /home/pi/.ethereum/geth.ipc
I0110 23:38:10.237027 node/node.go:411] HTTP endpoint opened: http://localhost:9002
I0110 23:38:20.225637 eth/downloader/downloader.go:326] Block synchronisation started
I0110 23:38:49.583631 core/blockchain.go:1067] imported 1 blocks,     0 txs (  0.000 Mg) in   14.018s ( 0.000 Mg/s). #2669 [76077955
I0110 23:38:49.622191 core/blockchain.go:1067] imported 5 blocks,     0 txs (  0.000 Mg) in  38.520ms ( 0.000 Mg/s). #2674 [76077955
```

geth on the Raspberry Pi.

This can be further verified by running commands in the `geth` console on both nodes as shown in the following screenshot. The `geth` client can be attached by simply running the following command on the Raspberry Pi:

```
$ geth attach
```

This will open the JavaScript `geth` console for interacting with the `geth` node. We can use `admin.peers` command to see the connected peers:

```
> admin.peers
[{
    caps: ["eth/62", "eth/63"],
    id: "44352ede5b9e792e437c1c0431c1578ce3676a87e1f588434aff1299d30325c233c8d426fc57a25380481c8a36fb3be2787375e932f
b4885885f6452f6efa77f",
    name: "Geth/drequinox/v1.5.2-stable-c8695209/linux/go1.7.3",
    network: {
      localAddress: "192.168.0.21:56550",
      remoteAddress: "192.168.0.19:30301"
    },
    protocols: {
      eth: {
        difficulty: 11719415397,
        head: "0x2d32c90b4c9dacea9a109b0ae52c1ebf511915bb618a2d3c55a80a63852e89f6",
        version: 63
      }
    }
}]_
```

geth console admin peers command running on Raspberry Pi

Similarly, we can attach to the `geth` instance by running the following command on the first node:

```
$ geth attach ipc:.ethereum/privatenet/geth.ipc
```

Once the console is available `admin.peers` can be run to reveal the details about other connected nodes as shown in the following screenshot:

```
> admin.peers
[{
    caps: ["eth/62", "eth/63"],
    id: "98ba36ecea7ff01803d634da45752abd25101f20a62f23427afc3f280017bc134833dd5ba400bb195ac6ed59c3b01
ca2a3f14638a52697a1bb1bf967fc84274",
    name: "Geth/raspberry/v1.5.6-stable-2a609af5/linux/go1.7.4",
    network: {
      localAddress: "192.168.0.19:30301",
      remoteAddress: "192.168.0.21:56512"
    },
    protocols: {
      eth: {
        difficulty: 11700186157,
        head: "0x1188f58b4900a1d771d333141ea9408d78400bb8e561494ab436519ae64e1e34",
        version: 63
      }
    }
}]
```

geth console admin peers command running on the other peer

Once both nodes are up-and-running further prerequisites can be installed to set up the experiment. Installation of Node.js and the relevant JavaScript libraries is required.

Installing Node.js

The required libraries and dependencies are listed here. First Node.js and npm need to be updated on the Raspberry Pi Raspbian operating system. For this the following steps can be followed:

1. Install latest Node.js on the Raspberry Pi using the following command:

   ```
   $ curl -sL https://deb.nodesource.com/setup_7.x | sudo -E bash -
   ```

   This should display output similar to the following. The output is quite large therefore only the top part of the output is shown in the following screenshot:

Node.js installation

2. Run the update via `apt-get`:

   ```
   $ sudo apt-get install nodejs
   ```

   Verification can be performed by running the following command to ensure that the correct versions of Node.js and npm are installed, as shown in the following screenshot:

npm and node installation verification

It should be noted that these versions are not a necessity; any of the latest version of npm and Node.js should work. However, the examples in this chapter make use of npm 4.0.5 and node v7.4.0, so it is recommended that readers use the same version in order to avoid any compatibility issues.

3. Install Ethereum `web3` npm, which is required to enable JavaScript code to access the Ethereum blockchain:

 Make sure that specific version of `web3` shown in the screenshot is installed or a version similar to this for example 0.20.2. This is important because by default version 1.0.0-beta.26 (at the time of writing) will be installed which is beta and is under development. Therefore `web3` 0.20.2 or 0.18.0 stable version should be used for this example. Readers can install this version by using `$ npm install web3@0.20.2`.

```
pi@raspberrypi:~/testled $ npm install web3
testled@1.0.0 /home/pi/testled
└─ web3@0.18.0
   └─ bignumber.js@2.0.7  (git+https://github.com/debris/bignumber.js.git#94d7146671b9719e00a09c29b01a691bc85048c2)

npm WARN testled@1.0.0 No repository field.
pi@raspberrypi:~/testled $
```

npm install web3

4. Similarly, npm `onoff` can be installed, which is required to communicate with the Raspberry Pi and control GPIO:

```
$ npm install onoff
```

```
pi@raspberrypi:~/testled $ npm install onoff --save
testled@1.0.0 /home/pi/testled
└─ onoff@1.1.1

npm WARN testled@1.0.0 No repository field.
pi@raspberrypi:~/testled $
```

Onoff installation

When all the prerequisites are installed, hardware setup can be performed. For this purpose, a simple circuit is built using a breadboard and a few electronic components.

The hardware components are listed as follows:

- **LED**: The abbreviation of **Light Emitting Diode**, this can be used as a visual indication for an event.
- **Resistor**: A 330 ohm component is required which provides resistance to passing current based on its rating. It is not necessary to understand the theory behind it for this experiment; any standard electronics engineering text covers all these topics in detail.

- **Breadboard**: This provides a means of building an electronic circuit without requiring soldering.
- **T-Shaped cobbler**: This is inserted on the breadboard as shown in the following photo and provides a labeled view of all **General Purpose I/O** (**GPIO**) pins for the Raspberry Pi.
- **Ribbon cable connector**: This is simply used to provide connectivity between the Raspberry Pi and the breadboard via GPIO. All these components are shown in the following picture:

Required components

Circuit

As shown in the following picture, the positive leg (long leg) of the LED is connected to pin number **21** of the GPIO, and the negative (short leg) is connected to the resistor, which is then connected to the **ground** (**GND**) pin of the GPIO. Once the connections are set up the ribbon cable can be used to connect to the GPIO connector on the Raspberry Pi simply.

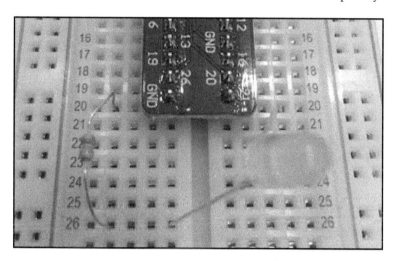

Connections for components on the breadboard

Once the connections are set up correctly, and the Raspberry Pi has been updated with the appropriate libraries and Geth, the next step is to develop a simple, smart contract that expects a value. If the value provided to it is not what it expects it does not trigger an event; otherwise if the value passed matches the correct value, the event triggers which can be read by the client JavaScript program running via Node.js. Of course, the Solidity contract can be very complicated and can also deal with the Ether sent to it, and if the amount of Ether is equal to the required amount, then the event can trigger. However, in this example, the aim is to demonstrate the usage of smart contracts to trigger events that can then be read by JavaScript program running on Node.js, which then, in turn, can trigger actions on IoT devices using various libraries.

The smart contract source code is shown as follows:

```
1   pragma solidity ^0.4.0;
2 ▾ contract simpleIOT {
3       uint roomrent = 10;
4       event roomRented(bool returnValue);
5 ▾     function getRent (uint8 x) public returns (bool) {
6 ▾         if (x==roomrent) {
7               roomRented(true);
8               return true;
9           }
10      }
11  }
```

Solidity code for simple IOT

The online Solidity compiler (Remix IDE) can be used to run and test this contract. The **Application Binary Interface (ABI)** required for interacting with the contract is also available in the **Details** section as shown in the following screenshot:

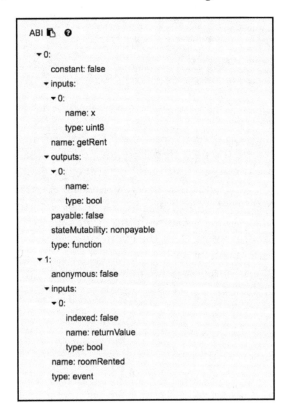

ABI from Remix IDE

The following is the ABI of the contract:

```
[
    {
        "constant": false,
        "inputs": [
            {
                "name": "x",
                "type": "uint8"
            }
        ],
        "name": "getRent",
        "outputs": [
            {
                "name": "",
                "type": "bool"
            }
        ],
        "payable": false,
        "stateMutability": "nonpayable",
        "type": "function"
    },
    {

        "anonymous": false,
        "inputs": [
            {
                "indexed": false,
                "name": "returnValue",
                "type": "bool"
            }
        ],
        "name": "roomRented",
        "type": "event"
    }
]
```

There are two methods by which the Raspberry Pi node can connect to the private blockchain via the web3 interface. The first is where the Raspberry Pi device is running its own geth client locally and maintains its ledger, but with resource-constrained devices, it is not possible to run a full geth node or even a light node in a few circumstances. In that case, the second method, which uses web3 provider can be used to connect to the appropriate RPC channel. This will be shown later in the client JavaScript Node.js program.

A comparison of both of these approaches is shown in the following diagram:

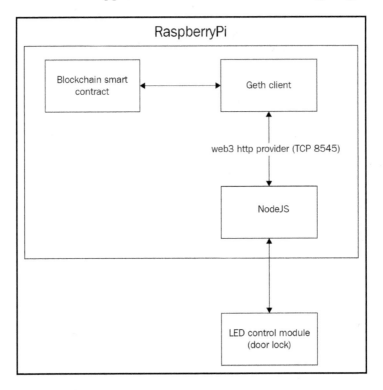

Application architecture of room rent IoT application (IoT device with local ledger)

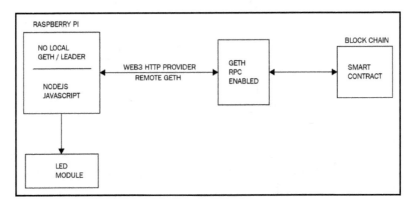

Application architecture of room rent IoT application (IoT device without local ledger)

There are obvious security concerns which arise from exposing RPC interfaces publicly; therefore, it is recommended that this option is used only on private networks and if required to be used on public networks appropriate security measures are put in place, such as allowing only the known IP addresses to connect to the geth RPC interface. This can be achieved by a combination of disabling peer discovery mechanisms and HTTP-RPC server listening interfaces.

More information about this can be found using geth help. The traditional network security measures such as firewalls, **Transport Layer Security** (**TLS**) and certificates can also be used but have not been discussed in this example. Now Truffle can be used to deploy the contract on the private network ID 786 to which at this point the Raspberry Pi is connected. Truffle deploy can be performed simply by using the following shown command;

```
$ truffle migrate
```

It should produce the output similar to the following screenshot:

```
imran@drequinox-OP7010:~/iotcontract$ truffle migrate --reset
Running Migration: 1_initial_migration.js
  Deploying Migrations...
  Migrations: 0xdd8a88072aa4ff49b62c25d6f6f2207b731aee76
Saving successful migration to network...
Saving artifacts...
Running migration: 2_deploy_contracts.js
  Deploying simpleIOT...
  simpleIOT: 0x151ce17c28b20ce554e0d944deb30e0447fbf78d
Saving successful migration to network...
Saving artifacts...
```

Truffle deploy

Once the contract is deployed correctly, JavaScript code can be developed that will connect to the blockchain via web3, listen for the events from the smart contract in the blockchain, and turn the LED on via the Raspberry Pi. The JavaScript code of the index.js file is shown as follows:

```
var Web3 = require('web3');
if (typeof web3 !== 'undefined')
{
    web3 = new Web3(web3.currentProvider);
}else
{
    web3 = new Web3(new
Web3.providers.HttpProvider("http://localhost:9002"));
    //http-rpc-port
```

```
    }
var Gpio = require('onoff').Gpio;
var led = new Gpio(21,'out');
var coinbase = web3.eth.coinbase;
var ABIString =
'[{"constant":false,"inputs":[{"name":"x","type":"uint8"}],"name":"getRent"
,"outputs":[{"name":"","type":"bool"}],"payable":false,"stateMutability":"n
onpayable","type":"function"},{"anonymous":false,"inputs":[{"indexed":false
,"name":"returnValue","type":"bool"}],"name":"roomRented","type":"event"}]'
;
var ABI = JSON.parse(ABIString);
var ContractAddress = '0x975881c44fbef4573fef33cccec1777a8f76669c';
web3.eth.defaultAccount = web3.eth.accounts[0];
var simpleiot = web3.eth.contract(ABI).at(ContractAddress);
var event = simpleiot.roomRented( {}, function(error, result) { if (!error)
{
    console.log("LED On");
    led.writeSync(1);
}
});
```

Note that in the preceding example the contract address
`'0x975881c44fbef4573fef33cccec1777a8f76669c'` for variable `var`
`ContractAddress` is specific to the deployment and it will be different when readers run this example. Simply change the address in the file to what you see after deploying the contract.

Also, note that the HTTP-RPC server listening port on which Geth has been started on Raspberry Pi. By default, it is TCP port `8545`. Remember to change this according to your Raspberry Pi setup and Geth configuration. It is set to `9002` in the preceding example code because Geth running on Raspberry Pi is listening on `9002` in the example. If it's listening to a different port on your Raspberry Pi, then change it to that port:

```
web3 = new Web3(new Web3.providers.HttpProvider("http://localhost:9002"));
```

When Geth starts up it shown which port it has HTTP endpoint listening on. This is also configurable with `--rpcport` in `geth` by specifying the port number value as a parameter to the flag.

This JavaScript code can be placed in a file on the Raspberry Pi, for example, `index.js`. It can be run by using the following command:

```
$ node index.js
```

This will start the program, which will run on Node.js and listen for events from the smart contract. Once the program is running correctly, the smart contract can be invoked by using the Truffle console as shown in the following screenshot.

In this case, the getRent function is called with parameter 10, which is the expected value:

```
truffle(development)> simpleiot.getRent(10)
'0x71f550949a4c5168af7b9f7f84fada99bccc20a123779642e5e8c0c0127266ee'
```

Interaction with the contract

After the contract is mined, roomRented will be triggered, which will turn on the LED.

In this example, it is a simple LED, but it can be any physical device such as a room lock that can be controlled via an actuator. If all works well, the LED will be turned on as a result of the smart contract function invocation as shown in the following picture:

Raspberry Pi with LED control

Also, on node side it will display output similar to the one shown here:

```
$ node index.js
LED On
```

As demonstrated in the preceding example, a private network of IoT devices can be built that runs a `geth` client on each of the nodes and can listen for events from smart contracts and trigger an action accordingly. The example shown is simple on purpose but demonstrates the underlying principles of an Ethereum network that can be built using IoT devices along with smart contract-driven control of the physical devices.

In the next section, other applications of the blockchain technology in government, finance, and health will be discussed.

Government

There are various applications of blockchain being researched currently that can support government functions and take the current model of e-government to the next level. First, in this section, some background for e-government will be provided, and then a few use cases such as e-voting, homeland security (border control), and electronic IDs (citizen ID cards) will be discussed.

Government or electronic government is a paradigm where information and communication technology are used to deliver public services to citizens. The concept is not new and has been implemented in various countries around the world, but with blockchain, a new avenue of exploration has opened up. Many governments are researching the possibility of using blockchain technology for managing and delivering public services including but not limited to identity cards, driving licenses, secure data sharing among various government departments and contract management. Transparency, auditability, and integrity are attributes of blockchain that can go a long way in effectively managing various government functions.

Border control

Automated border control systems have been in use for decades now to thwart illegal entry into countries and prevent terrorism and human trafficking.

Machine-readable travel documents and specifically biometric passports have paved the way for automated border control; however current systems are limited to a certain extent and blockchain technology can provide solutions. A **Machine Readable Travel Document (MRTD)** standard is defined in document ICAO 9303 (`https://www.icao.int/publications/pages/publication.aspx?docnum=9303`) by the **International Civil Aviation Organization (ICAO)** and has been implemented by many countries around the world.

Each passport contains various security and identity attributes that can be used to identify the owner of the passport and also circumvent attempts at tampering with the passports. These include biometric features such as retina scan, fingerprints, facial recognition, and standard ICAO specified features including **Machine Readable Zone** (**MRZ**) and other text attributes that are visible on the first page of the passport.

One key issue with current border control systems is data sharing whereby the systems are controlled by a single entity and data is not readily shared among law enforcement agencies. This lack of the ability to share data makes it challenging to track suspected travel documents or individuals. Another issue is related to the immediate implementation of blacklisting of a travel document, for example, when there is an immediate need to track and control suspected travel documents. Currently, there is no mechanism available to blacklist or revoke a suspected passport immediately and broadcast it to the border control ports worldwide.

Blockchain can provide a solution to this problem by maintaining a blacklist in a smart contract which can be updated as required and any changes will be immediately visible to all agencies and border control points thus enabling immediate control over the movement of a suspected travel document. It could be argued that traditional mechanisms like PKIs and peer-to-peer networks can also be used for this purpose, but they do not provide the benefits that a blockchain can provide. With blockchain, the whole system can be simplified without the requirement of complex networks and PKI setups which will also result in cost reduction. Moreover, blockchain based systems will provide cryptographically guaranteed immutability which helps with auditing and discourages any fraudulent activity.

The full database of all travel documents perhaps cannot be stored on the blockchain currently due to scalability issues, but a backend distributed database such as BigchainDB, IPFS, or Swarm can be used for that purpose. In this case, a hash of the travel document with the biometric ID of an individual can be stored in a simple smart contract, and a hash of the document can then be used to refer to the detailed data available on the distributed filesystem such as IPFS. This way, when a travel document is blacklisted anywhere on the network, that information will be available immediately with the cryptographic guarantee of its authenticity and integrity throughout the distributed ledger. This functionality can also provide adequate support in anti-terrorism activities, thus playing a vital role in the homeland security function of a government.

A simple contract in Solidity can have an array defined for storing identities and associated biometric records. This array can be used to store the identifying information about a passport. The identity can be a hash of MRZ of the passport or travel document concatenated with the biometric record from the RFID chip. A simple Boolean field can be used to identify blacklisted passports. Once this initial check passes, further detailed biometric verification can be performed by traditional systems and eventually when a decision is made regarding the entry of the passport holder that decision can be propagated back to the blockchain, thus enabling all participants on the network to immediately share the outcome of the decision.

A high-level approach to building a blockchain-based border control system can be visualized as shown in the following diagram. In this scenario, the passport is presented for scanning to an RFID and page scanner which reads the data page and extracts machine-readable information along with a hash of the biometric data stored in the RFID chip. At this stage, a live photo and retina scan of the passport holder is also taken. This information is then passed on to the blockchain where a smart contract is responsible for verifying the legitimacy of the travel document by first checking its list of blacklisted passports and then requesting more data from the backend IPFS database for comparison. Note that the biometric data such as photo or retina scan is not stored on the blockchain, instead only a reference to this data in the backend (IPFS or BigchainDB) is stored in the blockchain.

If the data from the presented passport matches with what is held in the IPFS as files or in BigchainDB and also pass the smart contract logical check, then the border gate can be opened.

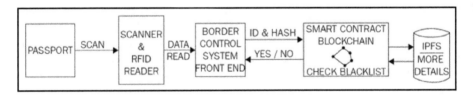

Automated border control using blockchain

After verification, this information is propagated throughout the blockchain and is instantly available to all participants on the border control blockchain. These participants can be a worldwide consortium of homeland security departments of various nations.

Voting

Voting in any government is a key function and allows citizens to participate in the democratic election process. While voting has evolved into a much more mature and secure process, it still has limitations that need to be addressed to achieve a desired level of maturity. Usually, the limitations in current voting systems revolve around fraud, weaknesses in operational processes, and especially transparency. Over the years, secure voting mechanisms (machines) have been built which make use of specialized voting machines that promised security and privacy, but they still had vulnerabilities that could be exploited to subvert the security mechanisms of those machines. These vulnerabilities can lead to serious implications for the whole voting process and can result in mistrust in the government by the public.

Blockchain-based voting systems can resolve these issues by introducing end-to-end security and transparency in the process. Security is provided in the form of integrity and authenticity of votes by using public key cryptography which comes as standard in a blockchain. Moreover, immutability guaranteed by blockchain ensures that votes cast once cannot be cast again. This can be achieved through a combination of biometric features and a smart contract maintaining a list of votes already cast. For example, a smart contract can maintain a list of already casted votes with the biometric ID (for example a fingerprint) and can use that to detect and prevent double casting. Secondly, **Zero-Knowledge Proofs** (**ZKPs**) can also be used on the blockchain to protect voters' privacy on the blockchain.

 Some companies are already providing such services, one example is `https://polys.me/blockchain/online-voting-system`. Recently, presidential elections were held in Sierra Leone using blockchain technology, making it the first country to use blockchain technology for elections (`https://www.coindesk.com/sierra-leone-secretly-holds-first-blockchain-powered-presidential-vote/`).

Citizen identification (ID cards)

Electronic IDs or national ID cards are issued by various countries around the world at present. These cards are secure and possess many security features that thwart duplication or tampering attempts. However, with the advent of blockchain technology, several improvements can be made to this process.

Digital identity is not only limited to just government-issued ID cards; it is a concept that applies to online social networks and forums too. There can be multiple identities used for different purposes. A blockchain-based online digital identity allows control over personal information sharing. Users can see who used their data and for what purpose and can control access to it. This is not possible with the current infrastructures which are centrally controlled. The key benefit is that a single identity issued by the government can be used easily and in a transparent manner for multiple services via a single government blockchain. In this case, the blockchain serves as a platform where a government is providing various services such as pensions, taxation, or benefits and a single ID is being used for accessing all these services. Blockchain, in this case, provides a permanent record of every change and transaction made by a digital ID, thus ensuring integrity and transparency of the system. Also, citizens can notarize birth certificates, marriages, deeds, and many other documents on the blockchain tied with their digital ID as a proof of existence.

Currently, there are successful implementations of identity schemes in various countries that work well, and there is an argument that perhaps blockchain is not required in identity management systems. Although there are several benefits such as privacy and control over the usage of identity information due to the current immaturity of blockchain technology, perhaps it is not ready for use in real-world identity systems. However, research is being carried out by various governments to explore the usage of blockchain for identity management.

Moreover, laws such as the right to be forgotten can be quite difficult to incorporate into blockchain due to its immutable nature.

Miscellaneous

Other government functions where blockchain technology can be implemented to improve cost and efficiency include the collection of taxes, benefits management and disbursement, land ownership record management, life event registration (marriages, births), motor vehicle registration, and licenses. This is not an exhaustive list, and over time many functions and processes of a government can be adapted to a blockchain-based model. The key benefits of blockchain such as immutability, transparency, and decentralization can help to bring improvements to most of the traditional government systems.

Health

The health industry has also been identified as another major industry that can benefit by adapting blockchain technology. Blockchain provides an immutable, auditable, and transparent system that traditional peer-to-peer networks cannot. Also, blockchain provides a cost-effective, simpler infrastructure as compared to traditional complex PKI networks. In healthcare, major issues such as privacy compromises, data breaches, high costs, and fraud can arise from lack of interoperability, overly complex processes, transparency, auditability, and control. Another burning issue is counterfeit medicines; especially in developing countries, this is a major cause of concern.

With the adaptability of blockchain in the health sector, several benefits can be realized, ranging from cost saving, increased trust, faster processing of claims, high availability, no operational errors due to complexity in the operational procedures, and preventing the distribution of counterfeit medicines.

From another angle, blockchains that are providing a digital currency as an incentive for mining can be used to provide processing power to solve scientific problems that can help to find cures for certain diseases. Examples include FoldingCoin, which rewards its miners with FLDC tokens for sharing their computer's processing power for solving scientific problems that require unusually large calculations.

 FoldingCoin is available at `http://foldingcoin.net/`.

Another similar project is called CureCoin which is available at `https://www.curecoin.net/`. It is yet to be seen that how successful these projects will be in achieving their goals but the idea is very promising.

Finance

Blockchain has many applications in the finance industry. Blockchain in finance is the hottest topic in the industry currently, and major banks and financial organizations are researching to find ways to adapt blockchain technology primarily due to its highly-desired potential to cost-save.

Insurance

In the insurance industry, blockchain technology can help to stop fraudulent claims, increase the speed of claim processing, and enable transparency. Imagine a shared ledger between all insurers that can provide a quick and efficient mechanism for handling intercompany claims. Also, with the convergence of IoT and blockchain, an ecosystem of smart devices can be imagined where all these things can negotiate and manage their insurance policies controlled by smart contracts on the blockchain.

Blockchain can reduce the overall cost and effort required to process claims. Claims can be automatically verified and paid via smart contracts and the associated identity of the insurance policyholder. For example, a smart contract with the help of Oracle and possibly IoT can make sure that when the accident occurred, it can record related telemetry data and based on this information can release payment. It can also withhold payment if the smart contract after evaluating conditions of payment concludes that payment should not be released. For example, in a scenario where an authorized workshop did not repair the vehicle or was used outside a designated area and so on and so forth. There can be many conditions that a smart contract can evaluate to process claims and choice of these rules depend on the insurer, but the general idea is that smart contracts in combination with IoT and Oracle can automate the entire vehicle insurance industry.

Several start-ups such as Dynamis have proposed smart contract-based peer-to-peer insurance platforms that run on Ethereum blockchain. This is initially proposed to be used for unemployment insurance and does not require underwriters in the model.

 It is available at `http://dynamisapp.com/`.

Post-trade settlement

This is the most sought-after application of blockchain technology. Currently, many financial institutions are exploring the possibility of using blockchain technology to simplify, automate, and speed up the costly and time-consuming post-trade settlement process.

To understand the problem better, the trade life cycle is described briefly. A trade life cycle contains three steps: execution, clearing, and settlement. Execution is concerned with the commitment of trading between two parties and can be entered into the system via front office order management terminals or exchanges. Clearing is the next step whereby the trade is matched between the seller and buyer based on certain attributes such as price and quantity. At this stage, accounts that are involved in payment are also identified. Finally, the settlement is where eventually the security is exchanged for payment between the buyer and seller.

In the traditional trade life cycle model, a central clearinghouse is required to facilitate trading between parties which bears the credit risk of both parties. The current scheme is somewhat complicated, whereby a seller and buyer have to take a complicated route to trade with each other. This comprises of various firms, brokers, clearing houses, and custodians but with blockchain, a single distributed ledger with appropriate smart contracts can simplify this whole process and can enable buyers and sellers to talk directly to each other.

Notably, the post-trade settlement process usually takes two to three days and has a dependency on central clearing houses and reconciliation systems. With the shared ledger approach, all participants on the blockchain can immediately see a single version of truth regarding the state of the trade. Moreover, the peer-to-peer settlement is possible, which results in the reduction of complexity, cost, risk, and the time it takes to settle the trade. Finally, intermediaries can be eliminated by making use of appropriate smart contracts on the blockchain. Also, regulators can also see view the blockchain for auditing and regulatory requirements.

 This can be very useful in implementing MIFID-II regulation requirements (`https://www.fca.org.uk/markets/mifid-ii`).

Financial crime prevention

Know Your Customer (**KYC**), and **Anti Money Laundering** (**AML**) are the key enablers for the prevention of financial crime. In the case of KYC, currently, each institution maintains their own copy of customer data and performs verification via centralized data providers. This can be a time-consuming process and can result in delays in onboarding a new client.

Blockchain can provide a solution to this problem by securely sharing a distributed ledger between all financial institutions that contain verified and true identities of customers. This distributed ledger can only be updated by consensus between the participants thus providing transparency and auditability. This can not only reduce costs but also enable meeting regulatory and compliance requirements in a better and consistent manner.

In the case of AML, due to the immutable, shared, and transparent nature of blockchain, regulators, can easily be granted access to a private blockchain where they can fetch data for relevant regulatory reporting. This will also result in reducing complexity and costs related to the current regulatory reporting paradigm where data is fetched from various legacy and disparate systems and aggregated and formatted together for reporting purposes. Blockchain can provide a single shared view of all financial transactions in the system that are cryptographically secure, authentic, and auditable, thus reducing the costs and complexity associated with the currently employed regulatory reporting methods.

Media

Critical issues in the media industry revolve around content distribution, rights management, and royalty payments to artists. For example, digital music can be copied many times without any restriction and any attempts to apply copy protection have been hacked in some way or other. There is no control over the distribution of the content that a musician or songwriter produces; it can be copied as many times as needed without any restriction and consequently has an impact on the royalty payments. Also, payments are not always guaranteed and are based on traditional airtime figures. All these issues revolving around copy protection and royalty payments can be resolved by connecting consumers, artists, and all players in the industry, allowing transparency and control over the process. Blockchain can provide a network where digital music is cryptographically guaranteed to be owned only by the consumers who pay for it. This payment mechanism is controlled by a smart contract instead of a centralized media agency or authority. The payments will be automatically made based on the logic embedded within the smart contract and number of downloads.

 A recent example of such an initiative is Musicoin (`https://musicoin.org`).

Moreover, illegal copying of digital music files can be stopped altogether because everything is recorded and owned immutably in a transparent manner on the blockchain. A music file, for example, can be stored with owner information and timestamp which can be traced throughout the blockchain network. Furthermore, the consumers who own a legal copy of some content are cryptographically tied to the content they have, and it cannot be moved to another owner unless permissioned by the owner. Copyrights and transfers can be managed easily via blockchain once all digital content is immutably recorded on the blockchain. Smart contracts can then control the distribution and payment to all concerned parties.

Summary

There are many applications of blockchain technology, and as discussed in the chapter they can be implemented in various industries to bring about multiple benefits to existing solutions. In this chapter, five main industries that can benefit from blockchain have been discussed. First IoT was discussed, which is another revolutionary technology on its own; and by combining it with the blockchain, several fundamental limitations can be addressed, which brings about tremendous benefits to the IoT industry. More focus has been given to IoT as it is the most prominent and most ready candidate for adapting blockchain technology.

Already, practical use cases and platforms have emerged in the form of **Platform as a Service (PaaS)** for blockchain-based IoT such as the IBM Watson IoT blockchain. IBM Blue Horizon is also now available for experimentation, which is a decentralized blockchain-based IoT network. Second, applications in the government sector were discussed whereby various government processes such as homeland security, identification cards, and benefit disbursements can be made transparent, secure, and more robust.

Furthermore, issues in the finance sector were discussed with possible solutions that blockchain technology could provide. Although the finance sector is exploring the possibilities of using blockchain with high energy and enthusiasm, it is still far away from production-ready blockchain-based systems. Finally, some aspects of the health sector and music industry were also discussed. All these use cases and much more in the industry stand on pillars provided by core attributes of blockchain technology such as decentralization, transparency, reliability, and security. However, certain challenges need to be addressed before blockchain technology can be adapted fully; these will be discussed in the next chapter.

16
Scalability and Other Challenges

This chapter aims to provide an introduction to various challenges that need to be addressed before blockchains can become a mainstream technology. Even though various use cases and proof of concept systems have been developed and the technology works well for many of the scenarios, there still is a need to address some fundamental limitations that are present in blockchains in order to make this technology more adaptable.

At the top of the list of these issues comes scalability and then privacy. Both of these are important limitations to address, especially as blockchains are envisioned to be used in privacy-demanding industries too. There are specific requirements around confidentiality of transactions in finance, law, and health, whereas scalability is generally a concern where blockchains do not meet the adequate performance levels expected by the users. These two issues are becoming inhibiting factors toward blockchain technology's wider acceptance.

A review of currently proposed and ongoing research in these two specific areas will be presented throughout this chapter. In addition to privacy and security, other challenges include regulation, integration, adaptability, and security in general. Although, in Bitcoin blockchain security is bulletproof and has stood the test of time, there still are some caveats that may allow security to be compromised to an extent in some subtle scenarios. Also, there are some reasonable security concerns in other blockchains, such as Ethereum, regarding smart contracts, denial of service attacks, and large attack surface. All of these will be discussed in detail in the following sections.

Scalability

This problem has been a focus of intense debate, rigorous research, and media attention for the last few years.

This is the single most important problem that could mean the difference between wider adaptability of blockchains or limited private use only by consortiums. As a result of substantial research in this area, many solutions have been proposed, which are discussed in the following section.

From a theoretical perspective, the general approach toward tackling the scalability issue generally revolves around protocol-level enhancements. For example, a commonly mentioned solution to Bitcoin scalability is to increase its block size. Other proposals include off-chain solutions that offload certain processing to off-chain networks, for example, off-chain state networks. Based on the aforementioned solutions, generally, the proposals can be divided into two categories: **on-chain solutions** that are based on the idea of changing fundamental protocols on which the blockchain operates, and **off-chain solutions** that make use of network and processing resources off-chain in order to enhance the blockchain.

Another approach to addressing limitations in blockchains has been recently proposed by Miller and others in their position paper *On Scaling Decentralized Blockchains* available at `https://doi.org/10.1007/978-3-662-53357-4_8`. In this paper, it is shown that a blockchain can be divided into various abstract layers called **planes**. Each plane is responsible for performing specific functions. These include the network plane, consensus plane, storage plane, view plane, and side plane. This abstraction allows bottlenecks and limitations to be addressed at each plane individually and in a structured manner. A brief overview of each layer is given in the following subsections with some references to the Bitcoin system.

Network plane

First, the network plane is discussed. A key function of the network plane is transaction propagation. It has been identified in the aforementioned paper that in Bitcoin, this plane underutilizes the network bandwidth due to the way transaction validation is performed by a node before propagation and duplication of transaction propagation, first in the transaction broadcast phase, and then after mining in a block.

It should be noted that this issue was addressed by BIP 152 (*Compact Block Relay*, `https://github.com/bitcoin/bips/blob/master/bip-0152.mediawiki`).

Consensus plane

The second layer is called the consensus plane. This layer is responsible for mining and achieving consensus. Bottlenecks in this layer revolve around limitations in PoW algorithms whereby increasing consensus speed and bandwidth results in compromising the security of the network due to an increase in the number of forks.

Storage plane

The storage plane is the third layer, which stores the ledger. Issues in this layer revolve around the need for each node to keep a copy of the entire ledger, which leads to certain inefficiencies, such as increased bandwidth and storage requirements. Bitcoin has a method available called **pruning**, which allows a node to operate without the need to keep the full blockchain in its storage. Pruning means that when a Bitcoin node has downloaded the blockchain and validated it, it deletes the old data that it has already validated. This saves storage space. This functionality has resulted in major improvements from a storage point of view.

View plane

Next on the list is the view plane, which proposes an optimization which is based on the proposal that bitcoin miners do not need the full blockchain to operate, and a view can be constructed out of the complete ledger as a representation of the entire state of the system, which is sufficient for miners to function. Implementation of views will eliminate the need for mining nodes to store the full blockchain.

Finally, the side plane has been proposed by the authors of the aforementioned research paper. This plane represents the idea of off-chain transactions whereby the concept of payment or transaction channels is used to offload the processing of transactions between participants but is still backed by the main Bitcoin blockchain.

The aforementioned model can be used to describe limitations and improvements in current blockchain designs in a structured manner. Also, there are several general strategies that have been proposed over the last few years which can address the limitations in current blockchain designs such as Ethereum and Bitcoin. These approaches are also characterized and discussed individually in the following section.

Block size increase

This is the most debated proposal for increasing blockchain performance (transaction processing throughput). Currently, Bitcoin can process only about three to seven transactions per second, which is a major inhibiting factor in adapting the Bitcoin blockchain for processing microtransactions. Block size in Bitcoin is hardcoded to be 1 MB, but if the block size is increased, it can hold more transactions and can result in faster confirmation time. There are several **Bitcoin Improvement Proposals** (**BIPs**) made in favor of block size increase. These include BIP 100, BIP 101, BIP 102, BIP 103, and BIP 109.

An excellent account of historic references and discussion is available at `https://en.bitcoin.it/wiki/Block_size_limit_controversy`.

In Ethereum, the block size is not limited by hardcoding; instead, it is controlled by a gas limit. In theory, there is no limit on the size of a block in Ethereum because it's dependent on the amount of gas, which can increase over time. This is possible because miners are allowed to increase the gas limit for subsequent blocks if the limit has been reached in the previous block. Bitcoin SegWit has addressed this issue by separating witness data from transaction data which resulted in more space for transactions. Other proposals for Bitcoin include Bitcoin Unlimited, Bitcoin XT and Bitcoin Cash. Readers can refer back to `Chapter 8`, *Introducing Bitcoin*, for more details.

For more information refer to the following links:

- `https://www.bitcoinunlimited.info`
- `https://bitcoinxt.software`
- `https://www.bitcoincash.org`

Block interval reduction

Another proposal is to reduce the time between each block generation. The time between blocks can be decreased to achieve faster finalization of blocks but may result in less security due to the increased number of forks. Ethereum has achieved a block time of approximately 14 seconds.

This is a significant improvement from the Bitcoin blockchain, which takes 10 minutes to generate a new block. In Ethereum, the issue of high orphaned blocks resulting from smaller times between blocks is mitigated by using the **Greedy Heaviest Observed Subtree** (**GHOST**) protocol whereby orphaned blocks (uncles) are also included in determining the valid chain. Once Ethereum moves to **Proof of Stake** (**PoS**), this will become irrelevant as no mining will be required and almost immediate finality of transactions can be achieved.

Invertible Bloom Lookup Tables

This is another approach that has been proposed to reduce the amount of data required to be transferred between the Bitcoin nodes. **Invertible Bloom Lookup Tables** (**IBLTs**) were originally proposed by Gavin Andresen, and the key attraction in this approach is that it does not result in a hard fork of Bitcoin if implemented. The key idea is based on the fact that there is no need to transfer all transactions between nodes; instead, only those that are not already available in the transaction pool of the syncing node are transferred. This allows quicker transaction pool synchronization between nodes, thus increasing the overall scalability and speed of the Bitcoin network.

Sharding

Sharding is not a new technique and has been used in distributed databases for scalability such as MongoDB and MySQL. The key idea behind sharding is to split up the tasks into multiple chunks that are then processed by multiple nodes. This results in improved throughput and reduced storage requirements. In blockchains, a similar scheme is employed whereby the state of the network is partitioned into multiple shards. The state usually includes balances, code, nonce, and storage. Shards are loosely coupled partitions of a blockchain that run on the same network. There are a few challenges related to inter-shard communication and consensus on the history of each shard. This is an open area for research.

State channels

This is another approach proposed for speeding up the transaction on a blockchain network. The basic idea is to use side channels for state updating and processing transactions off the main chain; once the state is finalized, it is written back to the main chain, thus offloading the time-consuming operations from the main blockchain.

State channels work by performing the following three steps:

1. First, a part of the blockchain state is locked under a smart contract, ensuring the agreement and business logic between participants.
2. Now off-chain transaction processing and interaction is started between the participants that update the state only between themselves for now. In this step, almost any number of transactions can be performed without requiring the blockchain and this is what makes the process fast and a best candidate for solving blockchain scalability issues. However, it could be argued that this is not a real on-blockchain solution such as, for example, sharding, but the end result is a faster, lighter, and robust network which can prove very useful in micropayment networks, IoT networks, and many other applications.
3. Once the final state is achieved, the state channel is closed and the final state is written back to the main blockchain. At this stage, the locked part of the blockchain is also unlocked.

This process is shown in the following diagram:

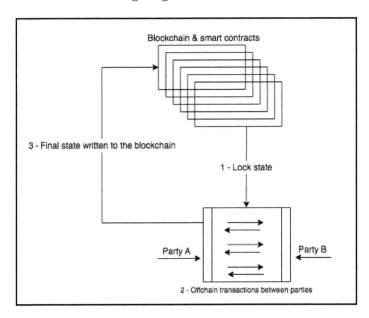

State channels

This technique has been used in the Bitcoin lightning network and Ethereum's Raiden.

Private blockchain

Private blockchains are inherently fast because no real decentralization is required and participants on the network do not need to mine; instead, they can only validate transactions. This can be considered as a workaround to the scalability issue in public blockchains; however, this is not the solution to the scalability problem. Also, it should be noted that private blockchains are only suitable in specific areas and setups such as enterprise environments where all participants are known.

Proof of Stake

Instead of using **Proof of Work (PoW)**, PoS algorithm based blockchains are fundamentally faster. PoS was explained in greater detail in `Chapter 10`, *Alternative Coins*.

Sidechains

Sidechains can improve scalability indirectly by allowing many sidechains to run along with the main blockchain while allowing usage of perhaps comparatively less secure and faster sidechains to perform transactions but still pegged with the main blockchain. The core idea of sidechains is called a two-way peg, which allows transfer of coins from a parent chain to a sidechain and vice versa.

Subchains

This is a relatively new technique recently proposed by Peter R. Rizun which is based on the idea of weak blocks that are created in layers until a strong block is found. Weak blocks can be defined as those blocks that have not been able to be mined by meeting the standard network difficulty criteria but have done enough work to meet another weaker difficulty target. Miners can build subchains by layering weak blocks on top of each other unless a block is found that meets the standard difficulty target.

At this point, the subchain is closed and becomes the strong block. Advantages of this approach include reduced waiting time for the first verification of a transaction. This technique also results in a reduced chance of orphaning blocks and speeds up transaction processing. This is also an indirect way of addressing the scalability issue. Subchains do not require any soft fork or hard fork to implement but need acceptance by the community.

The subchains research paper is available at
`https://www.ledgerjournal.org/ojs/index.php/ledger/article/view/`
`40`.

Tree chains (trees)

There are also other proposals to increase Bitcoin scalability, such as tree chains that change the blockchain layout from a linearly sequential model to a tree. This tree is basically a binary tree which descends from the main Bitcoin chain. This approach is similar to sidechain implementation, eliminating the need for major protocol change or block size increase. It allows improved transaction throughput. In this scheme, the blockchains themselves are fragmented and distributed across the network in order to achieve scalability.

Moreover, mining is not required to validate the blocks on the tree chains; instead, users can independently verify the block header. However, this idea is not ready for production yet and further research is required in order to make it practical.

The original idea was proposed in the research paper
`https://eprint.iacr.org/2016/545.pdf`.

In addition to the aforementioned general techniques, some Bitcoin-specific improvements have also been proposed by Christian Decker
(`https://scholar.google.ch/citations?user=ZaeGlZIAAAAJ&hl=en`) in his book *On the Scalability and Security of Bitcoin*. This proposal is based on the idea of speeding up propagation time as the current information propagation mechanism results in blockchain forks. These techniques include minimization of verification, pipelining of block propagation, and connectivity increase. These changes do not require fundamental protocol-level changes; instead, these changes can be implemented independently in the Bitcoin node software.

With regards to verification minimization, it has been noted that the block verification process is contributing toward propagation delay. The reason behind this is that a node takes a long time to verify the uniqueness of the block and transactions within the block. It has been suggested that a node can send the inventory message as soon as the initial PoW and block validation checks are completed. This way, propagation can be improved by just performing the first *difficulty check* and not waiting for transaction validation to finish.

Block propagation

In addition to the preceding proposal, pipelining of block propagation has also been suggested, which is based on the idea of anticipating the availability of a block. In this scheme, the availability of a block is already announced without waiting for actual block availability, thus reducing the round-trip time between nodes. Finally, the problem of long distances between transaction originator and nodes also contributes toward the slowdown of block propagation. It has been shown in the research conducted by Christian Decker that connectivity increase can reduce propagation delay of blocks and transactions. This is possible because, if at any one time the Bitcoin node is connected to many other nodes, it will result in reducing the distance between nodes and can speed up information propagation on the network.

An elegant solution to scalability issues will most likely be a combination of some or all of the aforementioned general approaches. A number of initiatives taken in order to address scalability and security issues in blockchains are now almost ready for implementation or already implemented. For example, Bitcoin **Segregated Witness (SegWit)** is a proposal that can help massively with scalability and only needs a soft fork in order for it to be implemented. The key idea behind so-called *SegWit* is to separate signature data from the transactions, which resolves the transaction malleability issue and allows block size increase, thus resulting in increased throughput.

Bitcoin-NG

Another proposal, Bitcoin-NG, which is based on the idea of microblocks and leader election, has gained some attention recently. The core idea is to split blocks into two types, namely leader blocks (also called key blocks) and microblocks:

- **Leader blocks**: These are responsible for PoW whereas microblocks contain actual transactions.
- **Micro blocks**: These do not require any PoW and are generated by the elected leader every block-generation cycle. This block-generation cycle is initiated by a leader block. The only requirement is to sign the microblocks with the elected leader's private key. The microblocks can be generated at a very high speed by the elected leader (miner), thus resulting in increased performance and transaction speed.

On the other hand, an Ethereum mauve paper written by Vitalik Buterin has been presented at Ethereum Devcon2 in Shanghai; it describes the vision of a scalable Ethereum. The mauve proposal is based on a combination of sharding and implementation of PoS algorithm. Certain goals such as efficiency gain via PoS, maximally fast block time, economic finality, scalability, cross-shard communication, and censorship resistance have been identified in the paper.

Mauve paper is available at `https://docs.google.com/document/d/1maFT3cpHvwn29gLvtY4WcQiI6kRbN_nbCf3JlgR3m_8/edit#`.

Plasma

Another recent scalability proposal is **Plasma**, which has been proposed by Joseph Poon and Vitalik Buterin. This proposal describes the idea of running smart contracts on root blockchain (Ethereum MainNet) and have child blockchains that perform high number of transactions to feedback small amounts of commitments to the parent chain. In this scheme, blockchains are arranged in a tree hierarchy with mining performed only on the root (main) blockchain which feeds the proofs of security down to child chains. This is also called a Layer-2 system, like state channels also operate on Layer 2, and not on the main chain.

 The research paper is available at `http://plasma.io`.

Privacy

Privacy of transactions is a much-desired property of blockchains. However, due to its very nature, especially in public blockchains, everything is transparent, thus inhibiting its usage in various industries where privacy is of paramount importance, such as finance, health, and many others. There are different proposals made to address the privacy issue and some progress has already been made. Several techniques, such as **Indistinguishability Obfuscation (IO)**, usage of homomorphic encryption, ZKPs, and ring signatures.

All these techniques have their merits and demerits and are discussed in the following sections.

Indistinguishability Obfuscation

This cryptographic technique may serve as a silver bullet to all privacy and confidentiality issues in blockchains but the technology is not yet ready for production deployments. IO allows for code obfuscation, which is a very ripe research topic in cryptography and, if applied to blockchains, can serve as an unbreakable obfuscation mechanism that will turn smart contracts into a black box.

The key idea behind IO is what's called by researchers a *multilinear jigsaw puzzle*, which basically obfuscates program code by mixing it with random elements, and if the program is run as intended, it will produce expected output but any other way of executing would render the program look random and garbage. This idea was first proposed by Shai and others in their research paper *Candidate Indistinguishability Obfuscation and Functional Encryption for all circuits*.

 This research paper is available at https://doi.org/10.1109/FOCS.2013.13.

Homomorphic encryption

This type of encryption allows operations to be performed on encrypted data. Imagine a scenario where the data is sent to a cloud server for processing. The server processes it and returns the output without knowing anything about the data that it has processed. This is also an area ripe for research and fully homomorphic encryption that allows all operations on encrypted data is still not fully deployable in production; however, major progress in this field has already been made. Once implemented on blockchains, it can allow processing on ciphertext which will allow privacy and confidentiality of transactions inherently. For example, the data stored on the blockchain can be encrypted using homomorphic encryption and computations can be performed on that data without the need for decryption, thus providing privacy service on blockchains. This concept has also been implemented in a project named *Enigma* which is available online at (https://www.media.mit.edu/projects/enigma/overview/) by MIT's Media Lab. Enigma is a peer-to-peer network which allows multiple parties to perform computations on encrypted data without revealing anything about the data.

 Original research is available at https://crypto.stanford.edu/craig/.

Zero-Knowledge Proofs

ZKPs have recently been implemented in Zcash successfully, as seen in `Chapter 10`, *Alternative Coins*. More specifically, **SNARK** (short for **Succinct Non-Interactive Argument of Knowledge**) have been implemented in order to ensure privacy on the blockchain.

The same idea can be implemented in Ethereum and other blockchains also. Integrating Zcash on Ethereum is already a very active research project being run by the Ethereum R&D team and the Zcash Company.

The original research paper is available at `https://eprint.iacr.org/2013/879.pdf`.
Another excellent paper is here
`http://chriseth.github.io/notes/articles/zksnarks/zksnarks.pdf`.

There is a recent addition to the family of ZKPs called **Zero-Knowledge Succinct Transparent Argument of Knowledge** (**ZK-STARKs**) which is an improvement on ZK-SNARKs in the sense that ZK-STARKs consume a lot less bandwidth and storage as compared to ZK-SNARKs. Also, they do not require the initial, somewhat controversial, trusted setup that is required for ZK-SNARKs. Moreover, ZK-STARKs are much quicker than ZK-SNARKs as they do not make use of elliptic curves and rely on hashes.

The original research paper for ZK-STARKs is available here `https://eprint.iacr.org/2018/046.pdf`.

State channels

Privacy using state channels is also possible, simply due to the fact that all transactions are run off-chain and the main blockchain does not see the transaction at all except for the final state output, thus ensuring privacy and confidentiality.

Secure multiparty computation

The concept of secure multiparty computation is not new and is based on the notion that data is split into multiple partitions between participating parties under a secret sharing mechanism which then does the actual processing on the data without the need of the reconstructing data on a single machine. The output produced after processing is also shared between the parties.

Usage of hardware to provide confidentiality

Trusted computing platforms can be used to provide a mechanism by which confidentiality of transaction can be achieved on a blockchain, for example, by using Intel **Software Guard Extension** (**SGX**), which allows code to be run in a hardware-protected environment called an **enclave**. Once the code runs successfully in the isolated enclave, it can produce a proof called a **quote** that is attestable by Intel's cloud servers. However, it is a concern that trusting Intel will result in some level of centralization and is not in line with the true spirit of blockchain technology. Nevertheless, this solution has its merits and, in reality, many platforms already use Intel chips anyway, therefore trusting Intel may be acceptable by some in some cases.

If this technology is applied on smart contracts then, once a node has executed the smart contract, it can produce the quote as a proof of correct and successful execution and other nodes will only have to verify it. This idea can be further extended by using any **Trusted Execution Environment** (**TEE**) which can provide the same functionality as an enclave and is available even on mobile devices with **Near Field Communication** (**NFC**) and a secure element.

CoinJoin

CoinJoin is a technique which is used to anonymize the bitcoin transactions by mixing them interactively. The idea is based on forming a single transaction from multiple entities without causing any change in inputs and outputs. It removes the direct link between senders and receivers, which means that a single address can no longer be associated with transactions, which could lead to the identification of the users. CoinJoin needs cooperation between multiple parties that are willing to create a single transaction by mixing payments. Therefore, it should be noted that, if any single participant in the CoinJoin scheme does not keep up with the commitment made to cooperate for creating a single transaction by not signing the transactions as required, then it can result in a denial of service attack.

In this protocol, there is no need for a single trusted third party. This concept is different from mixing a service which acts as a trusted third party or intermediary between the bitcoin users and allows shuffling of transactions. This shuffling of transactions results in the prevention of tracing and the linking of payments to a particular user.

Confidential transactions

Confidential transactions make use of Pedersen commitments in order to provide confidentiality. Commitment schemes allow a user to commit to some value while keeping it secret with the capability of revealing it later. Two properties that need to be satisfied in order to design a commitment scheme are binding and hiding.

Binding makes sure that the committer is unable to change the chosen value once committed, whereas the **hiding** property ensures that any adversary is unable to find the original value to which the committer made a commitment. Pedersen commitments also allow addition operations and preserve commutative property on the commitments, which makes it specifically useful for providing confidentiality in bitcoin transactions. In other words, it supports homomorphic encryption of values. Using commitment schemes allows the hiding of payment values in a bitcoin transaction. This concept is already implemented in the Elements Project (`https://elementsproject.org/`).

MimbleWimble

The MimbleWimble scheme was proposed somewhat mysteriously on the Bitcoin IRC channel and since then has gained a lot of popularity. MimbleWimble extends the idea of confidential transactions and CoinJoin, which allows aggregation of transactions without requiring any interactivity. However, it does not support the use of Bitcoin scripting language along with various other features of standard Bitcoin protocol. This makes it incompatible with existing Bitcoin protocol. Therefore, it can either be implemented as a sidechain to Bitcoin or on its own as an alternative cryptocurrency.

This scheme can address privacy and scalability issues both at once. The blocks created using the MimbleWimble technique do not contain transactions as in traditional Bitcoin blockchains; instead, these blocks are composed of three lists: an input list, output list, and something called **excesses** which are lists of signatures and differences between outputs and inputs. The input list basically references to the old outputs, and the output list contains confidential transactions outputs. These blocks are verifiable by nodes by using signatures, inputs, and outputs to ensure the legitimacy of the block. In contrast to Bitcoin, MimbleWimble transaction outputs only contain pubkeys, and the difference between old and new outputs is signed by all participants involved in the transactions.

Security

Even though blockchains are generally secure and make use of asymmetric and symmetric cryptography as required throughout the blockchain network, there still are few caveats that can result in compromising the security of the blockchain.

There are a few examples of transaction malleability, eclipse attacks, and the possibility of double spending in bitcoin that, in certain scenarios, have been shown to work by various researchers. Transaction malleability opens up the possibility of double withdrawal or deposit by allowing a hacker to change a transaction's unique ID before the Bitcoin network can confirm it, resulting in a scenario where it would seem that transactions did not occur. BIP 62 is one of the proposals along with SegWit that have suggested solutions to solve this issue. It should be noted that this is a problem only in the case of unconfirmed transactions, that is, scenarios where operational processes rely on unconfirmed transactions. In the case of normal applications that only rely on confirmed transactions, this is not an issue.

Information eclipse attacks in Bitcoin can result in double spending. The idea behind eclipse attacks is that the Bitcoin node is tricked into connecting only with the attacker node IPs. This opens up the possibility of a 51 % attack by the attacker. This has been addressed to some extent in Bitcoin client v0.10.1.

Smart contract security

Recently, a lot of work has been started in smart contract security and, especially, formal verification of smart contracts is being discussed and researched. This was all triggered especially due to the infamous DAO hack.

Formal verification is a process of verifying a computer program to ensure that it satisfies certain formal statements. This is now a new concept and there are a number of tools available for other languages that achieve this; for example, Frama-C (`https://frama-c.com`) is available for analyzing C programs. The key idea behind formal verification is to convert the source program into a set of statements that is understandable by the automated provers.

For this purpose, Why3 (`http://why3.lri.fr`) is commonly used, and a formal verifier for Solidity also makes use of that. An experimental but operational verifier is available in browser Solidity already.

Smart contract security is of paramount importance now, and many other initiatives have also been taken in order to devise methods that can analyze Solidity programs and find bugs. A recent and seminal example is Oyente, which is a tool built by researchers and has been introduced in their paper *Making Smart Contracts Smarter*.

Oyente is available at `https://github.com/melonproject/oyente`.

Several security bugs in smart contracts have been discovered and analyzed in this paper. These include transaction ordering dependence, timestamp dependence, mishandled exceptions such as call stack depth limit exploitation, and reentrance vulnerability. The transaction ordering dependency bug basically exploits the scenarios where the perceived state of a contract might not be what the state of the contract changes to after execution.

This weakness is a type of race condition. It is also called frontloading and is possible due to the fact that the order of transactions within a block can be manipulated. As all transactions first appear in the memory pool, the transactions there can be monitored before they are included in the block. This allows a transaction to be submitted before another transaction, thus leading to controlling the behavior of a smart contract.

Timestamp dependency bugs are possible in scenarios where the timestamp of the block is used as a source of some decision-making within the contract, but timestamps can be manipulated by the miners. Call stack depth limit is another bug that can be exploited due to the fact that the maximum call stack depth of EVM is 1,024 frames. If the stack depth is reached while the contract is executing then, in certain scenarios, the send or call instruction can fail, resulting in non-payment of funds. The call stack depth bug was addressed in the EIP 50 hard fork `https://github.com/ethereum/EIPs/blob/master/EIPS/eip-150.md`.

The reentrancy bug was exploited in the DAO attack to siphon out millions of dollars into a child DAO. The reentrancy bug basically means that a function can be called repeatedly before the previous (first) invocation of the functions has completed. This is particularly unsafe in Ether withdrawal functions in Solidity smart contracts.

In addition to the aforementioned bugs, there are several other problems that should be kept in mind while writing contracts. These bugs include that fact that if sending funds to another contract, handle it carefully because send can fail and even if throw is used as a *catch-all* mechanism, it will not work.

Other standard software bugs such as integer overflow and underflow are also quite significant and any use of integer variables should be carefully implemented in Solidity. For example, a simple program where uint8 is used to parse through elements of an array with more than 255 elements can result in an endless loop. This occurs because uint8 is limited to 256 numbers.

In the following sections, two examples of contract verification will be shown using Remix IDE, Why3 and Oyente respectively.

Formal verification and analysis

Security analysis of Solidity code is now available as a feature in the solidity online IDE called Remix. The code is analyzed for vulnerabilities and reported in the **Analysis** tab of the remix IDE:

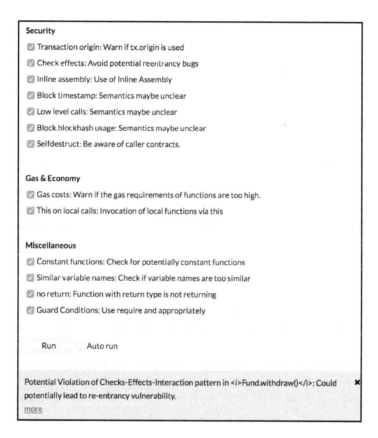

Remix IDE analysis options

A sample output of the same contract with reentrancy bug is shown in the bottom of the preceding screenshot.

This tool analyzes several categories of vulnerabilities including, security, gas, and economy. As shown in the preceding screenshot the analysis tool has successfully detected the reentrancy bug, details of which are shown at the bottom of the screen.

Why3 can also be used for formally analyzing Solidity code.

 Why3 is available at `http://why3.lri.fr/try/`.

In the following example, a simple Solidity code that defines the z variable as the maximum limit of uint is shown. When this code runs, it will result in returning 0, because uint z will overrun and start again from 0. This can also be verified using Why3, which is shown here:

```
1  pragma solidity ^0.4.8;
2 ▾ contract Overflow {
3      uint z;
4 ▾    function x() returns (uint y) {
5          z = 2**256-1;
6          return z+1;
7      }
8  }
```

This tab provides support for **formal verification** of Solidity contracts.
This feature is still in development and thus also not yet well documented, but you can find some information here. The compiler generates input
Please paste the text below into http://why3.lri.fr/try/ to actually perform the verification. We plan to support direct integration in the future.

```
(* copy this to http://why3.lri.fr/try/ *)

module UInt256
    use import mach.int.Unsigned
    type uint256
    constant max_uint256: int =
0xffffffffffffffffffffffffffffffffffffffffffffffffffffffffffffffff
    clone export mach.int.Unsigned with
        type t = uint256,
        constant max = max_uint256
end

module Address
    use import mach.int.Unsigned
    type address
    constant max_address: int = 0xffffffffffffffffffffffffffffffffffffffff (* 160_bit = 40 *)
    clone export mach.int.Unsigned with
        type t = address,
        constant max = max_address
```

Solidity online compiler with formal verification

Conversion from Solidity to Why3 compliant code used to be available in Solidity online compiler but it is no longer available. Therefore, the following example is only for completeness purposes and to shed light on an important class of bugs which can go undetected with traditional tools. In this example, integer overflow is shown as an example.

The following example shows that Why3 successfully checks and reports integer overflow errors. This tool is under heavy development but is still quite useful. Also, this tool or any other similar tool is not a silver bullet. Even formal verification generally should not be considered a panacea because specifications in the first place should be defined appropriately:

Why3

Oyente tool

Currently, Oyente is available as a Docker image for easy testing and installation. It is available at `https://github.com/melonproject/oyente` and can be downloaded and tested.

In the following example, a simple contract taken from Solidity documentation that contains a reentrancy bug has been tested and it is shown that Oyente successfully analyzes the code and finds the bug:

Contract with reentrancy bug, source: solidity documentation

This sample code contains a reentrancy bug which basically means that if a contract is interacting with another contract or transferring Ether, it is effectively handing over the control to that other contract. This allows the called contract to call back into the function of the contract from which it has been called without waiting for completion. For example, this bug can allow calling back into the withdraw function shown in the preceding example again and again, resulting in getting Ethers multiple times. This is possible because the share value is not set to 0 until the end of the function, which means that any later invocations will be successful, resulting in withdrawing again and again.

An example is shown of Oyente running to analyze the contract shown here and as can be seen in the following output, the analysis has successfully found the reentrancy bug. The bug is proposed to be handled by a combination of the Checks-Effects-Interactions pattern described in the solidity documentation:

Oyente tool detecting solidity bugs

Oyente is also available in analysis tools for smart contacts at `https://oyente.melon.fund`. A sample output is shown here.

With this example, we conclude our introduction to security and analysis tools for solidity. This is a very rich area of research and more and more tools are expected to be available with time.

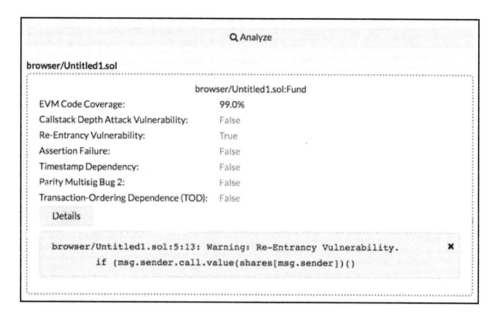

Oyente analysis

Summary

In this chapter, readers have been introduced to the security, confidentiality, and privacy aspects of blockchain technology. Privacy was discussed, which is another major inhibiting factor in adapting public blockchains for various industries. Next, smart contract security, which is a very hot topic currently, was discussed. It is a deep and extensive subject but a brief introduction on various aspects has been given, which should serve as a solid ground for further research in this area.

For example, formal verification on its own is a vast area for research. Furthermore, examples of formal verification have also been provided to give readers an idea of what tools are available. It should be noted that the tools mentioned earlier are under heavy development and lack various desirable features. Also, documentation is quite scarce; therefore, readers are encouraged to keep an eye on developments, especially around formal verification and developments related to the Ethereum mauve paper, as it is going to develop rapidly very soon. The field of blockchain security and especially smart contract security is so ripe now that a whole book can be written on the subject.

There are many experts and researchers in academia and the commercial sector exploring this area and soon there will be many automated tools available for the verification of smart contracts. There is an online tool available already at `https://securify.ch` which analyses smart contract code to find security vulnerabilities.

17
Building a Consortium Blockchain

Consortiums (an association, typically of several participants such as banks, e-commerce sites, government entities, hospitals, and so on) can use blockchain technology to solve many problems and make things faster and cheaper. Although they figure out how blockchain can help them, an Ethereum implementation of blockchain doesn't specifically fit them for all cases. Although there are other implementations of blockchain (for example, Hyperledger) that are built specially for consortium, as we learned Ethereum throughout the book, we will see how we can hack Ethereum to build a consortium blockchain. Basically, we will be using parity to build a consortium blockchain. Although there are other alternatives to parity, such as J.P. Morgan's quorum, we will use parity as at the time of writing this book, it has been in existence for some time, and many enterprises are already using it, whereas other alternatives are yet to be used by any enterprises. But for your requirements, parity may not be the best solution; therefore, investigate all the others too before deciding which one to use.

In this chapter, we'll cover the following topics:

- Why is Ethereum unfit for consortium blockchain?
- What is parity node and what are its features?
- What is the Proof-of-Authority consensus protocol and what types of PoA are supported by parity?
- How does the Aura consensus protocol work?
- Downloading and installing parity
- Building a consortium blockchain using parity

What is a consortium blockchain?

To understand what a consortium blockchain is, or, in other words, what kind of blockchain implementation consortiums need, let's check out an example. Banks want to build a blockchain to make money transfers easier, faster, and cheaper. In this case, here are the things they need:

1. **Speed**: They need a blockchain network that can confirm transactions in near-real time. Currently, the Ethereum blockchain network block time is 12 seconds, and clients usually wait for a couple of minutes before confirming a transaction.

2. **Permissioned**: They want the blockchain to be permissioned. Permissioning itself means various different things. For example: permissioning can include taking permission to join the network, it can include taking permission to to be able create blocks, it can also be taking permission to be able to send specific transactions and so on.

3. **Security**: PoW isn't secure enough for private networks as there is a limited number of participants; therefore, there isn't enough hash power produced to make it secure. So, there is a need for a consensus protocol that can keep the blockchain secure and immutable.

4. **Privacy**: Although the network is private, there is still a need for privacy in the network itself. There are two kinds of privacy:

5. **Identity privacy**: Identity privacy is the act of making the identity untraceable. The solution we saw earlier to gain identity privacy was to use multiple Ethereum account addresses. But if multiple Ethereum accounts are used, then smart contracts will fail ownership validation as there is no way to know whether all of these accounts actually belong to the same user.

6. **Data privacy:** Sometimes, we don't want the data to be visible to all the nodes in the network, but to specific nodes only.

Overall, in this chapter, we will learn how to solve these issues in Ethereum.

What is Proof-of-Authority consensus?

PoA is a consensus mechanism for blockchain in which consensus is achieved by referring to a list of validators (referred to as authorities when they are linked to physical entities). Validators are a group of accounts/nodes that are allowed to participate in the consensus; they validate the transactions and blocks.

Unlike PoW or PoS, there is no mining mechanism involved. There are various types of PoA protocols, and they vary depending on how they actually work. Hyperledger and Ripple are based on PoA. Hyperledger is based on PBFT, whereas ripple uses an iterative process.

Introduction to parity

Parity is an Ethereum node written from the ground up for correctness/verifiability, modularization, low footprint, and high performance. It is written in Rust programming language, a hybrid imperative/OO/functional language with an emphasis on efficiency. It is professionally developed by Parity Technologies. At the time of writing this book, the latest version of parity is 1.7.0, and we will be using this version. We will learn as much as is required to build a consortium blockchain. To learn parity in depth, you can refer to the official documentation.

It has a lot more features than go-ethereum, such as web3 dapp browser, much more advanced account management, and so on. But what makes it special is that it supports **Proof-of-Authority** (**PoA**) along with PoW. Parity currently su+-pports Aura and Tendermint PoA protocols. In future, it may support some more PoA protocols. Currently, parity recommends the use of Aura instead of Tendermint as Tendermint is still under development.

Aura is a much better solution for permissioned blockchains than PoW as it has better block time and provides much better security in private networks.

Understanding how Aura works

Let's see at a high level how Aura works. Aura requires the same list of validators to be specified in each node. This is a list of account addresses that participate in the consensus. A node may or may not be a validating node. Even a validating node needs to have this list so that it can itself reach a consensus.

This list can either be provided as a static list in the genesis file if the list of validators is going to remain the same forever, or be provided in a smart contract so that it can be dynamically updated and every node knows about it. In a smart contract, you can configure various strategies regarding who can add new validators.

The block time is configurable in the genesis file. It's up to you to decide the block time. In private networks, a block time as low as three seconds works well. In Aura, after every three seconds, one of the validators is selected and this validator is responsible for creating, verifying, signing, and broadcasting the block. We don't need to understand much about the actual selection algorithm as it won't impact our dapp development. But this is the formula to calculate the next validator, `(UNIX_TIMESTAMP / BLOCK_TIME % NUMBER_OF_TOTAL_VALIDATORS)`. The selection algorithm is smart enough to give equal chances to everyone When other nodes receive a block, they check whether it's from the next valid validator or not; and if not, they reject it. Unlike PoW, when a validator creates a block, it is not rewarded with ether. In Aura, it's up to us to decide whether to generate empty blocks or not when there are no transactions.

You must be wondering what will happen if the next validator node, due to some reason, fails to create and broadcast the next block. To understand this, let's take an example: suppose A is the validator for the next block, which is the fifth block, and B is the validator for the sixth block. Assume block time is five seconds. If A fails to broadcast a block, then after five seconds when B's turn arrives, it will broadcast a block. So nothing serious happens actually. The block timestamp will reveal these details.

You might also be wondering whether there are chances of networks ending up with multiple different blockchains as it happens in PoW when two miners mine at the same time. Yes, there are many ways this can happen. Let's take an example and understand one way in which this can happen and how the network resolves it automatically. Suppose there are five validators: A, B, C, D, and E. Block time is five seconds. Suppose A is selected first and it broadcasts a block, but the block doesn't reach D and E due to some reason; so they will think A didn't broadcast the block. Now suppose the selection algorithm selects B to generate the next block; then B will generate the next block on top of A's block and broadcast to all the nodes. D and E will reject it because the previous block hash will not match. Due to this, D and E will form a different chain, and A, B, and C will form a different chain. A, B, and C will reject blocks from D and E, and D and E will reject blocks from A, B, and C. This issue is resolved among the nodes as the blockchain that is with A, B and C is more accurate than the blockchain with D and E; therefore D and E will replace their version of blockchain with the blockchain held with A, B, and C. Both these versions of the blockchain will have different accuracy scores, and the score of the first blockchain will be more than the second one. When B broadcasts its block, it will also provide the score of its blockchain, and as its score is higher, D and E will have replaced their blockchain with B's blockchain. This is how conflicts are resolved. The chain score of blockchain is calculated using `(U128_max * BLOCK_NUMBER_OF_LATEST_BLOCK - (UNIX_TIMESTAMP_OF_LATEST_BLOCK / BLOCK_TIME))`. Chains are scored first by their length (the more blocks, the better). For chains of equal length, the chain whose last block is older is chosen.

You can learn more about Aura in depth at
`https://github.com/paritytech/parity/wiki/Aura`.

Getting parity running

Parity requires Rust version 1.16.0 to build. It is recommended to install Rust through rustup.

Installing rust

If you don't already have rustup, you can install it like this.

Linux

On Linux-based operating systems, run this command:

```
curl https://sh.rustup.rs -sSf | sh
```

Parity also requires the `gcc`, `git`, `libssl dev/openssl`, `libudev-dev`, and `pkg-config` packages to be installed.

OS X

On OS X, run this command:

```
curl https://sh.rustup.rs -sSf | sh
```

Parity also requires clang. Clang comes with Xcode command-line tools or can be installed with Homebrew.

Windows

Make sure you have Visual Studio 2015 with C++ support installed. Next, download and run the rustup installer from
`https://static.rust-lang.org/rustup/dist/x86_64-pc-windows-msvc/rustup-init.exe`, start "VS2015 x64 Native Tools Command Prompt", and use the following command to install and set up the `msvc` toolchain:

```
rustup default stable-x86_64-pc-windows-msvc
```

Downloading, installing and running parity

Now, once you have rust installed on your operating system, you can run this simple one-line command to install parity:

```
cargo install --git https://github.com/paritytech/parity.git parity
```

To check whether parity is installed or not, run this command:

```
parity --help
```

If parity is installed successfully, then you will see a list of sub-commands and options.

Creating a private network

Now it's time to set up our consortium blockchain. We will create two validating nodes connected to each other using Aura for consensus. We will set up both on the same computer.

Creating accounts

First, open two shell windows. The first one is for the first validator and the second one is for the second validator. The first node will contain two accounts and the second node will contain one account. The second account of first node will be assigned to some initial ether so that the network will have some ether.

In the first shell, run this command twice:

```
parity account new -d ./validator0
```

Both the times it will ask you to enter a password. For now just put the same password for both accounts.

In the second shell, run this command once only:

```
parity account new  -d ./validator1
```

Just as before, enter the password.

Creating a specification file

Nodes of every network share a common specification file. This file tells the node about the genesis block, who the validators are, and so on. We will create a smart contract, which will contain the validators list. There are two types of validator contracts: non-reporting contract and reporting contract. We have to provide only one.

The difference is that non-reporting contract only returns a list of validators, whereas reporting contract can take action for benign (benign misbehaviour may be simply not receiving a block from a designated validator) and malicious misbehavior (malicious misbehaviour would be releasing two different blocks for the same step).

The non-reporting contract should have at least this interface:

```
{"constant":true,"inputs":[],"name":"getValidators","outputs":[{"name":"","type":"address[]"}],"payable":false,"type":"function"}
```

The getValidators function will be called on every block to determine the current list. The switching rules are then determined by the contract implementing that method.

A reporting contract should have at least this interface:

```
[
{"constant":true,"inputs":[],"name":"getValidators","outputs":[{"name":"","type":"address[]"}],"payable":false,"type":"function"},
{"constant":false,"inputs":[{"name":"validator","type":"address"}],"name":"reportMalicious","outputs":[],"payable":false,"type":"function"},
{"constant":false,"inputs":[{"name":"validator","type":"address"}],"name":"reportBenign","outputs":[],"payable":false,"type":"function"}
]
```

When there is benign or malicious behavior, the consensus engine calls the reportBenign and reportMalicious functions respectively.

Let's create a reporting contract. Here is a basic example:

```
contract ReportingContract {
    address[] public validators =
[0x831647ec69be4ca44ea4bd1b9909debfbaaef55c,
0x12a6bda0d5f58538167b2efce5519e316863f9fd];
    mapping(address => uint) indices;
    address public disliked;

    function ReportingContract() {
        for (uint i = 0; i < validators.length; i++) {
            indices[validators[i]] = i;
        }
```

```
    }

    // Called on every block to update node validator list.
    function getValidators() constant returns (address[]) {
        return validators;
    }

    // Expand the list of validators.
    function addValidator(address validator) {
        validators.push(validator);
    }

    // Remove a validator from the list.
    function reportMalicious(address validator) {
        validators[indices[validator]] = validators[validators.length-1];
        delete indices[validator];
        delete validators[validators.length-1];
        validators.length--;
    }

    function reportBenign(address validator) {
        disliked = validator;
    }
}
```

This code is self-explanatory. Make sure that in the validators array replaces the addresses with the first address of validator 1 and validator 2 nodes as we will be using those addresses for validation. Now compile the preceding contract using whatever you feel comfortable with.

Now let's create the specification file. Create a file named spec.json, and place this code in it:

```
{
    "name": "ethereum",
    "engine": {
        "authorityRound": {
            "params": {
                "gasLimitBoundDivisor": "0x400",
                "stepDuration": "5",
                "validators" : {
                "contract": "0x0000000000000000000000000000000000000005"
                 }
            }
        }
    },
    "params": {
```

```
            "maximumExtraDataSize": "0x20",
            "minGasLimit": "0x1388",
            "networkID" : "0x2323"
    },
    "genesis": {
      "seal": {
        "authorityRound": {
          "step": "0x0",
            "signature": "0x000000000000000000000000000000000000000000
                000000000000000000000000000000000000000000000000000000000
                000000000000000000000000000000000000"
          }
        },
        "difficulty": "0x20000",
        "gasLimit": "0x5B8D80"
    },
    "accounts": {
        "0x0000000000000000000000000000000000000001": { "balance": "1",
"builtin": { "name": "ecrecover", "pricing": { "linear": { "base": 3000,
"word": 0 } } } },
        "0x0000000000000000000000000000000000000002": { "balance": "1",
"builtin": { "name": "sha256", "pricing": { "linear": { "base": 60, "word":
12 } } } },
        "0x0000000000000000000000000000000000000003": { "balance": "1",
"builtin": { "name": "ripemd160", "pricing": { "linear": { "base": 600,
"word": 120 } } } },
        "0x0000000000000000000000000000000000000004": { "balance": "1",
"builtin": { "name": "identity", "pricing": { "linear": { "base": 15,
"word": 3 } } } },
        "0x0000000000000000000000000000000000000005": { "balance": "1",
"constructor" : "0x606060405260406040519081016040528073831647" },
        "0x004ec07d2329997267Ec62b4166639513386F32E": { "balance":
"1000000000000000000000000" }
    }
}
```

Here is how the preceding file works:

- The engine property is used to set the consensus protocol and the protocol-specific parameters. Here, the engine is authorityRound, which is aura. gasLimitBoundDivisor determines gas limit adjustment and has the usual ethereum value. In the validators property, we have a contract property, which is the address of the reporting contract. stepDuration is the block time in seconds.

- In the `params` property, only the network ID is what matters; others are standard for all chains.
- `genesis` has some standard values for the `authorityRound` consensus.
- `accounts` is used to list the initial accounts and contracts that exist in the network. The first four are standard Ethereum built-in contracts; these should be included to use the Solidity contract writing language. The fifth one is the reporting contract. Make sure you replace the byte code with your byte code in the `constructor` param. The last account is the second account we generated in the validator 1 shell. It is used to supply ether to the network. Replace this address with yours.

Before we proceed further, create another file called as `node.pwds`. In that file, place the password of the accounts you created. This file will be used by the validators to unlock the accounts to sign the blocks.

Launching nodes

Now we have all basic requirements ready to launch our validating nodes. In the first shell, run this command to launch the first validating node:

```
parity  --chain spec.json -d ./validator0 --force-sealing --engine-signer
"0x831647ec69be4ca44ea4bd1b9909debfbaaef55c" --port 30300 --jsonrpc-port
8540 --ui-port 8180 --dapps-port 8080 --ws-port 8546 --jsonrpc-apis
web3,eth,net,personal,parity,parity_set,traces,rpc,parity_accounts --
password "node.pwds"
```

Here is how the preceding command works:

- `--chain` is used to specify the path of the specification file.
- `-d` is used to specify the data directory.
- `--force-sealing` ensures that blocks are produced even if there are no transactions.
- `--engine-signer` is used to specify the address using which the node will sign blocks, that is, the address of the validator. If malicious authorities are possible, then `--force-sealing` is advised; this will ensure that the correct chain is the longest. Make sure you change the address to the one you generated, that is, the first address generated on this shell.
- `--password` is used to specify the password file.

In the second shell, run this command to launch second validating node:

```
parity  --chain spec.json -d ./validator1 --force-sealing --engine-signer
"0x12a6bda0d5f58538167b2efce5519e316863f9fd" --port 30301 --jsonrpc-port
8541 --ui-port 8181 --dapps-port 8081 --ws-port 8547 --jsonrpc-apis
web3,eth,net,personal,parity,parity_set,traces,rpc,parity_accounts --
password "/Users/narayanprusty/Desktop/node.pwds"
```

Here, make sure you change the address to the one you generated that is, the address generated on this shell.

Connecting nodes

Now finally, we need to connect both the nodes. Open a new shell window and run this command to find the URL to connect to the second node:

```
curl --data '{"jsonrpc":"2.0","method":"parity_enode","params":[],"id":0}'
-H "Content-Type: application/json" -X POST localhost:8541
```

You will get this sort of output:

```
{"jsonrpc":"2.0","result":"enode://7bac3c8cf914903904a408ecd71635966331990c
5c9f7c7a291b531d5912ac3b52e8b174994b93cab1bf14118c2f24a16f75c49e83b93e0864e
b099996ec1af9@[::0.0.1.0]:30301","id":0}
```

Now run this command by replacing the encode URL and IP address in the enode URL to 127.0.0.1:

```
curl --data
'{"jsonrpc":"2.0","method":"parity_addReservedPeer","params":["enode://7ba.
.."],"id":0}' -H "Content-Type: application/json" -X POST localhost:8540
```

You should get this output:

```
{"jsonrpc":"2.0","result":true,"id":0}
```

The nodes should indicate 0/1/25 peers in the console, which means they are connected to each other. Here is a reference image:

```
2017-04-19 00:29:59  Imported #868 ec6f..dfa8 (0 txs, 0.00 Mgas, 0.57 ms, 0.56 KiB)
2017-04-19 00:30:04  Imported #869 980b..7964 (0 txs, 0.00 Mgas, 0.60 ms, 0.56 KiB)
2017-04-19 00:30:10  Imported #870 552c..4fd8 (0 txs, 0.00 Mgas, 0.51 ms, 0.56 KiB)
2017-04-19 00:30:15  Imported #871 2fed..27d4 (0 txs, 0.00 Mgas, 0.58 ms, 0.56 KiB)
2017-04-19 00:30:17     0/ 1/25 peers    309 KiB db  302 KiB chain  0 bytes queue    17 KiB
2017-04-19 00:30:19  Imported #872 834c..9d78 (0 txs, 0.00 Mgas, 0.49 ms, 0.56 KiB)
2017-04-19 00:30:25  Imported #873 62ee..6335 (0 txs, 0.00 Mgas, 0.48 ms, 0.56 KiB)
2017-04-19 00:30:29  Imported #874 8843..7a5d (0 txs, 0.00 Mgas, 0.51 ms, 0.56 KiB)
2017-04-19 00:30:35  Imported #875 9b7d..a9c9 (0 txs, 0.00 Mgas, 0.46 ms, 0.56 KiB)
2017-04-19 00:30:40  Imported #876 493b..9cc6 (0 txs, 0.00 Mgas, 0.65 ms, 0.56 KiB)
2017-04-19 00:30:45  Imported #877 a672..fe6f (0 txs, 0.00 Mgas, 0.53 ms, 0.56 KiB)
2017-04-19 00:30:47     0/ 1/25 peers    311 KiB db  302 KiB chain  0 bytes queue    17 KiB
2017-04-19 00:30:49  Imported #878 cedf..1ee5 (0 txs, 0.00 Mgas, 0.47 ms, 0.56 KiB)
2017-04-19 00:30:55  Imported #879 4381..8fcc (0 txs, 0.00 Mgas, 0.58 ms, 0.56 KiB)
2017-04-19 00:30:59  Imported #880 b383..ef90 (0 txs, 0.00 Mgas, 0.53 ms, 0.56 KiB)
2017-04-19 00:31:05  Imported #881 25cf..aeeb (0 txs, 0.00 Mgas, 0.46 ms, 0.56 KiB)
2017-04-19 00:31:10  Imported #882 8dee..ca2c (0 txs, 0.00 Mgas, 0.53 ms, 0.56 KiB)
2017-04-19 00:31:15  Imported #883 770a..f85b (0 txs, 0.00 Mgas, 0.53 ms, 0.56 KiB)
```

Permissioning and privacy

We saw how parity solves the issues of speed and security. Parity currently doesn't provide anything specific to permissioning and privacy. Let's see how to achieve this in parity:

1. **Permissioning**: A parity network can implement permissioning to decide who can join and who cannot by configuring each node's server to allow connections from only specific IP addresses. Even if IP addresses aren't blocked, to connect to a node in the network, a new node will needs an enode address, which we saw earlier, and that's not guessable. So by default, there is a basic protection. But there is nothing to enforce this. Every node in the network has to take care about this at its end. Similar permissioning for who can create blocks and who cannot can be done through a smart contract. Finally what kind of transactions a node can send is not configurable at the moment.

2. **Identity privacy**: There is a technique to achieve identity privacy by still enabling ownership checks. At the time of setting ownership, the owner needs to specify a public key of an un-deterministic asymmetric cryptography. Whenever it wants ownership checks to pass, it will provide an encrypted form of common text, which will be decrypted by the contract and see whether the account is owner or not. The contract should make sure the same encrypted data is not checked twice.

3. **Data privacy**: If you are using blockchain to just store data, you can use symmetric encryption to encrypt data and store and share the key with people who you want to see the data. But operations on encrypted data is not possible. And if you need operations on input data and still gain privacy, then the parties have to set up a different blockchain network completely.

Summary

Overall in this chapter, we learned how to use parity and how aura works and some techniques to achieve permissioning and privacy in parity. Now you must be confident enough to at least build a proof-of-concept for a consortium using blockchain. Now you can go ahead and explore other solutions, such as Hyperledger 1.0 and quorum for building consortium blockchains. Currently, Ethereum is officially working on making more suitable for consortiums; therefore, keep a close eye on various blockchain information sources to learn about anything new that comes in the market.

18
Current Landscape and What's Next

Blockchain technology is changing and will continue to change the way we conduct our day-to-day business. It has challenged existing business models and has the promise of great benefits regarding cost saving, and greater efficiency and transparency. This chapter will explore the latest developments, emerging trends, issues, and future predictions about this technology.

We finish this book by presenting some topics related to open research problems and improvements related to blockchain technology.

Emerging trends

Blockchain technology is under rapid change and intense development due to the deep interest in it by academics and the commercial sector. As the technology is becoming mature, a few trends have started to emerge recently. For example, private blockchains have recently gained quite a lot of attention due to their specific use cases in finance. Also, enterprise blockchains are another new trend that is aiming to develop blockchain solutions that meet enterprise-level efficiency, security, and integration requirements. Some of the trends are listed here and discussed.

Application-specific blockchains (ASBCs)

Currently, an inclination toward ASBCs is noticed, whereby a blockchain or distributed ledger is specially developed for only one application in mind and is focused on a specific industry, for example, Everledger, (`https://www.everledger.io`) which is a blockchain that has been developed to be used for providing an immutable tracing history and audit trail for diamonds and other high-value items. This approach thwarts any fraud attempts because everything related to ownership, authenticity, and value of the items is verified and recorded on the blockchain. This result is precious for insurance and law enforcement agencies.

Enterprise-grade blockchains

As blockchains in their original form are not ready for use at enterprise level due to privacy and scalability issues, a recent trend in developing enterprise-grade blockchains has emerged, whereby various companies have started to provide enterprise-grade blockchain solutions that are ready to be deployed and integrated at an enterprise level. Requirements such as testing, documentation, integration, and security are all addressed already in this type of solution and can be implemented with minimal or no change at the enterprise level.

This concept is in contrast to public blockchains, which are unregulated and do not meet specific enterprise-level security requirements. This also implies that enterprise-grade blockchains are usually supposed to be implemented in private configurations; however, public enterprise-grade blockchain implementation is also a possibility. In recent years, many technology start-ups have started to offer enterprise-grade blockchain solutions such as Bloq, Tymlez, Chain, Colu, ChainThat, ChromaWay and many others. This trend continues to grow, and years to come will see more technology initiatives like this.

Private blockchains

With the need for privacy and confidentiality, a major focus is on developing private distributed ledgers that can be used within a group of trusted participants. As public blockchains, due to their open and comparatively less secure nature, are not suitable for industries such as finance, medicine, and law, private blockchains hold the promise to address this limitation and bring end users one step closer to reaping the benefits of blockchains while meeting all security and privacy requirements.

Public blockchains are less secure because generally, they do not provide privacy and confidentiality services. Private blockchains allow the participants or a subset of participants to be in full control of the system, thus making it desirable for use in finance and other industries where privacy and control are required.

Ethereum can be used in both private and public modes, whereas there are a few projects that have been developed solely as private blockchains, such as Hyperledger and Corda. We discussed both of these in Chapter 13, *Hyperledger*.

Start-ups

In recent years, many technology start-ups have emerged that are working on blockchain projects and are offering solutions specific to this technology. There is a significant increase in the number of start-ups that are offering blockchain consultancy and solutions.

You can visit the link https://angel.co/blockchains, which currently shows a list of 1927 blockchain start-ups.

Strong research interest

Blockchain technology has stimulated intense research interest both in academia and the commercial sector. In recent years, the interest has dramatically increased, and now major institutions and researchers around the world are exploring this technology. This growth in interest is primarily because blockchain technology can help to make businesses efficient, reduce costs, and make things transparent. Academic interest is around addressing hard problems in cryptography, consensus mechanisms, performance, and addressing other limitations in blockchains.

As blockchain technology comes under the broader umbrella of distributed systems, many researchers from distributed computing research have focused their research on blockchain technology. For example, UCL has a dedicated department, the UCL Research Centre for Blockchain Technologies, which focuses on blockchain technology research.

Another example is the ETH Zurich distributed computing group (https://disco.ethz.ch) that has published seminal research regarding blockchain technology. A recent journal called the *Ledger Journal* has recently published its first issue of research papers.

It is available at `http://www.ledgerjournal.org/ojs/index.php/ledger`.

There are now teams and departments dedicated to blockchain research and development in various academic and commercial institutes.

Although the initiatives mentioned here are not an exhaustive list by any stretch of the imagination, it is still a solid indication that this is a subject of extreme interest for researchers, and more research and development is expected to be seen in 2018 and beyond. Another organization called **The Initiative for Cryptocurrencies & Contracts (IC3)**, is also researching smart contract and blockchain technologies. IC3 aims to address performance, confidentiality, and safety issues in blockchains and smart contracts and runs multiple projects to address these issues.

 More information about projects running in IC3 is available online at `http://www.initc3.org/`.

Standardization

Blockchain technology is not yet mature enough to be able to integrate with existing systems readily. Even, as the current technology stands, two blockchain networks cannot easily talk to each other. Standardization will help to improve **interoperability**, **adaptability**, and **integration** aspects of blockchain technology. Some attempts have been made recently to address this, and the most notable out of these attempts is the establishment of ISO/TC 307, which is a technical committee with the scope of standardizing blockchain and distributed ledger technology.

The aim of the committee revolves around increasing interoperability and data interchange between users, applications, and systems. On the other hand, the recent creation of consortia and open source collaborative efforts such as R3 and Hyperledger has helped with standardization of this technology by sharing ideas, tools, and code with other participants. R3 works with a consortium of more than 80 banks that all have similar goals, which in a way results in standardization. Hyperledger, on the other hand, has a reference architecture that can be used to build blockchain systems and is supported by the Linux Foundation and many other participants from the industry.

Another example is the open chain standard, which is a protocol developed for financial networks. The chain OS1 standard is already available, which was built in collaboration with major financial institutions around the world. This standard allows faster settlement of transactions and direct peer-to-peer transaction routing. It aims to address regulatory, security, and privacy requirements in blockchain technologies. OS1 also provides a framework for smart contract development and allows the participant to meet AML and KYC requirements easily.

Smart contract standardization efforts have also started with a seminal paper authored by Lee and others, which formally defines the smart contract templates and presents a vision for future research and necessities in smart contract related research and development.

This paper is available at `https://arxiv.org/abs/1608.00771v2`.

Moreover, some discussion on this topic has been carried out in `Chapter 16`, *Scalability and Other Challenges* and `Chapter 4`, *Smart Contracts*.

All of the efforts mentioned here are a clear indication that very soon, standards will emerge in the industry that will further make adoption of blockchain technology easier and quicker. Standards will also result in exponential growth of the blockchain industry because the availability of standards will eliminate hurdles such as interoperability.

Enhancements

Various enhancements and suggestions to further develop existing blockchains have been made over the last few years. Most of these suggestions have been made in response to security vulnerabilities and to address inherent limitations in blockchain technology. There are certain limitations in blockchain technology, such as scalability, privacy, and interoperability, that are required to be addressed before it can become mainstream like any other technology.

Recently, there have been tremendous efforts made toward addressing scalability issues in blockchain technology, which have been discussed in `Chapter 16`, *Scalability and Other Challenges*. Also, blockchain-specific improvement proposals such as **BIPs** (short for **Bitcoin Improvement Proposals**) and **EIPs** (short for **Ethereum Improvement Proposals**) are regularly made by developers to address various concerns in these systems.

Some recent and notable improvement proposals for both of these chains will be discussed later in the chapter. Moreover, recent advancements such as state channels are examples that blockchain technology is improving rapidly and very soon will evolve as a mature and more practical technology.

Real-world implementations

Many proofs of concept have been developed in recent years, especially in 2017, using blockchain technology. A few application-specific implementations emerged, such as Everledger for diamond tracking and filament for the IoT but are still lacking in various areas.

This seems not too far now as many proofs of concept have already been developed and proved to work; the next stage is to implement these in real-life scenarios. For example, recently, a group of seven banks agreed to build a **Digital Trade Chain** (**DTC**) that will simplify the trade finance process.

DTC related information is available at `http://www.bankingtech.com/2017/10/ibm-and-eight-banks-unleash-we-trade-platform-for-blockchain-powered-commerce/`.

Concrete, real-life, end-to-end implementations are also now becoming available, even in finance industry such as **Australian Securities Exchange** (**ASX**) replacing it legacy post trade system with blockchain.

The information regarding this project from ASX is available at `https://www.asx.com.au/services/chess-replacement.htm`.

Consortia

In recent years there has been various consortia and shared open source efforts started. This trend is expected to grow in the coming years, and more and more consortia, committees, and open source efforts will emerge soon. A prime example is R3, which has developed Corda with a consortium of the world's largest financial organizations.

Answers to technical challenges

Already, due to intense research effort and interest from the community in blockchain technology, answers to various challenges have started to emerge. For example, the concept of state channels has been developed as a response to scalability and privacy issues on the blockchain. Using state channels, the Bitcoin lightning network and Ethereum's Raiden are already almost ready for implementation.

 This is work in progress, however and updates are available here `https:/ /github.com/raiden-network/raiden/milestones`.

Moreover, various blockchain solutions emerged, such as Kadena, that directly addressed the confidentiality issues in blockchains. Other concepts such as Zcash, CoinJoin, and confidential transactions have also been developed and were discussed in `Chapter 10`, *Alternative Coins*. This trend will also continue to grow in years to come, and even if almost all fundamental challenges are addressed in blockchain technology, further enhancement and optimization will never stop.

Convergence

Convergence of other technologies with blockchains brings about major benefits. At their core, blockchains provide resilience, security, and transparency, which, when combined with other technologies, results in a very powerful technology that complements each other. For example, the IoT can gain major benefits when implemented via blockchains, such as integrity, decentralization, and scalability. **Artificial Intelligence** (**AI**) is expected to gain benefits from blockchain technology, and in fact, within blockchain technology, AI can be implemented in the form of **Autonomous Agents** (**AAs**). More examples and the aforementioned converging technologies would be discussed in detail in later sections in the chapter.

Education of blockchain technology

While blockchain technology has spurred a great interest among technologists, developers, and scientists throughout almost every industry around the world, there is a lack of formal learning resources and educational material. As this is a new technology, various courses are now being offered by various reputed institutions such as Princeton University that introduce the technology to anyone who wants to learn about this technology.

For example, Princeton University has started a cryptocurrency and digital currencies course that is delivered online (`https://online.princeton.edu/course/bitcoin-and-cryptocurrency-technologies`). Many private organizations are also offering similar online and classroom training courses. More efforts like this will be seen soon due to the popularity and acceptance of blockchain technology.

Employment

There is a recent trend emerging in the job market whereby recruiters are now looking for blockchain experts and developers who can program for blockchains. This is especially relevant to the financial industry, and recently many start-ups and large organizations have started to hire blockchain specialists. This trend is of course expected to grow as the technology gains more acceptance and maturity. There is also concern about the lack of blockchain developers, which undoubtedly will be addressed as the technology progresses and more and more developers either gain experience on a self-learning basis or gain formal training from some training providers.

Cryptoeconomics

New fields of research are emerging with blockchains, most notably, cryptoeconomics, which is the study of protocols governing the decentralized digital economy. With the advent of blockchains and cryptocurrencies, research in this area has also grown. Cryptoeconomics has been defined as a combination of mathematics, cryptography, economics, and game theory by Vitalik Buterin.

 There is an excellent presentation available at `https://vitalik.ca/files/intro_cryptoeconomics.pdf`.

Research in cryptography

Even though cryptography was an area of keen interest and research for many decades before Bitcoin invention, blockchain technology has resulted in renewed interest in this field. With the advent of blockchains and related technologies, there is a significant increase in the interest in cryptography also. Especially in the area of financial cryptography, new research is being carried out and published regularly.

Technologies such as ZKPs, fully homomorphic encryption, and functional encryption are being researched for their use in blockchains. In the form of Zcash, already ZKPs have been implemented for the first time at a practical level. It can be seen that blockchains and cryptocurrencies have helped with the advancement of cryptography and especially financial cryptography.

New programming languages

There is also an increased interest in the development of programming languages for developing smart contracts. The efforts are more focused on domain-specific languages, for example, Solidity for Ethereum and Pact for Kadena. This is just a start, and many new languages are likely to be developed as the technology advances.

Hardware research and development

When it was realized in 2010 that current methods are not efficient for mining bitcoins, miners started shifting toward optimizing mining hardware. These initial efforts included usage of GPUs, and then **Field-Programmable Gate Arrays** (**FPGAs**) were used after GPUs reached their limit. Very quickly after that, **Application-Specific Integrated Circuits** (**ASICs**) emerged, which increased the mining power significantly. This trend is expected to grow further as now there is more research into further optimizing ASICs by parallelizing and decreasing the die size.

Moreover, GPU programming initiatives are also expected to grow because new cryptocurrencies are emerging quite regularly now and many of them make use of PoW algorithms that can benefit from GPU processing capabilities. For example, recently Zcash has spurred interest in GPU mining rigs and related programming using NVIDIA CUDA and OpenCL. The aim is to use multiple GPUs in parallel for optimizing mining operations. Also, some research has been in the field of using trusted computing hardware such as Intel's **Software Guard Extensions** (**SGX**) to address security issues on blockchains. Also, Intel's SGX has been used in a novel consensus algorithm called **Proof of Elapsed Time** (**PoET**) which has been discussed in `Chapter 13`, *Hyperledger*. Another project, the 21 Bitcoin Computer, was developed, which serves as a platform for developers to learn Bitcoin technology and easily develop applications for the Bitcoin platform.

The hardware research and development trend are expected to continue, and soon many more hardware scenarios will be explored.

Research in formal methods and security

With the realization of security issues and vulnerabilities in smart contract programming languages, there is now a keen interest in the formal verification and testing of smart contracts before production deployments. For this, various efforts are already underway, including Why3 for Ethereum's Solidity. Hawk is another example that has been developed to allow smart contract confidentiality.

Alternatives to blockchains

As the blockchain technology advanced in recent years, researchers started to think about the possibility of creating platforms that can provide guarantees and services which a blockchain provides but without the need for a blockchain. This has resulted in development of R3's Corda, which in fact is not really a blockchain because it is not based on the concept of blocks containing transactions; instead, it is based on the concept of a state object that transverses throughout the Corda network according to the requirements and rules of the network participants representing the latest state of the network. Other examples include IOTA, which is an IoT blockchain which makes use of a **Directed Acyclic Graph** (**DAG**) as a distributed ledger named Tangle, instead of conventional blockchain with blocks. This ledger is claimed to have addressed scalability issues along with high-level security which even protects against quantum computing based attacks. It should be noted that Bitcoin is also somewhat protected against quantum attacks because the quantum attacks can only work on exposed public keys which are only revealed on the blockchain if both send and receive transactions are made. If the public key is not revealed, which is the case in unused addresses or the addresses that may have only used to receive bitcoins, then quantum safety can be guaranteed. In other words, using a different address for each transaction protects against quantum attacks. Also, in Bitcoin, it is quite easy to change to another quantum signature protocol if required.

Interoperability efforts

Recent realization of limitations around interoperability of blockchains has resulted in the development of systems that can work across multiple blockchains. A recent example is Qtum, which is a blockchain that is compatible with both Ethereum and Bitcoin blockchains. It makes use of Bitcoin's UTXO mechanism for transfer of value and an EVM for smart contracts. This means that Ethereum projects can be ported onto Qtum without requiring any change.

Blockchain as a Service

With the current level of maturity of cloud platforms, many companies have started to provide **Blockchain as a Service** (**BaaS**). The most prominent examples are Microsoft's Azure, where Ethereum blockchain is provided as a service, and IBM's Bluemix platform, that provides IBM BaaS. This trend is only expected to grow in the next few years, and more companies will emerge that provide BaaS. **Electronic Government as a Service** (**eGaaS**) is another example which is, in fact, BaaS but provides application-specific blockchains for governance functions (`http://egaas.org`). This project aims to organize and control any activity without document circulation and bureaucratic overhead.

Efforts to reduce electricity consumption

It is evident from Bitcoin's blockchain that the PoW mechanism is very inefficient. Of course, this computation secures the Bitcoin network but there is no other benefit of this computation, and it wastes much electrical energy. To reduce this waste, now there is more focus on greener options such as PoS algorithms which do not need enormous resources like Bitcoin's PoW algorithm. This trend is expected to grow, especially with PoS planned for Ethereum.

Other challenges

Apart from security and privacy, discussed in `Chapter 16`, *Scalability and Other Challenges*, several other hurdles should be addressed before the mainstream adoption of blockchains can be realized. These include regulation, government control, immature technology, integration with existing systems, and implementation costs.

Regulation

Regulation is considered one of the most significant challenges that need to be addressed. The core issue is that blockchains and especially cryptocurrencies are not recognized as a legal currency by any government. Even though in some cases, it has been classified as money in the US and Germany, it is still far from being accepted as a regular currency. Moreover, blockchains in their current state are not recognized as a platform that can be used by financial institutions. No financial regulatory body has yet accepted it as a platform that can be authorized to be used.

There are, however, various initiatives taken by regulatory authorities around the world to research and propose regulations. Bitcoin in its current state is fully unregulated, even though some attempts have been made by governments to tax the bitcoin. In the UK, under the EU VAT directive, bitcoin transactions are exempt from **Value Added Tax (VAT)**, but this may change after Brexit. However, **Capital Gains Tax (CGT)** may still be applicable in some scenarios.

Some regulation attempt is expected very soon from financial regulatory authorities generally regarding blockchain technology, especially after the recent announcement by the **Financial Conduct Authority (FCA)** in the UK that it may approve some companies that are using blockchain.

It is a general concern that the blockchain technology is not ready for production deployments. Even though the Bitcoin blockchain has evolved into a solid blockchain platform and is used in production, it is not suitable for every scenario. This is especially true in the case of sensitive environments such as finance and health. However, this situation is changing very quickly and we've already seen in this chapter various examples of new blockchain projects, that have been implemented in real life such as ASX blockchain post trade solution. This trend is expected to grow as ample efforts discussed previously in this chapter are being made to improve the technology and address any technical limitations such as scalability and privacy.

Security is also another general concern which has been highlighted by many researchers and is especially applicable to the finance and health sectors. A report by the **European Union Agency for Network and Information Security (ENISA)** has highlighted distributed ledger specific concerns that should be addressed.

The report is available at https://www.enisa.europa.eu/news/enisa-news/enisa-report-on-blockchain-technology-and-security.

Some concerns highlighted in the report include smart contract management, key management, **Anti Money Laundering (AML)**, and anti-fraud tools. Also, the need for **regulation**, **audit**, **control**, and **governance** has been highlighted in the report.

Integration with existing legacy systems is also a prime concern. It is not clear how blockchains can be integrated with the existing financial systems.

Hurdles toward adoption are more or less related to regulatory, security, and interoperability. Integration with existing systems can be carried out in several ways.

Dark side

With the key attributes of censorship resistance and decentralization, blockchain technology can help to improve transparency and efficiency in many walks of life, but this somewhat unregulated nature of this technology means that it can be used by criminals for illegal activities too. For example, compare a scenario where if some illegal content is published over the internet it can be immediately shut down by approaching the concerned authorities and website service providers, but this is not possible in blockchains.

Once something is there on the blockchain, it is almost impossible to revert it. This means that any unacceptable content, once published on the blockchain, cannot be removed. If the blockchain is used for distributing immoral content, then there is no way for anyone to shut it down. This poses a serious challenge and it seems that some regulation and control is beneficial in this scenario, but how can a blockchain be regulated? That is another critical question. It may not be prudent to create the regulatory laws first and then see if blockchain technology adapts to that because it might disrupt innovation and progress in this technology. It would be more sensible to let the blockchain technology grow first, just like the internet and when it reaches a critical mass then governing bodies can call for applying some regulation around the implementation and usage of blockchain technology.

There are various examples where the Dark Web is used in conjunction with bitcoin to perform illegal activities. For example, Silk Road, which was used to sell illegal drugs over the internet, used bitcoins for payments and the Dark Web using onion URLs which are only visible with Tor. Although Silk Road was shut down after months of effort by law enforcement agencies, new similar sites started to emerge. Now, other alternatives are available that similar offer services; as such, generally, this type of problem remains a big concern.

Imagine that an illegal website is on IPFS and a blockchain; there is no easy way of shutting it down. It is clear that absence of control and regulation can encourage criminal activity and similar issue like Silk Road will keep arising. Further development of totally anonymous transaction capabilities such as Zcash could provide another layer of protection for criminals but at the same time may be quite useful in various legitimate scenarios. It depends on that who is using the technology; anonymity can be good in many scenarios, for example in the health industry where patient records should be kept private and anonymous but may not be appropriate if it can also be used by criminals to hide their activities.

One solution might be to introduce intelligent bots or AAs or even contracts that are programmed with regulatory logic embedded within them. They are most likely to be programmed by regulators and law enforcement agencies and live on the blockchain as a means to provide governance and control. For example, a blockchain could be designed in such a way that every smart contract has to go through a controller contract that scrutinizes the code logic and provides a regulatory mechanism to control the behavior of the smart contract.

It may also be possible to get each smart contract's code to be inspected by regulatory authorities, and once a smart contract code has a certain level of authenticity attached to it in the form of certificates issued by a regulator, it can be deployed on the blockchain network. This concept of binary signing is akin to the concept of the already established concept of code signing whereby executables are digitally signed as a means to confirm that the code is bona fide and is not malicious. This idea is more applicable in the context of semiprivate or regulated blockchains, where a certain degree of control is required by a regulatory authority, for example, in finance. It means that there is some degree of trust required to be placed in a trusted third party (regulator) which may not be desirable due to deviation from the concept of full decentralization. However, to address this, the blockchain itself can be used to provide a decentralized, transparent, and secure certificate issuance and digital signing mechanism.

Blockchain research

While major innovations have been made in blockchain technology in recent years, the area is still very ripe for further research. Some selected research topics are listed as follows with some information about existing challenges and state of the art. Some ideas are also presented in the following subsections on how to address these issues.

Smart contracts

Significant progress has been made in this area to define the key requirements of smart contracts and development of templates. However, further research is required in the area of making smart contracts more secure and safe.

Centralization issues

This is true for especially Bitcoin mining centralization, there is a growing concern about how Bitcoin can be decentralized again.

Limitations in cryptographic functions

Cryptography used in the Bitcoin blockchain is exceptionally secure and has stood the test of time. In other blockchains, similar security techniques are used and are also very secure. However, specific security issues such as the possibility of generation and usage of duplicate signature nonces in elliptic curve digital signature schemes (leading to private key recovery attack), collisions in hash functions, and a possibility of quantum attacks that may break the underlying cryptographic algorithms remain an exciting area of research.

Consensus algorithms

Research in PoS algorithms or alternatives to PoW is also an important area of research. This is especially relevant due to the fact the current Bitcoin network's power consumption is expected to reach almost 125 TWh by the end of 2018. Currently it is almost equivalent to the country of Israel in terms of electricity consumption. It has also been suggested that instead of performing an inefficient or single-purpose type of work as is the case with Bitcoin's PoW, the network power can be used to solve some mathematical or scientific problems. Also, alternatives such as PoS algorithms have already gained much traction and are due to be implemented in major blockchains, for example, Ethereum's Casper. However, so far, PoW remains the best option for securing a public blockchain.

Scalability

A detailed discussion has already been carried out on scalability in `Chapter 16`, *Scalability and Other Challenges*; briefly, it is sufficient to say in this section that while some progress has already been made, still there is a need for more research to enable on-chain scalability and further improve off-chain solutions such as state channels. Some initiatives like block size increase and transaction-only blockchains (without blocks) have been proposed to address scalability issues that increase the capacity of the blockchain itself instead of using side channels. Examples of without blocks implementation include IOTA (Tangle). It is a DAG which is used to store transactions as compared to traditional blockchain solutions where a block is used to store transactions. This makes it inherently faster as compared to block-based blockchains such as Bitcoin where waiting time between block generations is at least approximately 10 minutes.

Code obfuscation

Code obfuscation by using indistinguishability obfuscation can be used as a means to provide confidentiality and privacy in the blockchain. However, this is still not practical, and major research effort is required to achieve this.

Notable projects

Following is a list of notable projects in the blockchain space that is currently in progress. In addition to these projects, there is also a myriad of start-ups and companies working in the blockchain space and offering blockchain-related products.

Zcash on Ethereum

A recent project by the Ethereum R&D team is the implementation of Zcash on Ethereum. This is an exciting project whereby developers are trying to create a privacy layer for Ethereum using ZK-SNARKs already used in Zcash project. With Zcash implementation on Ethereum, the aim is to create a platform that allows applications such as voting where privacy is of paramount importance.

It will also allow the creation of anonymous tokens on Ethereum that can be used in a number of applications.

CollCo

This is a project developed by Deutsche Borse which is based on the Hyperledger code base and is used for managing commercial bank cash transfers. **Collateralized Coin** (**CollCo**) provides a blockchain-based platform that allows real-time transfer of commercial bank money while still relying on traditional capabilities provided by Eurex Clearing CCP. This is a major project that can be used to address inefficiencies in the post-trade settlement processes.

Cello

As of February 2017, this is the most recent addition to Hyperledger project. This project aims to provide on-demand BaaS which will make deployments and management of multiple blockchains convenient and easy for users. It is envisioned that Cello will support all future and current Hyperledger blockchains, such as Fabric and Sawtooth Lake.

Qtum

This project is based on the idea of combining capabilities of Bitcoin and Ethereum blockchains. Qtum makes use of the Bitcoin code base but uses Ethereum's EVM for smart contract execution. Ethereum smart contracts can run using Bitcoin's UTXO (unspent transactions) model.

 It is available at `https://qtum.org/`.

Bitcoin-NG

This is another proposal for addressing scalability, throughput, and speed issues in the Bitcoin blockchain. **Next Generation** (**NG**) protocol is based on a mechanism of leader election which verifies transactions as soon as they occur, as compared to Bitcoin's protocols, where the time between blocks and block size are the key limitations concerning scalability.

Solidus

This is a new cryptocurrency which provides a solution for selfish mining while addressing scaling and performance issues. It also addresses confidentiality issues. It is based on permissionless Byzantine consensus. The protocol in its current state is comparatively complex and is an open area for research.

 Original research paper is available at `https://eprint.iacr.org/2017/317.pdf`.

Hawk

This is a project that is aiming to address privacy issues of smart contracts in blockchains. It is a smart contract system that allows encryption of transactions on the blockchain. Hawk can generate a secure protocol for interaction with blockchains automatically without the need for manually programming the cryptographic protocol.

Town-Crier

This is a project that is aiming to provide real-world, authentic feed into smart contracts. This system is based on Intel's SGX trusted hardware technology. This is a step further in Oracle design whereby smart contracts can request data from online sources while preserving confidentiality.

SETLCoin

This is a system built by Goldman Sachs and is filed for the patent under the *Cryptographic currency for securities settlement* application. As the name suggests, this cryptocurrency coin can be used for fast and efficient settlement. The technology makes use of virtual wallets to exchange assets over the network between peers and allows immediate settlement via ownership of SETLCoin.

TEEChan

This is novel idea of using **Trusted Execution Environments** (**TEEs**) to provide a scalable and efficient solution for scaling the Bitcoin blockchain. This is similar to the concept of payment channels whereby off-chain channels are used for faster transfer of transactions. The principal attraction in this idea is that it is implementable on Bitcoin blockchain without the need for any changes in the Bitcoin network because it is an off-the-chain solution.

There is, however, a small caveat that this solution does require trusting Intel for remote attestation (verification) as Intel's SGX CPUs are used to provide TEEs. This is not a desirable property in decentralized blockchains; however, it should be noted that the confidentiality of transactions is still preserved even if remote attestation is used as remote attester (Intel) cannot see the contents of the communication between users. This limitation makes it debatable that whether it is an entirely decentralized and trustless solution or not.

Falcon

Falcon is a project that helps Bitcoin to scale by providing a fast relay network for broadcasting Bitcoin blocks over the network. The core idea revolves around a technique to reduce orphan blocks, thus helping with the overall scalability of the Bitcoin network. The technique used for this purpose has been called application-level cut-through routing.

Bletchley

This project has been introduced by Microsoft, indicating the commitment by Microsoft to blockchain technology. Bletchley allows the use of Azure cloud services to build blockchains in a user-friendly manner. A major concept introduced by Bletchley is called cryptlets, which can be thought of like an advanced version of Oracles that reside outside the blockchain and can be called by smart contracts using secure channels. These can be written in any language and execute within a secure container.

There are two types of cryptlets: **utility cryptlets** and **contract cryptlets**. The first type is used to provide basic services such as encryption and basic data fetching from external sources, whereas the latter is a more intelligent version that is created automatically when a smart contract is created on the chain and resides off the chain but still linked to the on-chain contract. Due to this off-chain existence, there is no need to execute the contract cryptlets on all nodes of the blockchain network. Therefore, this approach results in increased performance of the blockchain.

 The whitepaper is available at https://github.com/Azure/azure-blockchain-projects/blob/master/bletchley/bletchley-whitepaper.md.

Casper

This is the Proof of Stake algorithm for Ethereum in development. Significant research has already been conducted in this area and is expected to be implemented in 2017. The nodes become bonded validators in a Casper-based Ethereum network and are required to pay a security deposit for them to be able to propose new blocks.

 Casper research paper is available at https://github.com/ethereum/research/blob/master/papers/casper-basics/casper_basics.pdf.

Miscellaneous tools

Some tools that have not been discussed previously are listed in the following subsections and introduced briefly to make readers aware of the myriad of development options available for blockchains. This list includes platforms, utilities, and tools that can be used for blockchain development.

Solidity extension for Microsoft Visual Studio

This extension provides IntelliSense, autocompletion, and templates for DApps, and works within the familiar Visual Studio IDE, making it easier for developers to familiarize themselves with Ethereum development.

 You can download this extension from: `https://marketplace.visualstudio.com/items?itemName=ConsenSys.Solidity`.

MetaMask

This is a DApp browser that is similar to Mist from a DApp browsing point of view but allows users to run Ethereum DApps within the browser without the requirement of running a full Ethereum node.

 This is available from `https://metamask.io/` and can be installed as a Chrome plugin.

Stratis

This is a blockchain development platform that allows the creation of custom private blockchains and works in conjunction with the main Stratis blockchain (Stratis chain) for security reasons. It allows provisioning of major blockchains such as Bitcoin, Ethereum, and Lisk easy. Also, it allows development using C# .NET technologies. It is also available via Microsoft Azure as BaaS.

This is available at `https://stratisplatform.com/`.

Embark

This is a development framework for Ethereum which allows similar functionality to Truffle. It allows automatic deployment of smart contracts, easier integration with JavaScript, and, especially, easier integration with IPFS. This is a very feature-rich framework, and many more functionalities are available. It can be installed via npm.

 This framework is available at GitHub: `https://github.com/iurimatias/embark-framework`.

DAPPLE

This is another framework for Ethereum that allows easier development and deployment of smart contracts by taking care of more complex tasks. It can be used for package management, contract building, and deployment scripting.

 This is also available via npm. It is also available via GitHub at `https://github.com/nexusdev/dapple`.

Meteor

This is a full-stack development framework for single-page applications. It can be used for Ethereum DApp development. There is a development environment available in meteor, and it allows easier and easy development of complex DApps.

 It is available at `https://www.meteor.com/` and Ethereum-specific DApp building information is available at `https://github.com/ethereum/wiki/wiki/Dapp-using-Meteor`.

uPort

This platform is built on Ethereum and provides a decentralized identity management system. This allows users to have full control over their identity and personal information. This is based on the idea of reputation systems enables users to attest each other and build trust.

 This is available at `https://www.uport.me/`.

INFURA

This project aims to provide enterprise-level Ethereum and IPFS nodes. INFURA consists of Ethereum nodes, IPFS nodes, and a service layer named Ferryman which provides routing and load balancing services.

Convergence with other industries

Convergence of blockchain with IoT has been discussed at length in `Chapter 16`, *Scalability and Other Challenges*. Briefly, it can be said that due to the authenticity, integrity, privacy, and shared nature of blockchains, IoT networks will benefit greatly from blockchain technology. This can be realized in the form of an IoT network that runs on a blockchain and makes use of a decentralized mesh network for communication to facilitate **Machine-to-Machine** (**M2M**) communication in real time. All this data which is generated as a result of M2M communication can be used in the machine learning process to augment the functionality of Artificially Intelligent DAOs or simple AAs. AAs can act as agents in a **Distributed Artificial Intelligence** (**DAI**) environment provided by a blockchain and can learn over time using machine learning processes.

AI is a field of computer science that endeavors to build intelligent agents that can make rational decisions based on the scenarios and environment that they observe around them. Machine learning plays a vital role in AI by making use of raw data as a learning resource. A key requirement in AI-based systems is the availability of authentic data that can be used for machine learning and model building. The explosion of data coming out IoT devices, smartphone's, and other data acquisition means that AI and machine learning is becoming more and more powerful.

There is, however, a requirement of authenticity of data. Once consumers, producers, and other entities are on a blockchain, the data that is generated as a result of interaction between these entities can be readily used as an input to machine learning engines with a guarantee of authenticity. This is where AI converges with blockchains. It could be argued that if an IoT device is hacked, it can send malformed data to the blockchain. This issue is mitigated because an IoT device is part of the blockchain (as a node) and has all security properties applied to it as a standard node in the blockchain network. These properties include incentivization of good behavior, rejection of malformed transactions, and strict verification of transactions and various other checks that are part of blockchain protocol. Therefore, even if an IoT device is somehow hacked, it would be treated as a Byzantine node by the blockchain network and would not cause any adverse impact on the network.

Moreover, the possibility of combining intelligent Oracles, intelligent, smart contracts, and AAs will give rise to **Artificially Intelligent Decentralized Autonomous Organizations (AIDAOs)** that can act on behalf of humans to run entire organizations on their own. This is another side of AI that can become norm in the future. However, more research is required to realize this vision.

Also, convergence of blockchain technology with other fields such as 3D printing, virtual reality, augmented reality, and the gaming industry is also envisaged. For example, in a multiplayer online game, blockchain's decentralized approach allows for more transparency and can ensure that no central authority is gaining unfair advantage by manipulating the game rules. All these topics are active areas of research currently and more interest and development are expected in these areas soon.

Future

The year 2017 was predicted to be the year when blockchain technology is implemented in real-world production environments and move from the **Proof of Concept** (**PoC**) and theoretical stage of previous years. It is true to some extent that companies have implemented some pilot projects but large-scale production implementations are yet to be seen. It is expected that within year 2018 we will see some organization implementing full scale blockchain based projects. In 2019, it is expected that almost 20% of central banks will be using blockchain.

 Original research is available here https://papers.ssrn.com/sol3/papers.cfm?abstract_id=3040224.

In years to come, this trend is only expected to grow. There are few careful predictions being made in the section that is based on the current advancement and speed of progress in the concerned field.

All of these predictions are likely to come true between the years 2020 and 2050:

- The IoT will run on multiple blockchains and will give rise to an M2M economy. This can include energy devices, autonomous cars, and house hold accessories.
- Medical records will be shared securely while preserving the privacy of patients between various private blockchains run by consortia of health providers. It may well be a single private blockchain shared among all service providers including pharmacies, hospitals, and clinics.
- Elections will be held via decentralized web applications with a backend of blockchains transparently and securely.
- Financial institutions will be running many private blockchains to share data between participants and for internal processes.
- Financial institutions will be making use of semiprivate blockchains that will provide identity information for AML and KYC functions and will be shared between many or all of the financial institutions around the world.
- Immigration and border control related activities will be recorded on the blockchain and passport control will be conducted via a blockchain shared between all ports of entries and border agencies around the world.
- Governments will run interdepartmental blockchain to provide government services such as pension disbursement, benefit disbursement, land ownership records, birth registrations and other citizen services. This way auditability, trust and sense of security will develop among citizens.
- Research in cryptography and distributed systems will reach new heights and universities, and educational establishment will offer dedicated courses on cryptoeconomics, cryptocurrencies, and blockchains.
- Artificially Intelligent DAOs will prevail on blockchains that will make rational decisions on behalf of humans.
- A publicly available regulated blockchain run by the government will be used on day-to-day basis by citizens to perform their day-to-day activities, for example tax payments, TV license registration and marriage registrations.
- BaaS will be provided as standard to anyone who wishes to run their business or day-to-day transactions on a blockchain. In fact, it could be envisaged that just like the Internet, blockchains will seamlessly integrate into our daily lives and people will be using them without knowing much about the underlying technology and infrastructure.

- Blockchains will normally be used to provide **Digital Rights Management (DRM)** services for arts and media and can be used to deliver content to the consumers, enabling direct communication between consumer and the producer. This will eliminate the need for any central party to govern the licensing and rights managing of valuable goods.
- Existing cryptocurrencies such as Bitcoin will continue to grow in value, and with the availability of state channels and scalability efforts, this trend is only expected to grow.
- Cryptocurrency investment will greatly increase, and a new cryptoeconomic society will emerge.
- Bitcoin value will reach tens of thousands of dollars per coin.
- Digital identities will be routinely managed on the blockchain, and different government functions such as voting, taxation, and funds disbursement will be conducted via blockchain-enabled platforms.
- Financial institutions and clearing houses will start to introduce blockchain based solutions for their customers in 2018.

Summary

Blockchains are going to change the world. The revolution has already started, and it is only expected to grow at an exponential scale. This chapter has explored various projects and the current state of blockchain technology.

First, a few trends were discussed that are expected to continue as the technology progresses further. There is deep research interest in blockchain technology by many researchers and organizations around the world, and some research topics have also been introduced in this chapter. Furthermore, convergence with other fields such as the IoT and AI has also been discussed.

Finally, some predictions regarding the growth of blockchain technology have been made. Most of these predictions are likely to come true within the next decade or so, while some may take a longer time. Blockchain technology has the potential to change the world, and a few positive signs have already been seen in the form of successful PoC implementations and a growing number of enthusiasts and developers taking an interest in this technology. Very soon, blockchains will be intertwined with our lives just as the Internet is now. This chapter is just a modest overview of the vast and tremendous potential of blockchains, and in the near future, exponential growth and further adoption of this technology is expected.

Other Books You May Enjoy

If you enjoyed this book, you may be interested in these other books by Packt:

Hands on Blockchain for Python Developers
Arjuna Sky Kok

ISBN. 9781788627856

- Understand blockchain technology and what makes it an immutable database
- Use the features of web3.py API to interact with the smart contract
- Create your own cryptocurrency and token in Ethereum using Vyper
- Use IPFS features to store content on the decentralized storage platform
- Implement a Twitter-like decentralized application with a desktop frontend
- Build decentralized applications in the shape of console, web, and desktop applications

Blockchain by Example

Bellaj Badr, Xun (Brian) Wu and Richard Horrocks

ISBN: 9781788475686

- Grasp decentralized technology fundamentals to master blockchain principles
- Build blockchain projects on Bitcoin, Ethereum, and Hyperledger
- Create your currency and a payment application using Bitcoin
- Implement decentralized apps and supply chain systems using Hyperledger
- Write smart contracts, run your ICO, and build a Tontine decentralized app using Ethereum
- Implement distributed file management with blockchain
- Integrate blockchain into existing systems in your organization

Leave a review - let other readers know what you think

Please share your thoughts on this book with others by leaving a review on the site that you bought it from. If you purchased the book from Amazon, please leave us an honest review on this book's Amazon page. This is vital so that other potential readers can see and use your unbiased opinion to make purchasing decisions, we can understand what our customers think about our products, and our authors can see your feedback on the title that they have worked with Packt to create. It will only take a few minutes of your time, but is valuable to other potential customers, our authors, and Packt. Thank you!

Index

www.ingramcontent.com/pod-product-compliance
Lightning Source LLC
La Vergne TN
LVHW081507050326
832903LV00025B/1405